Encore!

nashville

junior league of nashville, inc.

The purpose of the Junior League is exclusively educational and charitable and is:

to promote voluntarism;

to develop the potential of its members for voluntary participation in community affairs; and

to demonstrate the effectiveness of trained volunteers.

Proceeds from the sale of *Encore! Nashville* will be returned to the community through the Community Trust Fund of the Junior League of Nashville, Inc.

Additional copies may be obtained by writing:
Encore! Nashville
The Junior League of Nashville, Inc.
2202 Crestmoor Road
Nashville, Tennessee 37215

Copyright 1977
The Junior League of Nashville, Inc.
Nashville, Tennessee

First Edition
First Printing: 15,000 September 1977
Second Edition
First Printing: 20,000 October 1982

Library of Congress Catalog Number 82-083121.
International Standard Book Number 0-939114-68-2

Printed in the United States of America
by
Wimmer Brothers Fine Printing and Lithography

The Junior League of Nashville

proudly salutes Nashville as

Music City, USA! Encore! Nashville

is a tribute to the country music

celebrities who have done so much

to make the Nashville area such

an exciting place in which to live.

Encore! Nashville is an updated

revision of *Nashville Seasons' Encore.*

The 563 recipes included offer an

extensive selection of southern

cooking at its finest. Take your own

curtain calls with *Encore! Nashville.*

Vital information is found at the top of each recipe. Understanding that the time element is so important in all types of cooking, preparation times and/or baking times are listed. The baby chicken symbolizes the varying degrees of difficulty throughout the book.

quick and easy

average

worth the effort

table of contents

celebrities   7

beverages   37

hors d'oeuvres   47

soups and sandwiches   75

salads   109

eggs cheese rice and pasta   161

vegetables   187

seafood   221

poultry and game   263

meats   293

breads   331

cookies and candy   361

desserts   385

contributors   476

index   479

6

celebrities

celebrities

Alabama's Carob Brownies. . . . 9

Bill Anderson's Pumpkin
Ice Cream Pie. 10

Eddy Arnold's Coconut
Cream Pie. 11

Johnny Cash's "Old Iron Pot"
Family-Style Chili. 12

June Carter Cash's Vegetable
"Stuff". 13

Mama Cash's Chocolate
Bavarian Pie. 14

Rosanne Cash's Tuna
Casserole. 15

Tennessee Ernie Ford's Fresh
Apple-Nut Cake. 16

The Gatlin Brothers' Mexican
Meatball Soup. 17

Merle Haggard's Rainbow
Stew. 18

Grandpa Jones' Biscuits. 19

Brenda Lee's Trout Fillets. 20

Loretta Lynn's Cherry Pie. . . . 21

Barbara Mandrell's Seafood
Mold. 22

Ronnie Milsap's Chicken
Breast Casserole. 23

The Oak Ridge Boys'
Caramel Corn. 24

Dolly Parton's Brownie
Pudding. 25

Minnie Pearl's Chess Pie. 26

Jeannie C. Riley's Texas
Skyscraper Dessert. 27

Johnny Rodriguez's
Enchiladas. 28

T.G. Sheppard's Chicken-
Shrimp Supreme. 29

Hank Snow's Melting
Moments Cookies. 30

Ray Stevens' "Raymone's
Salad". 31

Sylvia's Flour Tortillas. 32

Mel Tillis' Hamburger Stew. . . 33

Porter Wagoner's Fudge. 34

Kitty Wells' Barbecued
Chicken In a Bag. 35

Tammy Wynette's Blueberry
Buckle. 36

alabama's carob brownies

Yield: 2 dozen bars

Temperature: 325°
Baking time: 23 minutes

1 (6-ounce) package carob nuggets
1/2 cup honey
2 eggs
1 banana, sliced
1/3 cup butter, softened
1 teaspoon vanilla
1 cup chopped nuts
1 cup whole wheat flour
1/2 teaspoon baking soda
1/2 teaspoon salt

Preheat oven to 325°. Place the carob, honey, eggs, banana, butter, and vanilla in a blender. Blend for 1 minute. In a large bowl, mix the nuts, flour, baking soda, and salt. Add the contents of the blender and mix well. Bake in a greased 12x8x2-inch baking pan. Do not overbake!

Submitted by Kelly Owen, wife of Randy Owen, lead vocalist for *Alabama*.

9

bill anderson's pumpkin ice cream pie

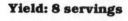

Yield: 8 servings

Preparation time:
10 minutes
plus 2 hours freezing
time

½ cup brown sugar
½ teaspoon cinnamon
¼ teaspoon nutmeg
1 (16-ounce) can pumpkin
1 quart vanilla ice cream, softened
Whipped topping, optional

In a large bowl of an electric mixer, blend together the brown sugar, cinnamon, nutmeg, pumpkin, and ice cream. Pour the mixture into a 9-inch pie pan and freeze. Serve topped with whipped topping, if desired.

eddy arnold's
coconut cream pie

Yield: 8 servings

Temperature: 350°
Baking time:
 12 to 15 minutes

2/3 cup sugar
1/2 teaspoon salt
2 1/2 Tablespoons cornstarch
1 Tablespoon flour
3 cups milk
1 cup coconut
3 egg yolks, slightly beaten
1 Tablespoon butter or
 margarine
1 1/2 teaspoons vanilla
1 (9-inch) pie shell, baked

In a large saucepan, mix the sugar, salt, cornstarch and flour. Gradually stir in the milk and cook over moderate heat, stirring constantly, until the mixture comes to a boil. Remove from heat and stir in 3/4 cup coconut, the egg yolks, butter, and vanilla. Pour into the pastry shell.

Meringue
3 egg whites
1/2 teaspoon vanilla
1/4 teaspoon cream of tartar
6 Tablespoons sugar

Beat the egg whites with vanilla and cream of tartar until soft peaks form. Add the sugar gradually, beating until stiff and all the sugar is dissolved. Spread meringue over the filled pie and seal to the edge of the pastry. Sprinkle with the remaining coconut and bake until golden brown.

Eddy Arnold

johnny cash's "old iron pot" family-style chili

Yield: 12 to 15 servings

**Preparation time:
45 minutes**

5 pounds sirloin steak,
  chopped
Shortening
3 packages chili seasoning
  mix
Chili powder and/or chili
  con carne seasoning to
  taste
Cumin
Thyme
Sage
Chopped onions
Chopped green chiles
3 or 4 (1-pound) cans
  kidney beans, undrained
3 or 4 (20-ounce) cans
  tomatoes, undrained
2 Tablespoons sugar
Garlic powder
Onion powder
Salt
1 (6-ounce) can tomato
  paste

In a large Dutch oven, brown the meat in shortening. Pour off the grease. Add chili seasoning and cook for 5 minutes over moderate heat. Add chili powder and/or chili con carne seasoning, spices, onion, green chiles, beans, tomatoes, and sugar. Season to taste with garlic powder, onion powder, and salt. If too spicy, add more tomatoes. Stir in the tomato paste. If it gets too thick, add water. Simmer, uncovered, for 20 minutes.

june carter cash's vegetable "stuff"

Yield: 8 servings

Preparation time:
45 minutes

1/3 cup flour
2 1/4 teaspoons salt
1/4 teaspoon freshly ground
  black pepper
2 medium green tomatoes,
  sliced 1/4 inch thick
2 zucchini, sliced
  1/4 inch thick
1/2 cup oil
1 large green pepper, sliced
1 pound potatoes, peeled
  and thinly sliced
1 cup chopped onions
4 Tablespoons butter or
  margarine
1 pound fresh mushrooms,
  sliced
1 teaspoon sugar
Freshly grated Parmesan
  cheese

Mix flour with 1 1/4 teaspoons salt and 1/8 teaspoon black pepper. Use this mixture to coat the tomato and zucchini slices. Set aside. In a very large skillet, heat 1/4 cup oil; add green pepper and saute for 2 minutes; remove and set aside. In the same skillet, saute the tomato and zucchini, a few slices at a time, until nicely browned (about 2 minutes on each side). Remove. Put 1/4 cup oil in the skillet and add potatoes, onion, and 1/2 teaspoon salt. Cook over medium heat and stir until the potatoes are tender, about 10 minutes. Remove. In the same skillet, melt butter and saute the mushrooms for 5 minutes. Stir in sugar and the remaining salt and pepper. Gently stir in the sauteed green pepper, tomatoes, zucchini, potatoes, and onion. Toss gently until well mixed. Reheat and serve topped with cheese.

June Carter Cash

mama cash's chocolate bavarian pie

Yield: 8 servings

Preparation time:
10 minutes
plus 4 hours chilling time

1 envelope unflavored
  gelatin
1/2 cup cold water
2 envelopes cocoa mix
1 Tablespoon instant coffee
1 cup evaporated milk,
  heated
1/2 cup evaporated milk,
  chilled
Chocolate shavings
2 Tablespoons low-calorie
  whipped topping

In a medium bowl, dissolve the gelatin in the water. Add cocoa mix, coffee, and the hot milk. Mix well and chill until thickened. With an electric mixer, beat the chilled mixture until fluffy. Add the cold milk and continue beating until smooth. Pour mixture into an 8-inch pie plate. Refrigerate until firm. Before serving, garnish with chocolate shavings and the whipped topping.

Note: Only about 94 calories per serving!

Mrs Ray Cash

rosanne cash's tuna casserole

Yield: 4 to 6 servings

Temperature: 425°
Baking time: 20 minutes

1 (10-ounce) package egg noodles or 5 ounces egg noodles and 5 ounces macaroni
1 can cream of mushroom, cream of chicken, or cream of celery soup
5 ounces milk
4 ounces sharp Cheddar cheese, shredded
1/2 cup mayonnaise
1 (17-ounce) can peas, undrained
1 (6 1/2-ounce) can tuna packed in water, drained
Cracker crumbs

Preheat oven to 425°. In a large saucepan, cook the noodles in boiling water. Drain and set aside. In the same saucepan, mix the soup and milk over medium heat; stir in the cheese until melted. Remove the pan from the heat. Add mayonnaise, peas, tuna, and noodles; mix thoroughly. Pour mixture into a 12x8x2-inch baking dish. Sprinkle with crumbs and bake.

Rosanne Cash

tennessee ernie ford's fresh apple-nut cake

Yield: 8 to 10 servings

Temperature: 300°
Baking time:
1 hour 10 minutes

2 eggs
1 cup oil
1¾ cups granulated sugar
2½ cups sifted self-rising
flour
1 cup chopped nuts
3 cups pared, chopped
apples
1 teaspoon cinnamon
1 teaspoon vanilla

Grease a 13x9x2-inch baking pan. Beat eggs, oil, and sugar together thoroughly. Add flour, nuts, apples, cinnamon, and vanilla; mix well. Turn the batter into the prepared pan and bake.

Cream Cheese Icing
2 (3-ounce) packages cream
cheese
¼ cup butter or margarine,
softened
1 (1-pound) box powdered
sugar
2 teaspoons vanilla

Blend the icing ingredients until smooth. Frost the cooled cake. Store in the refrigerator.

Tennessee Ernie Ford

the gatlin brothers' mexican meatball soup

Yield: 6 servings

Preparation time: 1 hour

1 egg, slightly beaten
1/2 cup chopped onion
1/4 cup cornmeal
1 (4-ounce) can green chiles, seeded, rinsed, and chopped
1 clove garlic, minced
3/4 teaspoon salt
1/4 teaspoon oregano
1/8 teaspoon pepper
1 pound ground beef

In a large bowl, combine the egg, onion, cornmeal, 1/2 the green chiles, garlic, salt, oregano, and pepper. Add the ground beef and mix well. Shape mixture into 48 meatballs, using 1 rounded teaspoon for each. Set aside.

3 cups water
1 (16-ounce) can tomatoes, undrained
1 (8-ounce) can tomato sauce
1/3 cup chopped onion
1 clove garlic, minced
1 Tablespoon sugar
1 1/2 teaspoons chili powder
1 1/2 teaspoons salt
1/4 teaspoon pepper
1/4 teaspoon oregano

In a Dutch oven, combine the water, tomatoes, tomato sauce, onion, the remaining green chiles, garlic, sugar, chili powder, salt, pepper, and oregano. Mix thoroughly and bring to a boil. Add the meatballs. Return to a boil. Cover, reduce heat, and simmer for 30 minutes.

Submitted by Janis Gatlin.

merle haggard's rainbow stew

Yield: 6 to 8 servings

Preparation time:
2¾ hours

3 pints water
1 teaspoon red food coloring
1 teaspoon green food coloring
1 teaspoon yellow food coloring
4 medium potatoes, peeled and diced into ¾-inch cubes
1 quart water
1¼ pounds lean stew meat, cubed
1 large carrot, sliced
1 teaspoon Worcestershire sauce
1 Tablespoon salt
¾ teaspoon white pepper
1 clove garlic, minced
½ teaspoon Italian seasoning
1 (20-ounce) can whole tomatoes, undrained
1 stalk celery, diced
1 large green pepper, chopped
1 medium red onion, diced
2 Tablespoons chopped parsley
1 (10-ounce) package frozen pea pods
2 Tablespoons oil
2 Tablespoons flour

Divide the 3 pints water equally among 3 small saucepans; put a different color in each and add ⅓ of the potatoes to each pan; let stand for about an hour. Boil until the potatoes are tender, but still firm; drain and set aside to cool. Bring 1 quart water to a boil in a large heavy kettle. Add the meat and simmer for 50 minutes. Add the carrot, Worcestershire sauce, salt, pepper, garlic, Italian seasoning, tomatoes, and celery. Simmer until the meat is tender. Add the green pepper, onion, parsley, and pea pods; stir thoroughly. Simmer for about 12 minutes. Mix the oil with the flour and add to the stew. Stir and simmer for about 2 minutes. Add potatoes, heat for about 15 minutes, and it's ready to serve with a silver spoon!

grandpa jones'
biscuits

Yield: 16 biscuits

Temperature: 450°
Baking time: 20 minutes

2 Tablespoons oil
1 cup buttermilk
2 cups self-rising flour

Mix the oil and the buttermilk well. Put the flour in a large bowl and add the buttermilk and oil gradually; stirring constantly. When the dough seems to be fairly stiff, turn onto a lightly-floured surface and knead gently about 8 times. Roll out to about a 1/2-inch thickness. Cut biscuits with a small glass dipped in flour and bake on a greased cookie sheet.

brenda lee's
trout fillets

Yield: 2 servings

Preparation time:
15 minutes

Salt
Pepper
2 trout or bass fillets
1 egg, well beaten
Dried bread crumbs
1/2 cup butter or margarine
Fresh lemon juice

Salt and pepper the fillets. Dip each fillet in the egg and roll in bread crumbs. Pan-fry in melted butter over medium heat. When golden brown, remove the fillets and place on a serving platter. Squeeze fresh lemon juice over the fillets and serve.

loretta lynn's cherry pie

Yield: 6 servings

Temperature: 450°, 350°
Baking time:
10, 30 minutes

Crust
2 cups sifted flour
1/4 teaspoon salt
1/4 cup hot water
2/3 cup shortening

Mix the flour and the salt. Take 1/3 of this mixture and form a paste with the hot water. Cut the shortening into the remaining flour mixture. Add paste to the dry mixture and blend. Roll out 1/2 the dough for the bottom crust. Line a 9-inch pie pan, trimming the edge to 1/2 inch.

Filling
2 1/2 cups canned cherries, undrained
1 cup sugar
1/8 teaspoon salt
1/2 teaspoon almond extract
2 Tablespoons quick-cooking tapioca
1 Tablespoon butter or margarine

Stir the filling ingredients together gently. Pour into the pastry-lined pie pan. Dot with butter. Roll out remaining dough; cover the filling and flute the edge. Prick the top crust with a fork and bake until golden brown.

barbara mandrell's seafood mold

Yield: 6 to 8 servings

Preparation time:
20 minutes
plus overnight chilling

1 (8-ounce) package cream cheese, softened
1/2 cup mayonnaise
1 cup sour cream
1/4 cup finely minced green pepper
1/4 cup finely minced celery
1/4 cup finely minced green onions
1 (4-ounce) jar pimentos, drained and minced
1/4 cup chili sauce
Tabasco sauce
1/2 teaspoon salt
1/2 Tablespoon Worcestershire sauce
1 envelope unflavored gelatin
2 Tablespoons fresh lemon juice
2 Tablespoons cold water
3 (6-ounce) packages frozen crab and shrimp, thawed and drained
Watercress or parsley

In a large bowl of an electric mixer, blend cream cheese, mayonnaise, and sour cream. Add green pepper, celery, green onions, pimentos, chili sauce, Tabasco sauce, salt, and Worcestershire sauce; mix thoroughly. Dissolve the gelatin in lemon juice and cold water. Heat this mixture in the top of a double boiler over hot water for 5 to 10 minutes, stirring occasionally. Gradually stir gelatin into the cheese mixture. Add the crab and shrimp and blend well. Pour into a 2-quart chilled and greased ring mold. Refrigerate overnight. Unmold and garnish with watercress or parsley.

Barbara Mandrell

ronnie milsap's chicken breast casserole

Yield: 6 servings

Temperature: 350°
Baking time: 30 minutes

2 (10-ounce) packages
frozen broccoli, cooked
and drained
2 cans cream of chicken
soup
1 cup mayonnaise
1 teaspoon lemon juice
6 chicken breasts, skinned,
boned, and fully cooked
1 cup shredded Cheddar
cheese
Bread crumbs

In a 12x8x2-inch baking dish,
mix together the broccoli, soup,
mayonnaise, and lemon juice.
Place the chicken on top of the
mixture and top with cheese and
bread crumbs. Bake.

Submitted by Joyce Milsap.

the oak ridge boys' caramel corn

Yield: 6 to 8 servings

Temperature: 250°
Baking time: 30 minutes

2 cups brown sugar
1/2 cup light corn syrup
1 cup butter or margarine
1/2 teaspoon cream of tartar
1 teaspoon baking soda
16 cups popcorn, popped
  and lightly salted

In a medium saucepan, combine the brown sugar, corn syrup, butter, and cream of tartar over low heat. Bring to a boil and boil for 5 minutes, stirring constantly. Remove the pan from the heat and add the baking soda. Pour the mixture over the popcorn and mix well. Spread on a cookie sheet and bake, stirring often. Store in an airtight container.

dolly parton's
brownie pudding

Yield: 6 to 8 servings

Temperature: 350°
Baking time: 40 minutes
plus 2 hours chilling time

1 cup sifted flour
3/4 cup granulated sugar
2 Tablespoons unsweetened
cocoa
2 teaspoons baking powder
1/2 teaspoon salt
1/2 cup milk
2 Tablespoons oil
1 teaspoon vanilla
3/4 cup chopped pecans
3/4 cup brown sugar
1/4 cup unsweetened cocoa
1 3/4 cups hot water

Sift together the flour,
granulated sugar, 2 Tablespoons
cocoa, baking powder, and salt
in a large bowl. Add the milk, oil,
and vanilla; mix until smooth.
Stir in the pecans and pour into
a greased 8-inch square baking
pan. Combine the brown sugar,
1/4 cup cocoa, and hot water and
pour over the batter. Bake. Cool
completely and then refrigerate.

Note: **This is best served really cold.**

minnie pearl's chess pie

Yield: 6 servings

Temperature: 300°
Baking time: 50 minutes

1/2 cup butter or margarine
1 1/2 cups sugar
3 eggs, beaten
1 Tablespoon cider vinegar
1 Tablespoon vanilla
1/2 teaspoon salt
1 (8-inch) unbaked pie shell

Combine the butter and sugar in saucepan over medium heat. Cook, stirring constantly, until very smooth. Remove the pan from the heat. Add the eggs and mix thoroughly. Stir in vinegar, vanilla, and salt; beat well with a wire whisk. Pour into pastry shell and bake.

minnie Pearl

jeannie c. riley's texas skyscraper dessert

Yield: 12 servings

Temperature: 350°
Baking time:
   15 to 20 minutes
   plus 3 hours chilling time

First Layer
1/2 cup butter or margarine, softened
1 cup chopped pecans
1 cup flour

Mix butter, pecans, and flour with a pastry blender or a food processor. Press on the bottom and sides of a 12x8x2-inch baking pan. Bake until lightly browned. Cool.

Second Layer
1 (8-ounce) package cream cheese, softened
1 cup powdered sugar
1 cup whipped topping

Blend cream cheese, powdered sugar, and whipped topping and spread evenly over cooled crust.

Third Layer
1 (3³/4-ounce) box instant chocolate pudding
2 1/2 cups milk

Blend the pudding mix and milk until smooth and spread over the second layer.

Fourth Layer
1 cup heavy cream
1/4 cup sugar
1 teaspoon vanilla

Whip the cream until light and fluffy. Add the sugar and vanilla; blend thoroughly. Spread over the top layer and chill.

'82

johnny rodriguez's enchiladas

Temperature: 350°
Baking time: 5 minutes

1 pound ground round
1/2 teaspoon salt
1 clove garlic, crushed
2 cups oil
1 package corn tortillas
1/2 cup chopped Bermuda onion
2 cups shredded Cheddar cheese
1 cup chopped olives
1 (8-ounce) can enchilada sauce
Chopped green onions, optional

Brown the meat in a large skillet over medium heat. Add salt and garlic, stir, and simmer. Heat the oil in a separate skillet over medium high heat. Fry the tortillas in the oil, approximately 15 seconds on each side. Drain and stack on paper towels. Fill each tortilla with 2 Tablespoons meat. Sprinkle with Bermuda onion, cheese, and olives. Spoon on 2 Tablespoons enchilada sauce for each portion. Fold in sides and fasten with a toothpick. When all tortillas are filled, place on a cookie sheet lined with foil. Cover each enchilada with the remaining sauce and sprinkle with the rest of the cheese and chopped green onions, if desired. Bake.

Note: This dish freezes beautifully.

t. g. sheppard's chicken-shrimp supreme

Yield: 8 servings

Preparation time:
  30 minutes

1/4 cup butter or margarine
1/2 pound fresh mushrooms, sliced
2 Tablespoons sliced green onions
2 cans cream of chicken soup
1/2 cup sherry
1/2 cup light cream
1 cup shredded Cheddar cheese
2 cups diced and cooked chicken
2 cups cooked shrimp
2 Tablespoons chopped parsley
Hot buttered rice

Melt the butter in a large saucepan; add the mushrooms and onions and saute for 5 minutes. Add the soup; gradually stir in the sherry and the light cream. Add the cheese and heat over low heat, stirring until the cheese melts. Add the chicken and shrimp and heat, but do not boil. Just before serving, stir in the parsley, and serve over the rice.

Note: This dish can be prepared ahead of time, refrigerated, and heated when ready to serve.

hank snow's melting moments cookies

Temperature: 300°
Baking time: 12 minutes

1 cup butter, margarine, or shortening
3/4 cup brown sugar
1 egg
1 teaspoon cream of tartar
1/2 teaspoon baking soda
2 cups flour
1 teaspoon vanilla

In a large bowl of an electric mixer, cream together the butter and the brown sugar. Add the egg and beat until fluffy. Add the cream of tartar, baking soda, and flour; mix until well blended. Stir in the vanilla and drop by teaspoons on an ungreased cookie sheet. Bake.

ray stevens' "raymone's salad"

Yield: 8 servings

Preparation time:
  30 minutes
  plus 2 hours chilling time

1/2 head iceberg lettuce, torn into pieces
1/2 head romaine lettuce, torn into pieces
3 small onions, chopped
1 green pepper, chopped
1 (8 1/2-ounce) can artichoke hearts, drained and chopped
1 (15-ounce) can asparagus tips, drained
4 radishes, thinly sliced
1 large tomato, cut into wedges
1 carrot, thinly sliced
2 large celery stalks, diced
2 hard boiled eggs, chopped
1 cup cottage cheese
Chopped sweet pickles
India relish
Bacon bits
2 Tablespoons avocado salad dressing
2 Tablespoons bleu cheese salad dressing
2 Tablespoons 1000 island salad dressing

Toss all ingredients together and chill.

sylvia's flour tortillas

Yield: 2 dozen tortillas

Preparation time:
20 minutes

4 cups flour
2 teaspoons salt
1/8 teaspoon baking powder
2/3 cup shortening
1 cup plus 3 Tablespoons
hot water

Combine flour, salt, and baking powder thoroughly. Cut in the shortening with a pastry blender until the mixture resembles coarse meal. Gradually stir in the water, mixing well. Shape the dough into 1 1/2-inch balls. Roll each ball out on a lightly-floured surface into a very thin circle, 6 inches in diameter. Heat an ungreased electric skillet to 375°. Cook tortillas for about 2 minutes on each side or until lightly browned. Pat the tortillas lightly with a spatula while browning the second side if they start to puff. Serve hot.

Note: **The tortillas can be cooked on an ungreased griddle or in a skillet over medium heat.**

m-m-m-mel tillis' hamburger stew

Yield: 4 to 6 servings

**Preparation time:
2 1/2 hours**

1 1/2 pounds ground beef
1 onion, chopped
5 or 6 carrots, sliced
3 medium potatoes, diced
2 cups sliced okra
Salt and pepper
1/4 teaspoon thyme
1/4 teaspoon oregano
1 cup water

Brown the ground beef in a large skillet; drain off grease. Stir in onion, carrots, potatoes, okra, salt, pepper, thyme, and oregano. Add water and bring to a boil. Reduce heat and simmer, uncovered, for about 2 hours.

Serving suggestion: Serve over hot fluffy rice.

Mel Tillis

porter wagoner's fudge

Yield: 20 pieces

Preparation time:
20 minutes
plus 1 hour chilling time

2 cups sugar
2 heaping Tablespoons
  cocoa
1/2 teaspoon salt
1/4 cup syrup
1/2 cup milk
2 Tablespoons butter or
  margarine
1 teaspoon vanilla
2 Tablespoons peanut
  butter
1/2 cup English walnuts,
  chopped

Combine the sugar, cocoa, salt, syrup, and milk in a large heavy saucepan. Bring to a boil over medium high heat. Stirring constantly, let the mixture continue to boil for another 4 to 5 minutes until the sugar is dissolved and it reaches a soft-ball stage. Remove the pan from the heat; stir in the butter and vanilla. Let cool at room temperature. Add the peanut butter and the walnuts; beat until creamy. Refrigerate for an hour and *hold a gun on yourself until you taste it! My mother taught me this when I was a boy and I've never forgotten it.*

kitty wells' barbecued chicken in a bag

Yield: 4 to 6 servings

Temperature: 375°
Baking time: 1 hour

Salt
Pepper
2 1/2 to 3 1/2 pounds fryer
  pieces

Sauce
2 Tablespoons catsup
2 teaspoons vinegar
2 teaspoons Worcestershire
  sauce
4 teaspoons water
2 teaspoons lemon juice
1/2 teaspoon red pepper
1 teaspoon prepared
  mustard
1 teaspoon paprika
1 teaspoon chili powder
2 teaspoons melted butter

Season the chicken and let stand at room temperature for 30 minutes. Meanwhile, combine all the ingredients for the sauce in a small bowl. Dip the chicken pieces in the sauce and place in a greased paper bag. Tie securely with a string to keep all the moisture inside the bag. Place on a cookie sheet and bake.

Note: Allow an additional 15 minutes baking time if the chicken is very cold.

Sincerely
Kitty Wells

tammy wynette's
blueberry buckle

Yield: 4 to 6 servings

Temperature: 375°
Baking time:
  45 to 50 minutes

2 cups sifted flour
2 teaspoons baking powder
1/2 teaspoon salt
3/4 cup sugar
1/4 cup butter or margarine,
  softened
1 egg
1/2 cup milk
2 cups fresh blueberries,
  stemmed

Sift together the flour, baking powder, and salt. In a blender or a food processor, cream the sugar and butter; beat in the egg. Add the flour mixture and the milk. Blend just until the dry ingredients are dampened. Fold in the blueberries. Pour mixture into a greased 9-inch square pan.

Topping
1/2 cup sugar
1/3 cup flour
1/2 teaspoon cinnamon
1/4 cup butter or margarine,
  softened

Blend topping ingredients and sprinkle over the blueberry mixture. Bake until a toothpick comes out clean. Loosen the edges, partially cool, and cut into squares.

beverages

beverages

Blender Ice Tea 40

Bloody Mary Mix 41

Boiled Custard 41

Breakfast in a Gulp 40

Cafe Mexicano 42

Christmas Cranberry Tea . . . 42

Coffee Punch 43

Do-It-Yourself Kahlua 43

Eggnog 44

Frozen Whiskey Sour 44

Mint Julep 45

Peach Smash 45

Sangria 46

Sunshine Tea 40

Super Slurping Punch 46

hints for beverages

Store your glasses in the freezer for 30 minutes before serving, to ensure frosty cold drinks.

Provide cloth napkins when serving Mint Juleps. The glasses are so very cold to hold for a long period of time!

Count on 350 ice cubes for 50 people: 1 pound per person.

Use the microwave to thaw frozen juice. Remove from container, place in microwave in serving pitcher. Microwave on high for 30 to 45 seconds; add water and serve.

Never fill wine glasses to the top. Serve only 1/2-full to allow the bouquet to fill the glass.

Store tea bags in jar with citrus peel, vanilla bean, or cinnamon sticks.

For large parties, use your empty washing machine for storing ice and cooling beer. No mess afterward.

To brew a perfect cup of tea, warm the teapot with boiling water and let stand for a few minutes. Drain and add 1 teaspoon tea leaves for each cup needed. Pour boiling water over the tea and let steep for 3 to 5 minutes before serving.

When serving lemon quarters or halves with tea, place in squares of cheesecloth to prevent squirting and to strain the seeds.

Store vodka in the freezer.

Freeze carbonated beverages in ice cube trays with a maraschino cherry to add color and fizz to a punch bowl.

Spice tea mix: 1/2 cup instant tea
          1 1/2 cups sugar
          2 (7-ounce) jars orange-flavored breakfast drink
          1 (12-ounce) package lemonade crystals
          1/2 teaspoon ground cloves
          1 teaspoon cinnamon

Mix thoroughly in a large bowl and store in a covered container. Use 1 to 2 teaspoons mix per 1 cup boiling water.

blender ice tea

Yield: 2 servings

Preparation time:
5 minutes

"Interesting new twist for tea"

2 cups cold water
1 1/2 Tablespoons instant tea
2 Tablespoons lemon or lime
   juice
4 maraschino cherries
2 teaspoons sugar
1 cup cracked ice

Blend all ingredients and serve over ice.

sunshine tea

Yield: 2 1/2 quarts

Preparation time:
Several hours

"Let the sun do all the work."

2 1/2 quarts water
5 tea bags
Mint

Fill glass jar with water, tea, and mint. Cover and set jar in the sun for several hours.

breakfast in a gulp

Yield: 1 serving

Preparation time:
5 minutes

"Good for sick children of all ages"

1 cup orange juice
1 egg
2 Tablespoons honey
2 ice cubes

Blend all ingredients on high speed for 5 seconds.

40

bloody mary mix

Preparation time:
10 minutes

"Not too spicy"

10 lemons
6 ounces Worcestershire
  sauce
10 drops Tabasco sauce
1 1/2 Tablespoons celery seed
3 Tablespoons salt
2 1/4 (46-ounce) cans
  vegetable juice
Vodka

Squeeze lemons into a gallon container. Add seasonings and fill to the top with vegetable juice. Lace with vodka.

boiled custard

Yield: 10 to 12 servings

Preparation time:
30 minutes
plus 2 hours chilling time

"Yummy"

1/2 gallon milk
9 eggs
1 1/2 cups sugar
Pinch salt
5 heaping teaspoons
  cornstarch
4 teaspoons vanilla

Heat milk in the top of a large double boiler. Beat eggs. Blend sugar, salt, and cornstarch and add to eggs. Pour a small amount of the hot milk over the egg mixture. Stir well. Combine with remaining milk and cook until thick. Flavor with vanilla and refrigerate until thoroughly chilled.

cafe mexicano

Yield: 12 servings

Preparation time:
20 minutes

"Your guests won't leave until this is all gone."

12 cups strong coffee
3 ounces chocolate syrup
1/4 cup sugar
1/2 teaspoon cinnamon
1/4 teaspoon nutmeg
1 1/2 cups coffee liqueur
Whipped cream
Cinnamon

Perk the coffee and remove the basket of the percolator. Add syrup, sugar, cinnamon, and nutmeg, stirring to dissolve. Add the liqueur. If not serving immediately, stir occasionally. Serve topped with whipped cream and a dusting of cinnamon.

Note: **This can be doubled or tripled, depending on the size of your coffee pot.**

christmas cranberry tea

Yield: 1 quart

Preparation time: 1 hour

"Great on a cold night"

1 quart fresh cranberries
2 quarts water
2 cups sugar
2 cups water
2 cinnamon sticks
1 cup orange juice
3 Tablespoons lemon juice
Vodka or light rum

Cook berries in 2 quarts water until mushy. Strain through cheesecloth 3 times and cool. Cook sugar with 2 cups water and cinnamon sticks to a medium syrup; cool. Add orange juice and lemon juice to the cranberry juice and strain again. Combine with the syrup. Heat before serving and spike with vodka or light rum, if desired.

coffee punch

Preparation time:
  10 minutes

"Milder than Irish coffee"

6 Tablespoons sugar
6 cups double-strength
  coffee
2 cups heavy cream,
  whipped
1 cup Jamaican rum
5 quarts vanilla ice cream

In a large bowl, add the sugar to the coffee; fold in whipped cream and rum. Place scoops of ice cream in a punch bowl. Add the coffee mixture and stir gently.

do-it-yourself kahlua

Yield: 1/2 gallon

Preparation time:
  30 minutes plus 2
  weeks standing time

"A delightful surprise"

3 cups water
4 cups sugar
1 vanilla bean
1 cup boiling water
2 ounces instant Yuban
  coffee
1 fifth 80-proof vodka

Boil 3 cups water and sugar for 20 minutes. Split vanilla bean lengthwise and add both halves to mixture. Cool. Combine boiling water with coffee and let cool. Add to sugar mixture. Add vodka and seal in a 1/2-gallon container. Let stand at room temperature for 2 weeks. Remove vanilla bean, strain, and bottle.

egg nog

Yield: 1 1/2 gallons

**Preparation time:
4 1/2 hours**

"A holiday tradition"

**12 eggs, separated
1 (1-pound) box powdered
  sugar
3 to 4 cups bourbon
2 quarts heavy cream
Nutmeg**

Beat the egg yolks until light in
color; gradually beat in the
sugar. Slowly add 2 cups
bourbon, beating constantly.
Cover and refrigerate 1 hour.
Add 1 to 2 cups bourbon and the
cream, beating constantly. Cover
and refrigerate 3 hours. Beat egg
whites until stiff, but not dry,
and fold them into cold mixture.
Serve sprinkled with nutmeg.

frozen whiskey sour

Yield: 8 servings

**Preparation time: 2 hours
  freezing time**

"Use your blender."

**1 (6-ounce) can frozen
  lemonade concentrate
12 ounces bourbon
18 ounces water
1 Tablespoon frozen
  orange juice
  concentrate**

Blend and freeze until ready to
serve. Mix in blender again right
before serving.

Note: **Use the empty lemonade can as a handy measure for
the bourbon and the water.**

mint julep

"A true Tennessee treat"

1/2 cup sugar
6 sprigs fresh mint
3 ounces ice water
18 ounces Sour Mash
  Whiskey (or a good
  bourbon)
Finely crushed ice

In a large glass container, sprinkle sugar over mint leaves and add ice water. Crush gently and let stand 30 minutes. Put a few of the crushed leaves in an empty quart bottle. Add the whiskey to the sugar mixture and stir gently. Pour through a funnel into the quart bottle; shake gently and tighten cap. Put in freezer for several hours. To serve, fill silver goblets or julep cups with finely crushed ice and the julep mix. Garnish with a sprig of mint and serve with a silver sipper or a short straw.

peach smash

Yield: 1 quart

**Preparation time:
  10 minutes**

"Very, very potent"

2 ripe peaches, pitted
1/3 (6-ounce) can frozen
  pineapple juice
3/4 cup light rum
Chopped ice

In blender or food processor, combine unpeeled peaches, cut into chunks, the pineapple juice, and the rum. Fill the container with chopped ice and blend again.

Note: **Those with a sweet tooth will want to add 1/4 cup sugar.**

sangria

**Preparation time:
20 minutes plus 2
hours chilling time**

"Marvelous accompaniment with a Mexican meal"

1/2 cup lemon juice
1/2 cup orange juice
1/2 cup sugar
1 (4/5-quart) bottle dry
red wine
1 (7-ounce) bottle club soda
Sliced bananas, oranges,
lemons, peaches,
strawberries, or pineapple
Ice cubes

Pour lemon and orange juice
into large pitcher. Add sugar and
stir to dissolve. Add wine and
refrigerate. When ready to serve,
add club soda, fruit, and ice
cubes.

Note: **To make Mock Sangria, substitute grape juice for the**
wine. If you're in a hurry, substitute fruit cocktail for the
sliced fruit.

super slurping punch

Yield: 32 servings

**Preparation time:
2 1/2 hours**

1 lemon, sliced
1 orange, sliced
1 (6-ounce) can frozen
lemonade, thawed
1 (6-ounce) can frozen
orange juice, thawed
6 ounces lemon juice
1 fifth bourbon
3 quarts lemon-lime
soft drink

Freeze lemon and orange slices
in an ice ring. Combine
lemonade, orange juice, lemon
juice, and bourbon and chill.
Pour over ice ring in a punch
bowl and add lemon-lime soft
drink just before serving.

hors
d'oeuvres

hors d'oeuvres

Appetizers
Artichoke Bottom First
  Course.................... 50
Avocados Stuffed with Curried
  Crabmeat................. 51
Broiled Chicken Liver
  Appetizers 51
Elegant Caviar Pie 52
Mexican Appetizer 52
Oysters Chez Elise........... 53

Canapes
Almond Cheese Strips 54
Apples with Bleu Cheese 55
Asparagus Roll-Ups 54
Bacon-Wrapped Shrimp 55
Brie en Croute............... 49
Buried Treasures 56
Krispie Cheese Wafers 57
Marinated Carrot Sticks 58
Marvelous Meatballs......... 58
Olive Cheese Balls 57
Oyster-Stuffed
  Mushrooms............... 59
Snowcapped Mushrooms 60
Stuffed Mushrooms
  Parmesan................. 61
Tasty Water Chestnuts....... 62
Toasted Artichoke
  Rounds.................. 53

Dips, Sauces, and Spreads
Beer Cheese................. 62
Beer Dip, Pumpernickel
  Surprise 63
Carousel Cheese Ball 64
Caviar Mousse 67
Chafing Dish Spinach with
  Oysters 65
Chicken Liver Pate 68
Chili Dip, Bacon-Wrapped
  Shrimp 55
Chili Roll................... 66
Christmas Cheese
  Spread................... 69
Crabmeat Hors d'Oeuvre
  Mold..................... 68
Crab Mousse 66
Dill Dip 69
Hot Clam Dip................ 70
Hot Crabmeat Dip 67
Jezebel Sauce 72
Layered Guacamole 71
Mexican Guacamole Dip 70
Pumpernickel Surprise 63
Shrimp Cocktail Spread 73
Shrimp, Mushroom, Artichoke
  Fondue 73
Something Special Hot Cheese
  Dip 72
Sour Cream Dip, Pumpernickel
  Surprise 63
Spinach Dip................. 74
Sweet 'n Sour Sauce 74

brie en croute

Temperature: 400°, 325°
Baking time:
  10, 20 minutes

"So good and different"

1 (2-pound) wheel Brie
  cheese
2 packages frozen puff
  pastry shells, thawed
1 egg yolk
1 Tablespoon water

Roll out 5 pastry rounds large enough to cover the bottom and sides of the cheese. Set dough on a buttered cookie sheet and place the cheese in the center, folding the dough up around the sides of the cheese. Roll out 4 more pastry rounds slightly larger than the top of the wheel, cover the top, and overlap the sides. Crimp the 2 sections together and seal. Use the remaining pastry, making a braid to cover where the sides are sealed. Flowers and leaves or other decorations may be added to the top, if desired. Prick the top and sides of the dough lightly, not touching the cheese inside. Brush wheel with a mixture of the egg yolk and water. Bake for 10 minutes at 400°. Reduce the oven to 325° and bake for 20 minutes or until golden brown. Let wheel sit for at least 2 hours at room temperature before serving.

Note: It is best to use a green wheel, as it matures during the baking time.

artichoke bottom first course

Yield: 5 to 7 servings

Preparation time:
15 to 20 minutes

"Ideal for ladies' brunch with salad and bread"

1 (7½-ounce) can artichoke bottoms
¼ cup butter or margarine
2 shallots, chopped
2 fresh mushrooms, thinly sliced
2 ounces prosciutto, finely chopped
2 teaspoons parsley, minced
2 teaspoons flour
⅓ cup milk
Pepper
Sherry or wine
2 ounces Gruyere cheese, shredded
Butter or margarine

Saute artichoke bottoms in butter briefly on each side. Remove artichokes from pan and saute shallots, mushrooms, and ham. Add parsley, stir in flour, and cook over low heat for 2 minutes, stirring constantly. Remove from heat and stir in milk. Return to heat and stir until thickened and smooth. Season to taste with pepper and sherry. Fill artichoke bottoms with mixture, sprinkle with cheese, and dot with butter. Run under broiler until cheese is melted and bubbly.

encore! nashville equivalents

1 pound brown sugar = 2½ cups, packed
1 pound cheese, shredded = 4 to 5 cups
15 to 18 graham crackers = 1 cup crumbs
1 lemon = 2 Tablespoons juice, 2 teaspoons rind
½ pound fresh mushrooms, = 2½ cups sliced
1 orange = 6 Tablespoons juice, 2 Tablespoons rind
1 pound powdered sugar = 3½ to 4 cups

avocados stuffed with curried crabmeat

Yield: 6 servings

Temperature: 350°
Baking time: 15 minutes

"An elegant first course"

2 Tablespoons butter or
  margarine
2 Tablespoons flour
1 cup milk
1/2 teaspoon curry powder
1/2 teaspoon grated onion
Salt and pepper
2 (6-ounce) packages frozen
  crab, thawed and drained
3 large avocados

Over medium heat, melt butter and add flour. Gradually add milk, stirring until smooth and thickened. Add seasonings and crabmeat. Halve avocados, remove seeds, and fill with crab mixture. Set avocados in a pan filled with boiling water an inch deep. Cover pan loosely and bake.

broiled chicken liver appetizers

Yield: 30 appetizers

Preparation time:
  10 minutes
  plus overnight chilling

"Crisp and delicious"

1/2 pound chicken livers
15 slices wafer-thin bacon
1 (8-ounce) can sliced water
  chestnuts, drained
2 1/2 ounces soy sauce
4 Tablespoons butter or
  margarine
Salt
Pepper

Halve each chicken liver and bacon slice. Stuff water chestnuts inside livers and then wrap with a bacon slice, securing with a toothpick. Marinate in the refrigerator overnight or for several hours in soy sauce and melted butter, seasoned with salt and pepper to taste. When ready to serve, broil about 5 minutes on each side or until bacon is well done.

51

elegant caviar pie

Preparation time:
1 1/2 hours

"For a very special occasion"

1 (8 or 9-inch) pie shell
1 (4-ounce) jar black
  lumpfish caviar
1 cup sour cream
Lemon juice
Scraped onion
Cayenne pepper
3 hard boiled eggs, grated
Paprika

Bake and cool pie shell. Spread caviar over the bottom. Season the sour cream with lemon juice, onion, and cayenne to taste. Spread this mixture over caviar. Cover with grated egg and sprinkle the top with paprika. Chill thoroughly and serve in wedges.

Note: The pie is also excellent served in tiny pastry shells for large cocktail parties. This method will yield 36 tarts.

mexican appetizer

Yield: 6 to 8 servings

Temperature: 400°
Baking time: 20 minutes

"So good you might want to eat this with a spoon"

1 onion, chopped
1 pound ground beef
1 (7-ounce) bottle taco
  sauce, red or green
1 (7-ounce) can green chiles,
  diced
1 (16-ounce) can refried
  beans
3 or 4 hard boiled eggs,
  chopped
1 (6-ounce) can black olives,
  pitted and sliced
2 cups shredded sharp
  Cheddar cheese

Brown onion and ground beef. Drain off fat. Stir in taco sauce and green chiles. Set aside. In a baking dish, layer refried beans, eggs, black olives (reserving some for the topping), and the meat mixture. Top with cheese and reserved olives. Bake until bubbly. Serve in a chafing dish.

oysters chez elise

Yield: 6 servings

Temperature: 400°
Baking time: 15 minutes

"Bake in a flat casserole and serve as a side dish."

3 to 4 dozen oysters
1/2 cup sherry
1/2 cup butter or margarine
1 large clove garlic, crushed
2 cups bread crumbs
3 Tablespoons finely
   chopped parsley
2 teaspoons grated lemon
   rind
Salt
Freshly ground pepper
Lemon wedges

Marinate oysters in sherry for an hour or more. In a medium saucepan, melt butter and stir in garlic, but do not brown. Stir in all other ingredients except lemon wedges and cook until the bread crumbs are golden. Spoon oysters into scallop shells and top with bread crumb mixture. Bake. Do not overcook. Serve immediately and garnish with lemon wedges.

toasted artichoke rounds

Yield: 24 to 32 rounds

Preparation time:
20 minutes

"Simply elegant"

24 to 32 small bread rounds
1 (8 1/2-ounce) can artichoke
   hearts, rinsed, drained,
   and quartered
1 cup shredded provolone
   cheese
1/2 cup mayonnaise
1 teaspoon salt
1/2 teaspoon lemon pepper
Paprika

Toast bread rounds. Place an artichoke quarter on each round. Mix cheese, mayonnaise, salt, and lemon pepper and spread on artichokes. Sprinkle lightly with paprika. Broil until bubbly and lightly browned.

53

almond cheese strips

Temperature: 400°
Baking time: 10 minutes

"Keep in the freezer for emergency entertaining."

6 slices crisp bacon, crumbled
1 (3-ounce) package sliced almonds, chopped
2 teaspoons Worcestershire sauce
1/2 pound sharp Cheddar cheese, shredded
1 cup mayonnaise
Salt and pepper
1 loaf thin-sliced white bread, crusts removed

Combine all ingredients except bread. Spread mixture on bread slices. Cut into strips, place on cookie sheets, and freeze. Once frozen, store in plastic bags in the freezer. When needed, remove from bags, place on cookie sheets, and bake.

asparagus roll-ups
Yield: 70 rolls

Temperature: 400°
Baking time: 25 minutes

"Great to keep on hand for unexpected guests"

1 large loaf of bread, sliced
1 egg
4 ounces bleu cheese
1 (8-ounce) package cream cheese, softened
2 (15-ounce) cans asparagus spears, drained
3/4 cup butter or margarine, melted

Remove crusts from bread and roll each slice with a rolling pin until flat. Mix egg and cheeses until fluffy. Spread on each bread slice. Place 1 asparagus spear on each slice of bread and roll up. Dip rolls in butter. Place on a cookie sheet, cover with plastic wrap, and freeze for an hour. Cut each roll into three sections. Bake.

apples with bleu cheese

Yield: 6 servings

Preparation time:
10 minutes

"An appetizer, a salad, or a dessert"

1 (8-ounce) package cream
   cheese
2 ounces bleu cheese
6 winesap apples
6 ounces walnuts, chopped
Paprika
Bibb lettuce

Soften cheeses and combine. Peel and core apples. Cut into wedges and spread with cheese mixture. Top with walnuts, sprinkle with paprika, and serve on lettuce leaves.

bacon-wrapped shrimp

Yield: 8 servings

Temperature: 500°
Baking time: 10 minutes

"Serve hot with icy cold chili dip."

Chili Dip
1 hard boiled egg, chopped
3/4 cup mayonnaise
3 Tablespoons chopped
   sweet pickle
1 Tablespoon chopped
   stuffed olives
1 1/2 teaspoons grated onion
1 Tablespoon chili powder

1 pound fresh shrimp,
   cooked
8 to 10 slices wafer-thin
   bacon
1/2 cup butter or margarine
1 clove garlic, finely minced
1 1/2 teaspoons chili powder

Combine ingredients for *Chili Dip*. Cover and refrigerate for at least an hour to blend flavors. Wrap each shrimp with half a bacon slice and reserve. When ready to serve, melt butter and saute garlic sprinkled with chili powder. Brush shrimp with butter mixture and bake in a preheated oven 3 inches from the heat. Baste several times with the butter mixture and bake until the bacon is well done, about 5 minutes on each side.

buried treasures

Preparation time:
15 minutes

"Definitely a show-stopper"

2 cups mayonnaise
1/2 cup horseradish, well
    drained
1/2 teaspoon monosodium
    glutamate
2 teaspoons dry mustard
2 teaspoons lemon juice
1/2 teaspoon salt
1 pound medium shrimp,
    cooked
1 pint basket small cherry
    tomatoes
1 (6-ounce) can pitted black
    olives, drained
1 (8-ounce) can water
    chestnuts, drained
1/2 pound whole mushrooms
1/2 head cauliflower, broken
    into bite-size florets

Combine mayonnaise with the
seasonings. Stir in other
ingredients and serve in a
shallow bowl with toothpicks.

Note: This is best made early in the day or the night before,
adding the cauliflower right before serving.

If you don't have a garlic press, mash peeled garlic between pieces of
waxed paper or plastic wrap with a handle or a large knife. The
garlic smell and juice won't be absorbed into your cutting board.

krispie cheese wafers

Yield: 5 dozen wafers

Temperature: 350°
**Baking time: 20 to 25
   minutes**

"Really good and different"

**1 pound sharp Cheddar
   cheese, shredded**
**1 cup butter or margarine,
   softened**
1 teaspoon salt
1/4 teaspoon cayenne pepper
2 cups sifted flour
2 cups rice cereal

Combine all ingredients except
cereal in mixer. Blend in cereal
by hand. Form into 1-inch balls
and press down with a fork.
Bake.

Variation: 1 cup chopped pecans may be added with the
cereal.

olive cheese balls

Yield: 20 to 30 balls

Temperature: 400°
Baking time: 10 minutes

"These can be made ahead and frozen."

**1 pound sharp Cheddar
   cheese, shredded**
1 cup flour
Red pepper to taste
**Worcestershire sauce to
   taste**
**20 to 30 pimento-stuffed
   olives, drained**

Mix cheese, flour, and
seasonings until mixture forms a
ball. Pinch off small pieces of
dough and press around olives.
Bake on greased baking sheets.

Note: If frozen, bake for 15 minutes.

marvelous meatballs

Yield: 50 to 60 meatballs

Preparation time:
30 minutes

"This may be made ahead and frozen."

1 pound ground chuck
1/4 cup quick oats
1 teaspoon monosodium glutamate
1/4 teaspoon salt
1 (8-ounce) can water chestnuts, chopped
1/4 teaspoon garlic salt
1/4 teaspoon onion salt
1 teaspoon soy sauce
Dash red pepper
1 egg, beaten
1/4 cup milk

Mix together all ingredients and shape into small meatballs. Brown them over low heat, turning carefully. Drain and serve with Jezebel Sauce or Sweet 'n Sour Sauce. Serve in a chafing dish with toothpicks.

marinated carrot sticks

Yield: 6 to 8 servings

Preparation time:
Marinate overnight

"Young turnips may be substituted or added to this."

3 Tablespoons vinegar
3 Tablespoons oil
1 clove garlic, crushed
3/4 teaspoon seasoned salt
1/4 teaspoon salt
Minced parsley, optional
8 small carrots

Combine first 6 ingredients in a jar. Slice carrots lengthwise and put in the jar with the marinade. Cover tightly and refrigerate overnight. Save the marinade and add to it later.

oyster-stuffed mushrooms

Yield: 3 dozen

**Preparation time:
30 minutes**

"An easy pick-up appetizer"

2 pounds fresh mushrooms
Butter or margarine
3 dozen oysters
1 Tablespoon finely minced
onion
1/4 cup sour cream
3 Tablespoons heavy cream
1/2 cup bread crumbs
1/2 teaspoon sherry
1/4 teaspoon minced parsley
1/4 teaspoon Worcestershire
sauce
Salt
1/4 teaspoon pepper
2 Tablespoons butter or
margarine
1/4 cup grated Parmesan
cheese

Cut stems from caps of mushrooms. Drop into boiling water and boil for 2 minutes; drain. Saute caps in butter until very tender. Place 1 oyster in each cap and broil for 3 minutes or until oyster is just done. Chop mushroom stems and combine with remaining ingredients except Parmesan. Top each oyster with a spoonful of the mixture, sprinkle with Parmesan, and broil until slightly brown. Serve hot.

An antipasto platter makes a beautiful hors d'oeuvre. Serve tuna, pepperoni slices, radishes, artichoke hearts, pickled peppers, honeydew, prosciutto, cherry tomatoes, and Italian bread sticks.

snowcapped mushrooms

Yield: 8 servings

**Preparation time:
20 minutes**

"Serve piping hot."

1 pound fresh mushrooms
2 Tablespoons butter or
   margarine
2 Tablespoons flour
3/4 cup milk
1/2 pound fresh crabmeat,
   drained
1/3 cup sliced almonds,
   toasted
2 Tablespoons chopped
   green onions
2 teaspoons sherry
Dash hot pepper sauce

Wipe mushrooms clean and remove stems. Melt butter. Add flour and milk, stirring until very thick. Add remaining ingredients, mixing well. Fill each mushroom cap with crab mixture. Broil until lightly browned.

Always serve caviar well-chilled in a bowl on a bed of shaved ice. Serve with buttered hot melba toast or crackers.

stuffed mushrooms parmesan

Yield: 4 to 6 servings

Temperature: 350°
Baking time: 20 minutes

"The pepperoni makes the difference."

12 large mushrooms
2 Tablespoons butter or margarine
1 small onion, finely chopped
1/2 cup diced pepperoni
1 small clove garlic, minced
1/2 cup cracker crumbs
3 Tablespoons grated Parmesan cheese
1 Tablespoon minced parsley
1/2 teaspoon seasoned salt
1/4 teaspoon oregano
Salt
Pepper
1/3 cup chicken broth

Wipe mushrooms with damp cloth. Remove and finely chop stems. Melt butter and add onion, pepperoni, garlic, and chopped mushroom stems. Cook this mixture over low heat until tender, but not brown. Add cracker crumbs, cheese, parsley, and seasonings. Mix well. Stir in chicken broth. Spoon into caps. Bake uncovered in a shallow, lightly greased baking pan.

Note: **Large mushrooms are good for a seated first course. Smaller mushrooms make better appetizers.**

Line silver dishes with glass bowls, doilies, or foil to prevent pitting.

tasty water chestnuts

Yield: 6 servings

Temperature: 375°
Baking time: 15 minutes
plus 12 hours chilling
time

"Allow enough time for marinating."

1 (8-ounce) can water
chestnuts
2 Tablespoons soy sauce
2 Tablespoons
Worcestershire sauce
4 Tablespoons lemon juice
1 Tablespoon seasoned salt
1 Tablespoon garlic powder
1/2 pound thinly sliced bacon

Drain water chestnuts. Mix soy sauce, Worcestershire, lemon juice, salt, and garlic powder and pour over water chestnuts. Marinate at least 12 hours or overnight in refrigerator. Wrap each water chestnut with 1/3 strip of bacon and secure with a toothpick. This may be done ahead of time. Place on cookie sheet lined with foil for easy cleaning. Pour remaining marinade over water chestnuts and bake until bacon is crisp.

beer cheese

Yield: 2 1/2 cups

Preparation time:
10 minutes

"A wonderful gift"

1 pound Cheddar cheese,
shredded
1 pound Swiss cheese,
shredded
1 clove garlic, crushed
1 Tablespoon dry mustard
2 teaspoons Worcestershire
sauce
1 cup beer

Combine all ingredients and mix well. Best made in an electric mixer or a food processor. Store in the refrigerator in a covered crock or jar.

62

pumpernickel surprise

"A fun beginning for your party"

Sour Cream Dip
2 cups sour cream
1 (4-ounce) jar red caviar
1 Tablespoon dill
1 Tablespoon Beau Monde
   seasoning
1 small onion, grated

Combine ingredients well in an electric mixer.

or

Beer Dip
3 (6-ounce) rolls sharp
   cheese
1 1/4 ounces Roquefort
   cheese
3 Tablespoons butter or
   margarine, melted
1/2 medium onion, minced
1 teaspoon Worcestershire
   sauce
1 cup warm beer

Combine all ingredients well in an electric mixer.

1 (2-pound) round loaf
   Pumpernickel

Hollow out a large unsliced loaf of pumpernickel to form a bowl. Tear removed bread into bite-size pieces for dipping. Fill center of loaf with either the Sour Cream Dip or the Beer Dip. Refrigerate until serving.

carousel cheese ball

"So pretty"

6 (8-ounce) packages cream
  cheese, softened
1/2 pound Roquefort cheese,
  crumbled
1/2 pound Cheddar cheese,
  shredded
1/2 cup chopped chives or
  green onions
1 clove garlic, minced

Garnishes
2 Tablespoons black caviar
2 Tablespoons chopped
  green olives
2 Tablespoons chopped
  parsley
2 Tablespoons crumbled
  bacon
2 Tablespoons chopped
  black olives

Divide cream cheese into 3
parts. Mix the first with
Roquefort, the second with
Cheddar, and the third part with
chives and garlic. Stack each
layer on top of the other and
shape into a ball. Mark the ball
with a knife and cover each
section with a different garnish.

Keep red spices (chili powder, paprika, and red pepper) in the
refrigerator for longer-lasting flavor and color.

chafing dish spinach with oysters

Yield: 12 servings

Preparation time: 30 minutes

"Just a touch of jalapeno"

2 (10-ounce) packages frozen spinach
4 Tablespoons butter or margarine
2 Tablespoons flour
2 Tablespoons chopped onion
1/2 cup evaporated milk
1/2 teaspoon black pepper
1 teaspoon celery salt
1 teaspoon garlic salt
1/2 teaspoon salt
Red pepper
1 teaspoon Worcestershire sauce
1 (6-ounce) roll jalapeno pepper cheese
1 1/2 pints fresh oysters, drained

Cook spinach until just tender; drain, reserving 1/2 cup liquid. In a large skillet, melt the butter; add flour and onion. Stir until onion is soft, but not brown. Add milk and spinach liquid slowly, stirring constantly. Add seasonings and cheese. Stir until cheese is melted. Mix in spinach and chopped oysters. Serve in chafing dish.

Snip bacon with scissors into 1/2-inch pieces before cooking. This eliminates the extra step of crumbling or chopping later.

chili roll

**Preparation time:
20 minutes**

"Zippy and crunchy"

**3/4 pound sharp Cheddar
   cheese, shredded
1 (3-ounce) package cream
   cheese, softened
2 cloves garlic, minced
1/4 teaspoon Worcestershire
   sauce
1/4 teaspoon salt
1/4 teaspoon onion juice
1/8 teaspoon cayenne pepper
3/4 cup finely chopped
   pecans
1 ounce chili powder**

Mix all ingredients except for
pecans and chili powder. Form
into rolls 1 1/2 inches thick. Roll
in the pecans, pressing in lightly.
Roll in chili powder and
refrigerate.

crab mousse

Yield: 20 servings

**Preparation time:
   30 minutes
   plus 6 hours chilling time**

"Party-perfect"

**2 Tablespoons cold water
1 envelope unflavored
   gelatin
1 pound fresh crabmeat,
   drained
2 (8-ounce) packages cream
   cheese, softened
2 Tablespoons grated onion
6 Tablespoons mayonnaise
1/2 teaspoon salt
1/2 teaspoon curry powder
2 Tablespoons lemon juice
1 Tablespoon
   Worcestershire sauce**

Stir cold water into gelatin. Place
container in a pan of hot water
and stir to dissolve the gelatin.
Combine all other ingredients.
Add gelatin, put into a mold, and
refrigerate for at least 6 hours.

caviar mousse

Preparation time:
15 minutes
plus 4 hours chilling time

"Fit for a king"

5 large hard boiled eggs,
   grated
1 (4-ounce) jar black
   lumpfish caviar
1 cup mayonnaise
½ cup sour cream
3 Tablespoons finely grated
   onion
1½ teaspoons
   Worcestershire sauce
2 Tablespoons lemon juice
⅛ teaspoon cayenne pepper
1 envelope unflavored
   gelatin
¼ cup cold water

Reserve part of the grated egg and the caviar for garnish. Combine mayonnaise, sour cream, eggs, and seasonings. Gently fold in caviar. Stir gelatin into cold water and heat to dissolve. Cool slightly and fold into caviar mixture. Pour into lightly oiled 3½ cup mold. Chill for at least 4 hours. Unmold and garnish with reserved egg and caviar.

hot crabmeat dip

Yield: 12 to 15 servings

Preparation time:
15 minutes

"Quite a treat"

5 ounces sharp Cheddar
   cheese, shredded
1 (8-ounce) package cream
   cheese
1 (6-ounce) package frozen
   Alaska King crab, thawed
   and drained
¼ cup light cream
½ teaspoon garlic salt
½ teaspoon cayenne pepper
½ teaspoon Worcestershire
   sauce

Melt cheeses in top of double boiler over hot water. Add remaining ingredients, mix thoroughly, and transfer to chafing dish.

crabmeat hors d'oeuvre mold

Yield: 8 to 10 servings

Preparation time: 3 hours

"Outstanding"

1 (8-ounce) package cream cheese
1 medium onion, finely minced
Tabasco sauce
Worcestershire sauce
1 (6-ounce) package frozen or fresh snow crab, drained
Catsup
Horseradish
Lemon juice
Parsley

Combine cream cheese, onion, Tabasco, and Worcestershire. Form into a thin loaf and chill. Before serving, pat crab into loaf. Top with a mixture of catsup, horseradish, and lemon juice. Garnish with parsley.

chicken liver pate

Yield: 3 cups

Preparation time:
  10 minutes
  plus 3 hours chilling time

"Good to keep on hand"

1 small onion, minced
1 cup butter or margarine, softened
1 pound chicken livers
1/2 cup red wine
1/4 teaspoon thyme
1/4 teaspoon salt
1/4 teaspoon pepper

Saute onion in 2 Tablespoons butter over medium heat. Add chicken livers and cook for 6 minutes, turning as necessary. Add wine and seasonings, reduce heat, and simmer for 3 minutes. Combine livers and remaining butter in a food processor or a blender until smooth. Put in a crock, cover, and chill well. Take out of refrigerator 1 hour before serving.

christmas cheese spread

Yield: 12 to 15 servings

**Preparation time:
Overnight**

"Festive and so easy"

6 ounces Roquefort cheese
1 (10-ounce) jar soft
   Cheddar cheese
1 (12-ounce) package cream
   cheese
2 Tablespoons finely minced
   onion
1 teaspoon Worcestershire
   sauce
1/2 cup minced parsley
1 cup finely chopped pecans
1/2 teaspoon cayenne
   pepper, optional

Let cheeses soften overnight at room temperature. Next day, combine with the remaining ingredients.

dill dip

Yield: 16 to 20 servings

**Preparation time:
5 minutes**

"Serve as a dip or thin slightly for a marvelous salad dressing."

1 (1-pound) carton cottage
   cheese
1 cup mayonnaise
2 Tablespoons fresh lemon
   juice
1 heaping teaspoon dill
   weed
1 teaspoon Beau Monde
   seasoning
3 Tablespoons finely
   chopped parsley
1 small onion, grated

Blend all ingredients in a blender or a food processor thoroughly. Chill.

hot clam dip

Temperature: 350°
Baking time: 30 minutes

"Serve hot with crackers."

1 (8-ounce) package cream
  cheese, softened
1 Tablespoon chopped
  chives
2 Tablespoons mayonnaise
1 (8-ounce) can minced
  clams, drained

Combine ingredients, place in a
serving dish, and bake.

mexican
guacamole dip

Yield: 8 servings

Preparation time:
  15 minutes
  plus 2 hours chilling time

"Sealed for freshness by the mayonnaise"

2 large ripe avocados
1 small onion, finely
  minced
1/4 teaspoon salt
1 Tablespoon lemon juice
1 (4-ounce) can chopped
  pimentos or 1 small
  tomato, seeded and
  chopped
2 Tablespoons chopped
  black olives
2 slices crisp bacon,
  crumbled
Mayonnaise

Peel, seed, and mash avocados.
Add next 5 ingredients, mix
well, and spread in serving dish.
Sprinkle with bacon and cover
completely with a thin layer of
mayonnaise. Chill. Before
serving, stir well.

70

layered guacamole

Yield: 6 cups

**Preparation time:
45 minutes**

"Your guests will lick the pan to get every little bit."

2 large ripe avocados
1/8 teaspoon garlic powder
1/8 teaspoon garlic salt
1 Tablespoon lemon juice
2 Tablespoons mayonnaise
1 cup sour cream
1 or 2 (8-ounce) jars picante sauce
3/4 cup chopped black olives
3 medium tomatoes, peeled and chopped
1 1/2 cups shredded Cheddar cheese
Crisp bacon, crumbled
1 (16-ounce) can refried beans

Peel, seed, and mash avocados; stir in garlic powder, garlic salt, lemon juice, and mayonnaise. Spread in a 12x8x2-inch dish. Spread the sour cream over the avocado mixture. Drain the picante sauce; spoon over the sour cream layer. Top with layers of olives and tomatoes; sprinkle with cheese and bacon. Force the refried beans through a pastry tube to make a festive border around the edge.

Note: **Vary the amount of picante sauce according to your taste.**

At cocktail parties, place lighted candles around the room to clear the air of smoke.

jezebel sauce

"Bewitching"

Yield: 3 1/2 cups

Preparation time: 1 hour

1 (16-ounce) jar apple jelly
1 (16-ounce) jar pineapple
  preserves
1 (5-ounce) jar horseradish
1 (1 1/2-ounce) can dry
  mustard

Mix all ingredients, cover, and
refrigerate. Serve with
meatballs, sausage, sliced ham,
or as a spread over cream
cheese.

something special
hot cheese dip

"Easily doubled or tripled"

Yield: 10 to 15 servings

Temperature: 350°
Baking time: 20 minutes

1/2 pound Cheddar cheese,
  shredded
1/2 pound processed cheese
  spread, shredded
1 large tomato, peeled and
  chopped
1 clove garlic, crushed
1 pound crisp bacon,
  crumbled
2 jalapeno peppers, seeded
  and chopped

Combine all ingredients, cover,
and bake in a glass dish.
Transfer to a chafing dish and
serve. This may be assembled a
day ahead, but do not cook until
serving time.

shrimp cocktail spread

Yield: 2 cups

Preparation time:
10 minutes

"Refrigeration improves the flavor and consistency."

1 pound fresh shrimp,
  cooked and chopped
1 cup mayonnaise
1 Tablespoon lemon juice
1 Tablespoon grated onion
2 Tablespoons prepared
  mustard
1 teaspoon Worcestershire
  sauce
1/2 teaspoon garlic salt
1/4 teaspoon seasoned salt
1/4 teaspoon salt

Mix ingredients in a blender or a food processor.

shrimp, mushroom, artichoke fondue

Yield: 10 servings

Preparation time:
20 minutes

"Everyone will dive right in."

4 Tablespoons olive oil
1 pound fresh shrimp,
  peeled and deveined
1 (2 1/2-ounce) jar whole
  mushrooms, drained
1 (8 1/2-ounce) can
  artichokes, drained
2 cloves garlic, minced
1 teaspoon oregano
2 Tablespoons lemon juice
2 Tablespoons salt
Pepper

In a large skillet, heat oil; add shrimp and mushrooms and cook until shrimp is pink. Add artichokes, garlic, and oregano. Stir in lemon juice, salt, and pepper to taste. Serve in a fondue dish with fondue forks or toothpicks.

spinach dip

Yield: 3 cups

Preparation time:
Chill overnight

"Serve in a hollowed-out sour dough loaf."

1 (10-ounce) package frozen
  chopped spinach, thawed
  and drained
1 package dry vegetable
  soup
1 cup sour cream
1 small onion, chopped
1 cup mayonnaise
1 (8-ounce) can water
  chestnuts, drained and
  chopped

Mix all ingredients and chill
overnight.

sweet 'n sour sauce

Yield: 2 cups

Preparation time:
5 minutes

"Serve with cocktail sausages or meatballs."

1 (10-ounce) jar currant
  jelly
1/3 cup prepared mustard

Combine jelly and mustard in
top of double boiler. Heat until
jelly melts.

soups

sandwiches

soups and sandwiches

Cold Soups

Avocado Vichyssoise 77
Cold Cream of Cucumber Soup 80
Cold Spinach Soup 79
Cream of Broccoli Soup 81
Easy Vichy 77
Gazpacho 82
Iced Melon Soup 78

Hot Soups

Artichoke-Oyster Soup 84
Asparagus Egg-Drop Soup 85
Avocado Vichyssoise 77
Black Bean Soup 87
Calcutta Mulligatawny Soup . . 88
Cheese Soup with Cauliflower . 89
Chicken Cheese Chowder 86
Cream of Broccoli Soup 81
Cream of Carrot Soup with
    Peas 90
Curry Tomato-Split Pea Soup . . 91
Hearty Clam Chowder 92
Hearty Sausage and Rice Soup 93
Italian Pesto Garden Soup 94
Lettuce Soup 95

Navy Bean Soup 96
Onion Soup 96
Seafood Gumbo 83
Super Simple Soup 86
Zucchini Soup 85

Sandwiches

Baked Sandwiches 97
Cheese Delights 98
Duke of Windsor Sandwiches 99
Hot Crabmeat Sandwiches. . . .100
Iced Cheese Sandwiches 104
Oyster or Shrimp Boats 101
Ribbon Sandwich Loaf 102
Shrimp and Cucumber
    Sandwiches 105
Super Dogs 105
Toasted Mushroom
    Sandwiches 108
The Well-Stuffed Pita Pocket . 106
    Club Supreme 107
    Mexican Salad 106
    Oriental Chicken Salad 107
    Sausage and Cheese 106

avocado vichyssoise

"Different and delicious"

Yield: 6 servings

**Preparation time: 1/2 hour
    plus 3 hours chilling time**

1 pound potatoes, peeled
    and sliced
2 leeks, sliced (white end
    only)
1 medium onion, sliced
4 cups chicken stock
1 cup heavy cream
2 medium avocados, peeled
    and mashed

Garnish
Parsley
Lemon slice
Thin slices of avocado

Combine potatoes, leeks, and onion in a large saucepan. Add chicken stock and cook vegetables until tender. Work broth and vegetables through a sieve or blend briefly in a blender or food processor. Transfer mixture back to saucepan; add cream and heat thoroughly. Do not boil. Place mashed avocados in a large bowl and gradually stir in hot soup, mixing well. Soup may be served immediately or chilled.

easy vichy

"It is as good as it is easy."

Yield: 4 to 6 servings

**Preparation time:
    5 minutes
    plus 2 hours chilling time**

1 can chicken broth
1 can cream of potato soup
1 cup sour cream
2 teaspoons minced onion
Chopped chives

Blend broth, soup, sour cream, and onion. Chill for several hours. To serve, garnish with chopped chives.

iced melon soup

Yield: 6 servings

**Preparation time:
10 minutes
plus 3 hours chilling time**

"Will become a summer favorite"

**2 cups finely chopped
  cantaloupe
1 cup finely chopped
  honeydew melon
2 cups fresh orange juice
1/3 cup fresh lime juice
3 Tablespoons honey
2 cups dry champagne**

**Garnish
1 cup heavy cream,
  whipped
Mint leaves
Strawberries**

In a blender or food processor, combine 1 cup cantaloupe, 1/2 cup honeydew, orange juice, lime juice, and honey. Blend until smooth. Pour into a large bowl. Add the champagne and stir in the remaining melon. Chill the mixture thoroughly. Serve in chilled bowls. Garnish with a spoonful of whipped cream, a mint leaf, and a strawberry.

Variation: Crenshaw melon can be used and is so delicious. Use 1 cup chopped cantaloupe and 1 cup chopped crenshaw melon.

Always taste cold soups before serving. Cold food tends to need more seasoning than hot food.

cold spinach soup

"A good summer stand-by"

1/2 cup finely chopped
   shallots
3 Tablespoons butter or
   margarine
2 (10-ounce) packages
   frozen chopped spinach
3 cans chicken broth
1 teaspoon salt
1/8 teaspoon pepper
Dash nutmeg
1 (8-ounce) package cream
   cheese, cut into cubes

Garnish
Lemon slices
Parsley sprigs

In a large skillet, saute shallots in butter until soft. Add spinach. Cover and cook over low heat for about 10 minutes or until spinach is completely thawed. Watch carefully. Add broth, salt, pepper, and nutmeg. Simmer for 5 minutes and cool. Pour part of the soup into blender; cover and blend until smooth. Pour into large saucepan. Repeat with remainder of the soup. Add cream cheese, heat, and whisk gently until cheese is melted. Pour into crockery or glass bowl and chill for at least 4 hours. When ready to serve, garnish with lemon slices and parsley sprigs.

Note: **This soup has more flavor if refrigerated overnight.**

cold cream of cucumber soup

Preparation time:
20 minutes
plus 3 hours chilling time

"Marvelous for a summer luncheon"

1 cup finely diced
** cucumbers, unpeeled**
1 cup peeled and diced
** potatoes**
2 cups chicken stock
Salt and pepper
1 Tablespoon curry powder,
** chopped mint, or dill weed**
2 cups light cream

Garnish
Freshly chopped chives if
** curry powder is used**
Freshly chopped mint or dill
** if respective seasoning**
** is used**

In a large saucepan, cook cucumbers and potatoes in the chicken stock with seasonings until the potatoes are tender. Blend quickly in a blender or a food processor. At this point, the soup can be frozen. To serve, add cream and mix thoroughly. Adjust seasonings and chill well.

Serve cold soups in bowls placed in crushed ice in larger bowls.

cream of broccoli soup

Preparation time:
45 minutes
plus 4 hours chilling time

"Perfect for any luncheon"

1/2 cup butter or margarine
1/2 cup chopped onion
2 (10-ounce) packages
frozen chopped broccoli,
thawed
2 cups chicken broth
3/4 teaspoon basil
1 1/2 teaspoons salt
1/4 teaspoon white pepper
1 1/2 Tablespoons fresh
lemon juice
1 cup light cream

Garnish
Thin slices of lemon
1/2 cup heavy cream,
whipped

In a heavy 3-quart pot, melt butter. Saute onion until transparent. Add broccoli, chicken broth, basil, salt, and white pepper. Cover and simmer for 15 minutes on medium low heat. Puree the soup well in a food processor or blender. Do 1/2 of the mixture at a time, returning mixture to pan. Add lemon juice and cream. Serve warm or cold. If serving cold, chill at least 4 hours. Top with garnishes.

gazpacho

Preparation time:
  10 minutes
  plus 1 hour chilling time

"Great all summer long"

6 tomatoes, quartered
1 cucumber, thickly sliced
4 Tablespoons wine vinegar
6 Tablespoons olive oil
1/4 cup lemon juice
2 cups chicken stock,
  slightly diluted
2 (10-ounce) cans vegetable
  juice
2 teaspoons salt
4 green onions, chopped
2 cloves garlic
1 green pepper, chopped
1/2 cup chopped parsley

Combine first 8 ingredients and toss. Spoon into a blender and blend for 15 to 30 seconds. Pour into jars or a suitable container and add remaining ingredients. Refrigerate for at least one hour or until thoroughly chilled. Remove garlic cloves before serving.

Note: **Substitute 1 (28-ounce) can tomatoes for the fresh tomatoes. Decrease vegetable juice to 1 (10-ounce) can.**

For an easy first course, serve cold soup in tall wine glasses before your guests are seated.

seafood gumbo

"Seafood lovers will adore it."

2/3 cup flour
2/3 cup oil
2 cups chopped onion
1 cup chopped bell pepper
1 cup chopped celery
1/4 cup chopped parsley
1/4 cup chopped green onion
 tops
3 quarts water
1 teaspoon gumbo file
1 teaspoon black pepper
1/2 teaspoon red pepper
1/2 teaspoon Tabasco sauce
4 teaspoons salt
2 pounds fresh shrimp,
 peeled
1 pound fresh crabmeat
1 to 2 pints oysters and
 liquid

In a large (5-quart or larger) heavy pot, mix flour and oil. Cook over medium heat until very dark brown, but not burned. This takes about 45 minutes. Add onion, bell pepper, and celery and cook until soft. Add parsley and green onion and mix well. Slowly add water, stirring constantly. Season with gumbo file, peppers, Tabasco, and salt. Simmer for at least an hour. (The longer the better!) About 30 minutes before serving, add seafood and heat through. It's ready to serve when the shrimp are pink and oysters are curled.

Serving suggestion: **Serve over fluffy white rice with a green salad and French bread, page 335.**

Add a pinch of brown sugar if the soup has too much salt.

artichoke-oyster soup

Preparation time: 5 hours

"This has a marvelous flavor."

1/2 cup butter or margarine
1 1/2 cups finely chopped onions
2 cups sliced mushrooms
4 Tablespoons freshly chopped parsley
1 1/2 teaspoons thyme
1 Tablespoon salt
3/4 teaspoon black pepper
1 cup dry white wine
1 (14-ounce) can water-packed artichoke hearts, drained and quartered
1 (6 1/2-ounce) jar marinated artichoke hearts, quartered and undrained
1 can cream of chicken soup
1 can cream of celery soup
2 soup cans water
6 bay leaves
1 pint oysters, drained
Parsley

In a heavy 4-quart pot, melt butter. Saute onions, mushrooms, and parsley until the onions are transparent. Add thyme, salt, pepper, wine, and artichokes. Gradually add canned soup, mixing well. Slowly add water, also making sure to mix well. Add bay leaves and simmer for at least 4 hours. An hour before serving, add oysters and continue to simmer until serving time. Remove bay leaves before serving. Garnish with parsley.

Remove grease from soup by dropping in ice cubes. The grease will cling to the cubes.

asparagus egg-drop soup

Yield: 4 to 6 servings

**Preparation time: 1 hour
plus 2 hours chilling time**

"A new twist to an old favorite"

4 cups well-seasoned
chicken stock
12 ounces fresh or frozen
asparagus tips, cooked or
1 (14-ounce) can whole
asparagus spears
1 egg, beaten
1 teaspoon sesame oil
1 teaspoon white wine or
cooking sherry
Salt and pepper
Chopped scallions

Bring stock to a full boil. Reduce heat and simmer. Drain asparagus and puree in blender or food processor. Add to stock, stirring until well blended. Bring to a boil again. Remove from heat and slowly add egg, breaking into pieces. Stir in sesame oil, wine, salt, and pepper. Serve hot or well chilled, topped with chopped scallions.

zucchini soup

Yield: 4 servings

**Preparation time:
30 minutes**

"Your guests don't have to know how easy this is."

3 medium zucchini, sliced
3 Tablespoons chopped
onion
4 cups chicken broth
1/4 teaspoon Italian
seasoning
1 (8-ounce) package cream
cheese
Salt and pepper

Garnish
**Thin lemon slices
Whipped cream**

Put zucchini, onion, broth, and seasoning in a deep skillet. Simmer until tender, but not mushy. Blend with cream cheese in a blender or food processor. Take care not to fill blender more than half full when blending ingredients. Add salt and pepper to taste and serve warm.

chicken cheese chowder

Yield: 4 servings

Preparation time:
30 minutes

"Terrific on a cold day"

1 cup finely grated carrots
1/4 cup chopped onion
4 Tablespoons butter or
   margarine
1/4 cup flour
2 cups light cream
1 can chicken broth
1 cup cooked and diced
   chicken
1 Tablespoon dry white wine
1/4 teaspoon celery seed
1/2 teaspoon Worcestershire
   sauce
1 cup shredded American
   cheese
Chopped chives

In large saucepan, saute carrots and onion in butter until tender. Blend in flour. Add cream and chicken broth slowly. Cook, stirring, until thickened and bubbly. Stir in chicken, wine, celery seed, and Worcestershire sauce. Heat through. Add cheese and stir until melted. Garnish with chopped chives.

super simple soup

Yield: 6 servings

Preparation time:
10 minutes

"Out of this world"

1 can tomato soup
1 can onion soup
1 can old-fashioned
   vegetable soup
1 can beef bouillon
1 (10-ounce) can chili
   without beans

Combine all ingredients in a saucepan, heat, and enjoy!

black bean soup

**Preparation time: 4 hours
plus overnight soaking
time**

"A hearty addition to any meal"

1 **pound dried black beans**
1/2 **gallon water**
1 **cup chopped onion**
1 **to 2 cloves garlic, minced**
1/2 **cup olive oil**
1 **large, meaty country ham
bone (if other type of ham
is used, add 1 teaspoon
salt)**
3 **bay leaves**
1 **Tablespoon salt**
1/4 **cup vinegar**
3 **cups cooked rice**

Garnish
Crumbled bacon
Chopped onion
Parmesan cheese, grated

Wash beans and soak overnight in water. Drain beans. Put 1/2 gallon fresh water and beans into heavy 4-quart pot. In a skillet, lightly saute onion and garlic in olive oil. Add the onion, garlic, ham bone, bay leaves, and salt to the beans. Simmer on low heat for about 3 hours, until beans are tender and liquid is thick. Remove bay leaves and ham bone and tear off meat. Return meat to soup. Puree the beans slightly with a potato masher. Just before serving, add vinegar. Serve soup over scoops of steaming rice in large soup bowls. Pass garnishes.

Vegetable water is great added to canned soup or to use as the cooking water when making soup.

calcutta mulligatawny soup

"Delicious and different"

1 (4 to 5 pound) chicken
1/2 cup flour
1/3 cup butter or margarine
1 1/2 cups chopped onion
2 cups chopped carrots
2 cups chopped celery
1 1/2 cups pared and chopped tart apples
6 cups cold water
1 1/2 Tablespoons hot curry powder
4 teaspoons salt
3/4 teaspoon mace
1/2 teaspoon pepper
1/2 cup grated coconut
1 cup apple juice
1 cup light cream
1 1/2 cups hot cooked rice
1/2 cup minced parsley

Wash chicken, pat dry, and cut into pieces. Roll pieces in flour, reserving excess flour. Saute chicken in butter in a Dutch oven until well browned. Remove chicken from pot and set aside. Put onion, carrots, celery, apples, and reserved flour in pot and cook, stirring, for 5 minutes. Add cold water, chicken, and seasonings to pot, stirring well. Bring to a boil, reduce heat, and simmer for 2 hours, covered. Remove from heat and skim fat from surface. Remove skin and bones from chicken pieces and cut into bite-size chunks. Set aside. Put half the soup through the blender until smooth. Return blended soup to pot along with chicken pieces. Stir in coconut, apple juice, and cream. Correct seasonings, if necessary. To serve, put 2 heaping Tablespoons of rice in each soup bowl, fill with soup, and top with minced parsley.

Note: **This soup is even better made ahead and reheated.**

cheese soup with cauliflower

Yield: 2 quarts

Preparation time: 2 hours

"The cauliflower goes totally undetected."

2 (10-ounce) packages
   frozen cauliflower
   or 1 small head, broken
   into florets
1 cup water
3 teaspoons cornstarch
3 cans chicken broth
6 chicken bouillon cubes
1/2 cup milk or light cream
1/3 cup chopped onion
4 Tablespoons butter or
   margarine
1 can cheese soup
3 carrots, finely grated
2 cups shredded sharp
   Cheddar cheese
1 teaspoon monosodium
   glutamate
1 teaspoon sugar
Dash Tabasco sauce
Dash nutmeg
Salt

Cook cauliflower in water until tender. Blend cauliflower and liquid in a blender or food processor until smooth. Transfer to a 4-quart saucepan. Add cornstarch and stir well. Add chicken broth, bouillon cubes, and milk; simmer. Saute onion in butter until soft and add to cauliflower mixture. When heated through and bouillon cubes have dissolved, add cheese soup, carrots, and cheese. Do not boil. Add seasonings to taste.

Note: **The soup may be thinned with more milk or thickened with flour or cornstarch, if needed.**

cream of carrot soup with peas

Yield: 4 to 6 servings

**Preparation time:
45 minutes**

"Delicious substitute for vegetables"

1/4 cup butter or margarine
1 1/2 pounds carrots,
 shredded
1 large bunch scallions,
 chopped
5 to 6 shallots, minced
1 small potato, peeled
 and chopped
1 clove garlic, minced
1/2 teaspoon tarragon
1/2 teaspoon chervil
1/4 teaspoon thyme
1/4 teaspoon bouquet garni
2 quarts chicken stock
1 cup light cream
1 (10-ounce) package frozen
 peas

Melt butter in large kettle over medium low heat. Add carrots, scallions, shallots, potato, garlic, and herbs. Cover and cook until vegetables are tender. Add chicken stock and bring to a boil. Transfer to a blender or food processor and puree. Return to pot and heat through, but do not boil. Add cream and peas and cook until peas are tender. Serve with garnishes.

Garnish
**Lemon slices topped with
 peas**
Freshly ground pepper

Variation: **This is equally as good without the peas. For a change, add strips of cooked ham.**

curry tomato-split pea soup

Yield: 4 servings

Preparation time: 1/2 hour plus 2 hours chilling time

"Perfect for any time of the year"

1 can tomato soup
1 can split pea with ham soup
1 cup light cream or heavy cream, if a richer soup is desired
1/2 teaspoon curry powder
1/2 teaspoon dry mustard
1/2 teaspoon Worcestershire sauce
Salt and pepper
Sprigs of parsley
Freshly ground pepper

Empty soups, cream, and seasonings into a saucepan. Cook over medium high heat, almost to boiling. Correct seasonings. Serve immediately or chill. Garnish with parsley and pepper.

Note: 1 soup can of water may be added for a thinner soup.

Soup garnishes: crumbled bacon; avocado cubes or slices; lemon, lime, or orange slices or grated rind; crumbled French fried onions; sour cream or yogurt flavored with herbs; flavored whipped cream; minced cashews, peanuts, almonds, or pistachios; minced herbs; poppy or caraway seeds; slivered pimento or olives.

hearty clam chowder

Yield: 4 to 6 servings

Preparation time: 1 hour

"Even if you're not wild about seafood, you'll love this soup."

4 slices bacon, cut into small cubes
3 green onions, chopped
5 medium potatoes, peeled and cut into 1/2-inch cubes
2 Tablespoons chopped green pepper
1 stalk celery, sliced
1 carrot, thinly sliced
1 clove garlic, minced
2 cups water
1 teaspoon salt
1/2 teaspoon black pepper
1 teaspoon Worcestershire sauce
4 drops Tabasco sauce
2 cups chopped raw clams with juice
2 cups light cream

In a large heavy kettle, saute bacon until crisp, drain grease. Add green onions, potatoes, green pepper, celery, carrot, and garlic. Pour in water and season with salt, pepper, Worcestershire, and Tabasco. Cover and simmer 20 minutes, or until potatoes are tender. Mash mixture well with potato masher or back of spoon. Add clams with juice and cream. Stir well and heat, but do not boil.

Serving suggestion: **Delicious with hot buttered pumpernickel and a tossed green salad.**

hearty sausage and rice soup

"Good for cold nights"

Yield: 8 to 10 servings

Preparation time: 3 hours

2 **Tablespoons olive oil**
2 **pounds Italian sausage (sweet or hot)**
2 **large onions, chopped coarsely**
2 **large green peppers, cut into strips**
2 **large carrots, cut into chunks**
2 **cloves garlic, minced**
1 **bay leaf**
1/4 **teaspoon thyme**
1/2 **teaspoon cumin**
2 **cups cooked rice**
8 **cups chicken stock**
1 **pound tomatoes, quartered**

Heat olive oil in Dutch oven over medium heat. Brown sausage and set aside. Drain fat, leaving 2 Tablespoons in pot. Add vegetables and cook, covered, about 15 minutes. Add garlic and herbs. Cover and cook another 5 minutes. Slice or crumble sausage and add to soup along with rice, chicken stock, and tomatoes. Reduce heat to low and simmer for 1 1/2 to 2 hours, partially covered. Remove the bay leaf before serving.

Note: **This is better made a day ahead.**

Variation: **For a heartier soup, add zucchini, peas, potatoes, or any other vegetable.**

italian pesto garden soup

Yield: 12 servings

Preparation time: 2 hours

"A feast by itself"

1/2 pound salt pork, diced
3 medium onions, diced
2 cloves garlic, crushed
1/4 cup olive oil
4 medium stalks celery,
   chopped
4 medium carrots, chopped
1 medium green pepper,
   chopped
8 cups chicken broth
4 cups cooked white beans
   or 2 (16-ounce) cans white
   beans, drained
1/2 cup minced parsley
1 bay leaf
Large pinch rosemary
1 pound sweet or hot
   sausage, sliced and
   cooked
1 cup small shell macaroni,
   uncooked
4 medium zucchini, thickly
   sliced
2 cups shredded spinach
1/4 cup Pesto sauce (recipe
   follows)
Salt and pepper
Parmesan cheese

(continued)

Saute salt pork. Drain off fat. Cook onions and garlic with the pork in the olive oil until limp. Add celery, carrots, and green pepper; toss to coat. Add broth, beans, parsley, and herbs. Bring to a boil and then simmer, uncovered for 10 minutes. Discard bay leaf. At this point, the soup may be cooled, covered, and refrigerated. If ready to serve, reduce heat to low. About 15 minutes before serving, add sausage, macaroni, zucchini, and spinach. Simmer for 10 minutes. Stir in pesto sauce and season with salt and pepper. Sprinkle each portion with Parmesan.

Pesto Sauce

1/3 cup walnut meats
2 large cloves garlic,
crushed
1/3 cup water
1 cup spinach leaves
1 cup fresh basil leaves,
lightly packed
1/2 cup olive oil
1/4 cup grated Parmesan
cheese
1 teaspoon salt

In a blender or food processor, combine walnut meats, garlic, and water. Gradually add spinach and basil alternately with olive oil. Blend until smooth. Blend in Parmesan and salt.

lettuce soup

Yield: 6 servings

Preparation time: 1 hour

"Divine"

2 cups shredded lettuce
1 cup water
1/2 cup chicken stock or
season water with chicken
base to taste
3 Tablespoons butter or
margarine
1 medium onion, grated
3 Tablespoons flour
4 1/2 cups light cream
Salt and pepper

In a covered saucepan, simmer the lettuce in water and chicken stock until lettuce is tender. Pour the lettuce and liquid into a double boiler and cook over low heat. In the saucepan first used, melt the butter and saute the onion until transparent. Add flour, mixing well. Stir in 1/2 cup light cream, blending well. Add onion mixture to lettuce. Gradually add the remaining cream, stirring constantly; blend thoroughly. Add salt and pepper to taste. Cook the soup over medium heat, until thick and hot, stirring constantly.

navy bean soup

Yield: 8 to 10 servings

Preparation time: 4 hours

"Your family will ask for thirds."

2 cups navy beans
1 ham hock
1 cup chopped onion
1 hot pepper pod
1 cup chopped carrots
3 quarts chicken stock
or
3 quarts water plus 10
chicken bouillon cubes
1 to 2 pounds cooked ham
pieces or sliced smoked
sausage
Salt and pepper

In a large kettle, put beans, ham hock, onion, pepper pod, and carrots in 3 quarts chicken stock. Cook for 2 hours over medium heat. Add ham or sausage; season to taste. Cook slowly for at least another hour. Partially mash beans and vegetables while cooking. Remove ham hock bone and skim off fat before serving.

onion soup

Yield: 6 servings

Preparation time: 2 hours

"The chicken broth makes this a little different."

3 Tablespoons bacon
drippings
4 large onions, finely
chopped
2 Tablespoons flour
1/2 teaspoon salt
1/8 teaspoon pepper
1 clove garlic, crushed
Sprig of parsley
Pinch of thyme
1 quart chicken stock
1 cup dry white wine
1 Tablespoon cognac
6 slices French bread,
toasted
Grated Parmesan cheese

In a deep saucepan, heat the bacon drippings. Add the onions and saute over medium heat until soft, but not browned. Add the flour, salt, pepper, and garlic. Cook until mixture turns a golden brown. Add parsley, thyme, chicken stock, and wine. Simmer for 45 minutes. Just before serving, add cognac. Serve in ovenproof bowls. Top each filled bowl with a piece of French bread and Parmesan cheese. Put the bowls under the broiler until the cheese melts.

baked sandwiches

Yield: 4 servings

Temperature: 300°
Baking time: 1 hour
plus overnight chilling

"Your family will love them."

8 slices bread
1/8 cup butter or margarine, softened
4 slices ham
4 slices Cheddar cheese
1/2 teaspoon dry mustard
3 eggs, slightly beaten
2 cups milk
1 teaspoon grated onion
1/2 teaspoon salt
1/8 teaspoon pepper
Dash Worcestershire sauce
Dash cayenne pepper

Trim crusts from bread and butter both sides well. Place 4 slices of bread in a buttered, square baking dish. Place a slice of ham on each piece of bread and cover with cheese. Top cheese with remaining slices of bread. Combine remaining ingredients and pour over bread. *Refrigerate overnight.* Spoon liquid over bread and bake, uncovered.

Note: Slices of tomato, green pepper, mushroom, avocado, or bacon may be layered between the ham and cheese to make a heartier sandwich.

A 1-pound loaf of bread has approximately 20 slices; 1 sandwich loaf averages 34 slices.

cheese delights

Temperature: 450°
Baking time:
   10 to 15 minutes
   plus 3 hours freezing
   time

"Wonderful flavor"

1 pound sharp Cheddar
   cheese, shredded
1 cup milk
2 eggs, beaten
2 teaspoons onion juice
Salt
Cayenne pepper
2 Tablespoons finely
   chopped parsley
1 Tablespoon
   Worcestershire sauce
4 Tablespoons flour
1/4 cup butter or margarine,
   melted
12 to 16 slices of white,
   whole wheat, or light
   rye bread

Melt cheese in the top of a double boiler. Add milk, eggs, onion juice, salt, cayenne, parsley, Worcestershire, and flour, mixing well. Mixture must get hot throughout and bubble lightly. Remove from heat and cool. Refrigerate to thicken. Mixture will look funny at this stage, but will be fine once it cools. When mixture is cold, spread thickly between slices of bread. Place sandwiches on waxed paper. Freeze. After freezing, sandwiches may be wrapped for storage or may be baked. Thaw slightly. Brush with melted butter and bake.

Variation: **Remove the crusts from the bread, quarter the sandwiches, bake, and serve piping hot as an hors d'oeuvre.**

duke of windsor sandwiches

Yield: 2 servings

**Preparation time:
30 minutes**

"Different and delicious"

**⅛ cup butter or margarine,
   softened
6 pieces thinly sliced bread,
   crusts removed
2 pineapple slices, dabbed
   with butter and run
   under broiler
2 Tablespoons chutney
4 slices turkey, white meat
4 pieces bacon, cooked
   but not too crisp
½ pound Cheddar cheese,
   cubed
Milk, optional
Parsley**

Spread butter lightly on bread and toast slightly. Place 2 slices of bread in a square baking pan. On each, place a slice of pineapple spread with chutney and top with second bread slice. On this bread layer, place 2 turkey slices and 2 bacon slices. Add the third layer of bread. Melt cheese (a small amount of milk may be added) in the top of a double boiler and pour, hot, over the 2 sandwiches. Put under broiler for 5 minutes or until bubbly. Garnish with parsley.

Note: **Drained peach halves filled with extra chutney are very good served with this sandwich.**

hot crabmeat sandwiches

Yield: 6 to 8 servings

Temperature: 325°
Baking time:
   15 to 20 minutes

"Husbands will like it as much as the ladies."

1 (8-ounce) package cream
   cheese
1 (6-ounce) package frozen
   crabmeat, thawed and
   drained
1 teaspoon grated onion
2 Tablespoons fresh lemon
   juice
1 teaspoon Worcestershire
   sauce
1/4 teaspoon Tabasco sauce
Salt and pepper
6 to 8 pieces Holland Rusk
2 large tomatoes, sliced
   and drained
6 to 8 slices sharp Cheddar
   cheese
6 to 8 slices bacon, cooked
   and broken in half,
   optional

Combine the first 6 ingredients
in a medium bowl. Season with
salt and pepper, if desired.
Spread a generous portion of
crab mixture on each Holland
Rusk. Add a tomato, then top
with cheese and bacon. Bake.

Spread slices of bread with a thin layer of butter or margarine to
prevent filling from making the bread soggy.

oyster or shrimp boats

Yield: 4 servings

Preparation time: 1 hour

"They'll launch any party."

1 loaf French bread
1/2 cup butter or margarine, softened
1/2 teaspoon garlic powder
2 cups shredded lettuce
2 medium tomatoes, thinly sliced
1 pint fried oysters or 1/2 pound fried shrimp, tails removed (see index for fried oyster recipe- use for shrimp too)

Condiment choices
Cocktail sauce, see index
Mayonnaise
Mustard
Catsup
Tabasco sauce

Cut bread in half lengthwise. Hollow out the bottom half of the loaf. Combine butter and garlic. Spread a thin, but even, layer on both cut sides of the bread. Put the loaf halves under the broiler and brown buttered sides lightly. Place a bed of shredded lettuce in the hollow, then arrange sliced tomatoes on top of the lettuce. Top with oysters or shrimp. Top with the other half of bread. Cut into 4 sections.

To stretch butter, add ½ cup milk to 1 pound butter. Beat together until fluffy.

ribbon sandwich loaf

Yield: 12 servings

Preparation time: 4 hours

"Impressive and delicious"

1 day-old loaf of unsliced bread
¼ cup butter or margarine
2 cups egg salad filling
2 cups ham salad filling
2 cups chicken salad filling
1 (8-ounce) package cream cheese, softened
5 Tablespoons light cream

Garnishes
Sliced hard boiled eggs, almond slices, olives, and parsley

Remove crusts from bread and slice loaf lengthwise into 4 slices. Butter one side of 3 slices. Spread one slice of buttered bread with egg salad on one side only; top with another slice of buttered bread and spread with ham filling; top with the 3rd slice of buttered bread and spread with the chicken salad filling. Top with the remaining unbuttered slice of bread. Beat softened cream cheese with cream until fluffy. Frost top and sides of loaf. Garnish as desired. Chill for several hours, but do not freeze. The loaf may be refrigerated for several days.

Egg Salad Filling

4 hard boiled eggs, chopped
3 slices bacon, cooked and
   crumbled
1/3 cup mayonnaise,
   preferably homemade
Salt and pepper

Mix all ingredients together well.

Chicken Salad Filling

1 1/2 cups finely diced,
   cooked chicken
1 ounce Roquefort cheese,
   crumbled
1/4 cup sour cream
1/4 cup mayonnaise,
   preferably homemade
1/2 teaspoon fresh lemon
   juice
Salt

Mix all ingredients together well.

Ham Salad Filling

1 1/2 cups finely diced,
   cooked ham
1 Tablespoon Dijon mustard
1 Tablespoon red wine
   vinegar
1/2 clove garlic, crushed
2 Tablespoons olive oil
1/4 cup finely chopped celery

Mix all ingredients together well.

iced cheese sandwiches

Yield: 60 sandwiches

Temperature: 325°
Baking time: 15 minutes

"Great to have in the freezer for unexpected guests"

2 cups butter or margarine, softened
4 (5-ounce) jars soft Cheddar cheese
1 teaspoon Tabasco sauce
1 teaspoon onion powder
1 1/2 teaspoons Worcestershire sauce
1 teaspoon Beau Monde seasoning
1 1/2 teaspoons dill weed
2 1/2 loaves thinly sliced bread, crusts removed

Combine butter and cheese in a mixer until fluffy. Add remaining ingredients, except the bread. Spread 3 slices of bread with the mixture and stack on top of each other. Spread sides with mixture and cut into 4 squares. Spread mixture on the cut sides. Ice the remaining slices of bread as described above. Place on waxed paper and freeze. Remove to plastic bags and freeze until ready to use. Thaw and place on cookie sheet. Bake until edges are browned.

Flavored butter or mayonnaise: (ingredients per 1/4 cup butter or mayonnaise)
Lemon: 1 teaspoon lemon juice and 1/4 teaspoon grated lemon rind
Herb: 2 to 3 teaspoons fresh minced dill, chervil, basil, parsley, or watercress
Shrimp or anchovy: 1 teaspoon shrimp or anchovy paste
Mustard: 1 to 2 teaspoons prepared mustard
Horseradish: 1 teaspoon horseradish
Onion: 1 teaspoon finely grated onion
Garlic: 1/4 clove garlic, crushed

shrimp and cucumber sandwiches

Yield: 20 sandwiches

Preparation time:
   20 minutes
   plus overnight chilling

"They will disappear right before your eyes."

**2 cups finely chopped
   cooked shrimp
1 cup finely diced cucumber
1/2 cup minced onion
2 Tablespoons sour cream
4 Tablespoons mayonnaise
Salt and pepper
Cayenne pepper
Fresh lemon juice
Fresh chopped dill
20 slices white bread,
   crusts removed**

Mix ingredients except for the bread and refrigerate overnight to blend flavors. Spread on half the bread and top with the other half. Cut in halves and serve ice cold.

super dogs

Yield: 6 servings

**Temperature: 350°
Baking time:
   15 to 20 minutes**

"A sure fire hit with the kids"

**6 hot dogs
Mustard
Mashed potatoes
6 slices Cheddar or
   American cheese
Paprika**

Split hot dogs lengthwise. They can come directly from the freezer. Lay them open on a baking sheet and spread with mustard. Put several spoonfuls of mashed potatoes on each hot dog. Top with cheese and sprinkle with paprika. Bake.

Note: **Use an envelope of instant mashed potatoes for a quick lunch.**

the well-stuffed pita pocket

"A good way to make a meal fun."

Sausage and Cheese Filling

5 pita pockets
5 Tablespoons butter or margarine
1 pound bulk sausage
2 cups shredded mozzarella cheese

Cut open top of each pita pocket; put 1 Tablespoon butter in each and bake for 5 minutes at 350°. Saute sausage until brown and drain well. Stuff pockets with sausage and cheese. Bake for 10 minutes at 350° or until cheese is melted and bread is crispy.

Mexican Salad Filling

1 pound lean ground beef
2 Tablespoons butter or margarine
1 medium green pepper, chopped
1 medium Bermuda onion, chopped
2 teaspoons cumin
1 teaspoon coriander
5 ounces tomato sauce
Salt and pepper
1 large tomato, chopped
1 large avocado, peeled and chopped
4 jalapeno peppers, chopped, optional
4 pita pockets
1/2 cup shredded lettuce
1 cup shredded Cheddar cheese

Brown meat, drain, and set aside. Melt butter in a skillet and saute green pepper and onion until tender. Add meat, cumin, and coriander, mixing well. Add tomato sauce, salt, and pepper and remove from heat. Add tomato, avocado, and peppers, combining gently. Cut tops of pita bread and fill with meat mixture, leaving 1/2-inch empty for a layer of lettuce and then a sprinkling of cheese. Place pitas upright in a pan and heat in a 350° oven for 5 minutes or until the cheese is bubbly and the pitas are slightly browned.

Oriental Chicken Salad Filling

4 boned chicken breasts, cooked and diced
4 green onions, finely chopped
3 large mushrooms, thinly sliced
1/3 cup chopped almonds
1/2 cup halved green grapes
2 stalks celery, finely chopped
1/2 cup mandarin oranges, optional
1/2 cup pineapple chunks, optional
2/3 cup mayonnaise
1 teaspoon fresh lemon juice
1 teaspoon soy sauce
1 teaspoon chopped fresh ginger, optional
1/2 teaspoon minced garlic
1 1/2 Tablespoons white wine vinegar
Salt and pepper
4 pita pockets
1/2 cup raisins or parsley

Mix first eight ingredients together in a bowl. In a separate bowl, mix mayonnaise, lemon juice, soy sauce, ginger, garlic, vinegar, salt, and pepper. Pour over chicken mixture and mix. Refrigerate for one hour to allow flavors to blend. Adjust seasonings to taste. Slice tops of pita pockets and stuff with filling. Garnish with raisins and parsley.

Club Supreme Filling

1 cup julienned smoked turkey
1 cup julienned cooked ham
1 cup julienned Swiss cheese
1 cup crumbled cooked bacon
2 medium avocados, peeled and thinly sliced
1 pint cherry tomatoes, halved
1 cup shredded lettuce, optional

Combine turkey, ham, cheese, bacon, avocados, tomatoes, lettuce, and olives in a medium bowl. Pour dressing over mixture and toss lightly until meat and vegetables are coated. Refrigerate at least 1 hour so the flavors will combine. Open the tops of the pita pockets and fill with the club mixture. Garnish with parsley.

(continued)

¹/4 cup sliced black olives,
     optional
¹/2 cup dressing (bleu
     cheese, French, oil and
     vinegar, or 1000 island)
6 pita pockets
Parsley

Note: For variety, these fillings may be served on Kaiser rolls,
croissants, hollowed-out French bread, or bakery bread.

toasted mushroom sandwiches

Yield: 10 to 12 servings

**Preparation time:
     15 minutes
     plus overnight chilling**

"Great for luncheons"

2 (8-ounce) cans mushrooms
     or 1 pound fresh
     mushrooms, chopped
1 small onion, chopped
2 Tablespoons butter or
     margarine
2 Tablespoons flour
Dash red pepper
¹/4 teaspoon salt
20 to 24 bread rounds or
     squares
Melted butter or margarine

In a small saucepan, saute
mushrooms and onion in the
butter. Add flour and seasonings
and stir until slightly thick.
Spread between bread rounds or
squares and brush sandwich
tops with melted butter.
Refrigerate overnight, covered
with damp cloth. Before serving,
toast in a hot skillet.

salads

salads

Artichoke-Rice Salad 112
Broccoli Salad.............. 113
Buffet Cauliflower 112
Chilled Picnic Ratatouille.... 114
Cold Pea Salad 115
Crab Louis................. 117
Cucumber-Sour Cream
   Salad.................... 116
Curried Bean Sprout Salad .. 116
Curried Chicken Salad 115
German Potato Salad 118
Layered Gourmet Salad..... 119
Marinated Artichoke and
   Mushroom Salad 120
Marinated Broccoli 121
Marinated Crab 122
Marinated Onions 121
Melon Ball and
   Shrimp Salad 123
Mexican Delight 124
Prosciutto and Fresh Fruit... 125
Salade Nicoise.............. 127
Seafood Bombay Salad...... 126
Slaw 125
Spinach Salad.............. 128
Stuffed Avocado Salad 130
Tomato-Egg Tarragon Salad. 131
Croutons 128

Molded Salads
Artichoke-Asparagus Mold .. 132
Cranberry Port Wine Salad .. 133
Egg-Curry Mold 134
Fresh Blueberry Salad 134
Frozen Fruit Salad.......... 135
Frozen Tomato Salad 136
Gazpacho Salad Mold 137
Molded Egg Salad, Lorenzo
   Dressing................. 138
Spinach Souffle Mold 139
Tomato Soup Aspic 140
Vegetable Salad Mold 141

Dressings
Beau Jacques French
   Dressing................. 146
Blender Mayonnaise 142
Bleu Cheese Dressing I 144
Bleu Cheese Dressing II 145
Camille Dressing 145
Dijon Mustard Dressing 147
Dill Dressing 146
Fruit Salad Dressing 147
Honey-Mustard Dressing.... 148
Hot Bacon Dressing......... 143
Italian Dressing 148
Lorenzo Dressing........... 138
Maurice Salad Dressing 149
Mayonnaise................ 142
Must-Make Mayonnaise..... 143
Navy Salad Dressing........ 149
Parmesan Salad Dressing ... 150
Tomato-Roquefort Dressing . 144

Conserves
Apple Honey-Cointreau 152
Banana Jama 152
Blackberry Curd 153
Cherry Conserve 154
Green Pepper Jelly 155
Hot Pepper Jelly............ 154
Peach Rum Jam............. 156
Strawberry Preserves 156

Relishes
Carrot Chutney 159
Cranberry-Orange Relish.... 157
Squash Relish.............. 158

Pickles
Layered Pickles 157
Pickled Okra 160
Seven-Day Pickles 158
Zucchini Bread 'n
   Butter Pickles 159

peak seasons for fresh fruits and vegetables

Apples: January-April, September-December
Apricots: May-August
Avocados: January-June, September-December
Blueberries: May-August
Cherries: May-August
Grapes: July-December
Grapefruit: January-June, November-December
Lemons and Limes: May-August
Melons: May-October
Oranges: January-June
Peaches: May-October
Pears: July-December
Pineapples: March-August
Plums: May-October
Strawberries: March-June

Artichokes: March-June
Asparagus: March-June
Beans: May-August
Broccoli: January-April, September-December
Brussel Sprouts: January-February, September-December
Corn: May-October
Cucumbers: May-August
Eggplant: July-October
Peas: January-August
Peppers: May-October
Spinach: January-April
Summer Squash: May-October
Sweet Potatoes: September-December
Tomatoes: May-August
Winter Squash: September-December

artichoke-rice salad

Yield: 12 servings

Preparation time:
20 minutes plus
24 hours chilling time

"A great substitute for potato salad"

2 packages chicken-flavored rice
1 small green pepper, chopped
8 green onions, sliced
1 (2-ounce) jar stuffed olives, chopped
2 (6-ounce) jars marinated artichoke hearts, chopped, reserving liquid from 1 jar
2/3 cup mayonnaise
1 teaspoon curry powder, optional

In a medium saucepan, brown the rice slowly without using butter. Let the rice cool completely. In a medium bowl, add the green pepper, onions, olives, and artichokes to the cooled rice. Mix the artichoke marinade with the mayonnaise and the curry powder, if desired. Gently stir into the rice mixture. Cover and chill before serving.

buffet cauliflower

Yield: 4 servings

Preparation time:
15 minutes plus
30 minutes chilling time

"Easy and so attractive"

1 large head cauliflower
1 cup mayonnaise
1 Tablespoon lemon juice
Tabasco sauce
Garlic powder

In a medium saucepan, cook cauliflower in boiling, salted water until just tender. Drain, cool, and refrigerate for 30 minutes. In a small bowl, combine remaining ingredients. Ice cauliflower with mayonnaise mixture just before serving on a tray or in a deep bowl.

broccoli salad

Preparation time:
  30 minutes plus
  3 hours chilling time

"Wonderful with quiche"

2 bunches broccoli
1 (6-ounce) can ripe olives,
  sliced
1 medium onion, chopped
1/2 pound fresh mushrooms,
  sliced
Lemon pepper (be generous)
3 hard boiled eggs, chopped

Dressing No. 1
1 cup mayonnaise
1/4 cup frozen lemon juice

Dressing No. 2
1 cup sour cream
1 cup mayonnaise
1 cup crumbled Roquefort
  cheese
1/2 clove garlic, diced
1/2 teaspoon
  Worcestershire sauce
Dash Tabasco sauce
2 teaspoons sugar
1/2 teaspoon salt

Remove stems from the broccoli and break up heads into bite-size florets. Combine with olives, onion, mushrooms, and lemon pepper in a medium bowl. Mix ingredients for either dressing and toss with broccoli mixture. Cover and chill for 3 hours. Top with chopped eggs when ready to serve.

chilled picnic ratatouille

Yield: 6 servings

Preparation time:
30 minutes plus
6 hours chilling time

"Great with hamburgers or grilled chicken"

1/4 cup olive oil
2 cloves garlic, minced
1 onion, sliced
1 red or green pepper, cut into strips
3 medium zucchini, cut into 1/4-inch slices, unpeeled
1 medium eggplant, peeled and cubed
1 teaspoon oregano
2 teaspoons basil
Salt and pepper
3 tomatoes, peeled and cut into wedges
Chopped fresh parsley

Heat oil in a large skillet. Add garlic, onion, red or green pepper, and zucchini. Saute for 3 minutes or until onion is tender, stirring constantly. Add eggplant and seasonings. Cover and cook over medium heat for 15 minutes, stirring occasionally. Add tomato wedges, cover, and cook for 4 minutes. Chill for at least 6 hours or overnight in a covered bowl. Garnish with parsley and serve cold.

Always rub herbs, dried or fresh, briskly between fingers, to release flavor oils.

cold pea salad

Yield: 6 servings

Preparation time:
   30 minutes
   plus 1 hour chilling time

"A picnic surprise"

**2 (10-ounce) packages
   frozen peas
1/2 cup mayonnaise
1/2 cup sour cream
6 slices bacon, crisply fried
   and crumbled
6 green onions, sliced
1 hard boiled egg, chopped
1/2 teaspoon salt
Freshly ground pepper
Dash garlic powder**

Thaw the peas at room
temperature. Combine with
remaining ingredients and chill,
covered, for 1 hour.

curried chicken salad

Yield: 4 servings

**Preparation time: 1 hour
   plus 2 hours chilling time**

"Refreshing and delicious"

**6 chicken breasts
1 or 2 (11-ounce) cans
   mandarin oranges
1 cup seedless green grapes
1/2 cup cole slaw dressing
1/2 cup mayonnaise
2 teaspoons curry powder
Salt and pepper**

Bake or broil chicken; bone and
cube. In a medium bowl, add
oranges and grapes to the
chicken. In another bowl,
combine the dressing,
mayonnaise, curry powder, salt,
and pepper to taste. Pour this
mixture over the chicken and
fruit and toss. This should be
enough mixture to coat the
chicken and fruit generously; if
not, add equal amounts of
dressing and mayonnaise. Cover
and chill for at least 2 hours.

cucumber-sour cream salad

Yield: 4 servings

Preparation time:
10 minutes plus
3 hours chilling time

"Nice when the garden begins to produce"

2 to 3 cucumbers, peeled and cubed
1 small red onion, thinly sliced
1 cup sour cream
2 Tablespoons vinegar
1/2 teaspoon seasoned salt
1/4 teaspoon dill weed, optional
Freshly ground pepper

Mix all the ingredients together and refrigerate, covered, for 3 hours.

***Serving suggestion:* Serve stuffed in a tomato half or in an avocado half.**

curried bean sprout salad

Yield: 4 servings

Preparation time:
10 minutes plus
2 hours chilling time

"So very nutritious"

1/2 cup mayonnaise
2 Tablespoons soy sauce
1 teaspoon curry powder
1 teaspoon lemon juice
1/2 pound fresh bean sprouts
1/2 cup thinly sliced celery
2 Tablespoons sliced green onions
1 (2 1/4-ounce) package slivered almonds, toasted

Thoroughly blend mayonnaise, soy sauce, curry powder, and lemon juice. Combine bean sprouts, celery, and onions. Toss this mixture with the dressing; sprinkle with almonds and chill, covered, for 2 hours. Serve on lettuce leaves.

crab louis

"Good on any luncheon menu"

**1 cup homemade
   mayonnaise
1/4 cup heavy cream,
   whipped
1/2 cup chili sauce
1/4 cup chopped green
   pepper
1/4 cup chopped green
   onions
1/4 teaspoon salt
Lemon juice to taste (about
   4 teaspoons)
1 head lettuce
1 1/2 pounds fresh crabmeat,
   drained
4 large tomatoes, cut into
   wedges
4 hard boiled eggs, sliced**

Combine the first 5 ingredients. Season with salt and lemon juice. Arrange large lettuce leaves on plates. Shred remaining lettuce and place on top of leaves. Flake crabmeat and arrange on lettuce. Place tomato wedges and sliced eggs around the crabmeat. Spoon dressing over each portion.

Note: **The dressing is better if made a day ahead and chilled thoroughly.**

When a recipe calls for green onions, use part of the tops for added flavor.

german potato salad

Yield: 6 servings

Preparation time:
45 minutes plus
3 hours standing time

"A terrific change of pace"

6 medium red potatoes
6 slices bacon
3/4 cup sliced onion
2 Tablespoons flour
1 to 2 Tablespoons sugar
1 1/2 teaspoons celery seed
Dash pepper
3/4 cup water
1/2 cup vinegar
3 hard boiled eggs, sliced

Cook unpeeled potatoes in boiling water until tender. Drain, cool, and cut into thick cubes. Fry the bacon in a medium skillet until crisp; drain, reserving 1/3 cup drippings. Saute the onion in the bacon drippings until tender. Mix in flour and sugar, stirring well. Add celery seed, pepper, water, and vinegar, stirring constantly. Cook over medium high heat until the mixture boils. Pour this over the potatoes in a large bowl. Crumble the bacon and add to the salad, saving a little for garnish. Stir dressing and bacon into potatoes gently. Cover and let stand at room temperature for at least 3 hours. At serving time, garnish with reserved bacon and egg slices.

layered gourmet salad

**Preparation time:
30 minutes plus
overnight chilling**

"Always a favorite"

**8 cups shredded lettuce
12 hard boiled eggs,
chopped
1/2 pound Gruyere cheese,
shredded
1 1/2 cups diced celery
1 cup sliced shallots or
sliced green onions
1 (10-ounce) package frozen
peas, cooked, drained,
and chilled
1/2 pound fresh
mushrooms, sliced
1 pound bacon, fried,
drained, and crumbled**

Dressing No. 1
**2 cups mayonnaise
5 Tablespoons Dijon
mustard
5 Tablespoons lemon
juice
2 teaspoons
Worcestershire sauce
Salt and pepper**

Dressing No. 2
**1 cup Miracle Whip
1 cup mayonnaise
Salad seasoning
Pinch sugar
1/3 cup milk or light cream
Salt and pepper**

Place 1/2 of the lettuce in the
bottom of a large bowl. Layer 1/2
of each of the other ingredients.
Top with remaining lettuce,
layer with the other ingredients.
Mix either dressing well and
spread over the top of the salad,
sealing completely. Cover tightly
and chill overnight.

marinated artichoke and mushroom salad

Yield: 6 servings

Preparation time:
10 minutes plus
4 hours chilling time

"A zesty salad to pick up any dinner"

1 **pound medium mushrooms, quartered**
1 **(8½-ounce) can artichoke hearts, drained**
⅓ **cup chopped green onions**
1 **(2-ounce) jar stuffed olives, drained and sliced**
½ **cup olive oil**
½ **cup white wine vinegar**
1 **Tablespoon dry sherry**
½ **teaspoon salt**
¼ **teaspoon garlic salt**
¼ **teaspoon oregano**
¼ **teaspoon freshly ground pepper**

Drop mushrooms into boiling, salted water and boil for 1 minute. Drain and put in a bowl. Quarter artichokes and add to mushrooms. Add onions and olives. Combine the rest of the ingredients and pour over the vegetables. Cover and refrigerate for at least 4 hours, stirring occasionally. Drain vegetables well and spoon mixture on lettuce leaves to serve.

If using as a substitute for fresh herbs, double the quantity of dried herbs.

marinated broccoli

**Preparation time:
30 minutes plus
overnight chilling**

"A dream for a summer buffet"

**4 1/2 pounds fresh broccoli
1 1/2 cups oil
1 cup cider vinegar
1 Tablespoon sugar
1 Tablespoon dill weed
1 Tablespoon monosodium
    glutamate
1 teaspoon salt
1 teaspoon pepper
1 teaspoon garlic salt**

Cut broccoli into bite-size pieces. Cook in boiling water until tender, but still crisp. Combine remaining ingredients in a jar and shake vigorously. Pour mixture over broccoli and refrigerate, covered, overnight. Drain well and serve chilled.

marinated onions

Yield: 6 servings

**Preparation time:
10 minutes
    plus overnight chilling**

"Everyone loves this."

**2 cups water
3 Tablespoons sugar
3 cups white vinegar
3 to 4 white or red onions,
    thinly sliced and
    separated into rings
1/2 cup mayonnaise,
    preferably homemade
1 teaspoon celery seed
Freshly ground pepper
Salt**

Heat the water, sugar, and vinegar in a medium saucepan until sugar is dissolved; cool. Soak onions, covered, in this marinade overnight; drain well. In a medium bowl, mix mayonnaise, celery seed, pepper, and salt to taste. Stir onions into this mixture and serve.

Note: **Vidalia onions make this even better. These onions are delicious with cold roast beef.**

marinated crab

Preparation time:
   5 minutes
   plus 4 hours chilling time

"Heavenly"

1/4 **cup oil**
3 **Tablespoons tarragon**
   vinegar
1 1/4 **teaspoons salt**
3/4 **teaspoon freshly ground**
   pepper
1/4 **teaspoon dry mustard**
1/8 **teaspoon thyme**
1/4 **teaspoon basil**
1 **Tablespoon minced**
   parsley
1 1/4 **cups chopped onion**
2 **Tablespoons lemon juice**
1 **pound lump crabmeat**

Combine all ingredients except crabmeat; mix well. Pour over crabmeat in a medium bowl and marinate, covered, for at least 4 hours in the refrigerator.

Note: **Although crabmeat is very perishable, it will keep up to 5 days in marinade.**

Never marinate in aluminum pans.

melon ball and shrimp salad

Yield: 6 to 8 servings

Preparation time:
30 minutes plus
2 hours chilling time

"Light and luscious"

2 pounds shrimp, cooked
and peeled
2 Tablespoons fresh lemon
juice
2 teaspoons grated onion
1 1/2 cups chopped celery
1 1/2 teaspoons salt
1 cup mayonnaise
1 1/2 Tablespoons curry
powder
6 Tablespoons sour cream
1 large honeydew melon,
cut into balls
1 large cantaloupe, cut
into balls
Bibb lettuce
Shredded coconut, optional

Combine first 6 ingredients. Blend curry powder with sour cream. Add this to shrimp mixture, mix well, and chill for several hours. Fold in melon balls just before serving. Arrange on a bed of lettuce and garnish with coconut, if desired.

mexican delight

**Preparation time:
30 minutes**

"A meal in itself"

2 pounds ground beef
**1 head lettuce, torn into
   bite-size pieces**
8 green onions, sliced
2 tomatoes, chopped
**1 avocado, peeled and
   chopped**
1 (4-ounce) can taco sauce
**1 (10-ounce) can enchilada
   sauce**
**1 (8-ounce) can tomato
   sauce**
**1 (8-ounce) package tortilla
   chips**
**1 (16-ounce) can kidney
   beans, drained**
**2 cups shredded Monterey
   Jack cheese**

Brown ground beef, drain, and keep warm. Combine lettuce, onions, tomatoes, and the avocado. Place taco, enchilada, and tomato sauces in a small pan and heat. Line a large salad bowl with tortilla chips. Cover with a layer of ground beef, lettuce mixture, beans, and cheese. Pour the hot sauce mixture over salad, toss, and serve immediately.

Tomatoes have a better flavor if not refrigerated.

prosciutto and fresh fruit

Yield: 8 to 10 servings

**Preparation time:
15 minutes**

"Any fresh melon may be used."

**16 to 20 paper-thin slices
  prosciutto**
**1 fresh pineapple, peeled
  and sliced lengthwise
  into spears**
**1 small honeydew melon,
  peeled and sliced into
  spears**
Grape leaves or bibb lettuce
2 to 3 limes, quartered

Wrap prosciutto around the pineapple spears and around the honeydew spears. Serve on grape leaves or bibb lettuce with a wedge of lime.

slaw

Yield: 6 servings

**Preparation time:
10 minutes plus
4 hours chilling time**

"A food processor makes this so easy."

1 medium cabbage
3 carrots
1 medium onion
1 1/2 teaspoons salt
2 Tablespoons sugar
3 Tablespoons vinegar
3/4 cup mayonnaise

Grate the cabbage, carrots, and the onion. Add salt, sugar, vinegar, and mayonnaise. Mix well and refrigerate, covered, for at least 4 hours. This is best made a day ahead.

Variation: For a little different consistency, add 1/2 cup cottage cheese.

seafood bombay salad

"Deliciously different"

1/2 cup French dressing
1/2 cup mayonnaise
4 teaspoons chutney
2 teaspoons lemon juice
2 teaspoons curry powder
Salt
Pepper
1 1/3 cups cooked, diced
    shrimp
1 1/3 cups crabmeat, cleaned
3/4 cup thinly sliced celery
4 teaspoons chopped
    peanuts, toasted
Romaine or bibb lettuce
    leaves
4 tomatoes cut into 8
    wedges each

Garnish
Asparagus spears
Sliced hard boiled eggs
Onion slices, separated
    into rings
Pitted black olives

Blend first 7 ingredients, set aside. In a medium bowl, mix the shrimp, crabmeat, celery, and peanuts. Combine with the dressing ingredients. Arrange large lettuce leaves on plates. Top with the tomato wedges. Mound seafood salad on each plate and garnish, as desired.

salade nicoise

Yield: 4 servings

Preparation time: 1 hour

"Delicious and low calorie too"

1/2 **cup olive oil**
1/2 **cup white wine vinegar**
4 **Tablespoons capers**
2 **teaspoons basil**
2 **teaspoons Dijon mustard**
1/2 **teaspoon salt**
1/4 **teaspoon pepper**
4 **medium red potatoes,
    boiled, drained, and
    thinly sliced**
1 **(7-ounce) can tuna,
    drained**
1/2 **cup fresh green beans,
    cooked but still crisp**
Bibb lettuce
2 **tomatoes, cut into wedges**
3 **hard boiled eggs, sliced**
Sliced black olives
Radishes
Anchovy fillets, optional

Mix the first 7 ingredients well for the dressing. Combine potato slices, tuna, and beans. Pour dressing over this and let stand for 30 minutes. To serve, arrange salad on a bed of lettuce. Garnish with tomato wedges, egg slices, olives, radishes, and anchovies.

Note: **315 calories per serving.**

croutons

Temperature: 250°
Baking time: 30 minutes

"Adds just the right touch to salads and soups"

1/4 cup butter or margarine
6 slices bread, frozen and
   cubed
Garlic salt

Melt butter in a large skillet. Add bread cubes and sprinkle generously with garlic salt; stir until evenly browned. Place croutons on a cookie sheet and bake.

spinach salad

Yield: 4 to 6 servings

Preparation time:
   30 minutes

"Always tasty with a choice of dressings"

1 pound fresh spinach
1 (8-ounce) can sliced water
   chestnuts, drained
1/2 pound fresh bean sprouts
1 pound bacon, cooked
   and crumbled
1/2 small onion, thinly
   sliced
2 hard boiled eggs, grated

Wash, dry, and remove stems from spinach and tear into pieces. Combine the spinach with the water chestnuts, bean sprouts, bacon, and onion. Combine and mix thoroughly ingredients of the dressing of your choice. Toss salad with dressing and top with grated eggs.

(continued)

Dressing No. 1

1/3 cup catsup
1/4 cup vinegar
1/2 cup sugar
1 cup oil
1 Tablespoon
  Worcestershire sauce
1 small onion or 4 green
  onions, chopped
Salt and pepper

Dressing No. 2

3 ounces Roquefort cheese,
  crumbled
1/2 cup mayonnaise
1/2 cup sour cream

Dressing No. 3

1 egg
1 Tablespoon grated
  Parmesan cheese
1 clove garlic, crushed
1 1/2 teaspoons Dijon
  mustard
1/2 cup lemon juice
1/2 cup oil
Salt and pepper

Note: These salad dressings are best made a day ahead.

1 lemon yields 2 Tablespoons juice and 2 teaspoons grated rind. Place a lemon in the microwave on high for a few seconds before cutting: you'll get more juice.

stuffed avocado salad

Yield: 8 servings

Preparation time:
20 minutes plus
2 hours chilling time

"Delicious luncheon fare"

4 large avocados
1 (12-ounce) package cream
cheese, softened
Salt
Worcestershire sauce
1/4 cucumber, peeled
and grated
1 Tablespoon grated onion
Light cream
8 large lettuce leaves
1 (8¹/2-ounce) can artichoke
hearts, drained
1 cup mayonnaise
3 Tablespoons chili sauce
Paprika or chopped parsley

Wash avocados and cut each in half. Remove pits. Combine cream cheese with salt, Worcestershire sauce, cucumber, onion, and cream; blend well. (Use only enough cream to soften cheese.) Stuff avocado halves and press together. Chill, covered, for several hours. Just before serving, peel and slice the stuffed avocados. Place on lettuce leaves and top each portion with an artichoke heart. Combine the mayonnaise with the chili sauce. Spoon this over the salad and sprinkle with paprika or chopped parsley.

Note: **This is equally good as a luncheon salad with seafood or as an accompaniment to a roast beef dinner.**

tomato-egg tarragon salad

Yield: 8 servings

**Preparation time:
30 minutes plus
overnight chilling**

"Adds color to your table"

1 **cup mayonnaise**
1 **teaspoon onion powder**
1 **teaspoon dried tarragon**
1/2 **teaspoon lemon juice**
1 **Tablespoon chopped
  chives**
1 **red onion, thinly sliced**
Bibb lettuce
3 **tomatoes, peeled and
  sliced**
4 **slices bratwurst sausage,
  cut into strips**
4 **slices pepper salami, cut
  into strips**
4 **hard boiled eggs, halved**
Chopped parsley

In a small bowl, combine
mayonnaise, onion powder,
tarragon, lemon juice, and
chopped chives; cover and
refrigerate overnight. Cover
onions with water and ice cubes.
Refrigerate for at least 6 hours,
adding ice cubes when needed. If
done the day before serving,
refrigerate onion slices in a jar of
ice water. On each plate, place
lettuce leaves, tomato slices, 1
sausage and salami slice, and
onion slices. Top each portion
with 1/2 a hard boiled egg, cut
side down. Spoon on the
tarragon mayonnaise and
sprinkle with chopped parsley.

artichoke-asparagus mold

**Preparation time:
20 minutes plus
overnight chilling**

"Just the right combination"

2 (10½-ounce) cans cut
  asparagus
2 envelopes unflavored
  gelatin
½ cup water
4 Tablespoons fresh lemon
  juice
1 teaspoon minced onion
2 teaspoons Worcestershire
  sauce
2 (15-ounce) cans artichoke
  hearts, drained and
  quartered
2 cups sour cream
1½ cups mayonnaise
2 hard boiled eggs, grated
1 (2¼-ounce) package
  slivered almonds
Salt
Black pepper
Red pepper

Drain asparagus, reserving
1½ cups of the liquid. Dissolve
gelatin in water. Heat asparagus
liquid, lemon juice, onion, and
Worcestershire sauce in a
medium saucepan. Stir in
gelatin and remove from heat.
In a large bowl, add the warm
mixture to the asparagus,
artichoke hearts, sour cream,
mayonnaise, eggs, and almonds.
Season to taste and pour into a
well-oiled 3-quart mold.
Refrigerate overnight.

cranberry port wine salad

Yield: 8 to 10 servings

**Preparation time: 1 hour
plus overnight chilling**

"A special treat with poultry"

1 (1-pound) can jellied
cranberry sauce, without
berries
2 cups cranberry juice
1 (6-ounce) and
1 (3-ounce) package
raspberry gelatin
1 cup cold water
1 cup port wine
1 (8-ounce) can water
chestnuts, drained
and finely chopped

Cream Cheese Sauce
1 (8-ounce) package cream
cheese, softened
Celery salt
Tabasco sauce
Onion juice
Worcestershire sauce
Light cream

In a small pan, melt the cranberry sauce over low heat. In a larger pan, bring cranberry juice to a boil. Stir gelatin into the cold water and add to the cranberry juice; stir well. Remove the pan from the heat and add the port wine and the cranberry sauce; refrigerate until the mixture begins to congeal. Add the water chestnuts, pour mixture into a 2-quart mold and chill overnight. Whip the cream cheese in a food processor or a blender; season to taste. Add enough cream for desired consistency. Serve the cream cheese sauce with the salad.

Pluck a leaf from the crown of a fresh pineapple. If it comes out easily, the fruit is ripe.

egg-curry mold

Preparation time:
15 minutes plus
4 hours chilling time

"A congealed salad at its best"

2 cups chicken broth
2 Tablespoons curry powder
2 envelopes unflavored
  gelatin
1/2 cup cold water
3/4 cup homemade
  mayonnaise
3/4 cup sour cream
3 hard boiled eggs, finely
  chopped
1 cup sliced, stuffed olives
Salt and pepper

Bring broth to a boil in a large saucepan. Stir in curry powder. Soften gelatin in cold water and then dissolve in the hot broth. Chill until mixture begins to thicken, about 1 hour. Blend mayonnaise and sour cream into the broth mixture. Fold in chopped eggs and olives, seasoning with salt and pepper, if needed. Pour into an oiled 1 1/2-quart ring mold and chill for 4 hours or until set.

fresh blueberry salad

Yield: 6 to 8 servings

Preparation time:
10 minutes plus
4 hours chilling time

"This may also be used as a light dessert."

2 (3-ounce) packages black
  cherry gelatin
3 cups boiling water
1 (8-ounce) can crushed
  pineapple, drained
1/4 cup maraschino cherries,
  drained and halved
2 cups fresh blueberries

In a 1 1/2-quart serving bowl, dissolve gelatin in boiling water; cool. Add pineapple and chill until thickened. Fold in cherries and blueberries. Chill until firm. Mix dressing ingredients and refrigerate for several hours or overnight.

(continued)

Dressing
1 cup miniature
  marshmallows
2 cups sour cream
1 teaspoon mayonnaise
1/2 teaspoon vanilla

When ready to serve,
stir dressing well and spoon over
blueberry mixture.

frozen fruit salad   Yield: 12 servings

Preparation time:
  15 minutes plus
  4 hours freezing time

"Substitute or add fruits of your choice."

1 (8-ounce) package cream
  cheese, softened
1 cup homemade
  mayonnaise
1 cup powdered sugar
1 cup sweet bing cherries,
  drained
1 cup canned pears,
  drained and chopped
1 cup chunk pineapple,
  drained
2 cups heavy cream,
  whipped

Combine the cream cheese and
the mayonnaise with an electric
mixer. Blend in the powdered
sugar, stir in the fruit, and fold in
the whipped cream. Freeze.

Note: For individual salads, this may be spooned into paper
muffin cups before freezing.

frozen tomato salad

Yield: 12 servings

Preparation time:
45 minutes plus
4 hours freezing time

"Perfect for the holidays"

5 tomatoes, peeled and
chopped
1 cup vegetable juice
1 (8-ounce) can crushed
pineapple, drained
1/2 cup minced onion
3 cups Miracle Whip
1 teaspoon celery salt
Cayenne pepper
Red food coloring, optional

Put tomatoes, vegetable juice, pineapple, and onion into a blender; blend for 1 minute. Pour 1/2 the mixture into a large mixing bowl. To the remaining mixture, still in the blender, add the Miracle Whip, celery salt, cayenne, and food coloring, if desired. Blend for 1 more minute. Combine both mixtures well and freeze in a 13x9x2-inch glass dish for 4 hours. Thaw for at least 30 minutes before serving.

Serving suggestion: **Serve on lettuce leaves with homemade mayonnaise. You may prefer to partially freeze to a sorbet-like consistency. Using an ice cream scoop, put scoops on a cookie sheet and return to the freezer. When serving, put a scoop in an avocado half on a bed of lettuce and garnish with homemade mayonnaise.**

To ripen pineapples, tomatoes, and avocados: place in a brown paper bag and leave in a warm place.

gazpacho salad mold

Yield: 6 to 8 servings

Ⓠ Ⓠ Ⓠ

Preparation time:
30 minutes plus
6 hours chilling time

"Excellent for a family cook-out"

3 envelopes unflavored gelatin
3 cups tomato juice
1/2 cup red wine vinegar
2 teaspoons salt
Tabasco sauce
1/2 medium green pepper, diced
2 medium tomatoes, peeled and diced
1/2 cup chopped celery
1/2 cucumber, peeled and diced
1 Tablespoon chopped chives
1/2 cup finely chopped red onion
3 large avocados
4 Tablespoons lemon juice
Watercress

In a large saucepan, sprinkle the gelatin over 3/4 cup tomato juice. Over low heat, stir constantly until the gelatin dissolves. Remove from heat. Stir in remaining tomato juice, vinegar, salt, and Tabasco to taste. Set pan in a bowl of ice, stirring occasionally, until the mixture thickens to a consistency of beaten egg whites. This will take about 15 minutes. Fold in the vegetables. Pour into a 2-quart mold that has been rinsed in cold water. Refrigerate for at least 6 hours. Before serving, peel and slice the avocados and brush them with lemon juice. Arrange avocados around the unmolded salad and garnish with watercress.

Serving suggestion: **Serve with *Mayonnaise*, page 142, *Blender Mayonnaise*, page 142, or *Must Make Mayonnaise*, page 143.**

molded egg salad, lorenzo dressing

Yield: 10 to 12 servings

Preparation time:
45 minutes plus
3 hours chilling time

"The dressing is a treasure."

2 envelopes unflavored
  gelatin
1/2 cup cold water
1 cup boiling water
12 hard boiled eggs
1 cup mayonnaise
2 teaspoons salt
1/4 teaspoon white pepper
1 Tablespoon lemon juice
2 Tablespoons chopped
  green pepper
2 Tablespoons chopped
  pimento
Fresh watercress

Lorenzo Dressing
1/4 cup tarragon vinegar
2 teaspoons salt
1/2 teaspoon English
  mustard
2 teaspoons
  Worcestershire sauce
3/4 cup oil
Dash Tabasco sauce
1/3 cup chili sauce
1 cup finely chopped
  watercress

Sprinkle gelatin over cold water; let stand for 10 minutes and then dissolve in boiling water. Sieve or rice the eggs into a large mixing bowl. Combine the mayonnaise, salt, pepper, lemon juice, green pepper, and pimento with the eggs and gelatin and turn into a greased 2-quart mold. Chill for 3 hours and serve on a bed of watercress. To prepare the dressing, mix all the ingredients except the watercress. Stir in the watercress just before serving over the egg salad.

Note: Using fresh watercress is vital for a truly fresh taste.

138

spinach souffle mold

Yield: 6 to 8 servings

Preparation time:
15 minutes plus
4 hours chilling time

"Such a pretty dish"

1 (3-ounce) package lemon
   gelatin
1 1/2 cups water
1/2 cup mayonnaise
1 1/2 Tablespoons vinegar
1 Tablespoon sour cream
1/4 teaspoon salt
1 cup chopped fresh spinach
1/2 cup chopped celery
3/4 cup cottage cheese
1 Tablespoon minced onion
Cherry tomatoes

Sprinkle gelatin over 1/2 cup cold water in a large bowl. Add 1 cup boiling water, mayonnaise, vinegar, sour cream, and salt. Blend thoroughly with an electric mixer, pour into a shallow 1-quart dish, and chill until the mixture starts to congeal around the edges. Return to the large bowl and beat until fluffy. Fold in the next 4 ingredients. Pour into a 1 1/2-quart ring mold and chill until firm. Fill the center of the mold with cherry tomatoes before serving.

To peel tomatoes: make a cross in the top with a sharp knife and drop the tomatoes in boiling water for a few seconds. This will make peeling much easier.

tomato soup aspic   Yield: 6 to 8 servings

Preparation time:
15 minutes plus
overnight chilling

"If you use less gelatin, this is a marvelous dip."

2 envelopes unflavored
  gelatin
1/2 cup cold water
1 can tomato soup
3 (3-ounce) packages cream
  cheese
1 cup chopped celery
1/2 cup chopped green
  pepper
1/2 cup chopped stuffed
  olives
1 Tablespoon grated onion
2 Tablespoons lemon juice
1 cup mayonnaise
1 Tablespoon
  Worcestershire sauce
1 or 2 teaspoons
  Tabasco sauce
2 cups cooked shrimp or
  lobster, optional
Salt

Soften gelatin in cold water. Heat soup in the top of a double boiler. Add the cream cheese and stir until cheese melts. Beat with an electric beater and add the gelatin. Stir well, adding remaining ingredients. Pour into a lightly oiled 1 1/2-quart mold and chill overnight.

Salt-free seasoning--Grind: 2 parts basil
                             2 parts savory
                             2 parts celery seed
                             2 parts sage
                             1 part thyme
                             1 part marjoram

vegetable salad mold

Yield: 12 to 14 servings

**Preparation time:
45 minutes plus
overnight chilling**

"Delicious served with curried mayonnaise"

6 beef bouillon cubes
4 1/2 cups boiling water
3 Tablespoons
  Worcestershire sauce
1/4 cup lemon juice
2 Tablespoons grated onion
Dash Tabasco sauce
1 Tablespoon sugar
Salt
3 1/2 envelopes unflavored
  gelatin
1/2 cup cold water
1 (15-ounce) can artichoke
  hearts, drained and
  quartered
3 (16-ounce) cans French
  style green beans, drained
1 small bunch carrots,
  sliced, cooked, and
  drained
1 head cauliflower, broken
  into florets, cooked,
  and drained
1 avocado, peeled and cubed
1 package mild Italian salad
  dressing, prepared with
  1/2 vegetable oil and
  1/2 olive oil

In a large saucepan, dissolve the bouillon cubes in 4 1/2 cups boiling water. Add Worcestershire sauce, lemon juice, onion, Tabasco sauce, sugar, and salt. Stir gelatin into 1/2 cup cold water and add to the bouillon mixture. Refrigerate until partially congealed. Stir the vegetables and the avocado into the dressing. To assemble the salad, put a thin layer of vegetables and avocado in a 2-quart mold and cover with a thin layer of bouillon mixture; repeat 3 times. Chill overnight.

blender mayonnaise

**Preparation time:
5 minutes**

"So easy and so good"

**1 egg
3/4 teaspoon salt
2 teaspoons fresh lemon
    juice or wine vinegar
2 dashes Tabasco sauce
1/2 teaspoon onion juice
Freshly ground pepper
1/2 cup vegetable oil
1/2 cup olive oil**

Blend the egg at top speed for 30 seconds. Add salt, lemon juice or wine vinegar, Tabasco sauce, onion juice, and pepper and blend for 15 seconds. Blending at high speed, remove the cover of the blender container and pour the combined oils into the center of the mixture in a very thin stream. Chill covered.

mayonnaise

Yield: 2 cups

**Preparation time:
10 minutes**

"Your family may never want store-bought mayonnaise ever again."

**1 teaspoon salt
1/4 teaspoon paprika
1/2 teaspoon dry mustard
Dash cayenne pepper
2 egg yolks
2 Tablespoons vinegar
2 cups oil
2 heaping Tablespoons fresh
    lemon juice**

Mix salt, paprika, dry mustard, and cayenne. Add egg yolks to this mixture and blend in a small bowl. Add vinegar and mix well. Add 1 cup oil, *1 Tablespoon at a time*, mixing after each addition. Add remaining oil and lemon juice and mix well. Refrigerate, covered.

Note: **The success of mayonnaise stems from the slow addition of oil to egg yolks. It's important to beat well after each addition with a wire whisk or with an electric mixer.**

must-make mayonnaise

Yield: 4 cups

**Preparation time:
5 minutes**

"A food processor specialty"

3 eggs
1 1/2 teaspoons salt
1 1/2 teaspoons sugar
1/3 teaspoon dry mustard
Pinch white pepper
Pinch red pepper
4 cups oil
2 Tablespoons vinegar
2 Tablespoons lemon juice

Using the metal blade of a food processor, mix eggs, salt, sugar, mustard, white, and red pepper. With machine on, add 2 cups oil, pouring very slowly. Slowly add vinegar, lemon juice, and the remaining oil. Let the machine run for 20 seconds after everything has been added. Store, covered, in the refrigerator.

Note: **This keeps 2 to 3 weeks in the refrigerator. If the mayonnaise refuses to thicken, dip a bowl in hot water, dry it thoroughly, and add 1 teaspoon Dijon mustard. Add 1 Tablespoon of the thin mayonnaise and beat with a wire whisk until well blended; beat in the rest of the mayonnaise, a little at a time, whisking after each addition.**

hot bacon dressing

Yield: 1 1/2 cups

**Preparation time:
10 minutes**

"Fabulous on spinach"

6 slices bacon, diced
1/2 cup minced onion
1/2 cup honey
2/3 cup cider vinegar
1 teaspoon salt
1/4 teaspoon white pepper

Fry bacon until brown and crispy in a large skillet or a 2-quart pan. Add all the other ingredients and heat to a boil, stirring constantly. This can be done ahead and reheated when ready to serve.

tomato-roquefort dressing

**Preparation time:
5 minutes**

"Delicious even on plain lettuce"

1/2 cup chili sauce
1 Tablespoon lemon juice
1/2 cup oil
1/2 cup crumbled Roquefort
  cheese
1 clove garlic, minced
1/2 teaspoon salt
1/2 teaspoon paprika
1 (8-ounce) can tomato
  sauce

Mix all ingredients in a blender or a food processor for 30 seconds. This will keep in the refrigerator for several months in a covered container.

bleu cheese dressing I

Yield: 2 1/2 cups

**Preparation time:
5 minutes**

"A delightful variation"

1 cup mayonnaise
1/3 cup oil
1/4 cup catsup
2 Tablespoons chopped
  onion
2 Tablespoons sugar
2 Tablespoons white vinegar
1 teaspoon Dijon or brown
  mustard
1/2 teaspoon salt
1/2 teaspoon paprika
1/4 teaspoon celery seed
Dash pepper
4 to 5 ounces bleu cheese,
  crumbled

Put all ingredients into a blender and blend until smooth. Refrigerate covered. Will keep for weeks.

bleu cheese dressing II

Yield: 2 cups

Preparation time:
  5 minutes plus
  2 hours chilling time

"A wee bit different"

1/2 cup mayonnaise
2 cups sour cream or plain
  yogurt
1/2 teaspoon pepper
1/2 teaspoon celery seed
1 teaspoon salt
1 teaspoon sugar
2 Tablespoons red wine
  vinegar
1 clove garlic
1/2 pound bleu cheese, well
  crumbled

Mix the mayonnaise, sour cream, and seasonings well. Fold in the bleu cheese. Refrigerate, tightly covered. Remove the garlic clove after several hours.

camille dressing

Yield: 1 1/2 cups

Preparation time:
  5 minutes plus
  2 hours chilling time

"Good and versatile"

1/3 cup red wine vinegar
3/4 cup oil
3 green onions, chopped
1/2 cup chopped parsley
3 heaping teaspoons creole
  mustard
1/2 teaspoon salt
1/2 teaspoon pepper

Put all the ingredients in a jar, cover, and shake well. Refrigerate for at least 2 hours before serving.

Variation: Bleu cheese may be substituted for the creole mustard.

145

beau jacques french dressing

Yield: 1 cup

**Preparation time:
5 minutes plus
1 hour standing time**

"Indescribably delicious"

1/2 cup sugar
1/4 cup red wine vinegar
1 Tablespoon fresh lemon
    juice
2 Tablespoons catsup
1/4 cup oil
1 teaspoon salt
1 teaspoon paprika
1 Tablespoon grated onion

Whisk all ingredients but the onion in a large mixing bowl. Add the onion and stir. Pour into a jar, cover, and keep upside down for 1 hour before refrigerating.

Note: **Fabulous over avocado and grapefruit sections. Equally good as a sauce with fried chicken or a base for baked chicken.**

dill dressing

Yield: 1 cup

**Preparation time:
10 minutes plus
1 hour chilling time**

"Fabulous on open faced sandwiches"

2 Tablespoons white wine
    vinegar
2 Tablespoons Dijon
    mustard
3/4 to 1 teaspoon salt
1/4 teaspoon pepper
Pinch sugar
1/2 clove garlic, minced
1/2 teaspoon dill weed
1/2 cup heavy cream
4 Tablespoons olive oil

Combine vinegar, mustard, salt, pepper, sugar, garlic, and dill. Heat cream and olive oil in top of a double boiler until hot, stirring constantly. Stir into first mixture and refrigerate for 1 hour.

146

dijon mustard dressing

Yield: 1 1/4 cups

Preparation time:
5 minutes

"Double this every time."

3/4 cup oil
1/4 cup cider vinegar
3 Tablespoons fresh lemon
   juice
1/2 clove garlic, minced
1/2 teaspoon monosodium
   glutamate
1/2 teaspoon salt
1/4 teaspoon pepper
3 heaping Tablespoons
   Dijon mustard

Mix all ingredients in a jar and
shake well or blend in a blender.
Refrigerate in a covered
container.

fruit salad dressing

Yield: 1 1/4 cups

Preparation time:
5 minutes plus
1 hour chilling time

"A summer favorite over fresh fruit"

1/4 cup sugar
1 teaspoon dry mustard
1 teaspoon salt
1/2 teaspoon celery or poppy
   seed
1 teaspoon grated onion
4 Tablespoons vinegar
1 cup chilled oil

Mix the first 5 ingredients with
1 Tablespoon vinegar in a small
bowl. Add the rest of the vinegar
and the oil alternately, beating at
medium to high speed with a
mixer. Refrigerate in a covered
jar for 1 hour. Shake well before
serving.

147

honey-mustard dressing

Yield: 5 cups

Preparation time: 5 minutes

"Great on any salad and a wonderful Christmas gift"

1/3 cup oil
1/3 cup Dijon mustard
1/3 cup honey
1 3/4 cups cider vinegar
2 cups mayonnaise
Onion salt
Celery salt
Cayenne pepper
1/2 teaspoon mustard seed, optional

Combine all ingredients in a food processor or in a blender. Refrigerate covered. This will keep for weeks.

italian dressing

Yield: 1 cup

Preparation time: 5 minutes plus 1 hour standing time

"Homemade is so much better."

2/3 cup olive oil
1/4 cup red wine vinegar
2 Tablespoons lemon juice
1 teaspoon salt
1 teaspoon sugar
1/2 teaspoon dried oregano, crushed
1/2 teaspoon crushed red pepper
1 clove garlic
1/4 teaspoon fennel seed, crushed

Combine all the ingredients. Beat or shake in a jar to mix. Let stand for 1 hour. Remove garlic clove. Strain before using, if desired. Store, covered, in the refrigerator.

maurice salad dressing

Yield: 2 1/2 cups

**Preparation time:
5 minutes**

"Especially good over a chef's salad"

**1/4 cup chopped dill pickles
3/4 cup mayonnaise
1/2 cup vinegar
3/4 cup mild olive oil
4 teaspoons chopped chives
4 teaspoons Worcestershire
    sauce
4 hard boiled eggs, chopped
Garlic powder**

Mix all ingredients well and
refrigerate in a covered
container.

navy salad dressing

Yield: 3 cups

**Preparation time:
5 minutes**

"Fabulous on any salad"

**1 teaspoon salt
1 teaspoon dry mustard
1 teaspoon sugar
1 teaspoon pepper
1 heaping teaspoon Beau
    Monde seasoning
1 Tablespoon
    Worcestershire sauce
2 Tablespoons catsup
2/3 cup wine vinegar
2 cups oil
1 clove garlic**

Mix all dry ingredients in a quart
jar. Add the remaining
ingredients, cover, and shake
well. Store unrefrigerated.
Remove garlic clove before
serving.

parmesan salad dressing

Yield: 2 cups

Preparation time:
10 minutes

"Good and hearty"

1 1/2 cups oil
2 eggs
1 teaspoon spicy steak
  sauce
1 teaspoon Heinz-57 sauce
1 teaspoon Worcestershire
  sauce
1 medium clove garlic,
  minced
1 Tablespoon lemon juice
1 Tablespoon vinegar
1/3 cup freshly grated
  Parmesan cheese
3 ounces bleu cheese,
  crumbled
4 or 5 drops Tabasco sauce
Salt and pepper

Shake all ingredients in a jar or
combine in a blender. Refrigerate
in a covered container.

Thin leftover dip slightly and use as a delicious salad dressing.

home canning notes

The process of home canning depends on the kind of food being canned. For fruits, tomatoes, and pickled vegetables, canning usually requires a boiling water-bath canner. For most jams, preserves, and pickles - foods which have enough sugar or vinegar to help prevent spoiling - use the oldest method, open-kettle canning.

First of all, your canning equipment must be in tip-top shape. Jars and lids must be flawless - no nicks, chips, or cracks. Discard any others. Use all new self-sealing lids or rubbers. Wash jars and lids, except those with sealing compounds, in hot, sudsy water and rinse (the dishwasher is perfect for this step). Some metal lids with sealing compound need boiling; others only need to be dipped in hot water. Follow the manufacturer's directions for this.

Water Bath Canner: You can use any large metal container with a tight-fitting cover that is deep enough to leave an inch or two of water over the tops of the jars and a little extra space for boiling. Use a rack to keep the jars from touching the bottom.

Open Kettle Canner:
1. Sterilize jars and lids by covering with warm water; heat to a boil and boil for 15 minutes. Follow the manufacturer's directions for sterilizing the self-sealing caps. Leave the jars in hot water until needed; remove 1 at a time.
2. Pack each sterilized jar to 1/2-inch from the top of the jar with the boiling product and liquid. Fill and seal only 1 jar at a time.
3. Wipe top and threads of jars with a clean cloth to remove all food particles. A speck of food or even a seed will break the seal.
4. Seal each jar immediately by placing a flat metal lid on the jar with the sealing composition next to the glass and screw the band tightly. Cool the jars right-side-up out of drafts.

Preserves - If not using canning jars and lids, seal jellies, jams, and preserves with a layer 1/8-inch thick of hot paraffin. Melt paraffin in the top of a double boiler; 1 Tablespoon paraffin to make 1/8-inch layer on a 6-ounce jelly glass. Prick any bubbles that appear. These form holes in the paraffin and result in a poor seal.

Pickles - Most pickles are canned by the open-kettle canning process, unless otherwise specified. **The flavor of almost all pickled produce is improved if it stands for 6 weeks before being used.**

151

apple honey-cointreau

Yield: 2 pints

Preparation time: 1 hour

"Serve over ice cream or even on French toast."

6 large tart apples, pared, cored, and cut up
3 cups sugar
1 Tablespoon honey
1 1/2 teaspoons grated orange rind
1/2 cup orange juice
2 Tablespoons Cointreau

Put apples through food chopper or processor, using coarse blade. Heat apples and all other ingredients, except Cointreau, and bring to a boil. Lower heat and simmer gently for about 45 minutes, stirring often. About 5 minutes before Apple Honey is done, add Cointreau. Do not boil after this. Pour into sterile jars and seal.

banana jama

Yield: 2 1/2 pints

**Preparation time:
30 minutes**

"Children love this on toast or with peanut butter."

6 cups sliced bananas
3 cups sugar
3/4 cup orange juice
1/3 cup lemon juice
2 strips orange peel
4 strips lemon peel
1 cinnamon stick
3 whole cloves

Combine all ingredients in a large kettle; cook over medium heat, stirring constantly until sugar has dissolved. Boil for 10 minutes. Reduce heat, still stirring, and cook for 15 to 20 minutes until mixture thickens. Put into sterilized jars, seal, invert for a few seconds, and then put jars upright to cool. This keeps the fruit from rising to the top. If the jam is to be stored longer than 6 months, put the jars in a boiling water bath for 10 to 15 minutes.

Note: A good way to use ripe bananas.

blackberry curd

Yield: 2 1/2 pints

**Preparation time:
30 minutes**

"Especially good made with wild blackberries"

1 **pound blackberries,
washed and hulled**
1/2 **pound cooking apples,
peeled, cored, and
chopped**
2 **Tablespoons fresh lemon
juice**
1 1/2 **cups butter or
margarine**
2 **cups sugar**
4 **large eggs**

Put fruit in a saucepan over very low heat and cook until the juices run and the fruit is tender. Puree the fruit. Strain the lemon juice into the top of a double boiler. Add pureed fruit, butter, and sugar. Stir over hot water until sugar has dissolved. Beat eggs and gradually add to fruit mixture. Cook gently, still stirring, until mixture thickens. Pour into hot, sterilized jars and seal. This keeps several months in the refrigerator.

Note: **This is an English recipe in the same category as lemon cheese or curd. It is delicious on slices of toasted pound cake, as a cake filling, or as a tart filling if it doesn't disappear by the spoonful out of the jar first!**

Grease the bottom of the pan to prevent sticking when making preserves.

cherry conserve

Yield: 3½ pints

**Preparation time:
30 minutes**

"A small jar of this and homemade bread make a wonderful gift."

**2 quarts sour cherries,
   pitted
1 cup raisins
2 cups sugar
1 teaspoon grated lemon
   peel
1 teaspoon grated orange
   peel
1 Tablespoon fresh lemon
   juice
1 cup walnuts or pecans**

Mix cherries, raisins, sugar,
lemon and orange peel and
simmer until thick and syrupy.
Add the lemon juice and nuts;
stir. Ladle into hot, sterilized
jars. Seal.

hot pepper jelly

Yield: 6 pints

**Preparation time:
10 minutes**

"A must to keep on hand to serve over cream cheese"

**3 large green peppers, cut
   and seeded
12 hot peppers, not seeded
1/3 cup water
3 cups cider vinegar
5 pounds sugar
Green food coloring
2 bottles liquid fruit pectin**

In blender or food processor,
pulverize peppers with water.
Combine this with cider vinegar
and sugar in a saucepan and boil
hard for 5 minutes. Add a few
drops of food coloring. Remove
from heat and add pectin. Pour
into sterile jars and seal.

***Note:* For a Christmasy touch, use red bell peppers, red hot
peppers, and red food coloring.**

green pepper jelly

Yield: 3 pints

**Preparation time:
15 minutes**

"Milder and sweeter than most"

4 green peppers, chopped
**8 small hot seasoning
peppers, ground**
1 1/2 cups white vinegar
7 1/2 cups sugar
1 bottle liquid pectin
**3 to 4 drops green food
coloring**

Put green and hot peppers in a blender or a food processor with enough vinegar to cover the blades. Blend thoroughly. Pour into a large saucepan with the sugar and the rest of the vinegar and boil for 6 minutes, stirring constantly. Add pectin and boil for 3 more minutes, still stirring. Remove from heat and add the food coloring. Pour into sterilized jars and seal.

Variation: This may be made with 6 to 6 1/2 cups sugar and a slight increase in the amount of vinegar.

Properly canned food stored in a cool, dry place will retain optimum eating quality for at least a year.

peach rum jam

Yield: 3 pints

Preparation time:
15 minutes

"Easy and delicious"

**3 pounds ripe peaches,
  peeled and finely chopped
  (about 4 cups)
1 box powdered pectin
5 cups sugar
1/4 cup light rum**

Combine peaches and fruit
pectin in a large saucepan. Bring
to a full boil over high heat,
stirring constantly. Add sugar
and boil hard for 1 minute.
Remove from heat, stir in rum,
skim off foam, and put in sterile
jars.

strawberry preserves

Yield: 3 pints

Preparation time:
15 minutes

"A gourmet preserve"

**3 (10-ounce) packages
  frozen strawberries,
  unsweetened
1/4 cup water
1 (1 3/4-ounce) package
  powdered pectin
6 cups sugar
1/3 cup rum, Grand Marnier,
  kirsch, Cointreau, or
  Triple Sec
3 Tablespoons fresh lemon
  juice**

Combine first 3 ingredients in a
kettle. Bring to a boil and stir for
1 minute. Stir in sugar and bring
to another boil that can not be
stirred down. Boil hard for 1
minute. Remove mixture from
heat; stir in rum and lemon
juice. Let stand for 5 minutes.
Skim off foam and pour into hot,
sterilized jars. Seal.

cranberry-orange relish

**Preparation time:
10 minutes**

"Very popular with children of all ages"

1 **pound fresh cranberries**
2 **cups sugar**
1/2 **cup water**
1 **teaspoon grated orange
   peel**
1/2 **cup orange juice**
1/2 **cup slivered almonds**

In a saucepan, combine all ingredients except almonds. Cook uncovered over medium high heat for 10 minutes or until cranberry skins pop. Stir occasionally. Remove from heat and stir in almonds. Cool. Store in covered containers in refrigerator until ready to serve, up to 6 months.

layered pickles

Yield: 8 pints

**Preparation time:
   10 minutes plus
   1 week standing time**

"Crisp and delicious"

1 **(1-gallon) jar whole sour
   pickles**
4 **teaspoons whole cloves**
2 **teaspoons mustard seed**
4 **cinnamon sticks, broken**
1 **garlic clove, minced**
3 **teaspoons celery seed,
   optional**
5 **pounds sugar**

Rinse pickles in cold water and drain well. Cut into 1/2-inch slices. Mix cloves, mustard seed, cinnamon sticks, garlic, and celery seed. Layer this alternately with the pickle slices and the sugar several times, in a large enamel pan. Cover and let stand for 24 hours. Stir contents once a day for another 6 days. The sugar will dissolve. The pickle is ready to eat or may be packed in sterilized jars.

squash relish

Preparation time:
  15 minutes plus
  1 hour standing time

"As pretty as it is good"

8 or more cups sliced
  yellow crookneck squash
1 cup sliced onion
2 green peppers, sliced
1 (7-ounce) jar pimentos,
  cut into strips
1/4 cup non-iodized salt,
  less if desired
2 cups white vinegar
3 cups sugar
2 teaspoons whole celery
  seed
2 teaspoons whole mustard
  seed

Combine squash, onion, peppers, pimento, and salt. Let stand for 1 hour. Drain. Bring vinegar, sugar, and spices to a boil. Add vegetables and bring to a second boil. Fill sterilized jars to within 1/2-inch of the top. Seal immediately.

seven-day pickles

Yield: 4 quarts

Preparation time:
  20 minutes plus 1
  week chilling time

"A good bread 'n butter pickle"

12 medium cucumbers,
  peeled and thinly sliced
8 small onions, thinly sliced
4 cups sugar
4 cups cider vinegar
1 1/2 teaspoons turmeric
1 1/3 teaspoons celery seed
1 1/3 teaspoons mustard seed
1/2 cup non-iodized salt

Make several layers of cucumbers and onions in each jar. Combine remaining ingredients and pour over layers, filling jars full. Screw tops on well. Refrigerate for a week before eating.

158

carrot chutney

Yield: 4 pints

Preparation time: 2 hours

"Especially good with curry dishes"

4 medium carrots, sliced
8 apples, peeled, cored, and sliced
1 lemon, quartered, seeds removed
1 onion, quartered
2 cups sugar or honey
2 teaspoons ground cloves
1 teaspoon ground ginger
2 cups vinegar
1/2 cup water

Process carrots, apples, lemon, and onion, using the metal blade of a food processor. Use quick on and off motions with the processor so that the vegetables aren't overprocessed. Combine this mixture with the remaining ingredients in a Dutch oven. Cook over low heat until thickened, about 1 1/2 hours. Ladle into sterile jars while hot; seal.

zucchini bread 'n butter pickles

Yield: 7 pints

Preparation time: 1/2 hour plus 1 hour standing time

"An interesting variation"

1 quart cider vinegar
2 cups sugar
1/2 cup salt
2 teaspoons celery seed
2 teaspoons mustard seed
1/2 teaspoon turmeric
5 pounds zucchini, sliced
1 1/2 pounds yellow onions, thinly sliced

In a large kettle, combine the first 6 ingredients. Cook over medium heat until sugar dissolves and mixture comes to a boil. Remove from heat, stir in zucchini and onions, and let stand for 1 hour. Heat mixture to boiling, reduce heat, and simmer for 3 minutes. Remove from heat and ladle zucchini and onions into jars. Fill each jar with liquid to 1/2-inch from top. Seal and process in a boiling water bath for 15 minutes.

159

pickled okra

**Preparation time:
10 minutes**

"Tastes like a Kosher dill pickle"

Garlic cloves
Crushed red pepper
Young okra pods
Dill seed or fresh dill sprigs
1 quart white vinegar
1 cup water
1/2 cup salt

Place 2 cloves of garlic and 2 teaspoons crushed red pepper in the bottom of each sterilized pint jar you plan to fill. Pack jars firmly with clean young okra pods from which part of the stem has been removed. If you remove all the stem, the okra will become slimy. Leave at least 1/4-inch stem on each pod. Add 1 Tablespoon dill seed or a fresh dill sprig to each jar. Bring vinegar, water, and salt to a boil. Lower heat and simmer for 5 minutes. Pour immediately over okra. Seal jars and let stand for 2 weeks. Refrigerate before serving to make the pickles crisp.

Choose fresh, firm fruit and young, tender vegetables for your canning.

eggs

cheese

rice and

pasta

eggs, cheese, rice and pasta

Eggs
Creole Eggs 163
Curried Swiss Eggs 163
Eggs Fox Hollow Farm 164
Fluffy Bacon-Cheese Omelet . 165
Kitchen Sink Frittata 166
Oven Omelet 170
Ranch Eggs 167
Spiced Eggs................ 166

Cheese
Camembert Souffle 168
Cheese Souffle 169
Green Chile Souffle 170
Make-in-Advance Cheese
    Pudding 171
Sour Cream Enchiladas 172

Quiches
Cheese-Spinach Luncheon
    Entree................... 173
Quiche Lorraine Dijon 174
Roquefort and Asparagus
    Quiche 176

Sour Cream Quiche......... 177
Variety Quiches 174
Zucchini Puff Pie 178

Rice
Brown Rice Enchiladas 179
Fried Rice.................. 180
Mexican Rice............... 181
Rice Pilaf 178
Rice with Green Chiles 181

Pasta
Baked Stuffed Manicotti
    Shells 182
Cheesy Noodles 183
Fettuccine 183
Make-Ahead Poppy Seed
    Noodles 184
Pasta Primavera............ 186
Spaghetti Frittata 184

creole eggs

Yield: 12 servings

**Preparation time:
45 minutes**

"Great for all those leftover Easter eggs"

1 (1-quart) can tomatoes
1 cup finely chopped celery
1 large onion, chopped
1 cup chopped mushrooms
2 green peppers, chopped
2 Tablespoons butter or
 margarine
4 Tablespoons flour
12 hard boiled eggs,
 quartered
1 cup buttered bread
 crumbs

Drain tomatoes, reserving juice. Over low heat, cook tomatoes, celery, onion, mushrooms, and peppers for 30 minutes. In a separate saucepan, melt butter, stir in flour, and cook until mixture becomes a smooth paste. Add reserved tomato juice and stir until thickened. Add eggs to vegetable mixture and remove from heat. Cover the bottom of a buttered 13x9x2-inch baking dish with a bit of the tomato sauce. Pour in the vegetable-egg mixture and cover with the rest of the tomato sauce. Sprinkle with bread crumbs and put under broiler until brown.

curried swiss eggs

Yield: 4 to 6 servings

**Temperature: 350°
Baking time: 30 minutes**

"A rich addition to breakfast"

1/4 pound Swiss cheese,
 shredded
2 Tablespoons butter or
 margarine
1/2 cup light cream
1/4 teaspoon salt
Dash white pepper
3/4 teaspoon curry powder
6 eggs, slightly beaten

Sprinkle cheese in a buttered 2-quart casserole. Dot with butter. Mix cream and seasonings together and pour 1/2 over the cheese. Pour in eggs and then the other 1/2 of the cream mixture. Bake until the eggs are set.

163

eggs fox hollow farm

Yield: 4 servings

Preparation time: 50 minutes

"An elegant way to poach an egg"

4 slices bread, crusts removed, sauteed in butter
1 (10-ounce) package chopped spinach, cooked and drained
1/2 cup sour cream
1/2 medium onion, chopped and sauteed in butter
Salt and pepper
1/4 teaspoon nutmeg
2 Tablespoons Madeira
4 eggs, poached in water with 1/4 teaspoon tarragon vinegar
4 sliced mushroom caps, sauteed in butter
1 cup Hollandaise sauce, see index
1/3 cup bread crumbs
1/3 cup grated Parmesan cheese

Place the bread slices in individual, lightly buttered ramekins or in a 2-quart casserole. In a blender, puree the spinach, sour cream, onion, salt, pepper, nutmeg, and Madeira. Pour this mixture over the bread. Top with poached eggs, mushrooms, and Hollandaise. Lightly sprinkle with bread crumbs and cheese. Place under the broiler in the middle of the oven to brown for about 5 minutes. Watch carefully.

Note: This can stand for 30 to 45 minutes and be reheated in a 450° oven for 2 to 3 minutes before the final broiling step.

fluffy bacon-
cheese omelet

Yield: 6 servings

**Preparation time:
40 minutes**

"Use your electric skillet."

**6 slices bacon, chopped
1 small onion, minced
5 eggs, separated
Dash Tabasco sauce
1/4 teaspoon paprika
1 1/4 cups milk
3 Tablespoons flour
1/2 pound Cheddar cheese,
  shredded
1/4 teaspoon salt
1 Tablespoon chopped
  fresh parsley**

In an electric skillet, cook the
bacon until crisp; drain. In 2
Tablespoons bacon grease, saute
the onion over low heat until
soft. Turn off the heat. In a
medium bowl, beat the egg yolks
with the Tabasco, paprika, milk,
and flour. Add 2/3 of the cheese
and the salt. Pour the mixture
over the onions. Turn the heat to
250°, cover, and cook for 12 to
15 minutes until almost set.
Remove the lid and sprinkle the
omelet with the chopped bacon
and the remaining cheese. Cover
and cook for 5 more minutes,
until the cheese is melted.
Sprinkle with parsley and serve
at once.

kitchen sink frittata

Yield: 6 servings

**Preparation time:
30 minutes**

"Put anything in this."

1 pound sausage
4 cups peeled and sliced
   potatoes
1 large onion, sliced
8 eggs
1/2 teaspoon poultry
   seasoning

Fry sausage until crumbly in a skillet. Remove from pan with slotted spoon and set aside. Cook potatoes and onion in sausage drippings until crisp. Return sausage to pan. Add eggs beaten with poultry seasoning. Cook until set, then put under broiler until crusty.

spiced eggs

Yield: 10 to 12 servings

**Temperature: 350°
Baking time: 30 minutes**

"Great for brunch"

12 hard boiled eggs
1/2 cup mayonnaise
2 teaspoons vinegar
2 teaspoons prepared
   mustard
Salt and pepper

Cut eggs lengthwise, remove the yolks and mix with mayonnaise, vinegar, mustard, salt, and pepper. Spoon mixture back into egg halves and place in a 13x9x2-inch baking dish.

Sauce
3 Tablespoons butter
   or margarine
3 Tablespoons flour
1 1/2 cups milk
1/2 teaspoon salt
Dash white pepper
2 teaspoons prepared
   mustard
2 teaspoons horseradish
1/3 cup mayonnaise
Paprika

Melt butter in a saucepan. Add flour and stir until blended. Add milk gradually, stirring constantly. Cook until thick. Add salt, pepper, mustard, and horseradish. Cool slightly and add mayonnaise. Spoon sauce over eggs. Sprinkle paprika on top. Bake.

ranch eggs

**Preparation time:
30 minutes**

"Super brunch or Sunday night supper dish"

6 slices bacon
**4 green peppers, seeded
and cut into thin pieces**
2 large onions, thinly sliced
**4 tomatoes, skinned, seeded
and quartered**
1 clove garlic, minced
1/2 teaspoon salt
1/4 teaspoon pepper
12 eggs
1/2 cup light cream
**4 Tablespoons butter or
margarine**
Salt and white pepper
**8 slices bread, crusts
removed**
Butter or margarine
Chopped chives

In large skillet, fry bacon until crispy. Set aside. in 4 Tablespoons bacon fat, saute peppers and onion gently. When vegetables are soft, add tomatoes, garlic, salt, and pepper. When all vegetables are very soft, mash them with a fork. Set aside and keep warm. Beat eggs with cream. Heat butter in a skillet, turn heat to low and add egg-cream mixture. Stir over low heat until eggs are just set, but not dry. Add salt and white pepper to taste. Toast bread slices, butter lightly, and cut into small triangles. Mound scrambled eggs in center of warmed platter. Sprinkle with chives; crumble up bacon and sprinkle over eggs. Arrange tomato sauce in a border around eggs. Place toast triangles around outside edge of platter.

camembert souffle

Yield: 6 servings

Temperature: 350°
Baking time: 40 minutes

"Light as a feather"

1/4 cup chopped celery
2 Tablespoons sliced
   green onions
1 clove garlic, minced
3 Tablespoons butter or
   margarine
3 Tablespoons flour
1 teaspoon dry mustard
1/2 teaspoon salt
Dash pepper
1 cup milk
5 ounces Camembert
   cheese, rind removed
1/2 cup grated Parmesan
   or Romano cheese
5 egg yolks
7 egg whites

Saute celery, onion, and garlic in butter until tender in a medium saucepan. Stir in flour, mustard, salt, and pepper. Add milk; cook and stir until bubbly. Blend in cheeses and cook until just melted. Beat yolks for 5 minutes with an electric mixer. Beat in cheese mixture gradually. With clean beaters, beat whites to stiff peaks; fold in yolk mixture. Turn into a 2-quart ungreased souffle dish and bake.

Room-temperature *eggs* beat better and have greater volume than refrigerated eggs.

cheese souffle

"Never-fail"

**3 Tablespoons butter
   or margarine
3 Tablespoons flour
1 cup milk
1 teaspoon salt
1/8 teaspoon dry mustard
4 dashes nutmeg
2 dashes cayenne pepper
1/8 teaspoon white pepper
1/2 cup shredded Colby
   cheese
1/2 cup shredded Jarlsberg
   cheese
4 egg yolks, beaten
5 egg whites at room
   temperature
Grated Parmesan cheese**

Melt butter in a saucepan and blend in flour until consistency of smooth paste. Slowly add milk, stirring constantly with wire whisk. Cook over low heat until thickened. Mix in seasonings and cheeses and stir. Cool slightly. Add beaten egg yolks. May be done to this point several hours ahead. Beat egg whites until stiff, but still moist. Stir 1/3 beaten whites into cheese sauce. Fold in rest of whites carefully. Pour into a 1 1/2-quart souffle dish, buttered and dusted with Parmesan cheese. Bake until puffed and golden brown. Serve immediately.

To extend *egg yolks,* add 2 or 3 egg whites per yolk. White has few calories and no cholesterol.

oven omelet

Yield: 6 servings

Temperature: 350°
Baking time:
   35 to 40 minutes

"Leaves you free to prepare the rest of the meal"

8 slices bacon
6 green onions, thinly
   sliced
9 eggs
1 cup milk
1/2 teaspoon seasoned salt
3 cups shredded Monterey
   Jack cheese

Fry bacon until crisp; drain, reserving 1 Tablespoon drippings. Saute onions in drippings until limp. Beat eggs with milk and salt. Stir in crumbled bacon, onions, and 2 1/4 cups cheese. Pour into a buttered round 2-quart casserole; bake until set and the top is lightly browned. Sprinkle with remaining cheese and return to oven until cheese melts. Serve immediately.

green chile souffle

Yield: 8 to 10 servings

Temperature: 350°
Baking time: 35 minutes

"Everyone will ask for seconds!"

2 (8-ounce) cans whole
   green chiles
4 eggs
4 Tablespoons flour
1/2 teaspoon salt
1 cup evaporated milk
1 1/2 pounds sharp Cheddar
   cheese
1 (8-ounce) can tomato
   sauce

Cut chiles lengthwise and remove seeds. Place in 12x8x2-inch glass dish. Beat eggs. Add flour, salt, and milk and beat again. Slice 20 to 25 thin squares of cheese and set aside. Shred remaining cheese and add to egg mixture. Pour over chiles and bake for 25 minutes. Cover with tomato sauce and cheese squares placed in a checkerboard pattern. Bake for 10 more minutes.

make-in-advance cheese pudding

Yield: 6 servings

Temperature: 475°, 400°
Baking time:
   10, 25 minutes

"Ideal for the busy cook"

1/2 **cup butter or margarine**
1/2 **cup flour**
1 1/2 **teaspoons salt**
1/2 **teaspoon paprika**
Dash cayenne pepper
2 **cups milk**
1/2 **pound sharp Cheddar**
   cheese, shredded
8 **eggs, separated**

Melt butter in top of double boiler over boiling water. Add flour, salt, paprika, and cayenne; mix well. Gradually add milk, stirring constantly. Add cheese, stirring until melted. Remove from heat. Beat egg yolks until light and fold into sauce, stirring constantly. Beat egg whites until stiff, but not dry. Fold cheese mixture gently into egg whites. Pour into buttered 10-inch souffle dish and refrigerate up to 3 hours. Remove from refrigerator 20 minutes before baking. Bake in preheated 475° oven for 10 minutes. Reduce temperature to 400° and bake another 25 minutes.

When using a glass baking pan, lower the oven temperature by 25°.

sour cream enchiladas

Yield: 6 to 8 servings

Temperature: 375°
Baking time: 20 minutes

"A zippy change of pace"

3 cups sour cream
1 1/2 cups chopped green onions
1/2 teaspoon ground cumin
4 cups shredded sharp Cheddar cheese
12 tortillas
Oil
1 (10-ounce) can enchilada sauce

Blend together 2 cups sour cream, 1 cup chopped onion, cumin, and 1 cup cheese for filling. Fry each tortilla in hot oil over medium heat for only a few seconds until tortilla begins to blister; do not fry until crisp. Remove with tongs and immediately dip into heated enchilada sauce. Spoon a small amount of filling in center of each tortilla, roll up cigar style, and place with seams down in greased 13x9x2-inch casserole. Pour extra sauce over enchiladas. Sprinkle with remaining cheese. Casserole may be covered and refrigerated or frozen at this point. Allow to come to room temperature before baking. Bake uncovered. Garnish with sour cream and green onions.

Serving suggestion: Delicious served with Mexican rice and green salad topped with tomatoes and guacamole.

cheese-spinach luncheon entree

Yield: 8 servings

Temperature: 350°
Baking time: 45 minutes

"A meal in itself"

1/4 **pound fresh mushrooms, sliced**
1 **small zucchini, thinly sliced**
1 **small green pepper, diced**
5 **Tablespoons butter or margarine**
1 1/2 **cups diced ham**
1 **pound cottage cheese**
1 **cup shredded mozzarella cheese**
3 **eggs, lightly beaten**
1/2 **cup chopped spinach, cooked and drained**
2 **Tablespoons olive oil**
1 **Tablespoon dill weed**
Salt and pepper

Saute mushrooms, zucchini, and green pepper in 3 Tablespoons butter until soft. Add ham and saute 2 more minutes. Cool. In a large bowl, combine cottage cheese, mozzarella, eggs, ham mixture, spinach, olive oil, dill weed, salt, and pepper. Pour into buttered 9-inch pie plate and top with 2 Tablespoons melted butter. Bake until set.

Variation: **Olive oil, ham, and green pepper may be eliminated for a lighter dish.**

One pound of *cheese* shredded yields 4 cups.

quiche lorraine dijon

Yield: 6 servings

Temperature: 375°
Baking time:
   35 to 40 minutes

"Wonderful"

Filling
3 eggs, lightly beaten
1 cup light cream
7 slices bacon, fried crisp,
   drained, and crumbled
3 Tablespoons Dijon
   mustard
1/4 cup finely grated onion
1 cup shredded Swiss
   cheese
1/4 teaspoon salt

1 unbaked (9-inch)
   deep-dish pie shell
1 1/2 teaspoons fresh parsley

Combine the filling ingredients,
reserving some of the bacon for
the topping. Pour filling into pie
shell and bake. Sprinkle with
reserved bacon and parsley. Cool
for 5 to 10 minutes before
serving.

variety quiches

Yield: 6 servings

Temperature: 375°
Baking time:
   30 to 40 minutes

"The best ever"

1 1/2 cups heavy cream
4 eggs
1 teaspoon salt
1/4 teaspoon pepper
4 ounces Swiss cheese,
   shredded
1 (9-inch) deep-dish
   pastry shell, partially
   baked in 400° oven
   for 15 minutes

Blend cream, eggs, salt, and
pepper. Add cheese and mix
well. Line shell with chosen
ingredients and cover with
batter. Bake until brown and
puffy. Cool 10 minutes before
cutting.

Spinach

1 (10-ounce) package frozen
  spinach
4 Tablespoons butter or
  margarine
2 teaspoons lemon juice
2 cloves garlic, minced

Saute spinach in butter; add
lemon juice and garlic.

Chicken and Broccoli

3/4 cup diced, cooked
  chicken
3/4 cup chopped, cooked
  broccoli, drained
4 Tablespoons butter or
  margarine
2 teaspoons lemon juice

Saute chicken and broccoli in
butter and lemon juice.

Crab

1 (6 1/2-ounce) can crabmeat

Clean and drain crabmeat. No
need to saute.

Artichoke

1 (14-ounce) can artichoke
  hearts

Drain, cutting hearts in half.

Mushroom

3/4 cup sliced fresh
  mushrooms
4 Tablespoons butter or
  margarine
2 teaspoons lemon juice

Saute mushrooms in butter and
lemon juice.

Zucchini

2 medium zucchini, sliced
1 teaspoon dill

Arrange zucchini in shell.
Sprinkle with dill.

Note: **With some fillings, this may be too much custard. If so, bake in separate dish and enjoy when no one is looking. If cream is not available, substitute 1 cup milk and add an extra egg.**

roquefort and asparagus quiche

Yield: 6 servings

Temperature: 375°
Baking time:
   30 to 35 minutes

"Perfect for a luncheon"

1 (3-ounce) package
   Roquefort cheese,
   softened
2 (3-ounce) packages cream
   cheese, softened
2 Tablespoons butter or
   margarine
3 Tablespoons heavy cream
2 eggs, beaten
Salt and pepper
Cayenne pepper
1 (16-ounce) can asparagus
   spears, drained and
   patted dry
1 partially baked (9-inch)
   deep-dish pie shell
1/2 cup chopped green
   onions

Combine Roquefort, cream cheese, butter, and cream. Add eggs, beating until smooth. Stir in seasonings. Arrange asparagus in shell and pour cheese mixture over asparagus. Sprinkle with onions. Bake. Cool 10 minutes before serving.

Perfect *pasta:* Cook 8 ounces pasta in 6 cups boiling water with 4 teaspoons salt. Stir for 2 minutes. Cover pan, remove from heat, and let stand for 10 minutes before draining and rinsing.

sour cream quiche
Yield: 6 servings

Temperature:
 450°, 350°
Baking time:
 10, 30 minutes

"It's even better the next day!"

Lemon Pastry
1 1/2 cups flour
1/2 teaspoon salt
1/4 cup ice water
9 Tablespoons butter or
 margarine
1 rounded teaspoon
 shortening
1 Tablespoon fresh lemon
 juice
1 teaspoon grated lemon
 rind

Combine all ingredients in food processor or with pastry blender. Form a ball and roll out on lightly floured board. Place in pie or quiche pan and bake for 10 minutes at 450°.

Filling
6 strips of bacon, cut into
 1/2-inch pieces
1 medium onion, chopped
1 clove garlic, minced
1 1/2 cups shredded Gruyere
 or Swiss cheese
1/4 cup grated Parmesan
 cheese
4 eggs, lightly beaten
2 cups sour cream
1/4 teaspoon nutmeg
Salt and pepper

Fry bacon until crisp. Remove bacon and saute onion and garlic in drippings. Drain and mix with bacon. Combine cheese, eggs, sour cream, nutmeg, salt, and pepper. Spread half the bacon mixture in bottom of pastry shell. Pour in cheese mixture and top with remaining bacon. Bake for 30 minutes at 350°. Set aside for several hours and reheat for 20 minutes.

When using deep-dish *quiche* pans, add more time for baking.

zucchini puff pie

Yield: 6 to 8 servings

Temperature: 350°
Baking time: 25 minutes

"Excellent party fare"

1/2 onion, chopped
2 medium zucchini, chopped
2 eggs, beaten
1/2 cup dried bread crumbs
1 teaspoon salt
1/2 teaspoon pepper
Dash nutmeg
4 slices Swiss cheese
Parsley
Paprika

Combine onion, zucchini, eggs, bread crumbs, and seasonings. Layer zucchini mixture alternately with cheese in a lightly greased 8-inch square dish. Sprinkle with parsley and paprika. Bake.

Note: **May be baked in a deep-dish pan with or without pastry.**

rice pilaf

Yield: 8 to 12 servings

Temperature: 375°
Baking time: 1 hour

"Good with chicken, lamb, or fish"

6 Tablespoons butter or
   margarine
2 cups long grain rice
4 cups chicken broth or
   beef consomme
3/4 cup finely chopped
   celery
3/4 cup finely chopped
   carrots
3/4 cup finely chopped
   parsley
1/2 cup chopped green
   onions
1 pound mushrooms, sliced
1 cup almonds
Salt and pepper

Heat a 2-quart casserole in a 375°oven. In a large skillet over high heat, melt butter. Add rice and stir constantly until well coated and hot to the touch. Rice will be lightly browned in about 5 minutes. Remove casserole from oven. Boil broth or consomme and add rice slowly so it will not boil over. Pour rice and broth into casserole and bake, covered for 30 minutes. Add vegetables, nuts, salt, and pepper to casserole. Return to oven for another 30 minutes, uncovered.

brown rice enchiladas

Yield: 5 to 6 servings

Temperature: 350°
Baking time:
** 30 to 45 minutes**

"So nutritious and delicious"

2 Tablespoons oil
2 medium onions, chopped
1 large green pepper,
  chopped
1 stalk celery, chopped
1 carrot, finely chopped
1 1/2 cups cooked brown rice
1/2 teaspoon salt
3 cups cooked pinto beans
  with 1 1/2 to 2 cups juice
3 teaspoons chili powder
20 corn tortillas
1/2 cup to 1 cup oil
2 cups shredded Cheddar
  cheese

Heat oil in a large, heavy skillet over medium heat. Add vegetables and saute for 5 minutes. Add rice and salt. Heat beans and chili powder in another pan. Soften each tortilla in warm oil. Fill tortillas with a heaping Tablespoon of the rice mixture. Sprinkle on cheese. Roll. Arrange filled tortillas in a 13x9x2-inch baking dish. Pour seasoned beans over tortillas. Sprinkle top with more cheese. Bake.

Serving suggestion: **Serve with garnishes such as chopped fresh onions, shredded lettuce, shredded cheese, hot enchilada sauce, or chopped jalapeno peppers.**

Macaroni doubles in volume when cooked.
Noodles increase by 1/3 when cooked.
Rice triples in volume when cooked.

fried rice

"A marvelous combination"

Yield: 4 servings

Preparation time:
45 minutes

1/2 cup oil
1/2 cup chopped celery
1/2 cup sliced water
   chestnuts
1/2 cup sliced green onions
2 Tablespoons chopped
   parsley
3 cups cooked rice
1/2 cup cubed ham
   (Country ham is fabulous)
Salt and pepper
2 cups shelled shrimp
1/2 cup green peas
2 Tablespoons butter or
   margarine
4 eggs
2 Tablespoons water
3 Tablespoons soy sauce

Heat oil in wok or large skillet. Add vegetables. Stir-fry quickly for 3 to 4 minutes. Add rice and ham, mixing well. Season with salt and pepper. Add shrimp and green peas, stirring thoroughly. Melt butter in separate skillet. Beat eggs with water and add to melted butter. Let the eggs cook without stirring to make a pancake. Do not turn. Cut the pancake into thin strips and sprinkle over fried rice. Season with soy sauce.

Variation: Cover sliced hard boiled eggs with rice mixture for a change.

Cooked *rice* can be stored in the refrigerater for a week; in the freezer for as long as 3 months.

mexican rice

Yield: 8 servings

Temperature: 325°
Baking time: 45 minutes

"Colorful and festive"

5 Tablespoons bacon
   drippings
1 cup uncooked rice
1/2 medium onion, chopped
1/2 medium green pepper,
   chopped
3 cloves garlic, crushed
1/2 teaspoon cumin
1 (6-ounce) can tomato
   paste
1 teaspoon salt
1/2 teaspoon pepper
5 cups water

Heat drippings in a heavy skillet.
Add rice and saute until golden
brown, stirring frequently. Stir in
onion and green pepper; cook
about 5 minutes. Add garlic,
cumin, and tomato paste. Stir
well and season with salt and
pepper. Add water, cover, and
bake until liquid is absorbed.

rice with green chiles

Yield: 6 servings

Temperature: 350°
Baking time: 30 minutes

"Delicious served with Sour Cream Enchiladas"

1 cup rice, cooked and
   cooled
2 cups sour cream
Salt and pepper
3/4 pound Monterey
   Jack cheese, cubed
1 (10-ounce) can whole
   green chiles
2 Tablespoons butter
   or margarine
Milk, if needed
1/2 cup shredded Cheddar
   cheese

Combine rice and sour cream;
salt and pepper to taste. Arrange
half the rice mixture in a
12x8x2-inch dish and cover with
cubes of Jack cheese wrapped in
strips of green chiles. Top with
remaining rice mixture and dot
with butter. Add milk to moisten
if rice seems too dry. Sprinkle
with Cheddar cheese. Bake.

181

baked stuffed manicotti shells

Yield: 6 servings

Overnight chilling
Temperature: 375°
Baking time: 45 minutes

"A sensational combination"

14 manicotti shells, cooked and drained
2 1/2 pounds cottage cheese
1/2 cup Italian-flavored bread crumbs
1/2 cup grated Parmesan cheese
1/4 teaspoon salt
2 Tablespoons chopped parsley
1 egg, slightly beaten
2 Tablespoons olive oil
1 1/2 cups sliced onion
1 clove garlic, minced
1 (16-ounce) can tomatoes, undrained
1 (16-ounce) can tomato sauce
3/4 teaspoon oregano
1 teaspoon basil
3/4 pound Muenster cheese, thinly sliced

Rinse shells with cool water. Mix cottage cheese, bread crumbs, Parmesan cheese, salt, parsley, and egg until blended. In large skillet, heat oil and saute onion and garlic. Add tomatoes, tomato sauce, oregano, and basil. Stir well and bring to a boil. Pour into a 13x9x2-inch baking dish. Spoon cheese mixture into shells and arrange in sauce. Cover with foil and refrigerate overnight. Bring to room temperature and bake uncovered for 30 minutes. Top with Muenster cheese and bake 15 minutes more, or until cheese melts.

Variation: For a lighter dish, substitute *Basic Crepes*, page 354 for the manicotti shells.

cheesy noodles

Temperature: 350°
Baking time: 20 minutes

"Great with barbecued chicken, pork, or steak"

1 (8-ounce) package noodles
1 (8-ounce) package cream
  cheese, softened
1 cup sour cream
1 cup cottage cheese
1/4 cup chopped green
  onions
1 teaspoon salt
1/4 teaspoon pepper
Dash cayenne pepper
1/4 teaspoon garlic salt
2 teaspoons Worcestershire
  sauce
1 cup bread crumbs
1/4 cup melted butter

Cook noodles in boiling water and drain. In a large bowl of an electric mixer, blend cream cheese, sour cream, and cottage cheese. Add the remaining ingredients except the bread crumbs and butter. Toss the mixture lightly with the noodles. Place in a 2-quart casserole and top with bread crumbs and melted butter. Bake covered for 10 minutes. Remove the cover and bake for another 10 minutes.

fettuccine

Yield: 4 to 6 servings

Preparation time:
20 minutes

"Oh so rich"

1 (8-ounce) package
  fettuccine, cooked
  and drained
6 Tablespoons butter or
  margarine, melted
1 Tablespoon fresh lemon
  juice
1 cup heavy cream, heated
1/2 cup grated Parmesan
  cheese
1 egg yolk, beaten
Salt and pepper

Toss ingredients and serve warm.

make-ahead poppy seed noodles

Yield: 6 to 8 servings

Temperature: 400°
Baking time: 30 minutes

"Do ahead for a special dinner party!"

1 (8-ounce) package noodles
4 Tablespoons butter or margarine
1/2 cup slivered almonds
3 Tablespoons poppy seeds
2 Tablespoons lemon juice
Dash cayenne pepper
Butter or margarine

Cook noodles and drain. Melt butter, add almonds, and brown quickly. Add poppy seeds and lemon juice. Place noodles in ovenproof dish in which they'll be served. Pour the butter mixture over the noodles and toss gently. Sprinkle lightly with pepper. Dot with butter. Cover with aluminum foil. This can be done well before guests arrive. Bake.

Note: **This freezes beautifully. Bring to room temperature before baking.**

spaghetti frittata

Yield: 6 servings

Preparation time:
1 1/2 hours

"The taste of northern Italy"

Tomato sauce
2 pounds fresh, ripe tomatoes
2/3 cup chopped carrot
2/3 cup chopped celery
2/3 cup chopped onion
Salt
1/4 teaspoon sugar
1/2 cup olive oil

Halve the tomatoes lengthwise and cook in covered saucepan over medium heat for 10 minutes. Add carrot, celery, onion, salt and sugar. Simmer uncovered for 30 minutes. Puree everything in a food processor or blender, return to the pan, add olive oil, and simmer uncovered another 15 minutes.

(continued)

184

Frittata

1/2 pound spaghetti
3 Tablespoons butter or
margarine
1/2 cup grated Parmesan
cheese
2 Tablespoons chopped
parsley
3 eggs
Salt
Freshly ground black
pepper
2 Tablespoons butter or
margarine

Cook spaghetti until firm to the touch. Drain. Toss with 3 Tablespoons butter, Parmesan, and parsley. Beat eggs lightly with salt and pepper and mix with spaghetti. Melt 1 Tablespoon butter in 12-inch skillet over medium heat. Spread spaghetti evenly over bottom of pan. Cook for 3 minutes. Tilt pan slightly, bringing the edge closer to the center of the heat source. Rotate the pan every minute, turning and cooking until you have come around full circle. Place a round platter upside down over the pan; turn the pan over, letting the frittata come out. Melt another Tablespoon of butter in the pan and slide the uncooked side back into the pan. Repeat the method of tilting the pan so that the second side also has a golden crust. Cut into wedges and cover with tomato sauce.

Note: **If using canned tomatoes in the sauce, use 2 cups plus juice. Cook with vegetables as directed.**

Salt and hot water poured down the sink will help eliminate odors and remove grease from drains.

pasta primavera

Yield: 6 servings

Preparation time: 45 minutes

"A fabulous production"

1/2 cup unsalted butter
1 medium onion, finely
    chopped
1 large clove garlic, minced
1 pound thin asparagus,
    tough ends trimmed, cut
    diagonally into 1/4-inch
    pieces
1/2 pound mushrooms,
    sliced
6 ounces cauliflower,
    broken into small florets
1 medium zucchini, cut into
    1/4-inch rounds
1 small carrot, halved
    lengthwise, cut diagonally
    into 1/8-inch slices
1 cup heavy cream
1/2 cup chicken stock
2 teaspoons basil
1 cup frozen tiny peas,
    thawed
2 ounces prosciutto
5 green onions, chopped
Salt and freshly ground
    pepper
1 pound fettuccine, cooked
    al dente and drained
1 cup freshly grated
    Parmesan cheese

Heat wok or large skillet over medium high heat. Add butter, onion, and garlic and saute. Mix in asparagus, mushrooms, cauliflower, zucchini, and carrot. Stir-fry for 2 minutes. Reserve some of the vegetables as garnish. Increase heat to high. Add cream, stock, and basil, allowing mixture to boil about 3 minutes. Stir in peas, prosciutto, and green onions. Cook 1 more minute. Season to taste with salt and pepper. Add pasta and cheese, tossing thoroughly. Turn onto large serving platter and serve immediately.

Note: **Vegetables can be chopped several hours in advance, wrapped, and refrigerated.**

vegetables

vegetables

Asparagus-Artichoke Casserole 189
Asparagus Parisienne 190
Easy Asparagus 189
Oriental Vegetable Casserole . . . 191
Red Beans with Rice 192
California Baked Beans 190
Oven-Baked Beans 191
Burgundy Beets 195
Broccoli and Cauliflower
   Casserole 193
Broccoli Puff 194
Carrots and Onions with
   Madeira 196
Orange Carrots 195
Celery Amandine 197
Cornmeal Mush 198
Southern Corn Pudding 198
White Corn Casserole 199
Cheesy Eggplant 199
Ratatouille with Sausage 200
Excellent Mushroom
   Casserole 201
Golden Mushrooms 202
Mushroom Florentine 202
Mushrooms on Toast 204
Souffleed Mushrooms 203
Hungarian Poppy Seed Onions . 209
Buddha's Feast 206
Peas Oriental 205
Sherried Peas and Mushrooms . 204

Cheese-Stuffed Peppers 207
Cinderella's Golden Potato
   Casserole 208
Party Wine Potatoes 208
Sweet Potatoes Caramel 207
Spinach Elegant 209
Spinach Pie 210
Spinach Souffle 210
Lemon Squash with Walnuts 211
Summer Squash au Gratin . . 212
Winter Squash Casserole 213
Colony Club Zucchini 214
Zucchini and Spring Onions . 215
Zucchini Puree 216
Zucchini Souffle 215
Fried Tomatoes in Golden
   Sauce 217
Mushroom-Stuffed Tomatoes 216
Tomatoes Supreme 218
Tomato Pie 218

Accompaniments
Bourbon Peaches 219
Cranberry Frappe 197
Hot Fruit Casserole 219

Sauces
Blender Hollandaise 220
Tangy Vegetable Sauce 220

asparagus-artichoke casserole

Yield: 8 servings

Temperature: 325°
Baking time: 20 minutes

"Can also be served cold"

2 pounds fresh asparagus, cooked and drained or 2 (15-ounce) cans asparagus with tips, drained
2 (6-ounce) cans marinated artichoke hearts, drained and quartered
1 cup sliced fresh mushrooms
1 (2-ounce) jar pimentos, chopped
1 (8-ounce) bottle creamy Italian salad dressing

Place asparagus in a 12x8x2-inch glass baking dish. Place artichokes and mushrooms on the top, spreading evenly. Arrange chopped pimentos over the mixture, cover with the salad dressing, and bake.

easy asparagus

Yield: 6 servings

Temperature: 325°
Baking time:
   20 to 25 minutes

"The very best method"

24 to 32 spears fresh asparagus
Salt and pepper
1/2 cup butter or margarine

Wash asparagus and trim dry ends. Lay on a piece of aluminum foil, sprinkle with salt and pepper, and dot with butter. Wrap and seal foil well and bake.

Variation: **For an added touch, sprinkle 1/2 cup grated Parmesan cheese and a little paprika on top of the asparagus about 5 minutes before the end of the baking time. Broil until golden brown.**

189

asparagus parisienne

Yield: 8 to 10 servings

Temperature: 375°
Baking time: 30 minutes

"Don't let Spring pass without giving this a try."

2 pounds fresh asparagus
Salt
1/4 pound Parmesan cheese, grated
2 cups sour cream
Pepper or cayenne
2 Tablespoons bread crumbs
4 Tablespoons butter or margarine
Paprika

Cook asparagus in salted water until just tender. Drain. Layer asparagus and cheese several times in a buttered 9-inch square casserole, ending with a layer of asparagus. Season sour cream with pepper and cover layers. Sprinkle with bread crumbs, dot with butter, and top with paprika. Bake until golden brown.

california baked beans

Yield: 6 servings

Temperature: 400°
Baking time: 1 hour

"A change with cheese"

1 (1-pound) can kidney beans, drained
6 slices bacon, partially cooked and chopped
1 (21-ounce) can pork and beans
1/2 cup catsup
1/2 cup brown sugar
1/4 teaspoon cumin
1/2 teaspoon chili powder
1 onion, chopped
1 cup shredded Cheddar cheese

Combine all ingredients except cheese in a 3-quart casserole or bean pot. Bake for 45 minutes uncovered. Sprinkle with cheese, cover, and bake for 15 minutes more.

oven-baked beans

Yield: 4 servings

Temperature: 300°
Baking time: 50 minutes

"Place hot dogs on the top for an easy supper."

1 (18-ounce) jar brick oven
  baked beans
1 teaspoon dry mustard
1 Tablespoon brown sugar
2 Tablespoons chili sauce
  or barbecue sauce
4 slices bacon, chopped

Combine beans, mustard, brown sugar, and chili sauce in a 2-quart casserole. Top with bacon and bake. Brown under the broiler before serving.

oriental vegetable casserole

Yield: 8 servings

Temperature: 400°
Baking time:
  30 to 35 minutes

"An unusual variation"

2 pounds green beans, fresh
  or frozen French style
1 medium onion, chopped
Butter or margarine
2 cups cream of mushroom
  or cream of celery soup
1 cup sliced water
  chestnuts, drained
1 cup sliced bamboo
  shoots, drained
Salt and pepper
1/4 cup grated Parmesan
  cheese
1 (3-ounce) can French fried
  onion rings, crushed

Cook the beans in boiling water until just tender. Drain. Saute the onion in butter until limp; mix with the soup. Layer 1/2 the beans, soup, water chestnuts, bamboo shoots, salt, and pepper in a 12x8x2-inch baking dish. Sprinkle with 1/2 the cheese and layer the same ingredients again. Bake for 25 minutes. Remove from the oven and cover with the onion rings. Bake 5 to 10 minutes longer until golden brown.

191

red beans with rice

"For hearty appetites"

1 (1-pound) can red kidney
    beans, undrained
1 (1-pound) ham, cut into
    bite-size pieces
1 ham bone, optional
4 cloves garlic
1 teaspoon oregano
1 medium green pepper,
    chopped
1 large onion, chopped
4 stalks celery, chopped
Bay leaf
Red pepper, hot sauce,
    or 2 whole pepper pods
Seasoned salt
2 cups cooked rice

Place all the ingredients except the rice in a large kettle and simmer for about 4 hours or until the gravy thickens. Remove the ham bone, garlic cloves, bay leaf, and pepper pods before serving over the rice.

Any vegetable, fresh or frozen, may be cooked in the oven. Place in a covered dish; add salt, pepper, and 2 Tablespoons butter or margarine. Bake approximately 45 minutes at 350°.

broccoli and cauliflower casserole

Yield: 8 to 10 servings

Temperature: 350°
Baking time:
    25 to 30 minutes

"A great combination"

1 **head fresh broccoli or 2
    (10-ounce) packages
    frozen broccoli spears**
1 **head fresh cauliflower or
    2 (10-ounce) packages
    frozen cauliflower**
1 **can cream of asparagus
    soup**
1 **cup sour cream**
1 **cup shredded sharp
    Cheddar cheese**
Paprika

Cook vegetables in water until crisp, but tender. Drain. Layer broccoli and cauliflower, separated into florets, in a buttered 13x9x2-inch baking dish. Mix soup and sour cream and pour over the vegetables. Sprinkle with cheese and paprika. Cover and bake.

Note: **If doubling the recipe, use 1 can cream of asparagus soup and 1 can celery soup.**

While cooking cauliflower, avoid odors by adding a slice of bread. Pour off with the water.

broccoli puff

Yield: 8 servings

Temperature: 350°
Baking time: 45 minutes

"Elegant enough for a dinner party"

1 **head fresh broccoli or 2 (10-ounce) packages frozen broccoli**
1 **can cream of mushroom soup**
1/2 **cup mayonnaise**
2 **eggs, beaten**
1 1/2 **cups shredded sharp Cheddar cheese**
2 **Tablespoons minced onion**
1/2 **teaspoon salt**
1/4 **teaspoon pepper**
1/4 **teaspoon monosodium glutamate**
1 **cup cheese-flavored cracker crumbs**
2 **Tablespoons butter or margarine**

In a large saucepan, cook the broccoli in boiling water until just tender; drain and chop. Combine the broccoli with the remaining ingredients, except the crumbs and the butter. Pour the mixture into a buttered 2-quart casserole, sprinkle with crumbs, dot with butter, and bake.

Note: **Cook the fresh broccoli in the microwave: cook on high for 8 minutes, covered, with 1/2 cup water in the pan.**

Variation: **3/4 cup chopped pecans may be added for a nutty flavor.**

burgundy beets

Yield: 4 servings

Preparation time:
1 1/4 hours

"An elegant way to serve beets"

1/4 cup sugar
1/4 cup dry red wine
1/4 teaspoon salt
Dash white pepper
1 1/2 teaspoons cornstarch
2 Tablespoons lemon juice
1 (16-ounce) can tiny whole
  beets, drained
1 Tablespoon butter or
  margarine

Combine sugar, wine, salt, and pepper in a saucepan. Make a paste of cornstarch and lemon juice and blend it with the sugar mixture. Heat, stirring constantly, until thickened and clear. Add beets and butter and heat through. Remove from heat and let sit for at least an hour so that the beets will absorb the sauce. Reheat when ready to serve.

orange carrots

Yield: 6 servings

Temperature: 400°
Baking time: 15 minutes

"Especially good with game or pork"

6 oranges
2 pounds carrots, sliced
2 Tablespoons butter or
  margarine
1/2 teaspoon salt
1/4 teaspoon powdered
  cloves
1 Tablespoon butter or
  margarine
1/2 cup sugar
1/4 cup water

Cut tops from the oranges 1/4 of the way down. Cook the carrots in boiling water until tender; drain and mash. Add 2 Tablespoons butter, salt, cloves, and the grated rind from the orange tops. Scrape out the pulp from the oranges, saving the pulp from 2 oranges. Fill shells with the carrot mixture and dot with butter. Heat the reserved pulp with the sugar and water. Place the shells in a 13x9x2-inch baking dish, drizzling with the hot syrup. Bake for 15 minutes, basting often.

carrots and onions with madeira

"Serve with your favorite roast."

**5 slices bacon, cut into
1/2-inch strips
4 Tablespoons butter or
margarine
2 1/4 pounds carrots,
thickly sliced
12 tiny onions
Salt and pepper
4 sprigs parsley
1/2 teaspoon thyme
Bay leaf
6 teaspoons Madeira wine
Chopped parsley**

Place bacon strips in a small saucepan and cover with cold water. Bring just to the boiling point. Drain bacon and rinse with cold water. Melt butter in a deep skillet. Add carrots and onions. Cook until nicely browned. Season with salt and pepper. Make a bouquet garni of cheese cloth filled with 4 sprigs parsley, thyme, and a bay leaf. Add this to the carrots and onions along with the bacon and the Madeira. Cover and cook over low heat for 35 minutes. Place vegetables on a serving platter and sprinkle with chopped parsley.

Add 1/2 teaspoon sugar to corn, peas, tomatoes, or carrots when cooking to enhance the flavor.

celery amandine

Yield: 6 servings

**Preparation time:
30 minutes**

"An unusual side dish"

1/2 cup butter or margarine
4 cups diced celery
Salt and pepper
**2 Tablespoons chopped
chives**
2 Tablespoons grated onion
**1 cup blanched, slivered
almonds**
**1/2 teaspoon finely chopped
garlic**
**2 Tablespoons dry white
wine**

Melt 1/4 cup butter in a large pan;
add celery, salt, and pepper.
Cover and cook over low heat
until celery is tender. Watch
carefully, stirring frequently to
prevent scorching. Add chives
and onion. Melt remaining
butter in another pan; add
almonds and cook over medium
heat until browned. Add garlic
and wine; cook for 1 minute.
Pour over celery and serve.

cranberry frappe

Yield: 1 quart

**Preparation time:
30 minutes plus
24 hours freezing time**

"A marvelous substitute for cranberry sauce"

**1 (16-ounce) package
cranberries, washed**
2 1/2 cups water
1 1/4 to 1 1/2 cups sugar
**1 envelope unflavored
gelatin**
1/4 cup cold water
1 Tablespoon lemon juice
**2 egg whites, beaten,
optional**

Place cranberries in 2 1/2 cups
water; cook until cranberries
pop. Pour into a blender and
puree. Return to saucepan; add
sugar and heat until sugar
melts. Dissolve gelatin in cold
water and add to mixture with
lemon juice. Freeze for 1 day.
Add beaten egg whites, if
desired, to partially frozen
mixture to make it fluffy.

Note: **This is most conveniently frozen in a 12x8x2-inch dish.**

197

cornmeal mush

Yield: 4 to 6 servings

Temperature: 350°
Baking time: 35 minutes

"A cross between cornbread and a corn souffle"

1 (8½-ounce) can cream
   style corn
½ cup oil
1 cup sour cream
1 cup self-rising cornmeal
½ teaspoon salt
2 eggs

Mix ingredients, blending well.
Pour into a pre-heated, greased
iron skillet and bake until the
top is brown. The outside will be
crunchy with a moist inside.

Note: If self-rising cornmeal is not available, use regular
cornmeal plus ½ teaspoon salt and 1 level teaspoon baking
powder.

southern corn pudding

Yield: 6 servings

Temperature: 350°
Baking time: 1 hour

"Traditionally delicious"

2 cups white corn, freshly
   scraped
½ cup milk
2 Tablespoons sugar
½ teaspoon baking powder
1 teaspoon salt
2 eggs, beaten
1 rounded Tablespoon
   cornstarch
¼ cup butter or margarine

Mix all ingredients. Pour into a
greased 1-quart casserole. Bake
until barely firm.

Note: An entire hour may not be necessary.

white corn casserole

Temperature: 350°
Baking time:
  45 to 50 minutes

"Good with duck, lamb, or pork"

1/2 **cup butter or margarine**
1/3 **cup sugar**
1/2 **cup flour**
2 **eggs, separated**
1/2 **teaspoon salt**
1 1/2 **cups milk**
6 **ears white corn, freshly
  scraped, or 2 (10-ounce)
  packages frozen white
  corn, thawed**

Cream butter, sugar, flour, and egg yolks. Add salt and milk; mix well. Stir in corn. Beat egg whites and fold in carefully. Pour mixture into a buttered 1 1/2-quart casserole and bake for 45 to 50 minutes. Turn off oven, cover casserole with aluminum foil, and let sit until mixture is set.

cheesy eggplant

Yield: 6 servings

Temperature: 350°
Baking time: 45 minutes

"Light and delicious"

1 **medium eggplant, peeled
  and chopped**
4 **Tablespoons chopped
  onion**
1 **teaspoon salt**
2 **eggs, separated**
1 **cup shredded Cheddar
  cheese**
2 1/2 **Tablespoons milk**
2 **Tablespoons butter or
  margarine, melted**
1/2 **cup grated Parmesan
  cheese**
2 **slices bread, toasted and
  crumbled**

In a large saucepan, boil eggplant in water until tender. Pour off water; add onion and salt. Mash mixture and cool. Mix the egg yolks, Cheddar cheese, milk, and butter; add to the eggplant mixture. Beat the egg whites until frothy and fold in carefully. Pour into a greased 1 1/2-quart casserole, top with Parmesan cheese and bread crumbs, and bake.

ratatouille with sausage

Yield: 8 servings

Temperature: 350°
Baking time: 55 minutes

"A hearty gourmet dish"

1 large eggplant, peeled and
  cut into strips
4 medium zucchini, cut into
  1/2-inch slices
Flour
Olive oil
3 large onions, sliced
3 cloves garlic, minced
3 green peppers, diced
4 large tomatoes, peeled,
  seeded, and cut into strips
1/2 cup finely chopped
  parsley
1 teaspoon oregano
1 teaspoon thyme
1 teaspoon basil
Salt and pepper
6 sweet or mild Italian
  sausages
Fresh parsley

Dredge eggplant and zucchini in flour. Heat oil in a large heavy pan and briefly saute eggplant and zucchini in several batches over medium high heat. Set aside. In the same pan, saute onion, garlic, and green pepper until soft. Save pan for browning the sausages. Layer the sauteed vegetables, tomatoes, parsley, and seasonings in a 3-quart casserole. Stir gently to mix. Cover and bake for 35 minutes. Meanwhile, brown sausages, drain, and cool. Slice 1/4-inch thick and return to pan. Saute 2 to 3 minutes on each side. After vegetables have baked for 35 minutes, add sausage, pushing most of the slices down into the mixture. Bake uncovered for 20 minutes. Garnish with parsley.

Note: **The flavor improves by baking 24 hours ahead and refrigerating. Bring to room temperature before reheating in the oven or the microwave.**

excellent mushroom casserole

Yield: 6 to 8 servings

Temperature: 300°
Baking time: 40 minutes

"The name says it all."

1 (8-ounce) package macaroni, cooked and drained (no salt added)
1 pound sharp Cheddar cheese, shredded
1 can golden mushroom soup
1/2 soup can milk
12 large fresh mushrooms, chopped or 1 (8-ounce) can mushroom pieces and stems, drained
1 cup sour cream
1 (2-ounce) jar pimentos, chopped
1 small onion, finely chopped
Ritz cracker crumbs
1/2 cup butter or margarine

Mix first 8 ingredients well. Spread in a buttered 1 1/2-quart casserole. Sprinkle with cracker crumbs and dot with butter. Bake.

Variation: **To add even more zest, saute mushrooms in butter and Worcestershire sauce before adding to the casserole.**

To parboil, boil partially for only a short time; precook.

golden mushrooms

Yield: 6 servings

Temperature: 350°
Baking time: 40 minutes

"Marvelous with just about everything"

1 clove garlic, minced
2 teaspoons chopped onion
2 cups butter or margarine
3/4 teaspoon Worcestershire sauce
1/2 teaspoon dried rosemary
1/2 teaspoon salt
1/2 teaspoon pepper
2 pounds fresh mushrooms with stems removed

Saute garlic and onion in butter. Stir in Worcestershire sauce, rosemary, salt, and pepper. Place mushrooms in a 13x9x2-inch baking dish. Cover with the butter mixture and bake.

mushroom florentine

Yield: 6 servings

Temperature: 350°
Baking time: 20 minutes

"A very special spinach dish"

1 pound fresh mushrooms
1 Tablespoon butter or margarine
2 (10-ounce) packages frozen chopped spinach, cooked and drained
1 teaspoon salt
1/4 cup chopped onion
1/4 cup butter or margarine, melted
1 cup shredded sharp cheese
Garlic salt

Wipe mushrooms. Slice off stems and saute both caps and stems in 1 Tablespoon butter until browned. Line a shallow 10-inch casserole with the spinach which has been well seasoned with salt, onion, and melted butter. Sprinkle with 1/2 cup cheese. Arrange mushroom caps and stems over this. Season with garlic salt. Cover with remaining cheese and bake until cheese is melted and browned.

souffleed mushrooms

Yield: 10 to 12 servings

Temperature: 350°
Baking time: 20 minutes

"Elegant with Hollandaise sauce"

1 1/2 pounds mushrooms
6 eggs, separated
5 shallots, minced
1 Tablespoon flour
1/2 cup butter or margarine, melted
Salt
Freshly ground pepper
2 Tablespoons lemon juice
2 Tablespoons butter or margarine
1 Tablespoon lemon juice or 1 Tablespoon Worcestershire sauce

Wipe the mushrooms, setting 7 aside for the topping. Chop the remaining mushrooms finely. In a large bowl, beat egg yolks until fluffy and add shallots. Combine with mushrooms, flour, melted butter, salt, pepper, and 2 Tablespoons lemon juice. Beat egg whites until stiff and carefully fold into mushroom mixture. Pour into a greased 12-inch casserole or quiche pan and bake. Saute the reserved mushrooms in 2 Tablespoons butter and lemon juice or Worcestershire sauce. Arrange on top of the baked souffle and serve.

Clarified butter is used for sauteing delicate foods. This burns less easily than ordinary butter. Melt butter over low heat. Skim off the foam as it rises to the top. The remainder will be divided into a clear yellow liquid and a white residue which sinks to the bottom of the pan. Discard the white residue; the clear yellow liquid is clarified butter.

mushrooms on toast

Yield: 4 servings

Temperature: 375°
Baking time: 20 minutes

"Great for a first course or a luncheon dish"

6 Tablespoons butter or margarine, softened
1 Tablespoon chopped parsley
2 teaspoons lemon juice
1/2 teaspoon salt
Freshly ground pepper
4 (1/2-inch) slices French bread, toasted
1 1/2 pounds fresh mushrooms with stems removed
1/2 cup heavy cream
2 Tablespoons sherry

Combine butter, parsley, lemon juice, salt, and pepper. Place toast in individual casseroles and spread with 1/2 the butter mixture. Lightly toss mushroom caps with the remaining butter mixture and mound on toast slices. Drizzle with cream, cover, and bake until mushrooms are just tender. Sprinkle each serving with warmed sherry and serve.

sherried peas and mushrooms

Yield: 6 servings

Preparation time:
    20 minutes

"Couldn't be easier"

1/2 pound fresh mushrooms, sliced
3 Tablespoons butter or margarine
2 (10-ounce) packages frozen baby peas, cooked and drained
1/2 teaspoon marjoram or dill
1/4 teaspoon nutmeg
3 Tablespoons sherry

In a large skillet, saute the mushrooms in the butter until tender. Add the peas, marjoram or dill, nutmeg, and sherry; heat thoroughly and serve.

204

peas oriental

Temperature: 350°
Baking time:
    10 to 15 mintues

"Crunchy and creamy"

1/2 cup finely chopped onion
1/2 cup finely chopped celery
1/2 pound fresh mushrooms, sliced
1/4 cup butter or margarine
2 (10-ounce) packages frozen peas, cooked and drained
1 (8-ounce) can sliced water chestnuts, drained
1/2 pound fresh bean sprouts, optional
4 teaspoons soy sauce
1 can cream of mushroom soup
1/4 pound Cheddar cheese, shredded
1 (3-ounce) can French fried onion rings

Saute the onion, celery, and mushrooms in butter and mix with the peas. Add the water chestnuts, bean sprouts, if desired, and soy sauce. Stir in the soup. Turn into a buttered 13x9x2-inch casserole. Top with cheese and onion rings and bake until bubbly.

Peas like minced mint leaves added to them; also slivers of orange rind or nutmeg.

buddha's feast

Yield: 8 to 10 servings

**Preparation time:
35 minutes**

"An Oriental treat"

2 slices fresh ginger,
  chopped
1 teaspoon sugar
1 Tablespoon cornstarch
2 Tablespoons soy sauce
1/4 teaspoon salt
1/2 cup chicken stock
3 carrots, thinly sliced on
  the diagonal
1 green pepper, thinly
  sliced
1 jar miniature corn on the
  cob, halved lengthwise
1 (8-ounce) can sliced water
  chestnuts, drained
1/2 cup radishes, thinly
  sliced
1 cup snow peas
1 cup bean sprouts
3 or 4 mushrooms, thinly
  sliced
3 Tablespoons peanut oil
1 clove garlic
2 Tablespoons sherry or
  white cooking wine
Sesame seeds

Mix ginger, sugar, cornstarch, soy sauce, salt, and chicken stock; set aside. Prepare each vegetable and set aside. Add oil to a wok or a large skillet and heat until a piece of ginger sizzles but does not burn. Add garlic to the oil; stir for 30 to 40 seconds to flavor the oil and then remove the clove. Add carrots, green pepper, and corn; stir-fry for 1 to 2 minutes. Add water chestnuts and radishes; stir-fry for 1 to 2 minutes. Add snow peas, bean sprouts, and mushrooms; stir-fry for 30 seconds to 1 minute. If the vegetables are cooking too quickly, lower the heat. Add sherry and cornstarch mixture; stir until mixture thickens. Transfer vegetables to a serving platter and sprinkle with sesame seeds.

cheese-stuffed peppers

Yield: 8 servings

Temperature: 350°
Baking time: 35 minutes

"Stuffed peppers with a difference"

4 green peppers, halved
1/2 pound sharp Cheddar
  cheese, shredded
2 cups light cream
28 saltine crackers,
  crumbled
Dash red pepper, optional

Cook the peppers in boiling water for 5 minutes; drain. In the top of a double boiler, combine cheese, cream, crackers, and red pepper. Stir over hot water until mixture has the consistency of a stiff souffle. Stuff peppers with cheese mixture and bake until cheese is puffy. Serve immediately.

sweet potatoes caramel

Yield: 6 servings

Temperature: 325°
Baking time:
  25 to 30 minutes

"Wonderful with a turkey dinner"

3 medium sweet potatoes,
  peeled
1 cup granulated sugar
2 eggs, beaten
1 teaspoon vanilla
1/2 cup butter or margarine
1/3 cup milk

Caramel Topping
1 cup brown sugar
1 cup broken pecans
1/3 cup flour
1/3 cup butter or margarine,
  softened

Boil the potatoes in water until tender; drain. In a large bowl of an electric mixer, mash the potatoes; add the sugar, eggs, vanilla, butter, and milk. Blend until fluffy. Pour into a buttered 8-inch square casserole. Combine the topping ingredients and sprinkle over the potatoes. Bake.

cinderella's golden potato casserole

Yield: 8 servings

Temperature: 350°
Baking time: 25 minutes

"Prince Charming's favorite"

6 potatoes
2 cups shredded Cheddar
cheese
1/4 cup butter or margarine
2 cups sour cream
1/3 cup chopped green
onions
1 teaspoon salt
1/4 teaspoon white pepper
2 Tablespoons butter or
margarine

Cook the potatoes in boiling water until tender. Drain. When cooled, peel and shred coarsely. In a large saucepan, melt the cheese and 1/4 cup butter over low heat. Remove from the heat and blend in the sour cream, onion, salt, and pepper. Add the potatoes, toss lightly, and turn into a buttered 2-quart casserole. Dot with 2 Tablespoons butter and bake.

party wine potatoes

Yield: 8 servings

Temperature: 325°
Baking time: 20 minutes

"Delicious as a stuffing for twice-baked potatoes"

8 to 10 medium potatoes,
peeled
1 (8-ounce) package cream
cheese
1/2 cup sour cream
2 to 3 Tablespoons
vermouth
Salt and pepper
Butter or margarine
Chives

Boil potatoes in water until tender; drain. With an electric mixer, mash potatoes; add cream cheese and sour cream. Beat until light and fluffy. Add vermouth and season to taste. Spoon into a greased 2-quart casserole. Dot with butter and sprinkle with chives. Bake.

hungarian poppy seed onions

Yield: 6 servings

Temperature: 350°
Baking time: 1 hour

"Glorious"

**6 medium onions, thinly
  sliced**
1/2 teaspoon salt
1/4 teaspoon pepper
1 Tablespoon poppy seeds
**1 (3-ounce) package cream
  cheese, softened**
1/2 cup milk

Separate the sliced onions into rings and place in a 1-quart casserole. Sprinkle with salt, pepper, and poppy seeds. Blend cream cheese with milk until smooth. Pour this over the onions, cover, and bake.

spinach elegant

Yield: 6 servings

Temperature: 325°
Baking time: 20 minutes

"Men love this."

**1/2 pound fresh mushrooms,
  sliced**
Butter or margarine
**6 canned artichoke
  bottoms, drained**
**2 (10-ounce) packages
  frozen chopped spinach,
  cooked and drained**
**3 slices bacon, crisply fried
  and crumbled**
Salt and pepper
Nutmeg
**1/2 teaspoon dried minced
  onion**
**1 cup sour cream at room
  temperature**
**1/2 cup shredded sharp
  Cheddar cheese**

Saute mushrooms in butter. Line the bottom of an 8-inch square pan with the artichoke bottoms. Cover with spinach and top with bacon and mushrooms. Sprinkle with salt, pepper, nutmeg, and minced onion. Bake for 15 minutes. (The dish made to this point may be refrigerated or frozen.) Remove from the oven and cover with sour cream and cheese. Return to the oven for another 5 minutes.

spinach souffle

Yield: 4 to 6 servings

Temperature: 350°
Baking time: 35 minutes

"A ladies' luncheon favorite"

1/4 cup butter or margarine
1/4 cup flour
1/2 teaspoon salt
Pepper
3/4 cup milk
1 cup shredded Cheddar
  cheese
1 (10-ounce) package
  chopped spinach, cooked
  and drained
2 Tablespoons chopped
  onion
4 eggs, separated

In a large saucepan, combine butter and flour over low heat; stir until smooth and bubbly. Add salt, pepper, and milk; stir constantly over medium heat until thickened. Add cheese and stir until melted. Remove from heat. Add spinach and onion; gradually add egg yolks and cool. This much can be done ahead. Fold stiffly beaten egg whites into the spinach and pour into a slightly greased 2-quart souffle dish. Bake.

spinach pie

Yield: 8 servings

Temperature: 400°
Baking time: 25 minutes

"Perfect for a light meal"

1/2 (8-ounce) package cream
  cheese
1 cup light cream
1/2 cup soft bread crumbs,
  lightly packed
1/4 cup grated Parmesan
  cheese
2 eggs, lightly beaten
1 cup cooked spinach,
  drained and finely
  chopped
1 large onion, finely
  chopped

In a large bowl of an electric mixer, beat cream cheese until fluffy. Blend in light cream gradually. Add crumbs, Parmesan, and eggs; beat well. Stir in spinach. Saute onion and mushrooms in butter, stirring frequently. Season with salt and tarragon when vegetables are tender. Add to the spinach mixture. The dish may be made a day ahead up to this point.

(continued)

1/2 pound mushrooms,
  finely chopped
4 Tablespoons butter or
  margarine
3/4 teaspoon salt
1/2 teaspoon tarragon
1 unbaked (9-inch) pie shell

Pour filling into pastry shell and
bake on the lowest rack of the
oven. Let stand for 10 minutes
before cutting.

*lemon squash
with walnuts*

Yield: 6 servings

Preparation time:
  20 minutes

"Add more lemon, if you wish."

3 or 4 medium yellow
  summer squash
3 or 4 medium zucchini
1 bunch scallions
1 large clove garlic, minced
1/2 cup chicken stock
3 Tablespoons fresh lemon
  juice
1/2 teaspoon salt
2 Tablespoons sugar
1 1/2 teaspoons cornstarch
2 teaspoons grated lemon
  rind
3 Tablespoons peanut or
  corn oil
1/4 cup chopped walnuts

Wash, trim ends, and cut squash
and zucchini in half lengthwise.
Scrape out seeds and discard.
Cut crosswise into 1/2-inch
pieces; set aside. Cut scallion
greens into circles and set aside.
Chop scallion whites and mix
with garlic. Mix stock, lemon
juice, salt, sugar, cornstarch, and
lemon rind; set aside. Heat a
wok or skillet and add oil. Stir-
fry the garlic and the scallion
whites for about 10 seconds.
Add the squash and zucchini
and stir-fry to the tender, yet
crisp stage. Add stock mixture;
stir until thickened before
adding scallion greens. Transfer
to a serving plate and garnish
with walnuts.

211

summer squash au gratin

Yield: 6 servings

Temperature: 325°
Baking time: 25 minutes

"This freezes beautifully."

2 pounds summer squash or 2 (10-ounce) packages frozen summer squash
2 small onions, finely chopped
2 Tablespoons butter or margarine
2 hard boiled eggs, chopped
1/2 teaspoon salt
1/4 teaspoon white pepper
Dash cayenne pepper
Freshly ground black pepper
Dash nutmeg
1/4 teaspoon dry mustard
1 1/2 cups shredded Cheddar or Colby cheese

Wash, trim ends, and cut squash into thin slices. Bring squash to a boil in a small amount of water. Cook until just tender and drain. In a large skillet, saute onion in butter until clear. Add squash, eggs, seasonings, and 1/2 the cheese. Cook until excess moisture evaporates. Put into individual dishes or in a 1 1/2-quart casserole. Top with the rest of the cheese and bake.

Note: **This can be assembled early in the day and baked when needed.**

Crumb Topping: 1/2 cup butter or margarine
1 clove garlic, crushed
1 cup dry bread crumbs
1 cup chopped fresh parsley

winter squash casserole

Temperature:
 350°, 375°
Baking time: 1 to 2
  hours, 45 minutes

"A substitute for sweet potatoes"

2 large winter squash
1/2 cup butter or margarine
2 eggs, beaten
2 teaspoons pumpkin pie
  seasoning
Topping
1/4 cup light cream
1 cup brown sugar
3/4 cup pecans or Brazil
  nuts, chopped

Bake squash whole in a 350° oven for 1 to 2 hours, until a fork penetrates easily. Cut, remove seed, and skin. Mash the squash in an electric mixer or a food processor and mix in remaining ingredients. Put in a 2-quart casserole and cover with topping ingredients. Bake for 45 minutes.

Note: **Use 1/2 teaspoon cloves, 1/2 teaspoon cinnamon, 1/2 teaspoon ginger, and 1/2 teaspoon allspice instead of the pumpkin pie seasoning.**

Variation: **Bake the winter squash in the microwave! Cut in half and remove the seeds. Invert in a glass dish and microwave on high for 2 minutes per half. Turn cut side up and put 1 Tablespoon butter or margarine and 1 Tablespoon brown sugar in each half. Microwave for another 2 minutes per half. Season with salt and pepper just before serving.**

To scald milk, heat it to just below the boiling point.

colony club zucchini

Yield: 6 servings

Temperature: 350°
Baking time: 30 minutes

"Equally good served cold or hot"

1/4 cup olive oil
1 medium onion, chopped
or cut into rings
1 cup green pepper rings
1 clove garlic
2 Tablespoons minced
parsley
3 large ripe tomatoes,
peeled and chopped
Salt and pepper
2 medium zucchini
1/4 cup grated Parmesan
cheese
Freshly ground pepper

Heat oil in a skillet. Add onion, green pepper, garlic, and parsley. Saute until onion is golden. Remove garlic. Add tomatoes. Season with salt and pepper to taste and cook for 5 minutes. Wash and trim ends from zucchini; slice thinly without peeling. Alternate layers of zucchini and the tomato mixture in a 1 1/2-quart casserole. Sprinkle with cheese and pepper. Cover and bake.

Boil potatoes for 5 minutes before baking so it will take 1/2 the usual time.

zucchini and spring onions

Yield: 4 servings

**Preparation time:
20 minutes**

"Made for a warm evening"

**4 to 6 bunches spring
   onions, tops removed
Salt
2   medium zucchini, thinly
   sliced
1 Tablespoon butter or
   margarine
4 Tablespoons grated
   Parmesan cheese
Salt and white pepper
2 dashes nutmeg
Paprika
1/2 cup sour cream**

Cover and boil onions in salted water for 5 minutes. Add zucchini and boil an additional 5 minutes or until zucchini is transparent. Drain well. In a large skillet, melt butter; add cheese and seasonings. Stir in zucchini and onions and heat thoroughly. Before serving, stir in sour cream.

zucchini souffle

Yield: 8 servings

**Temperature: 325°
Baking time: 1 hour**

"Light and nutritious"

**1/3 cup butter or margarine
2 Tablespoons chopped
   onion
1/3 cup flour
2/3 cup milk
2/3 cup chicken stock
4   eggs, separated
1/4 pound Swiss cheese,
   shredded
3 cups finely grated raw
   zucchini, drained
Salt and white pepper
Worcestershire sauce
Nutmeg**

Melt butter in a large saucepan. Stir in onion and flour to form a paste. Slowly add milk and stock, stirring until smooth. Stir in lightly beaten egg yolks and Swiss cheese. Continue to stir over low heat until sauce is quite thick. Allow to cool and add zucchini. Fold in stiffly beaten egg whites. Add salt, pepper, nutmeg, and Worcestershire sauce to taste. Pour into a 2-quart souffle dish and bake.

215

zucchini puree

Yield: 8 servings

Temperature: 375°
Baking time: 20 minutes

"A food processor will make quick work of this."

4 cups sliced zucchini
Salt
2 shallots, chopped
2 medium onions, chopped
1/2 cup butter or margarine
4 eggs, beaten until fluffy
Salt
Freshly ground pepper
Nutmeg
1/2 teaspoon dill weed
3 or 4 Tablespoons bread
   crumbs
1 cup sour cream
1/2 cup shredded Cheddar
   cheese or grated
   Parmesan cheese
Paprika

Boil zucchini in salted water for about 5 minutes until tender but still crisp. Drain and puree in a blender or a food processor. Saute shallots and onion in butter and add to zucchini. Puree again. Add eggs, salt, pepper, nutmeg, dill weed, and bread crumbs. Pour into a greased 2-quart souffle dish or a quiche pan. Spread with the sour cream and sprinkle with cheese and paprika. Bake for 20 minutes and brown under the broiler.

mushroom-stuffed tomatoes

Yield: 6 servings

Temperature: 350°
Baking time: 15 minutes

"Make the day before, cover, and refrigerate."

6 medium tomatoes
2 Tablespoons butter or
   margarine
1/2 pound mushrooms,
   sliced
1/4 cup chopped onion
1/4 pound mozzarella
   cheese, shredded
Salt and pepper

Slice tops off tomatoes; hollow out and drain upside down. Melt butter and saute mushrooms and onion until tender. Layer cheese with mushroom-onion mixture in tomato cups, ending with a layer of cheese on the top. Sprinkle lightly with salt and pepper. Bake.

fried tomatoes
in golden sauce

Preparation time:
15 minutes

"Delicious even when tomatoes aren't in season"

1/2 cup butter or margarine
Salt and pepper
6 ripe tomatoes, halved
2 Tablespoons flour
1 cup light cream
1 cup shredded sharp
  Cheddar cheese
Paprika
1/4 cup chopped parsley

Melt butter in a large skillet. Salt and pepper the tomato halves; fry, skin side down, slowly over medium heat. When the tomatoes are tender, transfer to a 13x9x2-inch baking dish with a slotted spoon; keep warm in a slow oven. Brown the butter left in the skillet. Remove the skillet from the heat and stir in the flour with a wire whisk. Return to the heat and add cream gradually, stirring constantly until smooth. Season with salt and pepper. Add the cheese and stir until melted. Pour the sauce over the tomatoes. Keep warm in the oven or serve immediately sprinkled with paprika and chopped parsley.

1 cup medium cream sauce can be substituted for 1 can cream soup. Season the cream sauce with salt and pepper and other spices or herbs to suit your taste and complement the vegetables used.

tomatoes supreme

Yield: 4 servings

Temperature: 400°
Baking time: 15 minutes

"So colorful"

Salt and pepper
2 tomatoes, cut in half
1 (8-ounce) package cream cheese, softened
Chives
2 teaspoons butter or margarine, melted
4 teaspoons herb-seasoned stuffing mix

Salt and pepper each tomato half. Spread cut side of tomatoes with cream cheese. Sprinkle with chives. Add melted butter to stuffing mix and sprinkle on top of cream cheese. Place tomato halves in a shallow 9-inch square baking dish and bake.

tomato pie

Yield: 6 to 8 servings

Temperature: 425°
Baking time:
**   20 to 25 minutes**

"Also delicious without the crust as a casserole"

5 medium tomatoes, peeled, sliced, and drained
1 (9-inch) baked pie shell
1/2 cup mayonnaise
1 clove garlic, crushed
1/2 cup grated Parmesan cheese
1/4 teaspoon pepper
Basil
1/4 cup Ritz cracker crumbs
2 teaspoons butter or margarine

Arrange tomatoes in pie crust. Mix mayonnaise, garlic, cheese, pepper, and basil. Spread this mixture over the tomatoes. Sprinkle with cracker crumbs and dot with butter. Bake in a preheated oven.

bourbon peaches

Temperature: 300°
Baking time: 15 minutes

"Just enough zing"

1 (16-ounce) can peach
  halves
6 macaroons, crumbled
4 Tablespoons butter or
  margarine, melted
1 (1¾-ounce) package
  pecan halves
1 Tablespoon brown sugar
2 Tablespoons bourbon
Salt

Place peach halves in muffin tins to help keep their shape. Fill cavities with a mixture of the remaining ingredients and bake.

hot fruit casserole

Yield: 6 to 8 servings

Temperature: 350°
Baking time: 1 hour

"Rich and satisfying"

1 (29-ounce) can pear halves
1 (29-ounce) can peach
  halves
1 (20-ounce) can pineapple
  slices
1 cup sugar
2 Tablespoons flour
½ teaspoon nutmeg
½ teaspoon cinnamon
¼ cup sherry
Topping
½ cup rolled oats
½ cup flour
Salt
½ cup butter or margarine,
  melted

Drain fruit and cut pieces in half. Roll fruit in a mixture of sugar, flour, nutmeg, and cinnamon. Place in a buttered 13x9x2-inch glass dish. Pour sherry over the fruit. Combine rolled oats, flour, and salt; sprinkle over fruit. Drizzle with butter and bake.

blender hollandaise

Yield: 1 cup

**Preparation time:
10 minutes**

"Magnificent"

**3 egg yolks
2 Tablespoons fresh lemon
  juice
1/2 teaspoon salt
1/8 teaspoon pepper
1/2 cup butter or margarine,
  softened and cut into
  pieces
1 thin slice onion, optional
1 sliver garlic, optional
1/2 cup boiling water**

Put egg yolks, lemon juice, salt, pepper, and butter into a blender. Add onion and garlic, if desired. Blend until smooth. Add boiling water slowly as you continue blending. Pour mixture into the top of a double boiler and stir over hot water until thickened. Remove from heat and serve.

tangy vegetable sauce

Yield: 8 servings

**Preparation time:
10 minutes**

"Also marvelous as a dip"

**1 cup mayonnaise
2 hard boiled eggs, mashed
1 Tablespoon horseradish
1 teaspoon Worcestershire
  sauce
1 1/2 teaspoons parsley
  flakes
2 Tablespoons fresh lemon
  juice
Salt and pepper
Garlic salt
Celery salt
Onion salt**

Mix the first 6 ingredients and season to taste. Serve at room temperature.

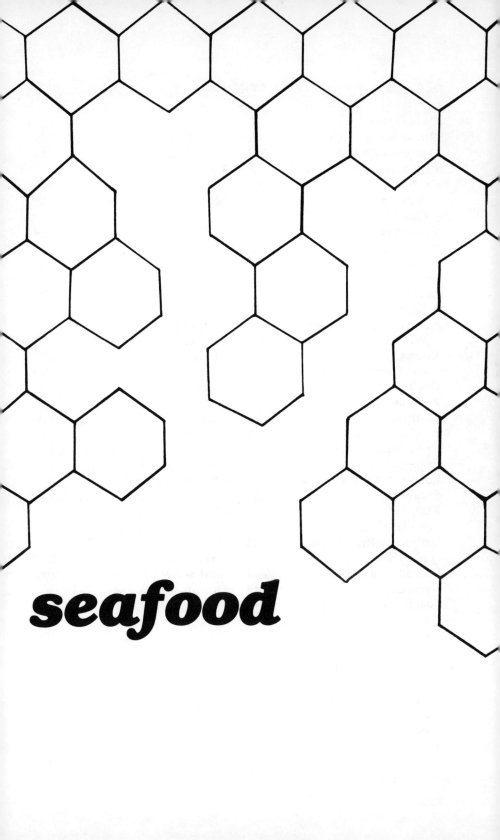

seafood

seafood

Casseroles
Crab-Shrimp au Gratin. . , . . . 225
Company Crab Casserole . . . 228
Crab Epicurean 226
Crab Imperial 224
Lobster, Shrimp, and Crab
   Casserole 259
Crabmeat Supreme. 227
Scalloped Oysters 229
Coquilles St. Jacques 232
Shrimp-Curry Casserole 251
Shrimp and Cheese
   Casserole 256
Shrimp with Mushrooms in
   Wine Sauce 257
Clams
Super Simple Clam Sauce . . . 228
Crab
Au Gratin. 225
Company Casserole 228
Elegant Crabmeat Crepes . . . 223
Epicurean 226
Imperial 224
Lobster, Shrimp Casserole. . . 259
Supreme 227
Fish
Baked Red Snapper. 236
Barbecued Red Snapper. 235
Broiled Sole 240
Flounder Florentine 242
Oven-Baked Bass or Crappie . 237
Poached Fillet of Sole with
   Grapes 239
Poached Salmon
   Mousseline 244
Redfish in Wine 234
Salmon Souffle. 245
Special Fish Fillets. 235
Stuffed Sole with Mushroom
   Sauce 238
Trout Creole 240
Trout in Foil. 241
Tuna Cooler. 246

Tuna Souffle 247
Turbot Turbon 243
Lobster
Boiled 260
Shrimp, Crab Casserole 259
Mussels
Provencales. 234
Oysters
Fried 230
Oyster Pie. 231
Oyster Souffle 230
Scalloped Oysters 229
Scallops
Coquilles St. Jacques 232
Elegant. 231
Italian 233
Shrimp
Au Gratin. 225
Barbecued 249
Boiled in Beer 248
Creole 250
Curry Casserole 251
Dilled Shrimp with
   Mushrooms. 252
Fried in Beer Batter 253
Lobster, Crab Casserole 259
Mandarin-Fried Shrimp with
   Peas. 254
Nantua 255
Shrimp and Cheese
   Casserole 256
Shrimp Boil Dinner 248
Shrimp with Lemon Sauce . . 258
Shrimp with Mushrooms in
   Wine Sauce 257
Sauces
Clam 228
Flemish 262
Green 261
Tartar 262
Watercress Mousseline. 261

elegant crabmeat crepes

Yield: 12 servings

Temperature: 400°
Baking time: 20 minutes

"Perfect for a luncheon or a light supper"

Filling
1/2 cup butter or margarine
1/2 cup minced green onions
2 pounds crabmeat, drained
Salt and pepper
1/4 teaspoon garlic powder
1/2 cup vermouth

Sauce
2/3 cup vermouth
1/4 cup cornstarch
1/4 cup milk
4 cups heavy cream
Salt and pepper
2 1/2 cups shredded Swiss
   cheese

16 crepes, see index

Melt the butter in a large skillet. Combine onion, crab, salt, pepper, and garlic powder and add to the butter. Add 1/2 cup vermouth and boil rapidly until almost all the liquid is evaporated. Pour into a bowl and set aside. In the same skillet used for the filling, add 2/3 cup vermouth and boil until this is reduced to 2 Tablespoons. Mix cornstarch and milk and add to the vermouth; heat thoroughly. Reduce heat and add cream slowly before adding salt and pepper. Thicken slightly and stir in 1 1/2 cups cheese. Blend until cheese melts. Mix 1/2 of the sauce with the filling ingredients. Put a large spoonful on each crepe and roll up, placing the seam side down in a 12x8x2-inch buttered baking dish. Spoon remaining sauce over crepes and sprinkle with the rest of the cheese. Bake until bubbly. Brown under the broiler.

223

crab imperial

Yield: 6 servings

Temperature: 350°
Baking time: 30 minutes

"A marvelous variation"

1/2 cup butter or margarine
4 Tablespoons flour
1/2 cup milk
2 cups light cream
1/2 teaspoon salt
1/2 teaspoon pepper
1 (4-ounce) can sliced mushrooms
1 (4-ounce) jar sliced pimentos
1/4 cup grated Parmesan cheese
1/2 cup dry sherry
1 pound crabmeat, drained
Buttered bread crumbs

In a large saucepan, melt the butter. Add flour, stirring until smooth. Gradually add milk and cream, stirring constantly. When this is very thick, add the remaining ingredients except the bread crumbs. Pour into a 2-quart casserole and top with bread crumbs. Bake.

A *roux* consists of equal amounts of butter or other fat and a starch such as flour, mixed together and cooked. Use a heavy pan to permit the butter to heat slowly. If you need a white roux, remove the pan from the heat before whisking in the flour. Cook over medium-low heat for about 2 minutes. For a golden roux, cook longer until golden in color.

Cooked shellfish freezes well, but do not reheat very long: it will become mushy or leathery.

crab-shrimp au gratin

Yield: 6 to 8 servings

Temperature: 375°
Baking time: 35 minutes

"Absolutely the best version"

1 clove garlic, minced
2 Tablespoons finely chopped shallots
1/4 cup butter or margarine
1/2 pound mushrooms, sliced
1/4 cup flour
1 teaspoon salt
1/2 teaspoon pepper
3/4 cup milk
1/2 pound sharp Cheddar cheese, shredded
2/3 cup dry white wine
1 pound crabmeat, drained
1 pound shrimp, cooked and cleaned
1 (9-ounce) package frozen artichoke hearts, drained
Paprika

In a deep skillet, saute garlic and shallots in butter until soft. Add mushrooms and simmer for 3 minutes. Add flour, salt, and pepper; stir. Gradually stir in milk and bring to a boil. Remove from heat and add 1/2 of the cheese. Stir until cheese melts; add the wine. Combine crabmeat, shrimp, and artichoke hearts into the cheese mixture. Pour into a 13x9x2-inch casserole, making sure that the seafood is evenly distributed. Top with remaining cheese and sprinkle with paprika. Bake.

225

crab epicurean

"As easy as it is delicious"

3 Tablespoons butter or
   margarine
2 Tablespoons chopped
   onion
1 cup sliced mushrooms
6 to 8 ounces crabmeat,
   drained
1/2 cup bread crumbs
2 Tablespoons finely
   chopped chives
1/4 teaspoon thyme
1/2 teaspoon salt
1/8 teaspoon pepper
1 cup light cream
1 egg yolk, beaten
1/2 cup buttered bread
   crumbs
Paprika

Melt butter and add onion and mushrooms. Stir over low heat for 5 minutes. Add crabmeat, bread crumbs, chives, and seasonings. Combine cream and egg yolk. Stir into crab mixture. Put into a 1 1/2-quart baking dish, top with buttered bread crumbs, and sprinkle with paprika. Bake until golden brown.

The most important thing to remember when cooking seafood is never to overcook.

crabmeat supreme   Yield: 4 servings

Temperature: 450°
Baking time: 10 minutes

"A taste of New Orleans"

3 Tablespoons butter or
  margarine
3 Tablespoons flour
1 cup light cream
1 egg yolk
Dash Tabasco sauce
1/2 cup white wine
1/2 to 1 cup shredded
  Cheddar cheese
1 Tablespoon chopped
  pimento, optional
1/8 teaspoon basil
1/2 teaspoon salt
1/4 teaspoon white pepper
1 pound crabmeat, drained
Paprika

In a medium saucepan, melt butter and blend in flour. Cook, stirring constantly for 2 to 3 minutes. In a small saucepan, bring cream to a boil. Add boiling cream, all at once, to the butter-flour mixture. Cook, stirring with a wire whisk, until sauce is smooth. Beat egg yolk lightly with the Tabasco sauce and stir into cream sauce. Stir over low heat for 5 minutes. Add the wine and cheese and stir until cheese melts. Add pimentos, seasonings, and crabmeat and mix well. Pour into a buttered 1 1/2-quart baking dish. Sprinkle with more cheese, if desired, and paprika. Bake.

Variation: Use 2 cups cream sauce, 1 pound shrimp, 1/2 pound crabmeat, and 1/2 pound lobster.

company crab casserole

Yield: 4 servings

Temperature: 350°
Baking time: 30 minutes

"A delightful summer meal"

1 Tablespoon butter or
  margarine
2 Tablespoons flour
1 1/2 cups milk
1 egg, beaten
1/2 cup chopped green
  pepper
Salt, pepper, and cayenne
  pepper
2 Tablespoons dry sherry
3 Tablespoons mayonnaise
1 teaspoon Dijon mustard
1 pound crabmeat, drained
Buttered bread crumbs

Melt butter and stir in flour. Gradually add milk, stirring constantly. Remove from heat and add egg, green pepper, salt, pepper, cayenne, and sherry. Return to stove and cook until thickened, but do not boil. Remove from heat and add mayonnaise, mustard and crabmeat. Pour into a 1 1/2-quart casserole and top with bread crumbs. Bake.

super simple clam sauce

Yield: 4 servings

Preparation time:
20 minutes

"Serve this over your favorite pasta."

2 (7 1/2-ounce) cans minced
  clams
1/4 cup olive oil
1/4 cup butter or margarine
2 cloves garlic, crushed
2 Tablespoons chopped
  parsley
1 teaspoon salt

Drain clams, reserving 3/4 cup liquid. In a skillet, slowly heat oil and butter. Add garlic and saute until golden brown. Stir in clam liquid, parsley, and salt. Bring to a boil, reduce heat, and simmer uncovered for 10 minutes. Add the clams and simmer for 2 to 3 minutes.

scalloped oysters

Temperature: 400°
Baking time: 20 minutes

"Great for everyday or for a special occasion"

2 pints oysters
6 Tablespoons light cream
Salt and pepper
Paprika
Tabasco sauce
Chopped celery, optional
1/2 cup dry bread crumbs
1 cup cracker crumbs
1/2 cup butter or margarine, melted

Drain oysters well, reserving liquor from 1 pint of the oysters. Combine liquor with cream, seasonings, and celery, if desired. Mix bread and cracker crumbs; combine with melted butter. Grease a 1 1/2-quart casserole and sprinkle the bottom with a layer of the crumbs. Layer half the oysters, cover with half the cream mixture, and top with half the crumbs. Repeat layers and bake.

Note: **Make casserole ahead and heat when ready to serve.**

Variation: **Omit the oyster liquor, add 1 cup light cream, and use 1 (8-ounce) package oyster crackers in place of the crumbs.**

A sauce made with cream will be thicker and richer than one made with milk or stock.

fried oysters

Preparation time:
20 minutes

"A quick and tasty treat"

1 pint standard or select oysters
3/4 cup white cornmeal
1 teaspoon salt
1/2 teaspoon black pepper
Oil

Cocktail Sauce
1 quart catsup
1/2 cup creamy horseradish
1/4 cup Worcestershire sauce
1/2 Tablespoon sugar
1/4 cup lemon juice
3/4 Tablespoon salt
1 Tablespoon Tabasco sauce

Drain oysters. Mix cornmeal with salt and pepper. Roll oysters in cornmeal until evenly covered. Fry oysters in enough hot oil (360° to 375°) to cover, in 2 batches. Wait a few minutes between batches to allow the oil to return to the high temperature. The oysters are ready when they are golden brown. Combine all the ingredients for the cocktail sauce. Serve the oysters with cocktail sauce. To store the sauce, refrigerate in a covered jar.

oyster souffle

Yield: 6 servings

Temperature: 350°
Baking time: 30 minutes

"Elegant and unusual"

1 pint oysters
3 Tablespoons butter or margarine
3 Tablespoons flour
1 cup milk
1 teaspoon salt
1/8 teaspoon pepper
Pinch nutmeg
3 eggs, separated

Drain and chop oysters. Melt butter in a saucepan and blend in flour. Add milk and bring to a boil, stirring constantly. Cool for 3 minutes. Add oysters, seasonings, and beaten egg yolks. Beat egg whites until stiff, but not dry. Fold into the oyster mixture. Pour into a 1 1/2-quart casserole and bake until a knife inserted in the center comes out clean.

oyster pie

Yield: 4 servings

Temperature: 425°
Baking time: 30 minutes

"The whole family will love this"

3 Tablespoons butter
  or margarine
1 cup sliced mushrooms
2 stalks celery, chopped
3 Tablespoons flour
1 cup milk
1/2 teaspoon salt
Dash red pepper
Dash black pepper
Lemon juice
1 pint oysters, with liquor
Pastry for a 2-crust (8-inch)
  pie

Preheat oven to 425°. Melt butter and saute mushrooms and celery until soft. Stir in flour. Add milk and stir until very thick, almost dry. Add seasonings, lemon juice, and oysters with liquor. Stir until as thick as heavy cream. Line an 8-inch pie pan with pastry; fill with oyster mixture. Place pastry on top of pie and seal edges. Cut slits in the top of the crust to let steam escape.

scallops elegant

Yield: 4 servings

Preparation time:
15 minutes

"Incredibly good"

1 pound scallops
3 green onions, thinly sliced
2 Tablespoons minced
  parsley
1/4 teaspoon dill
3 Tablespoons butter or
  margarine
2 Tablespoons lemon juice
Salt
6 Tablespoons heavy cream
2/3 cup dry vermouth
1 (6 1/2-ounce) can artichoke
  bottoms, heated

Saute scallops, onion, parsley, and dill in butter and lemon juice for 3 minutes, in a large skillet. Lower the heat and add salt, cream, and vermouth. Heat, but do not boil, for 5 minutes. Heat artichoke bottoms in a small saucepan and drain. Serve scallops on hot artichoke bottoms.

coquilles st. jacques

Temperature: 400°
Baking time: 15 minutes

"An elegant appetizer as well"

1 cup dry white wine
1/4 teaspoon white pepper
1/2 teaspoon salt
1/2 bay leaf
2 Tablespoons chopped
  green onions
1 pound scallops
1/2 pound mushrooms, sliced
3 Tablespoons butter or
  margarine
4 Tablespoons flour
3/4 cup milk
2 egg yolks
1/2 cup heavy cream
1 Tablespoon lemon juice
Salt and pepper
Tabasco sauce
1 cup shredded Gruyere
  cheese

In a 2-quart saucepan, simmer the wine, pepper, salt, bay leaf, and onion for 5 minutes. Add scallops, mushrooms, and enough water to cover; simmer for 5 minutes. Remove scallops and mushrooms with a slotted spoon and boil liquid until only 1 cup remains. Strain and set aside. In a 12-inch skillet, melt butter and add flour to make a *roux.* Reduce heat and add wine mixture and milk, stirring constantly. Boil for 1 minute over medium high heat. Beat egg yolks into the cream and lemon juice. Slowly stir this into the wine mixture and boil for another minute. Season with salt, pepper, and Tabasco. Add scallops and mushrooms. Pour into a 2-quart casserole or 6 individual shells and sprinkle with cheese. Bake.

Note: **This can be prepared early in the day and heated when ready to serve.**

Thin sauce: 1 Tablespoon butter and flour: 1 cup liquid (cream soups)
Medium sauce: 1½ Tablespoons butter and flour; 1 cup liquid (most sauces)
Thick sauce: 3 Tablespoons butter and flour: 1 cup liquid (souffle base)

scallops italian

Yield: 4 to 6 servings

**Preparation time:
30 minutes**

"Delicioso"

3 Tablespoons olive oil
3 Tablespoons butter or
margarine
1 pound bay scallops
8 green onions, minced
1 white onion, minced
2 cloves garlic, minced
1 teaspoon dried tarragon
¼ teaspoon dried thyme
2 teaspoons dried basil
½ cup white wine
4 cups tomatoes, drained
and crushed
½ cup heavy cream
Salt and pepper
1 pound freshly cooked
linguine

Heat oil and butter in a large skillet over medium heat. Add scallops and saute until barely firm, about 2 minutes. Remove from skillet with a slotted spoon. Increase heat to medium high and saute onions until soft. Add garlic and herbs and mix well. Add wine and cook for 2 minutes. Stir in tomatoes and boil until mixture thickens, almost all liquid should be boiled away. Add cream, salt, and pepper and mix well. Toss with hot pasta. If the sauce is made ahead, put in scallops just before serving.

Serving suggestion: Serve with an avocado and grapefruit salad and hot crusty bread.

233

mussels provencales

**Preparation time:
45 minutes**

"This is a real treasure."

2 to 3 quarts mussels
  (about 4 pounds)
3 Tablespoons butter
  or margarine
1 small onion, chopped
3 cloves garlic, minced
1/2 cup chopped celery
1 (1-pound) can Italian
  tomatoes, undrained
1/2 cup chopped parsley
1/8 teaspoon pepper
1 cup dry white wine

To clean the mussels, scrub the shells and remove beard. (The beard is really loose strands of fine seaweed-like material clinging to the mussels.) In the butter, saute onion, garlic, and celery until soft. Add tomatoes and simmer for 15 minutes. Add parsley, pepper, and white wine and bring to a boil. Add mussels, cover, and simmer for 5 to 7 minutes or until the shells open. The broth may be prepared early in the day, adding the mussels right before serving.

Serving suggestion: **Serve in a bowl with the broth spooned over the mussels. Accompany with hard rolls or French bread.**

redfish in wine

Yield: 4 servings

**Temperature: 350°
Baking time: 30 minutes**

"Also very good cooked on the grill"

4 redfish fillets
1 small onion, sliced
1 medium tomato, sliced
4 large mushroom caps
4 ripe olives
Salt and pepper
1 cup dry white wine

Place each fillet in an aluminum foil packet. Top each with a slice of onion, a slice of tomato, a mushroom cap, a ripe olive, salt, and pepper. Add 1/4 cup wine to each packet, seal the foil, and bake.

barbecued red snapper

Yield: 6 to 8 servings

Preparation time:
1 3/4 hours

"Delightfully different for a summer cookout"

1/2 cup butter or margarine
4 Tablespoons grated onion
2 Tablespoons chopped
    parsley
2 Tablespoons
    Worcestershire sauce
4 Tablespoons fresh lemon
    juice
Tabasco sauce
2 (2-pound) red snappers
Salt and pepper

Melt butter in a saucepan and add onion, parsley, Worcestershire sauce, lemon juice, and Tabasco. Season fish with salt and pepper. Place on a sheet of aluminum foil and pour sauce over the fish. Seal foil. Place on a covered grill for 1 hour, turning twice. Remove fish from the foil and place directly on the grill. Baste with sauce still in foil. Cook until the fish is flaky (about 30 minutes).

Note: The cooking time will vary according to the size of the fish and the temperature of the grill. Any fresh fish is delicious prepared this way.

special fish fillets

Yield: 4 servings

Temperature: 400°
Baking time: 15 minutes

"Divinely delicious"

4 (6-ounce) fish fillets;
    speckled trout, redfish,
    or your choice
Salt
Pepper
Worcestershire sauce
1/2 cup butter or margarine
4 Tablespoons fresh lemon
    juice
2 to 3 cloves garlic, minced

Season fillets with salt, pepper, and Worcestershire sauce. In a small saucepan, melt the butter and add lemon juice and garlic. Place the fish fillets in a 9-inch square baking dish. Pour butter sauce over fish and bake.

baked red snapper   Yield: 6 to 8 servings

Temperature: 325°
Baking time: 1 hour

"A gourmet's delight"

1/4 cup finely chopped onion
1/2 cup finely chopped celery
2 Tablespoons butter or
margarine
2 chicken bouillon cubes
1/2 cup water
3 cups bread crumbs
1/4 teaspoon poultry
seasoning
2 eggs, beaten
2 Tablespoons chopped
parsley
1 teaspoon salt
1/8 teaspoon paprika
1 teaspoon dill seed
4 Tablespoons capers
3 pounds red snapper, head
left on
Butter
Salt and pepper
Flour
Paprika
Bacon
Butter or margarine

(continued)

Saute onion and celery in 2 Tablespoons butter until clear, but not brown. Add the bouillon cubes dissolved in water and simmer for 5 minutes. Stir in bread crumbs. Add poultry seasoning, eggs, parsley, 1 teaspoon salt, 1/8 teaspoon paprika, dill seed, and 4 Tablespoons capers. Moisten with additional chicken stock, if necessary. This can be done a day ahead. Rub the fish, inside and out, with butter, salt, and pepper. Dredge fish in flour and sprinkle all sides with paprika. Cut 3 gashes in the sides of the fish, force slices of bacon into the cuts, stuff with dressing, and sew up loosely. Place the fish in a shallow pan lined with 2 slices of bacon. Bake, basting frequently with a mixture of 2 parts hot water and 1 part butter.

Caper and Egg Sauce

**11 Tablespoons butter
  or margarine**
3 Tablespoons flour
1/2 teaspoon salt
Cayenne pepper
1 1/2 cups milk
3 egg yolks
**2 Tablespoons fresh
  lemon juice**
4 Tablespoons capers

Melt 3 Tablespoons butter in the top of a double boiler. Add flour, salt, and cayenne to taste; stir until blended. Pour milk slowly into the pan, beating with a wire whisk until smooth. Cook over hot water until thickened. Remove from heat, beat in egg yolks, and reheat to thicken slightly. Remove from heat and add 1/2 cup butter, 1 Tablespoon at a time, lemon juice, and capers. Serve with the red snapper.

oven-baked bass or crappie

Yield: 4 servings

Temperature: 425°
**Baking time:
  10 to 15 minutes**

"Crisp and tasty"

**8 whole fish, cleaned
  and scaled**
1 cup light cream
1 cup corn flake crumbs
1 teaspoon salt
1/2 teaspoon pepper
**1/2 cup butter or margarine,
  melted**
**4 Tablespoons fresh lemon
  juice**
**4 Tablespoons chopped
  parsley**

Dip fish in cream and then roll in cornflake crumbs seasoned with salt and pepper. Place fish in a 13x9x2-inch casserole. Combine butter, lemon juice, and parsley. Pour butter mixture over fish and bake.

stuffed sole with mushroom sauce

Yield: 6 servings

Temperature: 350°
Baking time:
** 20 to 25 minutes**

"A simple gourmet dish"

1 (7-ounce) can salmon, drained and flaked
2 Tablespoons minced parsley
2 Tablespoons chopped chives
1/2 teaspoon tarragon
1/2 teaspoon paprika
2 Tablespoons fresh lemon juice
6 sole fillets (or flounder)
3 Tablespoons butter or margarine, melted

Mushroom Sauce
1/4 cup butter or margarine
1/4 pound mushrooms, sliced
1/2 cup minced onion
3 Tablespoons flour
1 1/4 cups milk
1 teaspoon salt
1/8 teaspoon white pepper

Mix salmon, parsley, chives, tarragon, paprika, and lemon juice. Spread mixture on sole fillets. Roll up in jelly roll fashion, beginning with the tail; secure with a toothpick. Place sole in a 12x8x2-inch buttered baking dish and brush with melted butter. Bake until fish flakes easily with a fork. Remove from oven and drain. For mushroom sauce, melt butter in a skillet; saute the mushrooms and onion. Add flour and mix well. Slowly add milk, stirring constantly, until thickness of heavy cream. Season and pour over the fish.

Note: This recipe is especially good if fresh herbs are used.

poached fillet of sole with grapes

Yield: 6 to 8 servings

Temperature:
400°, 350°
Baking time: 10 minutes

"Refreshingly light"

2 cups milk
8 (6-ounce) sole fillets
1/2 pound fresh mushrooms,
sliced
3 shallots, finely chopped
1/4 cup butter or margarine
2 cups white seedless
grapes
3 Tablespoons butter or
margarine
4 Tablespoons flour
2 Tablespoons fresh lemon
juice
Thyme
Salt and pepper
Paprika

Preheat oven to 400°. In a shallow oven proof pan, heat milk to just below the boiling point and poach the fillets in it for 5 minutes. Saute mushrooms and shallots in 1/4 cup butter in a medium pan. Drain milk from fillets and reserve. Top fillets with mushrooms, shallots, and grapes. Make a thick cream sauce melting 3 Tablespoons butter and stirring in flour and reserved milk until smooth. Add lemon juice and seasonings. Pour this mixture over the fillets, reduce oven temperature to 350° and bake until fish is flaky. Sprinkle with paprika before serving.

***Variation:* Flounder is also delicious prepared in this way.**

broiled sole

"Easy to make and enjoy"

2 pounds sole fillets
2 Tablespoons lemon juice
1/2 cup grated Parmesan
   cheese
1/4 cup butter or margarine,
   melted
3 Tablespoons mayonnaise
3 Tablespoons chopped
   green onions
1/4 teaspoon salt
Dash Tabasco sauce

Brush fillets with lemon juice
and let stand for 10 minutes.
Broil about 4 inches from heat
for 6 to 8 minutes. Combine
Parmesan, butter, mayonnaise,
onion, and seasonings. Remove
fish from the oven and spread
with Parmesan mixture. Broil for
2 to 3 minutes until golden
brown.

trout creole

"Easy, elegant, and so impressive"

6 Tablespoons butter or
   margarine
1 small onion, chopped
1 clove garlic, minced
1/4 green pepper, chopped
1 tomato, peeled and
   chopped
1 Tablespoon fresh lemon
   juice
Salt and pepper
Cayenne pepper
4 trout fillets
Paprika

Melt butter; add onion, garlic,
and green pepper and cook until
tender. Add tomato, lemon juice,
and seasonings. Cook over low
heat for 7 to 10 minutes. This
can be done ahead. Pour sauce
over the fish in a 12x8x2-inch
baking dish. Sprinkle with
paprika and bake.

Note: **This is a low calorie favorite.**

trout in foil

Yield: 4 servings

Temperature: 375°
Baking time: 20 minutes

"Enjoyed by all old enough to handle the bones"

3 Tablespoons finely
   chopped onion
1 1/2 cups chopped
   mushrooms
3 Tablespoons chopped
   parsley
10 Tablespoons butter or
   margarine
Salt
Freshly ground pepper
4 fresh Brook Trout, whole
   (6 ounces each)
Olive oil
4 thin slices lemon
4 Tablespoons dry white
   wine

Saute onion, mushrooms, and parsley in 4 Tablespoons butter until onion is transparent; season with salt and pepper. Stuff the trout with the mixture. Cut sheets of aluminum foil large enough to surround each fish completely. Brush foil with 2 Tablespoons melted butter mixed with a little olive oil. Place fish in center of each piece of foil. Sprinkle each fish with salt and pepper, top with slice of lemon, and cover with a mixture of 4 Tablespoons butter and the white wine. Bring the foil up over each fish and double fold the edges to form a tight packet. Close the ends securely so that the juices will not escape. Place on a baking sheet and bake. To serve, split edges of foil and roll back.

Substitutes: Redfish: broiled - sole, striped bass, brook trout, whitefish baked - haddock, swordfish, turbot, red snapper
   Red Snapper: yellowtail, gray snapper
   Pompano: red snapper, redfish, bluefish, mackerel, halibut, turbot
   Flounder: sole, yellowtail, turbot, lemon sole
   Speckled trout: bass, brook trout, perch, scampi

flounder florentine

Yield: 6 servings

Temperature:
350, 425°
Baking time:
12, 5 minutes

"Easier than it appears"

1 1/2 pounds frozen flounder fillets
2 (10-ounce) packages frozen chopped spinach, cooked
2 teaspoons salt
Freshly ground pepper
5 Tablespoons butter or margarine
3 Tablespoons lemon juice
1/4 teaspoon nutmeg
1 cup water
1 medium onion, thinly sliced
1 bay leaf
Milk or cream
3 Tablespoons flour
Butter or margarine
Salt and pepper
1/2 cup grated Parmesan cheese
Paprika

Defrost the fish in the refrigerator. Drain the spinach and add 1 teaspoon salt, pepper, 2 Tablespoons butter, 1 Tablespoon lemon juice, and nutmeg. Spread fillets in a 13x9x2-inch dish. Over the fish, pour the water mixed with 2 Tablespoons lemon juice, 1 teaspoon salt, pepper, onion, and the bay leaf. Bake for 12 minutes at 350°. Remove from the oven and drain liquid into a 2-cup measuring cup, discarding onion and bay leaf. Add enough milk or cream to the liquid to make 1 1/2 cups. In a small saucepan, melt 3 Tablespoons butter over medium heat; add flour and stir. Gradually add liquid and stir until the mixture bubbles. Dot the fish with butter and sprinkle with salt and pepper. Cover with spinach and pour sauce on the top. Sprinkle with cheese and paprika. Bake for 5 to 6 minutes at 425°.

Note: **This is an extremely good way to prepare frozen fish. Except for the final 5 minutes, everything can be done ahead.**

turbot turbon

"Magnificent"

2 (6-ounce) turbot fillets
1/4 teaspoon salt
1/8 teaspoon white pepper
4 Tablespoons fresh lemon
   juice
2 Tablespoons flour
3 Tablespoons butter or
   margarine
1/2 cup champagne
1 egg yolk, beaten
1/2 cup sliced seedless
   green grapes
1/2 recipe puff pastry, see
   index
1 egg, beaten

Season fillets with salt, pepper, and 2 Tablespoons lemon juice. After 5 minutes, dust with 1 Tablespoon flour. Saute fillets in butter for 5 minutes and remove from skillet. Add the rest of the flour to the butter over low heat. Slowly stir in champagne, remaining lemon juice, and egg yolk. Stir until very thick, almost like a paste. Add grapes and pour over the fish. Cut 2 (8-inch) circles from prepared puff pastry. Place fish and sauce in center of 1 circle, leaving 1 inch clear around the edge. Moisten edges slightly and place other circle on top. Seal the pastry by making indentations around the rim with a blunt knife. Cut a 1/4-inch hole in the top of the pastry. Refrigerate for 45 minutes. Brush with beaten egg and bake in a parchment-lined 8-inch round baking dish for 45 minutes. Turn off the oven, leave the door closed, and cook for another 15 minutes. If you don't want to serve this immediately, place the fish in a warming oven or crack the oven door, with the oven turned off, after 45 minutes.

poached salmon mousseline

Yield: 6 servings

Preparation time: 1 hour

"A continental classic"

Court Bouillon
2 quarts water
2 cups clam juice
4 cups white wine
4 Tablespoons salt
2 stalks celery, sliced
8 peppercorns
1 bay leaf
2 carrots, sliced
1 medium onion, thinly sliced
6 salmon steaks

In a large saucepan, bring court bouillon ingredients to a boil and simmer for 30 minutes. Strain and discard vegetables. Adjust salt and pepper, if necessary. This may be done ahead. Place the salmon in the bouillon to cover and cook at the lowest simmer until a meat thermometer reaches 160° degrees. Remove the skin and the dark meat at the backbone.

Mousseline Sauce
3 egg yolks
2 teaspoons lemon juice
Salt and white pepper
1/2 cup butter or margarine, melted and cooled slightly
1 cup heavy cream, whipped

While the fish are cooking, prepare the mousseline sauce. In a food processor or a blender, beat the egg yolks. Add lemon juice, salt, and pepper. Add the butter and blend until just mixed. Keep warm in the top of a double boiler until ready to serve. When ready to serve, fold in the whipped cream and serve over the salmon.

To saute halibut or salmon steaks, measure the thickness and allow 10 minutes cooking time per inch.

salmon souffle

**Temperature:
400°, 375°
Baking time: 30 minutes**

"A family favorite from a can, but suitable for guests too"

**4 Tablespoons butter
or margarine
1 Tablespoon grated
Parmesan cheese
2 Tablespoons chopped
onion
3 Tablespoons flour
3/4 cup shredded salmon,
canned or freshly cooked,
drained, reserving liquid
Milk
1/2 teaspoon salt
1/8 teaspoon pepper
1 Tablespoon tomato paste
1/2 teaspoon oregano
4 egg yolks
1/2 cup shredded Swiss
cheese
5 egg whites**

Preheat oven to 400°. Butter a 6-cup souffle dish with 1 Tablespoon butter, sprinkle with Parmesan cheese, and refrigerate until needed. Saute onion in remaining butter. Add flour and stir for 2 minutes. In another pan, boil 1 cup liquid composed of salmon liquid and enough milk to measure 1 cup. Remove from heat and add to the flour mixture. Season with salt, pepper, tomato paste, and oregano. Return to a boil and boil for 1 minute. Remove from heat and beat in egg yolks, 1 at a time. Add the salmon and all but 1 Tablespoon of the Swiss cheese. Beat the egg whites until stiff. Stir 1/4 of the egg whites into the salmon mixture, then fold in the rest. Pour into a mold and sprinkle with remaining cheese. Souffle will keep for 1 hour at room temperature under a large inverted bowl or for 2 to 3 hours in the refrigerator covered with plastic wrap. When ready to cook, set in the middle of a preheated oven, turn heat down to 375°, and bake.

tuna cooler

**Preparation time:
20 minutes**

"Perfect for a summer picnic"

**6 cups cooked shell
  macaroni
1/4 cup white wine vinegar
3/4 cup olive oil
1/2 teaspoon freshly ground
  black pepper
1 teaspoon salt
1 Tablespoon fresh basil
1 Tablespoon chopped
  parsley
1/4 cup chopped onion
3 ripe tomatoes, cut into
  wedges
1 (7-ounce) can white tuna,
  drained
4 hard boiled eggs, cut
  into wedges
1 medium green pepper,
  sliced into rings
Grated Parmesan cheese**

Toss pasta with vinegar, oil,
pepper, salt, basil, parsley, and
onion. Place in a deep serving
dish or salad bowl and garnish
with the remaining ingredients.
Toss at the table and serve.

tuna souffle

"Makes tuna taste very special"

1 slice white bread,
   moistened
2 (7-ounce) cans white tuna,
   drained
1/4 cup butter or margarine
1/4 cup flour
1 cup milk, warmed
1 teaspoon Mei Yen
   seasoning or monosodium
   glutamate
1 teaspoon chopped
   parsley
1/4 teaspoon salt
1/8 teaspoon white pepper
1 Tablespoon sliced green
   onions
2 egg yolks, well beaten
1/2 teaspoon baking powder
2 egg whites, beaten
1/2 cup shredded mild
   Cheddar cheese
Finely crushed cracker
   crumbs

In a colander, moisten bread with cold water and gently press out. In a large mixing bowl, combine tuna and bread. Over low heat, melt butter; blend in flour with a wire whisk and slowly add warmed milk, stirring constantly. Add Mei Yen seasoning, parsley, salt, pepper, and onions and cook until sauce comes to a boil. Remove from heat and beat in the egg yolks. Add baking powder and sauce to the tuna mixture and blend with an electric mixer on medium speed. Fold in the beaten egg whites and shredded cheese. Pour into a buttered 1 1/2-quart casserole. Lightly sprinkle with cracker crumbs and bake.

boiled shrimp in beer

Yield: 6 servings

Preparation time:
15 minutes

"Scrumptious"

1 quart beer
1 1/2 cups water
6 scallions, sliced
2 cups chopped celery
1 Tablespoon salt
2 hot peppers
2 lemons, halved
2 Tablespoons vinegar
Crab boil
3 pounds fresh shrimp
   in shells

Place all ingredients in a deep kettle except the shrimp. Bring to a boil, add shrimp, and cook until the shrimp turn pink; about 5 minutes after the liquid returns to a boil. Drain and serve. Let everyone peel his own.

Serving suggestion: Garnish with parsley and serve with Cocktail Sauce, page 230.

shrimp boil dinner

Yield: 10 servings

Preparation time:
45 minutes

"With a salad, this is a complete meal."

2 packages crab boil
6 lemons, halved
1 Tablespoon Tabasco sauce
2 to 3 Tablespoons ice
   cream salt
20 new potatoes
15 onions, unpeeled
10 ears of corn, shucked
   and halved
6 pounds fresh, unpeeled
   shrimp

In a large roaster filled half full with water, bring the crab boil, lemon halves, Tabasco, and salt to a boil. Add the new potatoes and onions and boil until the potatoes are tender. Add corn. When corn is tender, add the shrimp. The shrimp is ready when it turns pink. This will take only a few minutes after the water has come to a full boil again. Drain and serve.

barbecued shrimp

**Preparation time:
1 hour, 5 minutes**

"Everyone peels his own and will eat more than you think."

**2 pounds fresh shrimp
   in shells
2 cups Italian salad
   dressing or enough
   to cover**

In a large crockery bowl, marinate shrimp in the dressing for 1 hour, no longer. Drain well and put on skewers. Cook over medium hot coals for about 5 minutes.

**Sauce
1/2 cup butter or margarine
1/4 cup Worcestershire
   sauce
1 Tablespoon cornstarch
1/4 cup lemon juice**

Melt the butter over low heat. Stir in Worcestershire sauce. Mix cornstarch with the lemon juice and stir this mixture into the butter. Continue stirring until the sauce is as thick as heavy cream. Serve in individual bowls for dipping with the shrimp.

To minimize the odor, drop fresh celery leaves in with boiling shrimp.

creole shrimp

**Preparation time:
20 minutes**

"Wonderful on a cold, wintry night"

1/2 large onion, chopped
1/2 medium green pepper,
  chopped
4 Tablespoons butter or
  margarine
2 Tablespoons flour
1 can tomato soup
1 (20-ounce) can tomatoes
5 medium stalks celery,
  chopped
1 Tablespoon
  Worcestershire sauce
1 Tablespoon spicy steak
  sauce
1 teaspoon salt
Tabasco sauce
2 pounds shrimp, cooked
  and peeled
1/2 cup sliced green olives

In a deep skillet, saute onion and green pepper in butter. Add flour and stir until golden brown. Add remaining ingredients except for the shrimp and the olives. The sauce may be done ahead to this point. When ready to serve, add shrimp and olives and heat thoroughly.

Serving suggestion: Serve over fluffy rice.

Defrosting frozen fish in milk improves the flavor.

shrimp-curry casserole

Yield: 6 to 8 servings

Temperature: 325°
Baking time: 30 minutes

"An exotic flavor"

3 Tablespoons butter or margarine
4 Tablespoons flour
2 cups chicken stock
1/2 cup thinly sliced onion
1/4 cup thinly sliced green pepper
1/2 pound mushrooms, sliced
1/4 cup butter or margarine
1 teaspoon Worcestershire sauce
3 drops Tabasco sauce
1 teaspoon curry
2 pounds shrimp, cooked and peeled
1 (6-ounce) box long grain and wild rice with seasonings, cooked

In a small saucepan, melt 3 Tablespoons butter; stir in flour. Add chicken stock and cook until mixture thickens. In a medium saucepan, saute vegetables in 1/4 cup butter until soft; add seasonings and stir. Combine shrimp, rice, cream sauce, and vegetables. Pour into a buttered 2-quart casserole and bake.

dilled shrimp
with mushrooms

Yield: 6 servings

**Preparation time:
20 minutes**

"You'll receive applause for this."

1 **pound medium raw
  shrimp, heads removed**
1/4 **pound mushrooms,
  sliced**
1 **Tablespoon butter or
  margarine**
Salt and pepper
3 **Tablespoons brandy,
  optional**
1 **cup heavy cream**
1/2 **teaspoon dill**
1 **egg yolk**
1/8 **teaspoon cayenne pepper**
1 **Tablespoon fresh lemon
  juice**
3 **cups cooked rice or
  pasta**

Shell shrimp and rinse well.
Saute mushrooms in butter in a
deep skillet for 2 or 3 minutes.
Add shrimp, salt, and pepper.
Cook over medium heat until
shrimp turn pink. Sprinkle with
brandy, if desired, and ignite.
Remove shrimp and mushrooms
from the skillet. Add to skillet 3/4
cup cream. Cook over high heat,
stirring until liquid thickens.
Add dill, 1/4 cup cream, and the
egg yolk and stir. Add cayenne,
lemon juice, shrimp, and
mushrooms; blend. Serve over
rice or pasta.

Variation: **To stretch this recipe to feed 8, add 1/4 cup
mushrooms and an additional Tablespoon of butter.**

fried shrimp in beer batter

Yield: 4 servings

**Preparation time:
20 minutes**

"This batter is also delicious on vegetables."

Batter
1/2 cup flour
1/2 cup beer
Salt
Pepper
3/4 teaspoon paprika

**1 pound fresh shrimp,
    peeled**
Flour

Sweet and Sour Sauce
**1 (12-ounce) jar apricot
    preserves**
1/4 cup white vinegar
3 dashes Tabasco sauce

Garnish
Lemon wedges
Parsley

Mix batter ingredients. Dredge shrimp in flour; dip in batter. Fry in deep oil at 375° for 3 to 4 minutes; drain. Puree sweet and sour sauce ingredients in a blender or a food processor. Serve with the shrimp garnished with lemon wedges and parsley.

For crustier fried fish, soak fish in milk before coating. This also takes out the fishy taste.

mandarin-fried shrimp with peas

Yield: 4 servings

**Preparation time:
20 minutes**

"Low calorie and festive too"

**1 pound fresh shrimp
1 Tablespoon salt
4 Tablespoons peanut oil
2 small pieces ginger
1 clove garlic, crushed
10 ounces snow peas,
   fresh or frozen
1 Tablespoon dry sherry**

Sauce
**4 Tablespoons water
4 Tablespoons soy sauce
1 Tablespoon cornstarch**

Soak shrimp for 10 minutes in cold water with salt. Shell and devein shrimp. Dry shrimp and cut in half, if large. Heat skillet or wok to 350° and add oil. Stir-fry ginger and garlic until light brown. Add shrimp and stir-fry 2 to 3 minutes. Add peas and sherry and fry about 4 minutes. Mix sauce ingredients; add to the wok and cook for 2 minutes. Remove ginger.

***Serving suggestion:* Serve on a bed of fluffy rice.**

When buying fresh fish, the flesh should be firm and have no pronounced odor.

shrimp nantua

Yield: 8 servings

**Preparation time:
45 minutes**

"Definitely worth the effort"

Shrimp Butter
**1/2 pound shrimp, cooked
and cleaned**
**1/2 cup butter or margarine,
melted**
1 Tablespoon lemon juice

Sauce Nantua
**2 Tablespoons butter or
margarine**
3 Tablespoons flour
**2 cups white fish stock or
chicken broth with
vermouth**
1 cup heavy cream
1 1/2 teaspoons tomato paste
Salt and pepper

**1 1/2 pounds shrimp,
peeled and deveined**
**3 Tablespoons butter or
margarine**
Paprika
Salt and pepper
Dill

For shrimp butter, place shrimp in blender. Add melted butter and lemon juice; puree. Transfer mixture to a saucepan and heat over medium heat thoroughly. Strain the shrimp butter into a bowl, season to taste, and chill. To prepare sauce nantua, heat butter and stir in flour. Add boiling white fish stock. Stir until smooth. Add heavy cream, bring to a boil, and lower heat to a simmer until liquid is reduced to 2 cups. Stir in bits of shrimp butter, tomato paste, salt, and pepper. This makes 2 cups. In a skillet, toss 1 1/2 pounds shrimp with butter over medium heat until shrimp turns pink. Add paprika, salt, and pepper to taste. Moisten shrimp with 1/2 cup sauce nantua and garnish with sprigs of dill. Serve the remaining sauce separately.

Note: **Everything may be done ahead of time except for cooking the shrimp. Do this at the last minute so that the shrimp will remain tender.**

shrimp and cheese casserole

Yield: 6 servings

Standing time: 3 hours
Temperature: 350°
Baking time: 1 hour

"A perfect brunch or luncheon dish"

6 slices trimmed white bread, cubed
1/2 pound sharp cheese, sliced
1 1/2 pounds shrimp, cooked and peeled
1/4 cup butter or margarine, melted
2 cups milk
3 eggs, beaten
1/2 teaspoon dry mustard
Salt and pepper
Cayenne pepper

Arrange bread, cheese, and shrimp in layers in a 2-quart shallow casserole. Pour melted butter over this. Mix milk, eggs, mustard, salt, pepper, and cayenne; drizzle over casserole. Let stand for 3 hours or overnight in the refrigerator. Bake covered until set.

Note: If recipe is doubled, use a 3-quart casserole.

Coat your hands with salt to make it easier to handle freshly caught fish.

shrimp with mushrooms in wine sauce

Yield: 4 servings

Preparation time: 15 minutes

"A light Italian dish"

3 Tablespoons butter or margarine
1/2 pound mushrooms, thinly sliced
1 Tablespoon fresh lemon juice
Salt and pepper
1 pound shrimp, peeled and deveined
Flour
1/2 cup butter or margarine
2 large cloves garlic, minced
1/2 cup dry white wine
1/2 cup minced parsley
Worcestershire sauce
Tabasco sauce
Salt and pepper

Melt 3 Tablespoons butter in a heavy 12-inch skillet. Add mushrooms and sprinkle with lemon juice, salt, and pepper. Cover skillet and cook until mushrooms are tender, about 5 minutes. Remove mushrooms from the pan and set aside. Dust the shrimp lightly with flour. Melt remaining 1/2 cup butter in the same skillet used for the mushrooms. Saute shrimp for 1 minute. Add garlic and mushrooms to the shrimp and saute for 30 seconds. Add wine and boil until liquid is reduced by half. Add the parsley, Worcestershire sauce, Tabasco sauce, salt, and pepper. Stir until well combined and serve immediately.

***Serving suggestion:* This is marvelous over buttered noodles.**

shrimp with lemon sauce

**Preparation time:
10 minutes**

"Tangy and different"

**2 pounds large shrimp,
    peeled
1/2 cup butter or margarine
1/2 cup chicken broth
1/4 teaspoon tarragon
1 Tablespoon chopped
    parsley
2 Tablespoons fresh lemon
    juice
2 teaspoons grated lemon
    rind
1 clove garlic, minced
1 1/2 Tablespoons sherry**

In a 12-inch skillet, saute shrimp in butter for about 5 minutes. Add the remaining ingredients, except the sherry, and cook for another 5 minutes. Add the sherry and serve immediately.

***Serving suggestion:* Serve over rice cooked with chicken broth and flavored with green onions.**

lobster, shrimp, and crab casserole

Yield: 8 servings

Temperature: 400°
Baking time: 25 minutes

"Very special"

4 Tablespoons butter or margarine
1 clove garlic, minced
4 Tablespoons flour
1/2 teaspoon salt
3 drops Tabasco sauce
2 cups milk
1 (4-ounce) jar chopped pimentos
1/2 pound sharp Cheddar cheese, shredded
1/2 pound fresh crabmeat, drained
1 pound shrimp, cooked and peeled
1/2 pound lobster meat
Butter

In a large saucepan, melt butter and saute garlic. Blend in flour, salt, Tabasco, and milk; stirring constantly until mixture thickens. Add pimentos and 1/2 the cheese. Add seafood, mix well, and pour into a buttered 13x9x2-inch casserole. Sprinkle with remaining cheese, dot with butter, and bake.

Fish frozen in water for up to 1 year may be sold as fresh. Ask and find out what you are getting, especially if you plan to freeze it.

boiled lobster

"A real classic"

6 (1¾-pound) live lobsters
1 Tablespoon salt
1½ cups butter or
margarine, melted
6 lemons, cut into wedges

Put live lobsters in an 8-quart pot, cover with cold water, and add salt. Cover pot and place over high heat. Bring to a boil and boil for 5 minutes. Gently reduce heat to a simmer and cook covered for another 15 to 20 minutes, depending on the size of the lobsters. When ready, lift out the lobsters, drain, and rub the shells with a little melted butter to make them shine. Split each body in half down the middle, removing the long dark line (intestine) and the stomach (near the eyes). Serve hot with butter and lemon wedges.

Variation: **If you want to do this ahead, serve chilled lobster with a sauce of ½ cup Dijon mustard and 1 cup mayonnaise.**

Rub your hands with a slice of lemon to remove the fishy smell.

green sauce

Yield: 10 to 12 servings

Preparation time:
  20 minutes
  plus 1 hour chilling time

"Eye-appealing and taste-tempting"

4 Tablespoons butter or margarine
4 medium onions, minced
2 large cloves garlic, minced
2 cups chopped fresh parsley
2 cups sour cream
Lime juice
Salt and pepper
Tabasco sauce

Melt butter; add onions and garlic and simmer until transparent. Stir in parsley and simmer for 10 minutes. Remove from heat; stir in sour cream and season to taste with lime juice, salt, pepper, and Tabasco. Store, covered, in the refrigerator. Chill at least 1 hour before serving.

Serving suggestion: **Pour over chilled shrimp.**

watercress mousseline

Yield: 1 cup

Preparation time:
  15 minutes
  plus 2 hours chilling time

"Serve with cold poached salmon."

2 bunches watercress
2/3 cup heavy cream
Salt
Freshly ground pepper

Remove leaves from watercress. Place in cold water in saucepan and simmer for 10 minutes. Rinse well in cold water, drain, and pass through a fine sieve. Bring cream to a boil, add sieved watercress, and season to taste. Chill, covered, for at least 2 hours. Before serving, whisk until thick and smooth.

flemish sauce

"Serve over poached or broiled fish."

4 Tablespoons butter or
  margarine
2 teaspoons Dijon mustard
2 Tablespoons fresh lemon
  juice
Salt and pepper
2 teaspoons chopped
  parsley
1 teaspoon chopped chives
Dash nutmeg
4 egg yolks

In the top of a double boiler,
combine butter and all other
ingredients except egg yolks.
Stir over simmering water until
the butter melts. Beat egg yolks
until lemon-colored; whisk into
the butter mixture. Continue
whisking until the sauce
thickens.

tartar sauce

"Perfect for so many fish dishes"

1 cup mayonnaise
2 Tablespoons white wine
1 Tablespoon chopped
  capers
1 Tablespoon chopped
  parsley
1 Tablespoon chopped green
  olives
1 Tablespoon chopped sour
  pickles
1 Tablespoon chopped
  chives
1 Tablespoon chopped
  pimento
1/2 teaspoon tarragon
1/2 teaspoon chervil
Paprika

Combine all ingredients well.
Chill, covered, for at least 1 hour
before serving.

poultry

poultry and game

Apricot-Glazed Chicken 267
Baked Cornish Hens........ 289
Bearnaise Sauce 267
Breast of Chicken au
    Champagne 268
Chicken and Mushroom
    Crepes Florentine 265
Chicken Bombay........... 269
Chicken Breasts in Vermouth
    and Tarragon--New Sauce
    Verte.................... 270
Chicken Breasts with Cheese
    and Herbs 276
Chicken Cordon Bleu....... 272
Chicken Creole 273
Chicken Cutlets............ 274
Chicken Divan 275
Chicken Jerusalem 278
Chicken Plus 272
Chicken Rollade 277
Chicken Stuffed with Cream
    Cheese 278
Country Captain 279
Crunchy Chicken Squares .. 280

Deep-Frying Chicken
    Batter 286
Hickory-Smoked Barbecued
    Chicken 287
Iced Chicken Breasts 282
Italian Chicken 283
Lemoned Chicken.......... 271
Mock Turtle Doves--Stuffed
    Chicken Breasts in
    Mushroom Sauce 281
Oriental Chicken........... 284
Poulet Etouffe en Croute 266
Rock Cornish Game Hens... 288
South of the
    Border Chicken 285

Game
Baked Quail in Wine........ 292
Dove in White Wine 289
Duck...................... 290
Live Oak Duck 291
Grand Marnier Sauce for
    Fowl 291

chicken and mushroom crepes florentine

Yield: 6 to 8 servings

Temperature: 350°
Baking time: 40 minutes

"Truly worth the effort"

3/4 pound chicken breast, cooked and boned
10 ounces fresh or frozen spinach
1/2 pound mushrooms
1/2 cup butter or margarine
2 shallots, finely chopped
5 Tablespoons flour
2 cups milk
1 cup heavy cream
Salt and black pepper
Cayenne pepper
1/4 teaspoon nutmeg
1 1/2 cups shredded Swiss cheese
12 to 16 crepes, see index
1/2 cup grated Parmesan cheese

Chop the chicken finely. Cook spinach, drain thoroughly, and chop. Wipe mushrooms and chop. Heat 2 Tablespoons butter and add shallots. Cook for 2 minutes before stirring in mushrooms. Heat until liquid is almost evaporated. In a large saucepan, melt remaining butter and whisk in flour until light brown. Add milk gradually and stir. When mixture is thick and smooth, stir in cream, salt, pepper, cayenne, and nutmeg. In a large bowl, combine chicken, spinach, and mushroom mixture; add 1/2 the sauce or enough to hold mixture together. Add Swiss cheese to the rest of the sauce. Spoon a thin layer of the cheese sauce over the bottom of a 12x8x2-inch baking dish. Place a spoonful of the chicken mixture on each crepe. Roll crepes and arrange seam side down in dish. Cover with remaining sauce and sprinkle with Parmesan. Either cover tightly and freeze or bake. If frozen, bring to room temperature before baking.

poulet etouffe en croute

Temperature: 325°
Baking time:
   15 to 20 minutes

"Easy to do ahead"

6 chicken breast halves,
   skinned and boned
1 cup chicken broth
1 cup water
3 cups dry white wine
1/2 cup unsalted butter
3 Tablespoons finely
   chopped parsley
1/4 teaspoon white pepper
12 frozen puff pastry
   rounds, thawed
6 slices baked ham
6 slices Swiss cheese
2 (10 1/2-ounce) cans
   asparagus tips,
   well-drained
1 egg yolk
1 Tablespoon water

In a large bowl, marinate the chicken in the broth, 1 cup water, and 2 cups wine; cover and refrigerate for at least 3 hours. After the chicken has marinated, melt the butter in a deep skillet. Add 1 cup wine, parsley, and pepper. Poach chicken on both sides and simmer uncovered over medium heat for 25 to 30 minutes. Croute assembly per chicken breast: roll 2 puff pastry rounds together on a lightly floured surface to form a circle 7 1/2 to 8 inches in diameter. Butterfly the breast half and arrange in the center of the dough, leaving 2 inches of dough on all sides of the breast. Top chicken with 1 slice of ham, 1 slice of cheese, and 1/3 can of asparagus. Roll the ham and cheese ends over the asparagus. Fold the pastry ends over the center as you would do to the ends of a package. Place each croute, seam side down, on a greased cookie sheet. At this point they may be covered and refrigerated until ready to bake. When ready to bake, mix egg yolk and water together well and brush croutes with the mixture. Bake until golden brown. Serve immediately with Bearnaise sauce.

bearnaise sauce

Yield: 1 cup

**Preparation time:
10 minutes**

"Serve with Poulet Etouffe en Croute."

3 Tablespoons dry vermouth
  or dry white wine
1 Tablespoon tarragon
  vinegar
1/2 teaspoon dried tarragon
1/4 teaspoon freshly ground
  black pepper
1 Tablespoon finely chopped
  green onions
3 egg yolks
1 1/2 Tablespoons fresh
  lemon juice
1/4 teaspoon salt
Cayenne pepper
1/2 cup unsalted butter,
  melted
1 Tablespoon capers

Combine the first 5 ingredients in a small saucepan over medium heat. Reduce liquid by two-thirds. In a blender, mix egg yolks, lemon juice, salt, and cayenne. Turn on low speed and very slowly add hot butter in a steady stream, with motor running. When mixed well, add the wine mixture and blend on high speed for 10 seconds. Stir in capers and serve immediately or refrigerate and reheat in the top of a double boiler.

apricot-glazed chicken

Yield: 6 to 8 servings

**Temperature: 325°
Baking time: 1 hour**

"A marvelous combination"

6 to 8 chicken breasts,
  halved
1 (8-ounce) bottle Russian
  dressing
1 clove garlic, minced
1 (9-ounce) jar apricot
  preserves
1 package dry onion soup
  mix
2/3 cup water

Place chicken, skin side down, in a 13x9x2-inch baking dish. Mix remaining ingredients. Pour 1/2 the sauce over chicken. Bake for 30 minutes. Turn pieces over and spread with remaining sauce. Bake for 30 minutes.

breast of chicken au champagne

Yield: 4 servings

**Preparation time:
45 minutes**

"Wonderful"

**4 chicken breasts, skinned
  and boned**
1/4 cup flour
1 teaspoon salt
1/2 teaspoon pepper
1/2 cup butter or margarine
**1/2 pound fresh mushrooms,
  sliced**
1 cup light cream
1/2 cup champagne

Place breasts between pieces of waxed paper and pound until slightly flattened. Mix flour, salt, and pepper. Roll breasts in mixture and shake off excess flour. Brown breasts in butter over medium heat. Add mushrooms, cover, and cook over low heat for 10 minutes. Drain off butter, add cream, and simmer for another 10 minutes. Transfer breasts to warm serving plates. Add the champagne to the liquid in the skillet. Bring to a rapid boil and stir until creamy. If sauce becomes too thick, add a little milk.

Use white wine or white vermouth for poaching and braising poultry.

chicken bombay

Yield: 8 to 10 servings

Temperature: 350°
Baking time: 1 1/2 hours

"The apple, raisins, and almonds add marvelous texture and flavor."

1/4 cup butter or margarine
1/4 cup chopped onion
1 small apple, peeled
and chopped
1/2 cup raisins
1/8 teaspoon ginger
1 to 2 teaspoons curry
powder
1/4 teaspoon salt
1/3 cup slivered almonds,
toasted
1 1/2 cups cooked rice
8 to 10 whole chicken
breasts, boned, with skin
Melted butter or margarine
Salt and pepper
Paprika, optional

Melt butter; add onion and apple and simmer until tender. Remove from heat and add raisins, ginger, curry powder, salt, almonds, and rice, blending well. Fill breasts with mixture and fold over so that filling will not fall out. Place in a 13x9x2-inch baking dish and brush tops with melted butter. Sprinkle with salt and pepper and, if desired, paprika. Cover and bake for 1 hour. Remove cover and bake for another 1/2 hour.

Gravy
1 can cream of chicken
soup
1 teaspoon curry powder
1/4 cup chutney

While baking, heat soup, curry powder, and chutney for gravy and serve with chicken.

Any kind of poultry can be marinated before cooking to heighten the flavor.

chicken breasts in vermouth and tarragon

Yield: 6 servings

**Preparation time:
30 minutes**

"Served at the 1981 Herb Day sponsored by the Nashville Herb Society"

2 cups water
1/4 cup dry vermouth
1 teaspoon dried tarragon
or 1 Tablespoon fresh
tarragon
1 medium carrot, sliced
1 celery stalk, sliced
3 large green onions,
chopped
2 chicken bouillon cubes
Salt
White pepper
3 whole chicken breasts,
halved and boned

Place all ingredients, except chicken, in a deep skillet. Bring to a boil. Reduce heat and simmer for 5 to 10 minutes. Add chicken breasts and raise heat to medium until a slow simmer is reached. Reduce heat again to maintain a slow simmer. Cover and cook for 15 minutes for medium sized breasts and 20 minutes for larger ones. Turn off heat and let chicken cool slightly. Serve with *new sauce verte.*

Variation: Add 1 package unflavored gelatin dissolved in cold water to clarified stock and mix well. Arrange the chicken breasts and the vegetables in individual casseroles or in a 2-quart casserole. Pour stock mixture over the chicken and vegetables. Refrigerate until set, about 4 hours.

new sauce verte

3 Tablespoons Dijon
   mustard
1 Tablespoon white wine
   vinegar
2 Tablespoons water
1 cup olive oil
2 Tablespoons cold
   evaporated milk
1 teaspoon well drained
   capers
1/4 cup finely chopped
   parsley
1 teaspoon dried tarragon
1/4 teaspoon salt
White pepper
Lemon juice

In a food processor, combine first
3 sauce ingredients. Add oil, a
little at a time, alternating with
milk. When all milk and oil are
added, scrape down bowl and
add remaining ingredients.
Serve over chicken breasts.

Variation: Fold in 1/4 cup heavy cream, whipped, for a richer
sauce. This sauce is equally good served with steak.

lemoned chicken

Temperature: 350°
Baking time: 1 to 1 1/2 hours

"Fantastic"

1 chicken fryer
1/4 cup butter or margarine,
   melted
2 to 4 teaspoons grated
   lemon rind
1/4 cup lemon juice
1/4 cup olive oil
1/2 teaspoon salt
1/2 teaspoon freshly ground
   pepper
1/4 teaspoon oregano,
   optional

Place chicken in a 13x9x2-inch
casserole. Combine all other
ingredients and pour over the
chicken. Bake for 1 1/2 hours for a
whole chicken or for 1 hour for
chicken pieces. Baste every 15
minutes.

chicken cordon bleu

Yield: 6 servings

Preparation time: 2 hours

"Very attractive and tasty"

6 small chicken breasts, skinned and boned
Salt and pepper
6 thin slices ham
6 ounces Swiss cheese, cut into sticks
Flour
2 eggs, slightly beaten
1 cup finely crushed bread crumbs
4 Tablespoons oil
2 Tablespoons water

Pound chicken breasts to 1/4 inch thick. Sprinkle lightly with salt and pepper. Place a ham slice and a cheese stick on each breast. Tuck in sides and roll, pressing to seal well. Secure with toothpicks. Roll in flour, dip in eggs, and roll in bread crumbs. Cover and chill for 1 hour. In a large skillet, brown rolls in oil, about 5 minutes. Reduce heat and add water. Cover; simmer for 45 minutes or until tender. Remove the cover for the last 2 to 3 minutes.

chicken plus

Yield: 6 to 8 servings

Temperature: 300°
Baking time: 2 1/2 hours

"Perfect for buffet dinners"

2 cups sour cream
1 1/2 cans cream of celery soup
8 slices Canadian bacon
8 slices bacon
4 chicken breasts, boned, skinned, and halved
Parsley
Paprika

Combine sour cream and the soup; set aside. In a 13x9x2-inch baking dish, line the bottom with Canadian bacon. Wrap the bacon slices around the chicken breasts and place these on top of the Canadian bacon. Cover with the soup mixture. Bake, covered, for 2 hours. Uncover and bake an additional 30 minutes. Skim off any bacon fat before serving. Top each chicken breast with parsley and paprika.

chicken creole

"Tastes like jambalaya, but easier"

3 Tablespoons oil
1 cup chopped onion
2 cups chopped green
    pepper
3 Tablespoons chopped
    parsley
1 large clove garlic, minced
1 (16-ounce) can tomatoes,
    drained and chopped
2 cups chicken stock
1/2 teaspoon salt
1/4 teaspoon basil
1/2 teaspoon thyme
1/4 teaspoon cayenne pepper
2 bay leaves
1 cup brown or white rice
3 cups cubed, cooked
    chicken (add 2 bay leaves
    to cooking water)
1 cup cubed, cooked ham or
    sliced, smoked sausage,
    optional

Heat oil in a deep skillet. Saute onion, green pepper, parsley, and garlic until onion is transparent. Add tomatoes and cook for 2 minutes. Add chicken stock, salt, basil, thyme, cayenne, and bay leaves. Bring mixture to a boil. Stir in uncooked rice. Reduce heat and cover. Simmer for 15 minutes. Add chicken and simmer, covered, for 10 additional minutes, or until rice is tender. Remove bay leaves before serving.

A stewing chicken is ready when its meat is tender if pierced with a fork. Roasters, fryers, and broilers are ready when the meat is pierced deeply with a fork and the juices have no trace of a rosy color.

chicken cutlets

Overnight chilling
Temperature: 375°
Baking time: 30 minutes

"An elegant luncheon dish"

2/3 cup butter or margarine
2/3 cup flour
1 1/4 teaspoons salt
1 1/3 cups milk
1 1/3 cups chicken stock
1/3 cup Worcestershire
sauce
Thyme
Celery salt
10 cups cooked and diced
chicken
Bread crumbs
Eggs
Butter or margarine

Mushroom Sauce
1 pound fresh mushrooms,
sliced
6 Tablespoons butter or
margarine
6 Tablespoons flour
1 1/2 cups milk
1 cup chicken stock
1/4 cup dry sherry
Salt
Freshly ground pepper

In a large saucepan, melt butter over medium heat. Stir in flour and salt. Slowly add milk, chicken stock, Worcestershire sauce, thyme, and celery salt, stirring constantly. Cool before adding chicken. Chill overnight. Shape into cutlets. Roll each cutlet in fresh breadcrumbs and refrigerate until time to bake. At that time, dip in beaten eggs and more bread crumbs. Place on a greased baking sheet. Brush with melted butter and bake. Serve with mushroom sauce.

Saute mushrooms in butter. Stir in flour and slowly add milk and stock. Stir until smooth and thickened. Add sherry, salt, and pepper to taste.

chicken divan

"Should be re-named Divine"

Hollandaise Sauce
1 cup butter or margarine
6 egg yolks
2 Tablespoons fresh
   lemon juice
1 teaspoon salt
Dash cayenne pepper

Cream Sauce
4 Tablespoons butter
   or margarine
4 Tablespoons flour
2 cups milk
2 teaspoons Mei Yen
   seasoning
1 Tablespoon
   Worcestershire sauce
4 (10-ounce) packages
   frozen broccoli spears,
   cooked and drained
Grated Parmesan cheese
8 large chicken breasts,
   boned and cooked or meat
   from 1/2 cooked turkey
1/2 pint heavy cream,
   whipped

To prepare the Hollandaise sauce, combine 1 cup butter, egg yolks, lemon juice, salt, and cayenne in the top of a double boiler and cook over hot, not boiling, water. Stir until thickened. Set aside.

To prepare the cream sauce, heat butter, flour, milk, and Mei Yen seasoning in a saucepan. Stir until thickened. Add Worcestershire sauce and set aside. Place the broccoli in a 13x9x2-inch casserole and sprinkle with Parmesan cheese. Cover with the chicken breasts. Combine the Hollandaise, cream sauce, and whipped cream and pour over the casserole. Sprinkle the top generously with more Parmesan. Bake for 15 to 20 minutes, broiling during the last few minutes to brown the top.

Creamed chicken or turkey dishes will freeze, except for those containing hard boiled eggs.

chicken breasts with cheese and herbs

Yield: 4 to 6 servings

Temperature: 350°
Baking time: 35 minutes

"The tarragon enhances the flavor beautifully."

4 whole chicken breasts, halved, boned, and skinned
Seasoned salt
Monosodium glutamate
3/4 cup butter or margarine
1 teaspoon tarragon
1/2 teaspoon chopped parsley
1/2 teaspoon ground oregano
1/2 pound Monterey Jack cheese
1 cup flour
3 eggs, beaten
1 cup dry bread crumbs
1 cup sauterne wine

Place each piece of chicken between sheets of waxed paper and pound until very thin. Sprinkle with salt and MSG. Whip butter until fluffy and stir in tarragon, parsley, and oregano. Cut cheese lengthwise into 8 pieces. Spread 1/2 of herb butter on cheese. Place 1 piece of cheese on each piece of chicken and roll tightly. Coat chicken rolls in flour, dip in egg, and roll in bread crumbs. Place in a 12x8x2-inch baking dish and bake for 20 minutes. Melt remaining herb butter and stir in wine. Pour over chicken and bake 15 more minutes, basting occasionally.

1 (3 1/2-pound) chicken yields 3 cups diced cooked chicken.

chicken rollade

Temperature: 350°
Baking time: 50 minutes

"An old French recipe made easy"

4 or 5 large chicken breasts, boned, skinned, and halved
Pepper
1 cup flour
1 stalk celery
2 scallions
10 green olives
10 black olives, pitted
2 green peppers
1/2 cup unsalted butter
2 eggs, beaten
1 cup corn flake crumbs
1/4 cup oil
4 Tablespoons butter or margarine, melted
2 Tablespoons instant chicken broth
1/2 cup white sherry
1 teaspoon cornstarch mixed with 1 teaspoon water

Pound chicken breasts between pieces of waxed paper to flatten. Pepper and dip one side only into flour. Using a food processor or blender, mince the celery, scallions, olives, and green pepper finely. Spread the vegetable mixture on each breast, add a small portion of the butter, and roll up. Dip roll into egg and then into crumbs. Place rolls in a 12x8x2-inch baking dish and cover with oil and butter. Bake for 40 minutes. Dissolve chicken broth in sherry and simmer. Add cornstarch and simmer a few minutes longer. Pour over baked chicken and bake for another 10 minutes.

Note: **This may be prepared in the morning and refrigerated, brought to room temperature, and baked just before serving or baked in the morning and simply warmed before serving.**

chicken jerusalem

**Preparation time:
35 minutes**

"Delightful"

4 chicken breasts, boned
Flour
**4 Tablespoons butter or
margarine**
Salt
White pepper
Nutmeg
**1/4 pound mushrooms,
sliced**
**6 artichoke bottoms or
hearts, quartered**
1 cup sherry
1 pint heavy cream, heated
**Chopped parsley and
chives**

Roll chicken in flour and brown in butter in a large skillet. Season with salt, pepper, and nutmeg. Add mushrooms, artichokes, and sherry. Cover the skillet and simmer for about 15 minutes, until the chicken is tender. The wine should be almost evaporated. Add warm cream and stir well. Add finely chopped parsley and chives before serving.

chicken stuffed
with cream cheese

Yield: 3 to 4 servings

**Preparation time:
40 minutes**

"A creamy surprise inside"

**2 large chicken breasts,
halved, boned, and
skinned**
**1/2 (8-ounce) package cream
cheese, softened**
1 Tablespoon lemon juice
3 or 4 scallions, chopped
Salt and pepper
Flour
Butter, margarine, or oil

(continued)

Pound chicken between pieces of waxed paper. Mix cheese, lemon juice, and scallions; spread on each breast. Roll and secure with toothpicks. Coat with mixture of salt, pepper, and flour. Saute in butter, margarine, or oil for about 20 minutes. Remove chicken from pan and discard toothpicks.

Gravy
1 Tablespoon flour
Salt and pepper
1 cup water

Add flour, salt, pepper, and water to pan drippings. Stir over medium heat until thickened. Ladle over chicken and serve.

country captain

Yield: 4 to 6 servings

Temperature: 350°
Baking time: 45 minutes

"Great served with chutney or bread 'n butter pickles"

8 chicken breast halves, boned
1 teaspoon salt
1/4 teaspoon pepper
1/4 cup flour
4 Tablespoons butter or margarine
1 onion, thinly sliced
1 green pepper, slivered
1/2 teaspoon garlic powder
1 (28-ounce) can tomatoes
1 (16-ounce) can tomatoes
1 1/2 teaspoons salt
1 teaspoon white pepper
1 1/2 teaspoons curry powder
1 1/2 teaspoons thyme
3 Tablespoons raisins
Cooked rice
1/4 cup blanched almonds
1 1/2 teaspoons chopped parsley

Dredge chicken breasts in seasoned flour. In a large skillet, brown chicken in butter and remove. Brown onion and green pepper, adding more butter if needed. Add garlic powder, tomatoes, and seasonings and cook for 10 minutes. Place chicken in a 13x9x2-inch casserole and cover with the sauce. Bake covered. Stir raisins into the sauce at the end of the baking time. Serve breasts around a mound of rice. Cover with sauce. Sprinkle with almonds and parsley.

Note: **Can be cooked in a covered skillet over low heat until tender, about 30 to 45 minutes.**

crunchy chicken squares

Yield: 4 squares

Temperature: 350°
Baking time: 20 minutes

"Really creamy inside the flaky crust"

1 (3-ounce) package cream cheese
2 Tablespoons butter or margarine
2 cups chopped, cooked chicken
1/4 teaspoon salt
1/8 teaspoon pepper
2 Tablespoons milk
1 Tablespoon chopped pimento
1 Tablespoon chopped onion
1 Tablespoon chopped green pepper
1 (8-ounce) package crescent rolls
1/4 cup butter or margarine, melted
2 cups seasoned croutons, crushed

In a large bowl, blend cream cheese and butter. Add chicken, salt, pepper, milk, pimento, onion, and green pepper. Refrigerate. Separate crescent dough into 4 squares. Divide chicken mixture among the 4 squares. Pull 4 corners to the center of each, twist, and seal over the chicken mixture. Brush tops with melted butter and then sprinkle with the croutons. Bake on an ungreased baking sheet.

To clarify or degrease chicken stock, whip in 1 egg white. Heat over moderate heat and stir constantly until the egg white rises to the surface. Do not boil. Strain through cheesecloth.

Keep dental floss in your kitchen for a stronger and more hygienic method of trussing a turkey.

mock turtle doves (stuffed chicken breasts in mushroom sauce)

Yield: 4 servings

Temperature: 325°
Baking time: 1 1/2 hours

"Festive for the holidays"

2 cups prepared corn
  bread stuffing
4 whole chicken breasts,
  boned with skin left on
Salt and pepper
4 Tablespoons butter or
  margarine, melted

Sauce
2 Tablespoons butter or
  margarine
1/2 pound fresh mushrooms,
  sliced
1/4 cup minced onions
2 Tablespoons flour
1/2 cup light cream
1/2 teaspoon salt
Freshly ground pepper
1/2 cup sour cream
Tabasco sauce
Worcestershire sauce

Put 1/2 cup stuffing in the center of each breast. Fold the breast edges toward the center and secure with toothpicks. The breasts will resemble doves. Place chicken in a 9-inch square pan and sprinkle with salt and pepper. Pour melted butter over each breast and bake, uncovered. Baste once or twice.

In a medium saucepan, melt 2 Tablespoons butter and saute mushrooms and onion until tender. Set aside. Combine the remaining ingredients and heat in the top of a double boiler until thickened. Add mushroom mixture. Serve sauce over the chicken.

281

iced chicken breasts

Yield: 8 servings

Preparation time: 1 hour

"Great for a luncheon or on a hot summer evening"

4 chicken breasts, halved
2 cans chicken broth
1 (3-ounce) package cream
cheese with chives
1/4 cup mayonnaise
2 Tablespoons lemon juice
1/2 teaspoon grated lemon
rind
1/4 teaspoon salt
1 green onion, finely
chopped
Bibb lettuce leaves
2 to 3 large tomatoes,
peeled and chilled
Salt and pepper
2 large avocados
1/2 cup toasted slivered
almonds
Pitted ripe olives
Vinegar and oil dressing

Cook chicken breasts in broth and enough water to cover until tender. Drain, skin, bone, and refrigerate. Thoroughly mix cream cheese, mayonnaise, lemon juice, lemon rind, salt, and onion. Completely coat the rounded side of each breast with the cheese mixture. Arrange lettuce leaves on serving plates. Cut tomatoes into 8 thick slices and place on lettuce; sprinkle with salt and pepper. Top with chicken breasts. Halve and peel the avocados, cut each 1/2 into 4 slices, and arrange beside the chicken. Sprinkle chicken with almonds and garnish with olives. Pass the vinegar and oil dressing separately.

To keep fried chicken crisp, drain immediately after frying, place in a paper bag, and keep warm in the oven.

italian chicken

Yield: 6 to 8 servings

Temperature: 350°
Baking time: 40 minutes

"Zesty"

2 Tablespoons olive oil
1 Tablespoon butter or
margarine
6 to 8 chicken pieces
Salt and pepper
1 red onion, sliced
3 cloves garlic, crushed
1 small green pepper,
cut into strips
1 small eggplant, chopped
2 large tomatoes, chopped
1 teaspoon basil
1 teaspoon oregano
1/2 teaspoon thyme
1/2 cup chicken broth
3 cups cooked noodles or
rice
2 teaspoons cornstarch
1 Tablespoon water
1/3 cup grated Romano
cheese
3 Tablespoons minced
parsley

Heat 1 Tablespoon oil and butter in a heavy frying pan. Brown chicken well over medium heat. Salt and pepper lightly and transfer to a 13x9x2-inch casserole. Add remaining oil to frying pan and saute onion and garlic until softened. Add green pepper, eggplant, tomatoes, seasonings, and broth and bring to a boil. Pour over chicken, cover dish, and bake until chicken is tender. With slotted spoon, arrange chicken and vegetables on top of the noodles or rice. Heat remaining liquid. Mix cornstarch with water and stir into liquid to thicken. Pour over chicken. Sprinkle with cheese and garnish with parsley.

oriental chicken

Yield: 4 servings

**Preparation time:
30 minutes**

"A low calorie Chinese treat"

2 whole chicken breasts,
  skinned and boned
1 teaspoon plus
  3 Tablespoons peanut oil
1 teaspoon cornstarch
3/4 cup unsalted walnuts
  or slivered almonds
1/2 teaspoon salt
1/2 cup sliced mushrooms
3/4 cup sliced bamboo shoots
1 cup fresh snow peas
1 (8-ounce) can water
  chestnuts, drained
1/4 cup sliced onion
3/4 cup sliced celery
1/2 cup chicken broth
1/2 teaspoon sugar
1/4 teaspoon pepper
2 Tablespoons soy sauce
1 Tablespoon cornstarch
  mixed with 1 teaspoon
  water
Chinese noodles or cooked
  rice

Slice chicken thinly and mix with 1 teaspoon oil and 1 teaspoon cornstarch. Heat 3 Tablespoons oil in a wok or electric skillet. Brown nuts in oil; remove with slotted spoon. In remaining oil, cook chicken with salt over high heat. Add mushrooms, bamboo shoots, snow peas, water chestnuts, onion, celery, and broth. Stir-fry for 2 to 4 minutes. Add sugar, pepper, soy sauce, and cornstarch mixture; stirring until thickened. Return nuts and toss. Serve over Chinese noodles or rice.

To stir-fry: cut meat into bite-size pieces
cook quickly
serve immediately.

south of the border chicken

Yield: 6 to 8 servings

**Overnight chilling
Temperature: 300°
Baking time:
1 to 1 1/2 hours**

"This will be one of your favorites."

**4 large chicken breasts
6 corn tortillas
1 can cream of chicken
  soup
1 can cream of mushroom
  soup
1 cup milk
1 onion, finely chopped
1 (4-ounce) can diced green
  chiles
Tabasco sauce or jalapeno
  sauce
2 cups shredded Cheddar
  cheese**

Simmer chicken, covered, in a small amount of water until tender. Cool, skin, bone, and cut into bite-size pieces. Cut tortillas into 1-inch squares. Combine the soups, milk, onion, green chiles, and Tabasco sauce. In a buttered 13x9x2-inch baking dish, place layers of chicken, tortillas, and the soup mixture; alternating several times. Top with the shredded cheese. Refrigerate overnight, covered, and bake.

Variation: **Substitute 1 cup canned stewed tomatoes, undrained, for the milk.**

To cook poultry in water: season as desired, place in a kettle, and add just enough water to cover. Bring to a boil and skim off any froth from the surface. Reduce heat, cover, and simmer until the meat is tender (2 or 3 hours). Add sliced carrots, onions, celery, and a bay leaf to the water for more flavor.

deep-frying
chicken batter

Preparation time:
5 minutes
plus 1 hour standing
time

"A different taste for fried chicken"

1 cup flour
1/4 teaspoon salt
2 eggs, separated
3 Tablespoons olive oil or
melted butter or
margarine
1/2 cup beer or water
Freshly ground pepper

Mix all ingredients except egg whites. Let rest for 1 hour. Beat egg whites and fold in right before using. This is enough batter for 10 pieces of chicken.

Note: **This batter is also good for fish and onion rings.**

Note: **Fry chicken in a very large pan. Don't let the pieces touch each other. Chicken should cook about 15 minutes on each side; remove from the pan and drain on paper towels. Skim any floating material from the oil as it accumulates. When all the chicken is fried, sprinkle with additional salt to taste. Chicken is best not refrigerated and served at room temperature.**

hickory-smoked barbecued chicken

Yield: 4 to 6 servings

Temperature: 325°
Baking time: 1 hour

"A summer favorite"

Sauce
1/4 cup vinegar
1/2 cup water
2 Tablespoons brown sugar
1 Tablespoon prepared
   mustard
1 teaspoon salt
1/4 teaspoon cayenne pepper
1/2 teaspoon black pepper
2 Tablespoons fresh lemon
   juice
1 large onion, chopped
1/4 cup butter or margarine
1/2 cup catsup
2 Tablespoons
   Worcestershire sauce
1 1/2 teaspoons liquid smoke
1 broiler chicken, cut in
   pieces

Combine the first 10 ingredients in a saucepan. Boil for 20 minutes. Add catsup, Worcestershire sauce, and liquid smoke. Place chicken in a roasting pan. Pour 1/2 the sauce over the pieces and place in a preheated oven. Bake, turning and basting often with the remaining sauce.

To hasten cooking time, partially cook chicken in the microwave. Complete the cooking on the grill.

rock cornish game hens

Temperature: 350°
Baking time:
50 minutes

"The bacon bastes the hens and adds marvelous flavor."

1 (6-ounce) box long grain
   and wild rice
1 chicken bouillon cube
3/4 cup chopped mushrooms
2 Tablespoons butter or
   margarine
2 pieces sliced ham, cut into
   small strips
1/4 cup pistachio nuts,
   shelled
4 rock Cornish game hens
1/2 lemon
Salt
Pepper
8 strips bacon
Parsley

Cook rice, adding bouillon cube to the water. In a skillet, saute mushrooms in butter. Add ham, 1/2 of the prepared rice, and nuts. Refrigerate extra rice and reheat later to serve with the hens. Rub hens with the lemon inside and out and season with salt and pepper. Stuff hens with rice-ham mixture. Close with skewers and tie legs with string. Place 2 strips of bacon on top of each bird. Bake in a 12x8x2-inch casserole. Serve garnished with parsley.

baked cornish hens

Yield: 6 servings

Temperature: 350°
Baking time:
45 to 50 minutes

"This has a delicious orange flavor."

2 teaspoons salt
1 teaspoon sage
1 teaspoon nutmeg
1 clove garlic, minced
4 Tablespoons fresh lemon
   juice
6 Cornish hens at room
   temperature, halved,
   if desired
1 cup butter or margarine
1 cup orange juice

Combine spices, garlic, and lemon juice. Rub this mixture over the hens, inside and out. Melt the butter in a 13x9x2-inch casserole. Place hens in the pan and bake for 15 minutes. Turn, baste with orange juice, and bake for another 15 minutes. Turn again, baste, and bake for 15 to 20 minutes.

dove in white wine

Yield: 4 servings

Preparation time:
4 1/2 hours

"Grapes make it very special."

Salt and pepper
8 doves
Green grapes
6 Tablespoons unsalted
   butter
1 cup white wine
3 cups chicken stock
1 Tablespoon flour

Salt and pepper doves. Stuff each with several green grapes and 1 teaspoon butter. If doves have been skinned, this may be omitted. Soak in white wine for several hours. Reserve wine. Brown doves in remaining butter in a large pan. Reduce heat and add chicken stock. Cover and simmer for about 2 hours, until tender. Add flour and reserved wine to the gravy in the last 15 minutes.

duck

Yield: 2 small ducks
per person or
1 large duck
per person

Temperature: 375°
Baking time:
1 to 2 hours

"Loved by one and all"

Duck, large or small
Water
Lemon
Browning sauce
Dijon mustard
Salt
Freshly ground pepper
Chopped apple
Chopped onion
Chopped celery
Bacon strips

Soak duck for 2 hours in water with juice of a lemon added. Wash and dry duck, inside and out. Rub liberally, inside and out, with browning sauce. Rub outside with mustard. Salt and pepper, inside and out. Stuff duck with apple, onion, and celery. Place duck, breast up, on a sheet of aluminum foil. Cut a bacon strip in half and criss-cross breast; drizzling a little more browning sauce over the top. Seal foil, leaving a little space for steam. Place in shallow pan and bake for 1 hour and 20 minutes for a small duck and up to 2 hours for a larger one.

Note: **Adapt this recipe according to the number of ducks served.**

Note: **Cook ducks ahead, pull meat from the bones, and freeze in the gravy.**

live oak duck

**Preparation time:
2 1/2 hours**

"A fabulous change for the holidays"

4 teal ducks
1 lemon, sliced
Salt
Black or red pepper
4 cloves garlic
2 stalks celery
1 onion, quartered
1/4 cup bacon grease
1 can beef broth
1 can onion soup
1/2 cup orange juice
1/2 cup red wine
1/2 pound fresh mushrooms

Clean ducks, inside and out. Pat dry and rub with lemon slices. Season, inside and out. Stuff each bird with garlic, celery, and onion. Brown birds in bacon grease in a 5-quart dutch oven, starting with the breast. When browned, add broth, soup, juice, and wine. Cover and simmer about 2 hours, until breast meat begins to pull away from bone. 30 minutes before ducks are ready, add mushrooms and check seasonings.

grand marnier sauce for fowl

Yield: 6 to 8 servings

**Preparation time:
5 minutes**

"A gourmet touch"

2/3 cup brown sugar
2/3 cup granulated sugar
2 Tablespoons cornstarch
**2 Tablespoons grated
    orange rind**
**1 Tablespoon grated
    lemon rind**
1/2 teaspoon salt
1 1/2 cups orange juice
1/2 cup Grand Marnier
**Rind of 1/2 orange, cut into
    thin strips**

Combine sugars in a 1-quart saucepan; add cornstarch and stir. Add remaining ingredients and heat to a slow boil. Reduce heat and simmer until transparent and slightly thickened, about 4 minutes.

baked quail in wine

Yield: 4 servings

Temperature: 250°
Baking time: 1 1/2 to 2 hours

"Really moist and tender"

4 quail
Salt and pepper
1 cup flour
1/2 cup butter or margarine
1 cup white wine
1 can chicken broth

Shake quail in a paper bag with seasoned flour. In a large ovenproof skillet, brown quail in melted butter. Add wine and broth, cover, and bake for 1 1/2 to 2 hours.

Shotgun Sauce
3 ounces orange juice
   concentrate
1/2 cup currant jelly
Worcestershire sauce

Combine sauce ingredients and heat until the jelly melts. Pour over quail before serving or pass as gravy. Also delicious on wild rice.

Serving suggestion: **Serve quail with peach halves filled with raspberry preserves, covered with wine, and warmed in the oven.**

meats

meats

Casseroles and Sauces
Chili. 295
Houston's Italian Meat
  Sauce 297
Moussaka 298
Picadillo 299
Savory Souffle Roll 300
Spaghetti Bolognese Sauce . . 296
Steeplechase Casserole 302
Zucchini Lasagna 303

Beef
Barbecued Beef 305
Beef en Gelee 304
Beef Stroganoff. 306
Boeuf de Wellington 307
Brisket 308
Eye of Round or
  Tenderloin Rib Roast. 309
Marinated Eye of Round 310
Rib Roast with Artichoke
  Sauce 311
Shish Kebob 312
Steak Diane 308
Steak Teriyaki. 313

Lamb
Barbecued Lamb 314
Rack of Lamb with Dijon
  Sauce 315
Special Saucy Lamb 316
Spring Lamb Stew 317

Pork
Baked Ham with Plum
  Garnish 318
Barbecued Spareribs 322
Caper Sauce 323
Crown Pork Roast 319
Pork Chops in Wine 323
Pork Chop Stuffings 324
  Bleu Cheese
  Cheese and Fruit
  Dressing
  Spinach
Roast Pork with Sage 321
Stuffed Pork Chops 324
Stuffed Pork Loin 320

Veal
Lemon Veal 326
Scallopine with Mushrooms
  and White Wine 327
Veal Scallops Vermouth 326
Veal Smitane. 328

Accompaniments
Golden Gravy 329
Orange Mayonnaise 330
Raisin Sauce for Ham 330
Shallot Cream Sauce. 329

chili

Preparation time: 2 hours

"Perfect for an after-the-game party"

2 to 3 pounds ground chuck
1 large onion, minced
2 cloves garlic, minced
1 teaspoon oregano
1 teaspoon cumin seed
2 1/4 teaspoons chili powder
1 teaspoon sugar
1 (28-ounce) can whole
   tomatoes, undrained
2 (16-ounce) cans tomato
   sauce
Salt and pepper
1 teaspoon sage, optional

In a large, deep saucepan or a Dutch oven, saute chuck, onion, and garlic until lightly browned. Add remaining ingredients and bring to a boil. Lower heat and simmer for 1 1/2 hours, skimming off any grease. Adjust seasoning to taste.

Serving suggestion: **Serve with Cornbread, page 356.**

Oven temperatures:		
	warming	up to 200°
	slow	300°
	moderate	325° - 375°
	hot	400° - 450°
	very hot	475° - 550°

spaghetti bolognese sauce

Preparation time: 1 hour

"A really different flavor combination"

2 Tablespoons butter or margarine
2 Tablespoons olive oil
1 onion, finely chopped
4 strips lean bacon, diced
1 medium carrot, chopped
1 stalk celery, chopped
1 pound chuck, coarsely ground
2 chicken livers, minced
2 Tablespoons tomato puree
1/2 cup dry white wine
1 cup beef bouillon
1 bay leaf
1 strip lemon peel
Salt and pepper
1 clove garlic, crushed
1/4 cup light cream

In a Dutch oven or a large, deep saucepan, heat butter and oil. Add onion and stir until tender. Add bacon, carrot, and celery and saute until lightly browned. Add chuck and livers, stirring until lightly browned. Pour off grease. Add tomato puree, wine, bouillon, bay leaf, and lemon peel. Season with salt, pepper, and garlic. Cover and simmer for 40 minutes. Remove the bay leaf and the lemon peel and continue to simmer uncovered until sauce thickens, about 10 minutes. Stir in the cream just before serving.

Serving suggestion: Serve over spaghetti or small shell noodles sprinkled with freshly grated Parmesan cheese. Marinated hearts of palm on bibb lettuce are marvelous with this savory sauce.

houston's italian meat sauce

Yield: 12 servings

Preparation time: 3 hours

"Freeze part of this and enjoy again and again."

1/4 cup olive oil
1 teaspoon minced garlic
1 large onion, chopped
1 green pepper, chopped
2 pounds chuck, coarsely ground
1 pound Italian sausage, crumbled
1 (24-ounce) can Italian tomatoes, undrained
2 (6-ounce) cans tomato paste
3 Tablespoons sugar
2 teaspoons dried basil
2 teaspoons dried oregano
2 teaspoons salt
1/2 teaspoon pepper
1 1/2 cups sliced fresh mushrooms
Grated Parmesan cheese

In a large skillet, heat olive oil and saute garlic, onion, green pepper, chuck, and sausage until the meat is no longer pink. Combine tomatoes, tomato paste, sugar, herbs, salt, and pepper in a food processor or a blender. Blend into a chunky sauce, *do not over-process.* Thoroughly drain fat from meat mixture. Combine the chunky tomato sauce with the meat mixture in a Dutch oven. Bring to a boil and then simmer, uncovered, for 3 hours. Stir in mushrooms during the last 10 minutes of cooking. Sprinkle with Parmesan cheese and serve.

***Serving suggestion:* Serve over freshly cooked pasta with Onion Bread, page 337.**

moussaka

Temperature: 350°
Baking time: 40 minutes

"Complicated, but a meal in itself"

2 eggplants, peeled and
  cut into 1/3-inch slices
Milk
Salt and pepper
Flour
Oil
1 cup finely chopped onion
1 1/2 pounds ground chuck
1 clove garlic, minced
1 (16-ounce) can tomato
  sauce
1/2 teaspoon dried oregano
1 teaspoon dried basil
Salt and pepper
1 Tablespoon chopped
  parsley
2 Tablespoons bread
  crumbs
1/2 cup sliced mushrooms
2 Tablespoons butter or
  margarine
2 Tablespoons flour
2 cups milk
Salt and pepper
2 eggs
1/2 cup grated Parmesan
  cheese
1/2 cup shredded Cheddar
  cheese

Dip eggplant slices in milk and then in seasoned flour. In a large skillet, saute eggplant in oil until lightly browned on both sides. Remove eggplant and set aside. In the same skillet, saute onion, chuck, and garlic. Pour off grease and add tomato sauce, oregano, basil, salt, pepper, and parsley. Simmer for 30 minutes, remove from the heat, and stir in bread crumbs and mushrooms. In a medium saucepan, melt the butter and stir in flour. Add the milk, salt, and pepper and bring to a slow boil, stirring constantly. Remove from the heat and quickly stir in the eggs. Heat until cream sauce thickens. Layer 1/2 the eggplant in a 3-quart casserole. Sprinkle with 2 Tablespoons of each of the cheeses. Top with all of the meat mixture. Sprinkle with 2 Tablespoons of each of the cheeses. Top with the rest of the eggplant. Cover with the cream sauce and sprinkle with the remaining cheeses. Bake.

picadillo

"Best if made a day ahead and reheated"

1 medium onion, chopped
1 teaspoon oil
1 1/2 pounds ground beef
1 teaspoon salt
1 clove garlic, minced
1 to 2 teaspoons chili
  powder
1 (8-ounce) can tomato
  sauce
1/2 pound fresh mushrooms,
  sliced
1 (16-ounce) can whole
  tomatoes, undrained
2 Tablespoons vinegar
1 teaspoon sugar
1/2 teaspoon ground cumin
1 teaspoon cinnamon
1/2 cup raisins
Pinch ground cloves
1/2 cup sliced almonds

In a large, deep skillet or in an electric skillet, saute onion in the oil until soft; add beef and brown. Pour off grease and add the remaining ingredients except the almonds. Stir well, cover, and simmer for 1 1/2 hours. Stir in almonds just before serving.

Serving suggestion: **Serve in a chafing dish with corn chips as an hors d'oeuvre.**

Add 1 Tablespoon vinegar to the cold oil to reduce the cooking odor of deep frying.

savory souffle roll

Temperature: 400°
Baking time:
25 to 30 minutes

"Fantastic for an elegant brunch"

Butter or margarine
Flour
4 Tablespoons butter or
   margarine
1/2 cup flour
1/2 teaspoon salt
1/8 teaspoon white pepper
2 cups milk
5 eggs, separated

Grease, line with parchment paper, and grease again a 15x10x1-inch jelly roll pan. Dust lightly with flour. Melt 4 Tablespoons butter in a large skillet; blend in flour, salt, and pepper; stirring in milk gradually. Cook until thickened. Beat the yolks slightly. Add a little of the hot mixture while beating the egg yolks. Add yolks to the skillet and cook over medium heat for 1 minute, stirring constantly. Do not let it come to a boil. Cool to room temperature and stir. Beat egg whites until stiff and fold into the cooled mixture. Spread evenly in the prepared pan. Bake until puffed and golden brown. Meanwhile prepare the filling of your choice.

Seafood Filling

2 Tablespoons butter or margarine
4 shallots, finely chopped
3/4 cup chopped mushrooms
1 pound cooked shrimp, crabmeat, or lobster
2 Tablespoons fresh dill or 1 teaspoon dried dill
6 ounces cream cheese, softened
Salt and pepper

Melt butter in a medium skillet and saute shallots until tender. Add mushrooms and stir over medium heat for 3 minutes. Reserve part of the seafood for garnish and chop the rest. Add to the skillet with the dill. Stir in the cream cheese and season with salt and pepper.

Ham and Spinach Filling

2 Tablespoons butter or margarine
4 shallots, finely chopped
3/4 cup chopped mushrooms
1 (10-ounce) package frozen chopped spinach, cooked and drained
1 cup finely chopped ham
1 Tablespoon Dijon mustard
1/4 teaspoon nutmeg
6 ounces cream cheese, softened
Salt and pepper

Melt butter in a medium skillet and saute shallots until tender. Add mushrooms and stir for 3 minutes over medium heat. Add spinach, ham, mustard, and nutmeg. Stir in the cream cheese and season to taste with salt and pepper.

Once the souffle is baked, turn immediately onto a clean towel. Spread with either filling and roll up with the aid of the towel. Slide onto a platter, seam-side down, and serve.

Variation: **The fillings are also delicious served in puff pastry shells.**

Serving suggestion: **Serve with a fresh fruit salad and croissants.**

steeplechase casserole

Yield: 6 to 8 servings

Overnight chilling
Temperature: 350°
Baking time: 1 hour

"Perfect for a late night supper"

12 slices white bread, crusts removed
2 to 3 Tablespoons butter or margarine, softened
1/2 cup butter or margarine
1/2 pound fresh mushrooms, sliced
2 cups thinly sliced yellow onions
Salt and pepper
1 1/2 pounds mild bulk sausage
3/4 pound Cheddar cheese, shredded
5 eggs
2 1/2 cups milk
1 Tablespoon Dijon mustard
1 teaspoon dry mustard
1 teaspoon nutmeg
1 teaspoon salt
1/8 teaspoon pepper
2 Tablespoons finely chopped fresh parsley

Spread 1 side of each slice of bread with the softened butter and set aside. Melt 1/2 cup butter in a medium skillet and brown the mushrooms and onions over moderate heat for 5 minutes or until tender. Season to taste with salt and pepper, drain, and set aside. Cook the sausage in the same skillet or in the microwave; breaking it up into bite-size pieces. Drain well. In a greased 12x8x2-inch baking dish, layer half the bread (buttered side down), the mushroom mixture, the sausage, and the cheese. Repeat the layers. In a medium bowl, mix the eggs, milk, mustards, nutmeg, salt, and pepper. Pour this over the casserole, cover, and refrigerate overnight. Let stand at room temperature for 1 hour before baking. Sprinkle with parsley and bake uncovered until bubbly. Serve immediately.

Serving suggestion: **Serve with fresh fruit and *Sour Cream Coffee Cake*, page 352.**

zucchini lasagna

Temperature: 375°
Baking time: 40 minutes

"An economical delight"

1 ½ **pounds ground beef**
⅓ **cup chopped onion**
3 **(8-ounce) cans tomato**
  sauce
½ **teaspoon salt**
½ **teaspoon oregano**
¼ **teaspoon basil**
⅛ **teaspoon pepper**
4 **medium zucchini, peeled**
1 ½ **cups cottage cheese**
1 **egg**
2 **Tablespoons flour**
½ **pound mozzarella**
  cheese, shredded
Grated Parmesan cheese

In a large skillet, brown meat and onion over medium high heat. Pour off the fat and add the tomato sauce, salt, oregano, basil, and pepper. Heat to a boil, reduce the heat, and simmer for 5 minutes, stirring occasionally. Slice zucchini lengthwise into ¼-inch pieces. Combine cottage cheese and egg in a small bowl; mix well. In a 13x9x2-inch baking dish, place ½ the zucchini sprinkled with 1 Tablespoon flour. Top with the cottage cheese mixture and ½ the meat mixture. Repeat the zucchini layer and sprinkle with the remaining flour. Cover with the mozzarella cheese and add the remaining meat mixture. Sprinkle with grated Parmesan cheese and bake until hot and bubbly. Let stand for 10 minutes before serving.

Serving suggestion: Serve with *French Bread* page 335.

beef en gelee

Temperature: 350°
Baking time:
   40 to 50 minutes
   plus 6 hours chilling time

"An impressive party dish"

1 (5-pound) beef tenderloin
Salt and pepper
2 envelopes unflavored
  gelatin
3 cans beef consomme
1/2 cup dry white wine
2 cups sliced carrots,
  cooked but still crisp
2 cups sliced mushrooms
1 (6-ounce) jar marinated
  artichoke hearts,
  undrained
1 cup fresh cauliflower
  florets, cooked but still
  crisp
1 cup fresh broccoli
  florets, cooked but still
  crisp
1 cup Italian salad dressing,
  see index

The day before serving, season the beef with salt and pepper and bake in a glass 13x9x2-inch baking dish for 40 to 50 minutes. Cool and cut into very thin slices. In a small bowl, dissolve the gelatin in 1 can consomme; bring the rest of the consomme to a quick boil in a medium saucepan. Remove from heat; add the gelatin mixture and the white wine. Pour a thin layer of the gelatin into the bottom of a lightly oiled 15x10x1-inch jelly roll pan and chill until set. Place a layer of the sliced beef on top of the gelatin and arrange part of the carrots and mushrooms around each slice. Pour on another thin layer of the gelatin and chill until set. Repeat the process several times, saving 1/2 cup gelatin. Chill the layered meat for several hours. Combine the artichoke hearts, cauliflower, and broccoli and toss with dressing. Cover and chill. Chill the reserved gelatin in a 1-quart dish. When set, carefully remove the meat to a serving platter, using a long spatula. Garnish with chilled gelatin cut into cubes and the drained artichoke hearts, cauliflower, and broccoli.

barbecued beef

Yield: 10 to 12 servings

Temperature: 300°
Baking time: 5 hours

"Flexible cooking methods make this great for all schedules."

2 cups catsup
1/2 cup lemon juice
1/2 cup Worcestershire
   sauce
3 Tablespoons liquid smoke
2 cups water
2 teaspoons salt
1 (5 to 7-pound) beef
   brisket, fat removed

Combine the first 6 ingredients in a medium bowl for the sauce. Place brisket in a Dutch oven or a roaster and pour 2/3 of the sauce mixture over the meat. Cover and bake until tender. Discard the fat and shred or slice the meat. Return to the roaster and heat. When ready to serve, heat the reserved sauce and spoon over the meat.

Note: **Use a lower oven temperature and cook all day or cook in a crockpot on low all day or overnight.**

Serving suggestion: **Serve on warmed buns with *Slaw*, page 125.**

Tenderize a pot roast or stew meat by using hot tea as a cooking liquid.

beef stroganoff

"Chuck can be substituted for the tenderloin."

4 to 6 Tablespoons oil
**1 1/2 pounds sweet onions,
thinly sliced**
**1/2 pound fresh mushrooms,
sliced**
**1 (2-pound) beef tenderloin,
well trimmed and cut into
2-inch strips**
Salt and pepper
2 cups sour cream
1 Tablespoon Dijon mustard

Heat 2 Tablespoons oil in a large skillet; add the onion and mushroom slices. Stir and cook over medium high heat until soft and all the liquid has evaporated. Transfer onions and mushrooms to a bowl and keep warm. In the same skillet, heat 2 Tablespoons oil and add the beef strips in batches. Do not crowd them. Stir fry quickly until the meat is well browned. Transfer with a slotted spoon to the onion-mushroom mixture. Continue with the remaining meat, adding more oil if needed. Return onions, mushrooms, and meat to the skillet. Add salt and pepper to taste. Stir in the sour cream and mustard. Heat thoroughly, but do not boil. Serve immediately.

***Serving suggestion:* Serve over noodles, rice, or sauteed potatoes.**

boeuf de wellington

Temperature: 450°
Baking time: 10 minutes

"Your guests will think you cooked all day."

**4 beef fillets, 1-inch
thick
4 Tablespoons butter or
margarine
12 fresh mushrooms,
minced
1 cup water
1 beef bouillon cube
1 teaspoon Dijon mustard
Salt and pepper
4 frozen puff pastry shells,
thawed
1 egg white, slightly
beaten**

Sear the fillets in a large skillet in hot butter for 1 1/2 minutes per side. Remove from the pan and chill. Meanwhile, in a medium saucepan, cook the mushrooms in water with the bouillon cube for 15 minutes, covered, over medium high heat. Drain the mushrooms and mix with the mustard. Salt and pepper the fillets and spread with the mushroom-mustard mixture. Place the fillets on a cookie sheet and roll pastry shells out as thinly as possible and cover the tops and sides, but not the bottom, of each fillet with the pastry. Brush with beaten egg white and bake.

Note: **All but the final baking can be done ahead. Allow the meat to come to room temperature before baking.**

Variation: **A chicken liver pate can be substituted for the mushroom-mustard mixture.**

Serving suggestion: **Serve with *Bearnaise Sauce*, page 267, Boston lettuce with *Italian Dressing*, page 148, fresh broccoli, and cherry tomatoes sauteed in basil butter.**

brisket

"A real favorite for the whole family"

1 cup catsup
1 cup ginger ale
1 package onion soup mix
1 teaspoon spicy steak
   sauce
Salt and pepper
1 (2 1/2 to 3 pound) beef
   brisket
1/4 cup red wine

Combine the first 5 ingredients in a large Dutch oven. Add the brisket and turn to coat with the sauce. Bring to a slow boil over medium heat. Reduce heat to simmer and add wine. Cover and simmer for 2 hours. Add 1/4 cup water, if necessary, at the end of the cooking time if the sauce has been reduced too much.

steak diane

"A quick dish for 1 or more"

1/2 cup thinly sliced fresh
   mushrooms
2 1/2 Tablespoons butter or
   margarine
1 sirloin steak
1 Tablespoon cognac,
   heated
2 Tablespoons sherry

In a small skillet, saute mushrooms in 1 Tablespoon butter over low heat. Pound the meat with a mallet until 1/2-inch thick. Heat 1 1/2 Tablespoons butter in a chafing dish; add steak and cook very quickly, turning it once. Add cognac and flame. Add sherry and mushrooms; heat thoroughly. Place steak on a warmed platter and pour mushrooms and juices over it.

eye of round or tenderloin rib roast

Yield: 6 servings

Overnight chilling
Temperature: 500°
Baking time: 15 minutes,
**   2 hours**

"For very special occasions"

1 (3-pound) rolled rib
  roast or larger
Salt and pepper
1 cup red wine
1/2 cup butter or margarine,
  melted

Bring the roast to room temperature. Salt and pepper it heavily. Marinate in a mixture of the wine and butter overnight in a 2-quart glass or enamel pan, covered and refrigerated. Place meat on a roasting rack in the lower third of a preheated 500° oven. Bake for 5 minutes per pound. Turn off oven and *do not open the oven door.* Leave the roast in the oven for 2 hours or longer. If the meat is too rare, bake for 5 more minutes at 500° before serving.

Variation: **If using a tenderloin, make a foil tent over the meat so it won't be crusty on the outside. This will also prevent spattering in the oven. Remove the foil quickly when the oven is turned off, shut the door immediately, and do not reopen until ready to serve.**

Serving suggestion: **Serve with** *Cinderella's Golden Potato Casserole,* **page 208, and** *Easy Asparagus,* **page 189.**

marinated eye of round

Yield: 4 servings

Preparation time:
30 minutes
plus 4 hours chilling time

"A different grilled steak"

1/2 cup butter or margarine
Garlic salt
2 1/2 pounds eye of round
Freshly ground pepper
1/4 cup Worcestershire
   sauce
1/4 cup spicy steak sauce
3/4 cup bourbon
1 Tablespoon fresh lemon
   juice

Place meat in a large, deep skillet. Melt butter in a small skillet or in the microwave. Sprinkle garlic salt on the meat until it is white. Sprinkle with pepper until the top is black. Pour butter, Worcestershire sauce, and the steak sauce over the meat. Pour on bourbon to wash off the sauces and then cover with lemon juice. Boil on top of the stove until the alcohol is burned off, about 2 minutes after it reaches a boil. Remove from heat and marinate, covered, in the refrigerator for about 4 hours. Cook on the grill for 30 to 40 minutes, basting with the marinade.

Serving suggestion: Serve with *Mushroom Florentine*, page 202, and fresh fruit.

If reusing a marinade, strain it when you're through with it and refrigerate, but not for more than a day or two. Bring the marinade to a boil before reusing and cook for 3 to 4 minutes; cool to room temperature. Use it on the same kind of meat it was originally used for.

rib roast with artichoke sauce

Yield: 8 to 10 servings

Temperature: 300°
Baking time: 2 hours

"This sauce is delicious on anything at all."

1 (9-pound) standing rib roast
1/4 cup olive oil
2 Tablespoons ruby Port wine
2 teaspoons onion powder
1 teaspoon Italian herbs

Place meat in a roasting pan, rib side down to form a natural rack. Combine oil, 2 Tablespoons Port, onion powder, and herbs to form a paste. Rub the paste into the meat on all sides, being careful to cover fatty portions well. Bake for 2 hours for rare meat. Lift meat to a carving board and let rest while preparing the sauce.

Artichoke Sauce
Meat drippings
1 cup ruby Port
1 1/2 cups water
2 (9-ounce) packages frozen artichoke hearts
1 teaspoon salt
1 teaspoon Italian herbs
3 Tablespoons cornstarch

Remove the fat from the pan drippings; stir in 1 cup Port, 1 cup water, and the frozen artichoke hearts. Simmer until the artichokes are tender. Cut the artichokes into pieces. Add salt and herbs. Blend cornstarch with the remaining 1/2 cup water and slowly add this mixture to the pan. Cook, stirring constantly, until the mixture boils and thickens. Serve with the roast.

Note: **An alternate cooking method is to cook the roast 20 minutes per pound at 325° for medium rare or cook 5 minutes per pound at 500°. Turn off the oven and DO NOT open the oven door for 2 hours. With any method, always bring the roast to room temperature before beginning.**

shish kebob

**Preparation time:
20 minutes
plus overnight chilling**

"A summer favorite"

1 (2½-pound) sirloin
  or lamb, cubed
1 cup oil
½ cup soy sauce
¼ cup Worcestershire
  sauce
2 Tablespoons dry mustard
2 teaspoons salt
1 teaspoon pepper
¼ cup lemon juice
Garlic salt
1½ teaspoons dry parsley
Red and green peppers,
  cut into strips
Cherry tomatoes
Mushrooms
Small onions
Pineapple chunks

Marinate the sirloin or lamb in a mixture of oil, soy sauce, Worcestershire sauce, mustard, salt, pepper, lemon juice, garlic salt, and parsley in a 13x9x2-inch glass dish. Cover and refrigerate overnight. Place meat cubes on skewers alternating with peppers, tomatoes, mushrooms, onions, and pineapple. Cook on a grill or under the broiler.

Marinating meat in wine before cooking tenderizes the meat.

steak teriyaki

Preparation time:
20 minutes
plus 12 hours chilling
time

"So very easy"

1/4 cup soy sauce
3 Tablespoons honey
2 Tablespoons vinegar
1 1/2 teaspoons garlic
powder
1 1/2 teaspoons ground
ginger
3/4 cup oil
1 green onion, chopped
1 (1 1/2-pound) flank steak

In a medium bowl, mix soy sauce, honey, and vinegar; blend in the garlic powder and ginger. Add oil and onion and stir. Place meat in a 12x8x2-inch glass baking pan and cover with marinade. Refrigerate, covered, for at least 12 hours. Bring to room temperature before cooking on the grill. Baste with marinade while cooking, allowing 5 minutes per side for medium rare. Slice diagonally to serve.

***Serving suggestion:* Serve with *Zucchini and Spring Onions*, page 215.**

When grilling meat, count on 3/4 to 1 pound per serving for cuts with the bone in and 1/3 to 1/2 pound for boneless cuts.

barbecued lamb

"This is a nice change and wonderful as a leftover."

Barbecue Sauce
1/2 cup butter or margarine
1 onion, finely chopped
2 Tablespoons sugar
1/4 cup prepared mustard
1 Tablespoon
    Worcestershire sauce
2 Tablespoons soy sauce
1/4 cup lemon juice
1/4 cup catsup
Dash Tabasco sauce
Salt and pepper

1 leg or shoulder of
    lamb
Salt
Rosemary
1 clove garlic

In a medium saucepan, melt butter and saute onion. Stir in remaining sauce ingredients and heat thoroughly. Rub lamb with salt, rosemary, and garlic. Place in a roasting pan and cover with sauce. Bake for 30 minutes at 400°. Lower the heat to 300° and continue cooking, basting 2 or 3 times, until the meat is very tender, about 3 hours. Remove the meat from the pan and cool, reserving the sauce. Pull meat from the bone in chunks and discard any fat. The meat and the sauce may be refrigerated until ready to reheat and serve.

Serving suggestion: Serve with *Broccoli Salad*, page 113.

To retain moisture, salt after cooking is completed.

rack of lamb with dijon sauce

Yield: 6 to 8 servings

Temperature: 325°
Baking time: 3¹/2 hours

"Elegant enough for someone very special"

Salt and pepper
Rack of lamb

Dijon Sauce
4 Tablespoons Dijon
  mustard
¹/2 teaspoon salt
¹/4 teaspoon pepper
4 Tablespoons brown sugar
2 Tablespoons soy sauce
2 Tablespoons olive oil
¹/2 clove garlic, minced
¹/3 cup lemon juice

Salt and pepper the lamb and bake in a Dutch oven until a meat thermometer registers 160°. Combine all sauce ingredients in a small saucepan and heat. Baste the lamb with the sauce frequently.

Serving suggestion: Serve with boiled baby new potatoes sauteed in butter and parsley and fresh vegetables.

The size of the pot is essential. For roasting meats and vegetables, don't leave a wide space between the contents and the lid.

special saucy lamb

Temperature: 500°, 450°, 325°
Baking time:
15, 15 minutes,
2½ to 3 hours

"Makes a wonderful gravy"

1 leg of lamb
Salt and pepper

Sauce
¼ cup butter or margarine
¼ cup flour
¼ cup vinegar
1 clove garlic
2 cups water
1 Tablespoon
    Worcestershire sauce
1 Tablespoon salt
1 teaspoon sugar
¼ teaspoon red pepper

Gravy
2 Tablespoons flour
1 Tablespoon browning
    sauce
1 cup water

Score the lamb and season with salt and pepper. Place in an uncovered roasting pan, on a rack, in a 500° oven for 15 minutes. Lower the temperature to 450° and cook for 15 more minutes. In a medium saucepan, melt the butter and stir in ¼ cup flour until smooth. Slowly stir in vinegar; add the rest of the sauce ingredients and simmer for 5 minutes. Lower the oven temperature to 325° and baste the lamb with the sauce every 15 minutes for 2½ to 3 hours. Remove the lamb from the pan. Scrape the rack and the bottom of the pan and add 2 Tablespoons flour, the browning sauce, and the water, Heat thoroughly and serve with the lamb.

Serving suggestion: Serve with fluffy white rice and *Broccoli Puff*, page 194.

spring lamb stew

Preparation time:
2 1/2 hours

"Not the usual stew by any means"

3 Tablespoons butter or
   margarine
2 Tablespoons oil
4 pounds lamb shoulder,
   cut into 2-inch pieces
Salt and pepper
1/2 teaspoon thyme
1/2 teaspoon oregano
1 teaspoon chopped fresh
   parsley
4 Tablespoons flour
1 cup dry red wine
3 cups beef stock
2 large onions, chopped
2 Tablespoons butter or
   margarine
1 pound tomatoes, peeled,
   seeded, and chopped
2 cloves garlic, minced
1 Tablespoon sugar
Salt and pepper
1 bay leaf
1/2 pound fresh mushrooms
24 tiny new potatoes
24 small carrots, sliced
18 small white onions,
   peeled
1 (10-ounce) package frozen
   peas

Heat 3 Tablespoons butter and the oil in a large, heavy pot. Add meat a little at a time until it is all nicely browned. Add salt, pepper, thyme, oregano, and parsley. Sprinkle the meat with flour and stir over low heat for 10 minutes. Add the wine and beef stock and stir until smooth; set aside. In a medium skillet, saute onion in 2 Tablespoons butter until soft. Add the tomatoes, garlic, sugar, salt, and pepper. Simmer for 10 minutes and then add to the lamb with a bay leaf. Cover and simmer slowly for 1 1/2 hours. Pour into a colander set over a Dutch oven. Heat and reduce this liquid by 1/3, let cool, and skim off fat. Return lamb mixture from colander to the reduced sauce and add mushrooms, potatoes, carrots, onions, and peas. Simmer for 20 minutes and turn into a serving dish.

Note: Feel free to vary the vegetables according to your favorites and what is in season.

baked ham with plum garnish

Yield: 12 servings

Temperature: 350°
Baking time:
1 hour 10 minutes

"The ham may be marinated ahead of time."

1/2 a ham, boneless or
   semi-boneless, pre-cooked
Juice from 1 (17-ounce) can
   purple plums, reserving
   plums for garnish
1 cup brown sugar
1 teaspoon ground cloves
1/2 cup plum preserves
1/4 cup prepared mustard
8 to 12 large sprigs of
   parsley

Place ham in a large roasting pan, lined with enough foil to cover the ham. Pierce the ham all over with an ice pick. Mix plum juice, 1/2 cup brown sugar, and cloves. Pour over ham. Pull up foil, seal, and bake for 30 minutes. Open the foil and pour the marinade into a saucepan. Skim off the fat and add 1/2 cup brown sugar; boil until syrupy. Pour thickened marinade over ham and bake, uncovered, for 30 more minutes, basting frequently. Mix preserves and mustard together and spread over the ham. Bake for 10 minutes until the glaze is set. Serve on a platter garnished with the plums and parsley.

Serving suggestion: Serve with Zucchini Souffle, page 215.

crown pork roast

Yield: 10 servings

Temperature: 325°
Baking time: 3 hours

"An elegant entree without a lot of work"

**18 to 21 ribs, crown
  of pork**
1 cup apple cider

Stuffing
1 1/2 cups chopped celery
1 1/2 cups sliced mushrooms
1 cup butter or margarine
1 cup hot water
**1 (8-ounce) package herb
  stuffing**
1/2 cup chopped pecans
1/2 cup chopped onion
**2 apples, unpeeled, cored,
  and coarsely chopped**
**1 (2-ounce) jar sliced
  pimentos, drained**
1/2 cup chopped parsley
1/2 cup raisins
**1 (6-ounce) package long
  grain and wild rice,
  cooked**

Preheat oven to 325°. Place the crown, bones up, in a shallow roasting pan. Cook for 2 1/2 hours, basting occasionally with the cider. For stuffing, saute celery and mushrooms in butter for 2 to 3 minutes, in a small saucepan. In a large bowl, add water to herb stuffing; mix in all the other ingredients, adding the rice last. Stuff the center of the crown roast and bake for another 1/2 hour. If more fruit is desired, add 1/2 cup each chopped apricots and/or prunes.

Note: Remember to cover the tips of the roast and the stuffing with foil while baking to prevent drying and burning.

stuffed pork loin

Temperature: 350°
Baking time: 1 1/2 hours

"A classic enjoyed by all"

**4 1/2 to 5 pounds boned loin
of pork, center cut**
12 medium pitted prunes
**2 large tart apples, peeled,
cored, and chopped**
1 teaspoon lemon juice
Salt
Freshly ground pepper
**3 Tablespoons butter or
margarine**
3 Tablespoons oil
3/4 cup dry white wine
3/4 cup heavy cream
**1/3 to 1/2 cup red currant
jelly**

Ask the butcher to make a
pocket in the pork by cutting a
slit down the length of the loin
on the inside and to cover the
loin with netting. Place prunes
in a saucepan of cold water;
bring to a boil. Drain. Sprinkle
apples with lemon juice. Season
the prunes and apples with salt
and pepper. Alternating from
one end of the loin to the other,
stuff with apples and prunes. Fill
as firmly as possible. Sew up
both ends with heavy string. In a
Dutch oven, melt butter and oil
over medium heat. When the
foam subsides, add the loin,
turning to brown on all sides,
about 20 minutes. Remove the
meat from the pan and skim off
fat. Pour in wine and cream;
whisk, return meat to the pan,
and simmer for 5 minutes.
Cover and bake in a 350° oven
until the meat shows no
resistance when pierced with a
knife tip. Remove loin to a
heated platter. Skim fat from the
pan and bring the liquid to a
boil. When reduced to about 1 1/2
cups, add jelly. Reduce heat and
stir until the sauce is smooth.
Season, if necessary. Pour into a
heated gravy boat. Cut the string
from the pork and slice into
1-inch pieces.

roast pork with sage

Yield: 6 servings

Temperature: 350°
Baking time: 1 1/2 hours

"An unusually tangy flavor"

4 Tablespoons butter or
  margarine
2 1/2 pounds boneless
  pork roast
2 teaspoons fresh sage or
  1/2 teaspoon dried sage
4 Tablespoons sugar
6 Tablespoons red wine
  vinegar
3/4 cup chicken stock
1/3 cup fresh orange juice

At least 2 hours before serving time, melt butter in a Dutch oven over medium heat. Brown the roast on all sides. Remove the pan from the heat and add sage, sugar, vinegar, and chicken stock. Bake, uncovered, for 1 hour and 20 minutes or until a meat thermometer indicates the pork is done. Add the orange juice, basting the roast well, and return the roast to the oven for 10 more minutes. Degrease the pan juices and serve as gravy.

Serving suggestion: Serve with *Carrots and Onions with Madeira,* page 196.

Commercial stocks are usually saltier than the homemade kinds; dilute with beer, wine, or tomato juice.

barbecued spareribs

Preparation time: 2 hours plus 24 hours chilling time

"Good and juicy"

8 pounds spareribs, cut into serving pieces
3 cups beer
2 teaspoons chili powder
1 cup honey
2 teaspoons sage
1 1/2 teaspoons dry mustard
1 Tablespoon salt
2 Tablespoons lemon juice

Place ribs in a 13x9x2-inch baking dish. Mix remaining ingredients and pour over the ribs. Refrigerate for 24 hours, turning several times. Remove the ribs, reserving the sauce. Weave spareribs onto long skewers and place flat on the rack of a hot charcoal grill or broiler 4 inches from the heat. Cook, turning frequently, and brushing with the sauce, until browned. This usually takes 1 1/4 hours. Spareribs can be baked in a 300° oven for 1 1/2 hours.

***Serving suggestion:* Serve with *Marinated Onions,* page 121.**

Place breaded pork chops in the refrigerator for at least 30 minutes before baking.

pork chops in wine

Preparation time: 2 hours

"An inexpensive treat for company"

Salt and pepper
4 center cut pork chops,
**　1-inch thick**
Flour
3 Tablespoons butter or
**　margarine**
1 Tablespoon olive oil
2 Tablespoons minced green
**　onions**
1 cup dry white wine
1 cup water
1 Tablespoon minced fresh
**　parsley**

Salt and pepper the pork chops; lightly dredge in flour. Heat butter and oil in a heavy iron skillet and brown pork chops on both sides. Add onions, wine, and water. Lower the heat and simmer for 1 1/2 hours or until tender. Remove to a heated platter and sprinkle with parsley.

Serving suggestion: Serve with Spinach Elegant, page 209.

caper sauce

Yield: 1 1/2 cups

Preparation time:
**　10 minutes**

"Delightful with pork chops"

2 Tablespoons pork pan
**　drippings, butter, or**
**　margarine**
1/3 cup chopped onion
1 clove garlic, minced
2 Tablespoons chopped
**　green tops of scallions**
1/2 cup dry white wine
1 Tablespoon tomato paste
1 Tablespoon Dijon mustard
1/2 cup beef stock
4 to 6 Tablespoons capers

In a medium skillet, heat drippings; add onion, garlic, and scallions and saute for 1 to 2 minutes. Add wine and boil until reduced to 2 Tablespoons. Add tomato paste, mustard, and beef stock. Simmer for 2 minutes. Add capers and spoon over meat.

stuffed pork chops   Yield: 6 servings

Temperature: 350°
**Baking time: 1 hour and
5 minutes**

"Looks so much harder than it really is"

**6 pork chops, 1-inch
thick**
1/4 cup flour
Salt and pepper
**2 Tablespoons butter or
margarine**
**1 cup white wine or apple
cider**

Cut a pocket in each pork chop
for the stuffing. Fill pockets with
the stuffing of your choice. Salt
and pepper the pork chops. Roll
in flour and brown in butter in a
large skillet. Remove to a
13x9x2-inch baking dish. Add
wine to the skillet and stir until
smooth. Pour wine into the
baking dish with the pork chops.
Cover and bake for 45 minutes.
Remove the cover and bake for
20 minutes more. Remove the
pork chops to a serving platter.

Note: **The pan juices may be reduced and thickened with flour
and used as gravy.**

pork chop
stuffings

"Use your favorite to stuff pork chops or anything else."

Spinach Stuffing
**1 (10-ounce) package frozen
chopped spinach, thawed
and drained**
1/2 cup chopped onion
3/4 cup chopped mushrooms
1/2 teaspoon salt
1/4 teaspoon nutmeg
1/8 teaspoon pepper

Combine spinach stuffing
ingredients and put inside the
pork chops. Secure the openings
with toothpicks.

Bleu Cheese Stuffing

3 Tablespoons butter or
   margarine
1 Tablespoon chopped onion
1/4 cup chopped celery
1/2 cup crumbled bleu cheese
3/4 cup bread crumbs
1/8 teaspoon sage

In a small skillet, melt the butter; saute onion and celery until tender. Remove from the heat and stir in cheese, crumbs, and sage. Stuff mixture into the pork chops and secure with toothpicks. Spoon any remaining mixture on top of chops in the baking dish.

Cheese and Fruit Stuffing

1/2 cup shredded sharp
   Cheddar cheese
1/2 cup chopped apple
2 Tablespoons raisins
2 Tablespoons orange juice
1/4 teaspoon salt
1/8 teaspoon cinnamon
Melted butter
Orange marmalade

Combine the first 6 ingredients. Stuff in the pork chop pockets and secure. Glaze the pork chops with melted butter and marmalade during the last 10 minutes of baking.

Dressing Stuffing

1/2 cup finely chopped
   onion
1/2 cup finely chopped
   celery
1/4 cup butter or margarine
4 slices of bread, cubed
2 Tablespoons chopped
   parsley
1/2 cup dark raisins
1 teaspoon dried marjoram

In a small skillet, saute onion and celery in butter until the onion is golden. Stir in bread cubes. Remove from heat and add the remaining ingredients. Fill pockets and secure.

When breading meats, add a small amount of oil to the egg. This will seal the meat.

veal scallops vermouth

**Preparation time:
20 minutes**

"What could be better for your very favorite friends?"

2 pounds veal scallops
Flour
Salt and pepper
Oil
6 Tablespoons butter or
margarine
1/2 cup vermouth
1/3 cup lemon juice
1/2 to 1 pound mushrooms,
thickly sliced
1 (15-ounce) can artichoke
hearts, sliced

Cut scallops into small pieces (3 or 4 inches square). Dredge in flour, salt, and pepper. Heat enough oil to cover the bottom of a large skillet and brown the scallops quickly on each side. Add more oil if necessary. When all the veal is browned, remove from the pan, drain, and keep warm. In the skillet, add butter, vermouth, and lemon juice. Using a wooden spoon, scrape the bottom of the pan and stir the sauce well. Add the veal, mushrooms, artichokes, and reheat briefly before serving.

Serving suggestion: Serve with ***Poppy Seed Onions***, page 209.

lemon veal

Yield: 4 servings

**Preparation time:
5 minutes**

"An excellent low-calorie entree"

1 pound veal cutlets
Salt and pepper
1/4 cup butter or margarine
1 Tablespoon fresh lemon
juice
Chopped parsley

Pound cutlets to tenderize. Salt and pepper both sides. Heat butter in a large skillet over high heat until bubbly; add lemon juice and veal. Fry for 1 1/2 minutes on each side. Sprinkle with chopped parsley and serve immediately.

scallopine with mushrooms and white wine

**Preparation time:
15 minutes**

"Truly a gourmet dish"

**2 pounds veal scallops
Salt and pepper
Paprika
Flour
7 Tablespoons butter or
margarine
3 shallots, finely chopped
1/4 pound fresh mushrooms,
sliced
2/3 cup white wine
1 Tablespoon chopped
parsley
1 teaspoon chopped
tarragon**

Season scallops with salt, pepper, and paprika and roll in flour. In a large skillet, saute veal quickly in 6 Tablespoons butter and remove to a warm platter. Add shallots to the pan and stir over medium high heat for 2 minutes. Add mushrooms and stir for 3 minutes. Add 1/3 cup wine and cook until reduced by half. Add parsley, tarragon, and the remaining wine. Bring to a boil, swirl in the remaining Tablespoon of butter, and pour over the veal.

For subtle flavor, add wine at the beginning of cooking. For a more pronounced flavor, add wine near the end of heating or just before serving.

veal smitane

Yield: 6 servings

Temperature: 300°
Baking time:
  25 to 35 minutes

"Elegant for a small dinner party"

6 (4-ounce) veal cutlets
Salted flour
2 Tablespoons butter,
  margarine, or olive oil
6 shallots, finely chopped
2 Tablespoons butter or
  margarine
2 cups dry white wine
1 pound fresh mushrooms,
  quartered
1 Tablespoon butter or
  margarine
1 Tablespoon fresh lemon
  juice
1 cup sour cream

Coat cutlets lightly with salted flour. In a large skillet, cook veal in 2 Tablespoons butter or olive oil until both sides are golden brown. Place in a 13x9x2-inch baking dish and set aside. In the same skillet, saute the shallots in 2 Tablespoons butter until transparent over medium high heat. Add wine and scrape pan with a wooden spoon to loosen all the particles sticking to the bottom. Heat until the wine is reduced by 1/3 and pour this mixture over the cutlets. Cover and bake for 20 to 30 minutes. Saute mushrooms in 1 Tablespoon butter and lemon juice in the same skillet used before. Add to the cutlets and return to the oven for 5 more minutes. This can be made ahead up to this point and kept warm. At serving time; strain the sauce, add sour cream, reheat, and serve over cutlets.

***Serving suggestion:* Serve with *Asparagus-Artichoke Casserole*, page 189.**

Marinate veal in lemon juice for 1/2 hour to tenderize.

golden gravy

**Preparation time:
5 minutes**

"Great served with fillets or meatballs"

½ cup butter or margarine
**1 teaspoon instant beef
bouillon**
**2 Tablespoons fresh lemon
juice**
**3 or 4 dashes
Worcestershire sauce**
Chopped chives

Melt butter in a small pan. Add bouillon, lemon juice, Worcestershire sauce, and chopped chives to taste. Heat until the bouillon has dissolved.

shallot cream sauce

Yield: 4 servings

**Preparation time:
15 minutes**

"A must for all steak lovers"

**2 to 3 Tablespoons butter
or margarine**
**2 Tablespoons minced
shallots**
½ cup strong beef broth
½ cup brandy
½ cup heavy cream
Salt
Freshly ground pepper

Melt butter in a medium skillet. Add the shallots and sauté for 1 minute. Add the broth and brandy. Cook over high heat until reduced by half. Lower the heat, add the cream, and stir until the sauce thickens. Season to taste with salt and pepper. Serve immediately.

Note: **It's best if made in the same pan used for the steaks so that the brown bits in the bottom of the pan can be stirred into the sauce.**

orange mayonnaise

Yield: 1 cup

**Preparation time:
1 minute**

"Excellent with ham, turkey, or chicken"

1/2 cup mayonnaise
1/2 cup orange marmalade

Mix and enjoy.

Note: **Vary the sweetness with the amount of marmalade added.**

raisin sauce for ham

Yield: 3 1/2 cups

**Preparation time:
10 minutes**

"Spices up any type of ham"

1 cup sugar
1/2 cup water
1 cup raisins
2 Tablespoons butter or margarine
3 Tablespoons vinegar
1/2 Tablespoon Worcestershire sauce
1/2 teaspoon salt
1/8 teaspoon pepper
1/4 teaspoon ground cloves
1 (8-ounce) jar currant jelly

Heat sugar and water for 5 minutes in a medium saucepan over moderate heat. Let the mixture come to a boil and add the remaining ingredients. Stir until the jelly dissolves.

330

breads

breads

Bundt Bread. 333
Cheese French Bread. 334
Cinnamon-Raisin Bread 338
Coffee Can Bread. 339
Corn Bread 356
Danish Cheese Bread. 336
Easy Loaf Bread 340
French Bread. 335
Granola Bread 340
Honey-Whole Wheat
    Bread. 341
Onion Bread. 337
Plain White Bread. 343
Rye Bread 344
Whole Wheat Bread 342

Rolls
Beer Rolls 345
Czechoslovakian Kolaches. . . 346
Graham Rolls. 348
Ice Box Potato Rolls 345
Refrigerated Rolls-Sweet
    Rolls. 349

Biscuits
Easy Yeast Biscuits. 347

Muffins
Easy Schnecker Muffins 350
Whole Wheat Muffins 342

Coffee Cakes
Almond-Apricot Coffee
    Cake. 351
Sour Cream Coffee Cake 352
Spicy Marble Coffee
    Cake. 353

Basic Crepes. 354
Buttermilk Waffles 355
Lightest-Ever French
    Toast 351
Overnight Pancakes. 355
Popovers. 356

Tea Breads
Applesauce Bread. 359
Banana-Nut Bread 357
Date-Nut Bread 358
Lemon Bread. 358
Orange Tea Bread 360
Pumpkin Bread. 357
Strawberry Bread. 359
Zucchini Bread 360

bundt bread

Yield: 2 loaves

Temperature: 350°
Baking time:
   30 to 35 minutes

"This makes a beautiful loaf that easily pulls apart."

3/4 cup sugar
1 1/2 teaspoons salt
1 cup shortening
1 cup boiling water
1 cup warm water
1 Tablespoon sugar
2 packages yeast
6 cups flour
2 eggs, well beaten
1/2 cup butter or margarine

Cream together first 4 ingredients and let cool. Mix together the next 3 ingredients and set aside. When the sugar, salt, shortening, and water mixture cools, add 2 cups of the flour and the eggs. Stir well and add the yeast mixture. Gradually add the other 4 cups of flour and stir well. Cover and allow to rise 45 minutes. Punch down. At this point the dough may be refrigerated (well covered, 1 or 2 days). For each loaf, butter a bundt pan. Melt 1/4 cup butter. Take 1/2 dough and roll out on a floured board to a 1/4-inch to a 1/2-inch thick circle. Cut into biscuits with a biscuit cutter. Dip each biscuit in melted butter and stand up in pan (very close) making a full circle. Cover and let rise 3 1/2 to 4 hours. Bake.

Place a small dish of warm water in the oven while bread is baking to keep crust from getting too hard.

cheese french bread

Yield: 1 loaf

Temperature: 400°
Baking time: 30 minutes

"This adds a different twist to French bread."

1 package yeast
1 teaspoon sugar
1 cup warm water
2 cups flour
1/2 cup cake flour
1 teaspoon salt
1 1/2 ounces Jarlsberg or
  Swiss cheese, shredded
1 egg
1/2 teaspoon salt

Dissolve yeast and sugar in water. Combine flour and 1 teaspoon salt. Place 2 cups of flour mixture in workbowl of food processor. Add 1/2 of liquid and turn machine on and off 4 times. Add the remaining flour except for 1/4 cup, the cheese, and the remaining liquid. Turn on and off 4 times and then process until ball is formed. If mixture is too sticky, add remaining flour. Knead dough by running machine for 40 seconds. Place dough in a greased bowl, turning to grease top. Cover and let rise until doubled, at least 1 hour. Roll out to desired length, roll up tightly starting with long side. Pinch seams together. Place seam side down on a greased cookie sheet. Cover, let rise until doubled, at least 1 hour. Make diagonal slashes across loaf. Mix egg and 1/2 teaspoon salt for glaze. Brush over top and sides. Bake.

If bread bakes unevenly you could be using old dark pans; you might have too much dough in the pan; you may be crowding the oven shelf; or your temperature may be too high.

french bread

Yield: 2 loaves

Temperature: 400°, 350°
Baking time:
  15, 30 minutes

"Terrific"

1 package yeast
1/4 cup warm water
1 cup water
1/2 cup milk
2 teaspoons salt
1 Tablespoon sugar
1 Tablespoon shortening
5 cups (about) flour
1 egg white

Add yeast to warm water and set aside. Heat, but do not boil, water and milk. Add salt, sugar, and shortening and stir together. Sift 4 cups flour, add all liquids, and stir until well blended. Turn out onto floured board and knead in about 1/2 to 1 cup flour to make firm dough. Place in bowl, covered, in a warm place and let dough rise until doubled. Punch down, knead for a few minutes and shape into 2 long French loaves. Slash tops with sharp knife and let rise again. Bake in 400° oven for 15 minutes and then at 350° for 30 minutes or until done. Brush the tops of the loaves with egg white about 5 minutes before removing from the oven.

Note: Wrap in foil and freeze as soon as bread cools. To reheat, place frozen bread in foil in a preheated 350° oven for 15 minutes.

danish cheese bread

Yield: 2 loaves

Temperature: 375°
Baking time:
   30 to 35 minutes

"A Nordic treat"

2 cups milk
2 Tablespoons sugar
1 Tablespoon salt
2 Tablespoons butter or
   margarine
1/2 cup warm water
2 packages yeast
5 cups flour
2 cups rolled oats
3 cups (3/4 pound) shredded
   Danish cheese (Tybo,
   Samsoe, Fontina, or
   Creamy Havarti)
1 egg white
2 teaspoons poppy seeds

Scald milk; stir in sugar, salt, and butter. Cool to lukewarm. Pour warm water into large mixing bowl. Sprinkle in yeast; stir until dissolved. Add milk mixture, then flour and oats; mixing well with beater or wooden spoon. Turn out onto floured board; knead until smooth and elastic, about 10 minutes. Place in a greased bowl, turning dough to grease top. Cover with a damp towel and allow to rise in a warm place until doubled in bulk (about 45 to 60 minutes). Punch down, cover, and let rest 10 minutes. Divide dough in half; roll each piece to a rectangle twice the length of the pan (about 18 x 16 inches). Reserving 1/2 cup of the cheese for tops of loaves, arrange remaining cheese on dough, dividing evenly. Roll up dough, from short side, jelly roll fashion, sealing edge and ends. Place seam side down in 2 greased

(continued)

9x5x3-inch loaf pans. Cover and let rise in warm place until doubled in bulk, about 45 minutes. Brush gently with lightly beaten egg white. Sprinkle reserved cheese and poppy seeds on top. Bake in preheated oven until golden brown. For additional crustiness, remove loaves from pans. Return to oven rack for five minutes; cool on racks.

onion bread

Yield: 2 loaves

Temperature: 375°
Baking time: 40 minutes

"A unique bread that sent raves through the testing group"

4 to 4¹/2 cups flour
2 packages yeast
¹/3 cup non-fat dry milk
1¹/2 cups hot water
2 Tablespoons shortening
2 Tablespoons sugar
1 package dry onion
  soup mix
¹/3 cup grated Parmesan
  cheese
1 egg

In food processor, combine 2 cups flour and yeast. In a saucepan, heat milk, water, shortening, sugar, soup mix, and cheese. Pour into dry mixture and then add egg. Turn machine on and off until well blended (about 30 to 40 seconds). Add flour gradually until a soft ball forms that is smooth and elastic. Cover dough and let rest for 20 minutes. Divide dough into 2 parts and place into 9x5x3-inch loaf pans. Cover and let rise until doubled in size (about 45 minutes). Preheat oven to 375° and bake until crust has browned and loaves draw away from the sides.

cinnamon-raisin bread

Yield: 2 loaves

2 to 24 hours chilling time
Temperature: 375°
Baking time:
    30 to 40 minutes

"Excellent toasted with butter for breakfast"

3 to 4 cups white flour
2 packages yeast
1/2 cup sugar
1 1/2 teaspoons salt
1/2 cup butter or margarine,
    softened
1 1/2 cups warm water
2 eggs
2 cups whole wheat flour
1/2 cup brown sugar
2 teaspoons cinnamon
1/2 cup raisins (soaked in
    orange juice)
1/4 cup butter or margarine,
    softened

Combine 2 cups flour, yeast, sugar, and salt; stir to blend. Add 1/2 cup butter and water; beat with an electric mixer at medium speed for 2 minutes. Add eggs and 1 cup flour and beat at high speed for 1 minute. Gradually stir in whole wheat flour with wooden spoon, adding just enough flour to make a soft dough. If needed, add a little more white flour. Turn out onto a floured board. Knead 5 to 10 minutes until dough is smooth and elastic. Let rest 20 minutes covered with plastic wrap and towel. Now combine the brown sugar, cinnamon, and raisins. Punch down dough, divide in half, roll into 2 (5x10-inch) rectangles, and spread with 1/4 cup butter. Sprinkle raisin mixture over it, roll tightly, and place in 2 greased loaf pans. Refrigerate 2 to 24 hours, covered loosely with plastic wrap. Remove from refrigerator before preheating oven and bake.

coffee can bread

Yield: 2 loaves

Temperature: 350°
Baking time:
 45 to 50 minutes

"Makes great toast"

1 package yeast
1/2 cup warm water
1/8 teaspoon ginger
3 Tablespoons sugar
1 (13-ounce) can evaporated
 milk
1 teaspoon salt
2 Tablespoons oil
4 to 4 1/2 cups flour
Melted butter or margarine

Dissolve yeast in water in large bowl. Add ginger and 1 Tablespoon of the sugar. Let stand until bubbly, about 15 minutes. Add the rest of the sugar, milk, salt, and oil. Stir in 1 cup of the flour with a spoon; then add 1 cup of flour at a time using the electric mixer to beat mixture after each addition. When too stiff for mixer, add final flour and stir with a spoon. Dough should be too stiff to pour but too sticky to knead. Don't add too much flour. Grease the covers and insides of 2 (1-pound) coffee cans. Divide dough between them. Let dough rise in warm place until tops pop off, 45 to 60 minutes. Bake. Brush tops with melted butter and slip from cans to cool.

Note: **To warm, roll in foil and heat 20 minutes in warm oven.**

When greasing pans avoid using butter or margarine. Their salt and water cause sticking.

easy loaf bread

Yield: 1 loaf

Temperature: 350°
Baking time: 30 minutes

"For a yeast bread it is almost a 'quickie'."

1 package yeast
1/4 cup warm water
2 1/3 cups self-rising flour
1 cup sour cream
2 Tablespoons sugar
1 egg
2 teaspoons salt

Place yeast and water in large mixing bowl. Add 1 1/3 cups flour, sour cream, sugar, egg, and salt. Blend at low speed with mixer, add remaining flour, and turn to high speed. Pour into greased 9x5x3-inch loaf pan and let rise for about an hour. Bake.

granola bread

Yield: 2 loaves

Temperature: 350°
Baking time:
   30 to 35 minutes

"Fun for children to eat"

1 1/2 cups warm water
2 packages yeast
2 Tablespoons oil
1 to 2 Tablespoons honey
1 1/2 teaspoons salt
3 1/2 cups flour
1 1/2 cups granola cereal
Nuts and raisins, optional

Warm a large mixing bowl by rinsing it with hot water. Add warm water to bowl, sprinkle it with yeast, and allow mixture to stand a few minutes. Stir until yeast is dissolved. Add oil, honey, and salt and stir well. Add the flour, granola, and nuts or raisins, if desired. Mix thoroughly. Cover bowl with a towel and set in a warm place about 1/2 hour, or until doubled. Beat with a wooden spoon and put into 2 well greased 9x5x3-inch loaf pans. Let rise about 15 minutes; then bake. If top becomes too brown before done, cover lightly with foil. Cool; then wrap in foil until used.

Use non-white flours within 3-4 months. Store whole wheat, wheat germ, oatmeal, and soy in freezer.

honey-whole wheat bread

Yield: 2 loaves

Temperature: 375°
Baking time:
   40 to 50 minutes

"Can freeze and maintain freshness"

4 cups whole wheat flour
1/2 cup dry milk
2 teaspoons salt
2 packages yeast
2 teaspoons cinnamon
3 cups warm water
1/2 cup oil
1/2 cup honey
4 to 4 1/2 cups unbleached
   flour

Combine whole wheat flour, milk, salt, yeast, cinnamon, warm water, oil, and honey. Blend at low speed of mixer for 1 to 2 minutes; then medium speed for 2 minutes. By hand stir in unbleached flour, knead dough for 5 minutes on floured surface. Place dough in a greased bowl and cover with a damp towel. Let rise until doubled in bulk (40 to 60 minutes). Punch dough down and divide in half. Place each half in 9x5x3-inch loaf pans. Cover and let rise until doubled (30 to 40 minutes). Bake until the loaves sound hollow when thumped. Remove and cool on a rack.

whole wheat bread

Yield: 3 loaves

Temperature: 350°
Baking time: 1 hour

"Good and light"

2 packages yeast
1/2 cup warm water
2 cups milk
1/4 cup shortening
1/2 cup honey
2 teaspoons salt
4 cups whole wheat flour
4 cups unbleached white
  flour

In a large bowl, dissolve yeast in warm water. Heat milk and dissolve shortening, honey, and salt in it. When blended, put in a large bowl with yeast and add whole wheat flour and about 3 cups white flour. Mix well; then knead on floured board until dough becomes elastic, adding rest of flour as needed. Let rise in warm place until doubled. Punch down, form into 3 loaves, and let rise until doubled again. Bake in 9x5x3-inch greased pans. Cool on racks.

whole wheat muffins

Yield: 6 muffins

Temperature: 375°
Baking time:
  20 to 25 minutes

"Good sweet muffin"

2 cups whole wheat flour
1/4 cup sugar
1 teaspoon salt
3 teaspoons baking powder
1 cup milk
1 egg
3 Tablespoons butter or
  margarine, melted

Mix dry ingredients. Add milk, beaten egg, and melted butter. Beat well. Pour into greased muffin tins. Bake.

342

When making dough, wash hands, boards, and bowls with cold water. This will prevent sticking.

plain white bread

Yield: 3 to 4 loaves

Temperature: 425°
Baking time:
  25 to 30 minutes

"Nice basic loaf"

1 cup milk
1 cup water
3 Tablespoons shortening
1 Tablespoon salt
2 packages yeast
3 Tablespoons sugar
1 cup warm water
8 cups (about) sifted flour

Scald milk and water; pour over shortening and salt. Cool to lukewarm. In a separate bowl, dissolve yeast and sugar in warm, not hot, water. Add to milk mixture. Add 4 cups flour, mixing with a wooden spoon; then add remaining flour to make a stiff dough. Cover and let rise until doubled, about 1½ hours. Turn onto floured board and knead until smooth and elastic. Divide into 3 portions and shape to fit greased 9x5x3-inch loaf pans. Let rise until doubled. Bake for 25 or 30 minutes for large loaves, 15 to 20 minutes for small ones.

rye bread

"A good light rye bread"

1 package yeast
1/4 cup warm water
2 cups scalded milk
2 Tablespoons butter
or margarine
2 teaspoons salt
2 Tablespoons sugar
2 cups rye flour
4 cups white flour
1 Tablespoon caraway seeds
1 egg white
1 Tablespoon water

Put yeast in small bowl and dissolve in warm water. Pour scalded milk into large mixing bowl; add butter, salt, and sugar and stir to melt and dissolve. Let milk cool to lukewarm. Add dissolved yeast to milk. Stir in rye flour and enough regular flour to make a soft but not sticky dough. Add caraway seeds. Knead dough on lightly-floured surface until smooth, about 5 minutes. Form into a ball. Place in a clean greased bowl. Grease top of dough. Cover with wet cloth and set in warm place until doubled, about 1 hour. Punch down dough; knead briefly and divide dough in half. Form into 2 loaf shapes and fit into 2 greased 9x5x3-inch loaf pans. Cover and let rise until doubled, approximately 45 minutes. Beat egg white and water together and brush over tops of loaves. Bake.

Before slicing fresh bread run serrated bread knife under hot water, dry, and then use swift motions forward and backward until sliced through.

beer rolls

Yield: 10 rolls

Temperature: 350°
Baking time: 25 minutes

"Children love to make these."

4 cups biscuit mix
3 Tablespoons sugar
1 (12-ounce) can beer

Mix together all ingredients and fill greased muffin tins ¾ full; bake.

ice box potato rolls

Yield: 2½ dozen rolls

Overnight chilling
Temperature: 350°
Baking time: 15 minutes

"Impossible to eat just one"

½ cup mashed potatoes,
  reserving 1 cup potato
  water
½ cup shortening
1 cup warm water
2 packages yeast
2 eggs, beaten
½ cup sugar
2 teaspoons salt
6½ cups flour
Melted butter or margarine

Combine heated potato water and shortening and let stand until shortening is melted. In another bowl, mix warm water and yeast. Add potatoes, shortening mixture, eggs, sugar, and salt; mix well. Add ½ of the flour and stir. Gradually add enough of the remaining flour to make a stiff dough. Cover with plastic wrap and refrigerate overnight. Dough can remain in refrigerator up to 5 days. Roll out dough on floured surface. Cut, dip in melted butter, and fold over. Arrange on cookie sheet and let rise in warm place for 2 hours. Bake until golden brown.

czechoslovakian kolaches

Yield: 75 to 80 rolls

Temperature: 375°
Baking time: 10 minutes

"A treasured recipe"

1/2 cup granulated sugar
2 packages yeast
1 cup lukewarm milk
1 cup butter or margarine, melted
3 eggs
1 teaspoon salt
4 cups flour
Melted butter or margarine
Oil

Topping
1/2 cup granulated sugar
1/3 cup flour
4 Tablespoons butter or margarine

continued

Mix 1 teaspoon of the sugar with yeast and dissolve in the milk. Blend the rest of the sugar and 1 cup melted butter in an electric mixer. Add the eggs and beat well. Add salt to the flour. Add the flour and the milk alternately to the bowl, beating well. Place dough in a greased bowl, cover, and let rise in a warm place until doubled in size. You may let the dough rise in the refrigerator overnight. Either in the morning or after the dough has doubled, make balls the size of a large walnut and place on greased baking sheets. The dough will be soft and sticky. Flatten slightly with a pastry brush dipped in melted butter and a little oil. Let rise. Make an indentation in the center of each kolache and fill with 1 teaspoon of your favorite filling. With a pastry blender, mix topping ingredients until crumbly. Sprinkle this mixture over each roll. Let rise again. Bake until light, golden brown.

**Melted butter or
   margarine
Powdered sugar**

When baked; brush with melted butter, top with sifted powdered sugar, and cool on the pans.

> *Note:* **Use your imagination - Almond - use canned filling
>   Apricot - cook dried apricots and sweeten to taste
>   Cherry - use cherry pie filling
>   Date - grind dates and walnuts
>   Prune - cook prunes, mash, and add sugar to taste
>   (add chopped walnuts too)
>   Strawberry - use strawberry jam**

easy yeast biscuits

Yield: 3 dozen biscuits

**Overnight chilling
Temperature: 450°
Baking time: 10 minutes**

"This is a cross between a biscuit and a roll."

**1 package yeast
1/4 cup lukewarm water
4 cups flour
1 teaspoon baking soda
1 teaspoon salt
2 teaspoons baking powder
2 Tablespoons sugar
2 cups buttermilk
1 teaspoon light cream
1 cup shortening, melted
Melted butter or margarine**

Dissolve yeast in lukewarm water. Add sifted dry ingredients to the buttermilk, cream, and melted shortening. Then add yeast mixture and stir well. Let stand for 45 minutes. Cover and place in refrigerator for several hours or overnight. About 45 minutes to 1 hour before baking, roll out dough on floured surface and cut biscuits about 1/4-inch thick. Place on ungreased cookie sheet, brush tops with melted butter, and let stand at room temperature. Bake until brown on top.

graham rolls

Temperature: 350°
Baking time: 15 to 20 minutes

"Will melt in your mouth!"

2 packages yeast
1/2 cup warm water
2 eggs
1 Tablespoon salt
1 cup sugar
1 1/2 cups mashed potatoes
   (instant may be used)
1/2 cup milk
3 cups graham flour
   (whole wheat)
4 cups white flour
1 pinch baking powder
1 cup butter, margarine,
   or lard
1/2 cup butter or margarine,
   melted

Have all ingredients at room temperature. Dissolve yeast in warm water. In a food processor or a large bowl with an electric mixer, beat eggs. Add salt, sugar, and mashed potatoes. Add milk to yeast mixture to make 1 full cup; add to mashed potato mixture. Slowly add 2 cups graham flour and 1 cup white flour, mixing well. Add baking powder. Turn dough out on a lightly floured board. Work butter through dough with hands. Dry off hands; very slowly work the remaining white and graham flour into the dough. The dough needs to be firm, but not stiff; work more white flour into the dough if needed to make the desired consistency. Put dough in a bowl, cover and set in the refrigerator. Let rise 2 to 3 hours. Roll dough out on lightly floured board to 1/4 to 1/2-inch thick. Cut with a circular biscuit cutter and fold the circles in half. Place rolls on lightly greased baking sheets. Brush with melted butter and let rise for 1 hour at room temperature. Bake.

Note: **Make ahead and freeze! Bake for only 10 minutes if planning to freeze rolls. When planning to serve, thaw and finish baking at 325° until brown.**

refrigerated rolls-
sweet rolls

Yield: 2 1/2 dozen rolls

Overnight chilling
Temperature: 400° to 425°
Baking time:
7 to 10 minutes

"Absolutely divine and unfortunately irresistible"

2 cakes yeast
1 cup warm water
1 cup boiling water
1 cup shortening
2/3 to 1 cup granulated
  sugar
2 teaspoons salt
2 eggs, beaten
6 cups flour (unbleached)
Melted butter or margarine

Let yeast stand in warm water 5 minutes. Pour boiling water over shortening, sugar, and salt. Beat with a whisk and let cool. Add eggs. Stir dissolved yeast and water into the mixture. Add flour, 1 cup at a time, beating in the first 4 cups with whisk, then stirring in the remaining 2 cups. *Stir well* - cover. Refrigerate overnight. Roll out (not too thin). Cut. Dip in melted butter, fold, place in pan. Let rise 3 hours. Bake until light brown.

***Variation: Sweet rolls* - Roll dough into rectangle and brush with melted butter. Sprinkle generously with a mixture of cinnamon and sugar. Roll up like jelly roll and slice. Put in muffin tins sprayed well with pan coating or make a coffee cake by putting slices in a cake pan. Let rise 3 hours. Bake sweet rolls about 15 minutes at 350° to 375°. Bake coffee cakes 25 to 35 minutes at 350°. Cover with foil after 20 minutes to prevent burning.**

***Other fillings* - Add raisins to cinnamon rolls. Soak raisins in orange juice - drain on paper towels. Roll dough in rectangle, sprinkle with raisins - fold dough over, covering raisins, roll again.**

***Icing* - powdered sugar, water & lemon juice**
  powdered sugar, orange juice
  powdered sugar, sherry

easy schnecker muffins

Yield: 24 muffins

Temperature: 375°
Baking time:
  15 to 20 minutes

"A delightful breakfast treat"

4 Tablespoons butter
  or margarine
3/4 cup brown sugar
1 1/2 teaspoons light corn
  syrup
Pecan halves
2 cans crescent rolls
1 teaspoon cinnamon
1/2 cup raisins
1/2 cup pecans, finely
  chopped

Cream together butter, 1/4 cup brown sugar, and corn syrup. Coat miniature muffin tins heavily with this mixture. Place in each cup 1 pecan half. Roll crescent rolls into 2 rectangles (about 6x12 inches). Spread rectangles with mixture of: 1/2 cup brown sugar, cinnamon, raisins, and chopped pecans. Roll tightly as for jelly rolls, and seal seams. Slice each roll into 12 parts. Press into cups firmly. Let rise on top of stove until dough feels puffy (about 1 hour). Bake until golden brown. Turn upside down immediately.

Do not use a food processor when beating eggs as it makes them flat and do not use a food processor when making quick breads unless specifically told to do so as it makes the bread heavy.

lightest-ever french toast

"An easy and divine Saturday morning treat"

1 cup milk
6 eggs
1 Tablespoon vanilla
1/2 teaspoon cinnamon
1 teaspoon sugar
6 slices bread
2 Tablespoons butter or
   margarine

Beat together milk, eggs, vanilla, cinnamon, and sugar. Dip bread in mixture, soaking thoroughly. Fry in butter.

Note: Serve with melted butter and syrup.

almond-apricot coffee cake

Yield: 1 bundt pan cake

"Like the old "Sock-it-to-me" cake but better"

1 cup butter or margarine,
   softened
2 cups sugar
3 eggs
1 cup sour cream
1 teaspoon almond extract
2 cups flour
1 teaspoon baking powder
1/4 teaspoon salt
3/4 cup sliced almonds
1 (10-ounce) jar apricot
   preserves

Cream butter and sugar. Beat in eggs, one at a time. Fold in sour cream and almond extract. Sift together the flour, baking powder, and salt and fold into sour cream mixture. Place 1/2 the batter in a greased and floured bundt pan. Place 1/2 of the almonds over batter. Spoon 1/2 preserves over almonds. Spoon on rest of the batter. Add remaining preserves and top with remaining almonds. Bake. Cool on rack.

351

sour cream coffee cake

Yield: 2 cakes

Temperature: 350°
Baking time: 30 minutes

"This is our favorite of all coffee cakes."

1/2 cup butter or margarine
1 1/2 cups granulated sugar
2 eggs
1 cup sour cream
1 teaspoon vanilla
2 cups flour
1 teaspoon baking powder
1 teaspoon baking soda
1/2 cup brown sugar
1 teaspoon cinnamon
1 1/4 cups powdered sugar
3 Tablespoons milk
1/3 cup chopped nuts

Cream together butter and sugar with a mixer. Add eggs, sour cream, and vanilla. Combine flour, baking powder, and baking soda; add gradually to butter mixture. Put batter into 2 greased 8-inch round cake pans. Mix brown sugar and cinnamon together and sprinkle on top of batter. Bake. Remove from oven and cover with glaze of powdered sugar and milk. Then sprinkle with chopped nuts. Cool and remove from pans. If too sweet, eliminate powdered sugar and milk layer.

If making yeast bread that has to be refrigerated, rub the top with oil to prevent a hard crust from forming.

spicy marble coffee cake

Yield: 8 to 10 servings

Temperature: 350°
Baking time:
35 to 40 minutes

"A little different than the old standard coffee cake"

1/2 cup butter or margarine
3/4 cup sugar
1 egg
2 cups sifted flour
2 teaspoons baking powder
1/2 teaspoon salt
3/4 cup milk
1/2 teaspoon cinnamon
1/4 teaspoon nutmeg
1/8 teaspoon cloves
2 Tablespoons light
  molasses

Topping
1/2 cup brown sugar
1/4 cup chopped nuts
2 Tablespoons flour
1 teaspoon cinnamon
2 Tablespoons butter
  or margarine, melted

Cream together butter, sugar, and egg. Sift flour, baking powder, and salt. Add to creamed mixture alternately with milk. To half of the batter add cinnamon, nutmeg, cloves, and molasses. Spoon batters alternating into a greased 9x9-inch pan. Zigzag batter to create marble effect. Combine topping ingredients and sprinkle on top. Bake. Serve warm.

For a crunchy, nutty texture, replace about 1/2 cup of flour with 1/2 cup of cracked wheat.

If you need room temperature eggs for making dough, place them, in their shells, in a small bowl full of warm water.

basic crepes

Yield: 16 crepes

**Preparation time:
30 minutes
plus 3 hours chilling time**

"A good basic recipe to have on hand"

**1 cup cold milk
1 cup cold water
4 eggs
1 teaspoon salt
2 cups flour
4 Tablespoons butter or
   margarine, melted**

Blend all ingredients in blender and store in refrigerator for several hours. Heat a 6 to 7-inch crepe pan and grease with a bit of butter. Pour a scant 1/4 cup batter in pan and swirl until batter covers bottom of the pan. Cook until edges brown. Lift up to see if brown on bottom. Then turn with a spatula and cook until other side is lightly browned. Place crepe on plate and cover with piece of waxed paper. Re-grease pan and make the next crepe, stacking cooked crepes on top of each other with a piece of waxed paper in between.

Note: **Crepes may be frozen in airtight containers until ready to use. Thaw as many as needed and fill.**

buttermilk waffles

Yield: 8 to 10 waffles

**Preparation time:
10 minutes**

"Surprisingly light waffles"

2 cups self-rising flour
1 heaping teaspoon baking
powder
2 cups buttermilk (more if
batter is too thick)
1/2 cup oil
1 egg
1/2 teaspoon baking soda
1 Tablespoon water

Mix first 5 ingredients together until batter becomes smooth. At this point batter can be refrigerated until baking. Before baking, add baking soda, and water. Put waffle mixture into a pitcher for easier pouring onto the waffle iron.

Note: **Spray pan coating onto waffle iron before pouring batter each time to prevent sticking.**

overnight pancakes

Yield: 4 pancakes

**Preparation time:
Overnight plus
20 minutes**

"Very unusual and good"

1 slice bread
1 cup buttermilk
1 teaspoon baking soda
2 teaspoons sugar
1/2 teaspoon salt
1 teaspoon baking powder
1/2 cup flour
1 egg
2 Tablespoons butter or
margarine, melted

Soak bread in buttermilk overnight. Sift together soda, sugar, salt, baking powder, and flour. Add to milk mixture. Add egg and melted butter and beat. Cook on griddle.

Variation: **Fruits or nuts may be added.**

355

popovers

Yield: 10 popovers

Temperature: 400°, 350°
Baking time:
20, 10 minutes

"Can be filled with creamed chicken or eaten plain with butter and jelly"

2 eggs
1 cup flour
1/2 teaspoon salt
1 cup milk
1 Tablespoon butter or margarine, melted

Beat eggs slightly. Sift flour and salt and add alternating with milk to the eggs. Add butter and beat with egg beater until smooth and full of bubbles. Fill HOT greased muffin tins 1/2 full with batter. Bake 20 minutes at 400°. Lower heat to 350° and bake 10 minutes more, or until done.

corn bread

Yield: 1 (8-inch) round

Temperature: 400°
Baking time: 20 minutes

"Great to use for stuffing"

Bacon fat
1 egg, beaten
1 cup buttermilk
1 1/3 cups corn meal
1/2 teaspoon salt
1/2 teaspoon baking soda
1/2 teaspoon baking powder
2 Tablespoons bacon fat

Put enough bacon fat in a round 8-inch skillet to cover bottom. Heat skillet in oven until hot. Mix egg with buttermilk. Add corn meal, salt, soda, and baking powder. Mix well; add 2 Tablespoons bacon fat to mixture. Place in hot skillet and bake.

Variation: **A very good batter to use for corn sticks. Melt bacon fat in corn stick molds and bake for 10 minutes. Good and crunchy.**

banana-nut bread

Yield: 2 loaves

Temperature: 350°
Baking time: 1 hour

"This takes a little longer but is worth the effort."

²/₃ cup shortening
1 ¹/₂ cups sugar
2 eggs, separated
1 cup mashed bananas
1 ¹/₂ cups sifted flour
1 teaspoon baking soda
¹/₄ teaspoon salt
4 Tablespoons sour cream
¹/₂ teaspoon vanilla
¹/₂ cup nuts

Cream shortening and sugar.
Add beaten egg yolks and
bananas. Blend together flour,
soda, and salt. Add these slowly
to banana mixture. Add sour
cream, vanilla, and nuts. Fold in
beaten egg whites. Bake in 2
(8x4x3-inch) loaf pans.

pumpkin bread

Yield: 3 large loaves

Temperature: 350°
Baking time: 1 hour

"Brandelicious!"

3¹/₂ cups flour
1 teaspoon baking soda
1 teaspoon cinnamon
1 teaspoon nutmeg
1 teaspoon allspice
4 eggs
4 cups sugar
1 cup oil
1 (16-ounce) can pumpkin
²/₃ cup brandy
1 cup chopped dates
   (optional)
1 cup chopped nuts
   (optional)

Sift flour with soda and spices.
Set aside. Beat eggs well. Add
sugar gradually. Mix in oil, then
pumpkin. Blend flour mixture
and brandy alternately into egg
mixture. Fold in dates and nuts,
if desired. Bake in 3 greased
9x5x3-inch loaf pans.

Variation: **Bourbon may be used instead of brandy. However,
brandy is stronger and adds more flavor.**

lemon bread

Yield: 1 loaf

Temperature: 325°
Baking time: 1 hour

"An old time favorite that always brings comments."

1/2 cup butter or margarine
1 cup granulated sugar
2 eggs
1 1/2 cups flour
1 teaspoon baking powder
1/2 cup milk
4 teaspoons grated lemon
rind
4 Tablespoons fresh lemon
juice
1/2 cup powdered sugar

Cream together butter and sugar. Beat in eggs. Sift together flour and baking powder. Add this to the sugar mixture alternately with milk, mixing well. Add the grated rind and 2 Tablespoons fresh lemon juice. Bake in a greased 9x5x3-inch loaf pan. Remove and place on a rack. Pierce the top with a fork and pour a glaze of the remaining 2 Tablespoons lemon juice and the powdered sugar over the top of the cake. Let stand for a day wrapped in foil or plastic wrap.

Variation: Add 3/4 cup flaked coconut when the lemon juice is added.

date-nut bread

Yield: 1 loaf

Temperature: 300°
Baking time: 1 hour

"Once you've tried it, it will be your favorite."

1 cup boiling water
1 teaspoon baking soda
1 cup chopped dates
1 Tablespoon butter or
margarine
1 cup sugar
1 egg, beaten
1 3/4 cups flour
1 teaspoon vanilla
1 cup nuts, chopped

Mix boiling water and soda together. Add dates and let mixture soak while creaming butter and sugar together. Beat in egg and mix well. Add date mixture and blend well. Stir in flour, vanilla, and nuts, blending well. Place mixture in a well greased 9x5x3-inch loaf pan. Bake. Cool on rack.

applesauce bread

Yield: 1 loaf

Temperature: 350°
Baking time: 1 hour

"Deliciously different"

1 cup granulated sugar
1 cup applesauce
1/3 cup oil
2 eggs
3 teaspoons milk
2 cups sifted flour
1 teaspoon baking soda
1/2 teaspoon baking powder
1/2 teaspoon ground
   cinnamon
1/4 teaspoon salt
1/4 teaspoon ground nutmeg

Topping
1/4 cup brown sugar
1/4 teaspoon ground
   cinnamon

In a large mixing bowl, thoroughly combine sugar, applesauce, oil, eggs, and milk. Sift together flour, soda, baking powder, cinnamon, salt, and nutmeg. Add to applesauce mixture and beat until well combined. Pour batter into a well-greased and floured 9x5x3-inch loaf pan. For topping, combine brown sugar and cinnamon. Sprinkle evenly over batter. Bake. Remove from pan and cool on rack.

strawberry bread

Yield: 2 loaves

Temperature: 350°
Baking time: 1 hour

"Superbly delicious"

1 1/4 cups oil
3 cups flour
1 teaspoon baking soda
1 teaspoon salt
3 teaspoons cinnamon
2 cups sugar
3 beaten eggs
2 (10-ounce) packages
   frozen strawberries,
   thawed
1 cup chopped pecans

Mix all ingredients together and blend well. Stir in pecans, if desired. Pour mixture into 2 greased and floured 9x5x3-inch loaf pans and bake.

orange tea bread

Yield: 2 loaves

Temperature: 350°
Baking time: 50 minutes

"Blender's imperative--an all-time favorite"

3 cups sifted flour
4 teaspoons baking powder
3/4 teaspoon salt
1/3 cup soft shortening
1 egg
1/2 cup milk
1/4 cup orange juice
**1 medium unpeeled orange,
   diced**
1 cup sugar

Sift flour, baking powder, and salt into a mixing bowl. Place shortening, egg, milk, and orange juice in a blender. Add the unpeeled, diced orange, removing the large seeds. Add sugar. Cover and blend about 1 minute. Pour over the sifted mixture and mix until the mixture is moistened. Pour into 2 (8x4x3-inch) greased loaf pans and bake. Cool and let stand overnight before slicing.

zucchini bread

Yield: 2 loaves

Temperature: 325°
Baking time: 65 minutes

"A different tea bread"

3 cups flour
1 teaspoon salt
1 teaspoon cinnamon
1 teaspoon soda
1/4 teaspoon baking powder
1/4 teaspoon nutmeg
3 eggs
2 cups sugar
2 cups grated zucchini
1 cup oil
2 teaspoons vanilla
1 cup chopped nuts

Sift dry ingredients together; set aside. Mix all other ingredients except nuts. Add dry mixture and nuts. Put in 2 greased 9x5x3-inch loaf pans and bake.

cookies

candy

cookies and candy

Bar Cookies

Apricot Bars 363
Brownies Divine 363
Cheesecake Delights 365
Cheesy Cake Squares 364
Chess Cakes 364
Chewy Coconut Cookies . . 366
Lemon Squares 367
Linzer Bars 369
Oatmeal Bars
   Extraordinaires 368
Oatmeal Brownies 370

Drop Cookies

Fudge Drop Cookies 371
Ginger Snaps 371
Macaroons 372
Oatmeal Crispies 367

Rolled Cookies

Gingerbread Boys 373
Sugar Cookies 366

Special-Effect Cookies

Cigarettes Russes 375
Cream Cheese Cupcakes 376
Molasses Peppernuts 374
Rosettes 377
Spritz Delights 376
Tassies 378

Candy

Bon Bons 379
Caramels 380
Chocolate-Peanut
   Butter Balls 381
Microwave Fudge 379
Mother's Creamy Fudge 382
Peanut Butter Fudge 383
Southern Pralines 383
Toffee 384

apricot bars

Yield: 16 bars

Temperature: 350°
Baking time: 45 minutes

"Nutritious and delicious too"

Crust
1 cup flour
1/3 cup granulated sugar
1/2 cup butter or margarine,
  softened

Mix crust ingredients and press on bottom of 9-inch square pan. Bake for 20 minutes.

Filling
1 cup dried apricots
1 1/2 cups water
3 eggs
1 cup brown sugar
1/3 cup flour
1/2 teaspoon baking powder
1 teaspoon vanilla
Powdered sugar

Bring apricots and water to a boil. Reduce heat and cook for 15 minutes or until apricots can be mashed with a fork. Beat eggs and add brown sugar, beating again. Add flour, baking powder, vanilla, and drained apricots. Pour this on top of baked crust. Bake 25 minutes. Cool. Cut into bars and sprinkle with powdered sugar.

brownies divine

Yield: 32 squares

Temperature: 350°
Baking time: 40 minutes

"For thin people only"

4 eggs
2 cups sugar
1 cup butter or margarine
4 ounces unsweetened
  chocolate
1 cup flour, sifted
1 (6-ounce) package
  semi-sweet chocolate
  chips

Beat eggs and sugar until thick and light and the sugar is dissolved. Melt butter and chocolate. Cool slightly before adding to egg mixture. Stir in flour and chocolate chips. Spread into a greased 12x8x2-inch baking pan. Bake. Cut while still warm.

chess cakes

Yield: 24 squares

Temperature: 300°
Baking time: 45 minutes

"A real Nashville favorite"

1 (1-pound) box brown sugar
1 cup granulated sugar
1 cup butter or margarine,
  melted
4 eggs
2 cups flour
2 teaspoons baking powder
1/4 teaspoon salt
1 cup chopped pecans,
  optional

Powdered sugar

Stir together all ingredients.
Pour into a greased and floured
13x9x2-inch pan. Bake. Remove
from oven and sprinkle with
powdered sugar. Cool and cut
into squares.

cheesy cake squares

Yield: 36 bars

Temperature: 350°
Baking time: 35 minutes

"No need to tell anyone you used a cake mix!"

1 yellow cake mix
1 egg
1/2 cup melted butter or
  margarine
1 (8-ounce) package
  cream cheese
2 eggs
1 (1-pound) box powdered
  sugar

Combine cake mix, egg, and
melted butter. Press in bottom of
a greased 13x9x2-inch pan.
Blend cream cheese, eggs, and
powdered sugar. Drizzle over
bottom layer. Bake.

Variation: Use a variety of cake mixes to create a new treat
every time.

364

cheesecake delights

Yield: 16 bars

Temperature: 350°
Baking time: 40 minutes

"Great with after dinner coffee"

Crust
1/3 cup brown sugar
1 cup flour
1/2 cup chopped pecans
1/3 cup butter or margarine, melted

Mix brown sugar, flour, and pecans. Stir in melted butter. Reserve 1/3 cup of crumb mixture for topping. Pat remaining mixture into greased 8-inch square pan. Bake for 15 minutes.

Filling
1 (8-ounce) package cream cheese
1/4 cup sugar
1 egg
2 Tablespoons milk
1 Tablespoon lemon juice
1 teaspoon vanilla

Beat cream cheese and sugar until smooth. Add remaining ingredients and blend thoroughly. Pour over baked crust and top with reserved crumb mixture. Bake for 25 minutes more. Cool and cut into bars. Refrigerate, loosely covered.

Note: **These keep up to 3 days.**

A large egg is the safest size to use. Using extra large eggs usually means adding more flour; small eggs, a little less.

chewy coconut cookies

Yield: 16 bars

Temperature: 350°
Baking time: 35 minutes

"Coconutty and good"

Crust
1/2 cup butter or margarine
1/2 cup brown sugar
1 cup sifted flour

Cream butter and sugar. Stir in sifted flour. Press in bottom of a 13x9x2-inch pan and bake 10 minutes.

Topping
2 eggs
1 cup brown sugar
1 teaspoon vanilla
1 Tablespoon flour
1 teaspoon baking powder
1/2 teaspoon salt
1 cup flaked coconut

Beat eggs; add remaining ingredients. Spread on top of baked crust. Return to oven for 25 minutes or until top is golden brown. Cool, but cut while still warm.

Note: **A food processor or a blender makes this a snap.**

sugar cookies

Yield: 6 dozen

Temperature: 375°
Baking time: 10 minutes

"These are marvelous, plain or decorated."

1 cup butter or margarine
3/4 cup sugar
1 large egg
1 teaspoon salt
2 teaspoons vanilla
3 cups flour

Cream butter and sugar. Add remaining ingredients. Chill the dough. Roll out on a slightly-floured surface and cut into various shapes. Place cookies on greased cookie sheets and bake. Remove from oven when they start to brown slightly around the edges.

lemon squares

Yield: 36 bars

Temperature: 325°, 350°
Baking time:
15, 20 minutes

"The perfect dessert for every conceivable occasion"

Crust
2 cups flour
1 cup butter or margarine
1/2 cup powdered sugar

Blend crust ingredients well. Pat evenly on the bottom and slightly up the sides of a 13x9x2-inch pan. Bake at 325° for 15 minutes.

Filling
4 eggs
2 cups granulated sugar
1/2 teaspoon baking powder
4 Tablespoons flour
4 Tablespoons lemon juice
2 teaspoons grated lemon rind

Mix filling ingredients and pour over hot crust; bake in 350° oven for 20 minutes. Cool and cut into bars.

oatmeal crispies

Yield: 3 dozen cookies

Temperature: 350°
Baking time: 10 minutes

"Quite a treat"

3/4 cup granulated sugar
1/2 cup brown sugar
1/2 cup butter or margarine
1 egg
1/2 teaspoon vanilla
3/4 cup flour
1/2 teaspoon salt
1/2 teaspoon baking soda
1 1/2 cups quick oats
1/2 teaspoon cinnamon
1/4 cup granulated sugar

In a large bowl of an electric mixer, blend 1/2 cup granulated sugar, brown sugar, and butter. Add egg and vanilla and blend on high speed until mixture is white. Add flour, salt, baking soda and blend. Stir in oats. Shape lightly into walnut-sized balls and roll in cinnamon-sugar mixture. Bake.

Note: Take these out of the oven when they are still white in color. Don't let them bake too long.

oatmeal bars
extraordinaires

Yield: 60 bars

Temperature: 350°
Baking time: 30 minutes

"This will be one of your favorites."

1 cup butter or margarine **1 cup brown sugar** **1 cup granulated sugar** **2 eggs** **1 teaspoon vanilla** **1 1/2 cups flour** **1 teaspoon baking soda** **3 cups quick oats**	Combine ingredients thoroughly and pour into greased 17x11x1-inch jellyroll pan. Bake. Frost while still warm.

Frosting

5 Tablespoons butter or **margarine** **1 1/2 cups powdered sugar** **1 teaspoon vanilla** **Milk**	Brown the butter. Add powdered sugar, vanilla, and enough milk to get a spreading consistency.

Cookies from a cake mix: Add one or two eggs, 2 Tablespoons shortening, and 2 Tablespoons water for crisp cookies, or 1/4 cup water for soft cookies, to your favorite cake mix. Bake at 375° for 8 minutes.

linzer bars

Yield: 36 bars

1 1/2 hours chilling time
Temperature: 350°
Baking time: 45 minutes

"Very elegant"

1 1/2 cups flour
1/8 teaspoon cloves
1/4 teaspoon cinnamon
1 cup finely ground almonds
1/2 cup granulated sugar
1 teaspoon grated lemon
   peel
2 hard boiled egg yolks,
   mashed
1/2 pound unsalted butter,
   softened
2 raw egg yolks, lightly
   beaten
1 teaspoon vanilla
1 1/2 cups raspberry jam
1 egg
2 Tablespoons light cream
Powdered sugar

Combine the first 10 ingredients until the mixture is smooth. Form the dough into a ball, wrap in waxed paper, and refrigerate for at least 1 hour. Remove 3/4 of the dough from the refrigerator and press on the bottom and sides of a greased 12x8x2-inch pan. Spread the jam evenly over the bottom. Roll out the rest of the dough on a floured surface into a rectangle 1/4-inch thick. With a sharp knife, cut the dough into strips 1/2-inch wide, making a lattice on top of the jam. Beat the whole egg with cream and brush over the pastry strips. Refrigerate for 1/2 hour. Bake. Let cool for 5 minutes and sprinkle with powdered sugar.

Note: Serve at room temperature.

If you don't have self-rising flour, make your own. Combine 1 1/2 teaspoons baking powder and 1/2 teaspoon salt per one cup all-purpose flour.

oatmeal brownies

Yield: 24 bars

Temperature: 350°
Baking time: 35 minutes

"Very rich and sweet"

Oatmeal layer
1/2 cup flour
1/4 teaspoon baking soda
1/4 teaspoon salt
1 cup quick oats
1/2 cup brown sugar
1/2 cup melted butter or
    margarine

Combine oatmeal layer ingredients, spread in a greased 9-inch square pan, and bake for 10 minutes.

Brownie layer
1/3 cup butter or margarine
2 ounces unsweetened
    chocolate
2 eggs
1 cup granulated sugar
1/2 teaspoon salt
1 teaspoon vanilla
3/4 cup flour
1/2 cup chopped nuts,
    optional

Melt butter and chocolate over low heat or in microwave and cool. Beat eggs and stir in sugar, salt, and vanilla. Add chocolate mixture, flour, and nuts. Spread brownie mixture over baked oatmeal and bake for 25 minutes.

Icing
1 3/4 cups powdered sugar
1/4 cup butter or margarine,
    softened
2 Tablespoons milk
1 teaspoon vanilla

Combine icing ingredients and beat until smooth and creamy. Ice brownies after they have cooled.

Variation: For chocolate icing, add 1/4 cup cocoa. To make it even richer, use 1/3 cup butter and use cream instead of milk.

fudge drop cookies

Yield: 3 dozen

Temperature: 350°
Baking time:
    10 to 15 minutes

"Mmmmmmmmmmmm"

1 (8-ounce) package German
    Sweet Chocolate
1 Tablespoon butter or
    margarine
2 eggs
3/4 cup sugar
1/4 cup flour
1/4 teaspoon baking powder
1/4 teaspoon cinnamon
1/8 teaspoon salt
1/2 teaspoon vanilla
3/4 cup finely chopped
    pecans

In the top of a double boiler, melt the chocolate and butter over hot water; stir and cool. Beat eggs until foamy and add sugar, 2 Tablespoons at a time; beat until thickened (5 minutes with an electric mixer). Add chocolate mixture, flour, baking powder, cinnamon, and salt; blend. Stir in vanilla and pecans. Drop by teaspoons onto greased cookie sheets and bake. Remove from oven when cookies feel set when lightly touched.

ginger snaps

Yield: 8 dozen

Temperature: 350°
Baking time:
    10 to 12 minutes

"Chewy and irresistible"

1 cup sugar
3/4 cup butter or margarine
1 egg
4 Tablespoons molasses
1 teaspoon ginger
1 teaspoon cinnamon
1 teaspoon salt
2 teaspoons baking soda
2 cups flour, sifted
Sugar

Cream sugar and butter. Add egg and beat until fluffy before adding molasses and dry ingredients. Form into marble-sized balls and roll in sugar. Bake 1 inch apart on ungreased cookie sheets. Cool on wire rack.

Note: **To measure molasses, grease the tablespoon in which it is measured.**

macaroons

5 hours standing time
Temperature: 300°
Baking time: 30 minutes

"A marvelous family favorite"

1 (8-ounce) package almond paste
1 cup granulated sugar
1/3 cup egg whites
1/3 cup powdered sugar
2 Tablespoons flour

Blend almond paste and granulated sugar. Add egg whites, powdered sugar, and flour. Mix thoroughly. Drop by spoonfuls on cookie sheet covered with brown paper. Cover with a wet towel for 4 to 5 hours. Bake. Remove from oven. Place brown paper with cookies on a damp towel. When paper is slightly damp, cookies can be removed. Place in airtight container when still warm to retain chewy flavor.

Variation: Mix in 3 teaspoons grated lemon or orange rind.

Beat the egg first, if one egg needs to be divided.

gingerbread boys

Temperature: 375°
Baking time: 8 to 10 minutes

"Works of art"

1 cup butter or margarine
1½ cups granulated sugar
1 egg
4 teaspoons grated orange peel
2 Tablespoons dark corn syrup
3 cups sifted flour
2 teaspoons baking soda
2 teaspoons cinnamon
1 teaspoon ginger
½ teaspoon ground cloves
½ teaspoon salt

Mix cookie ingredients thoroughly. Chill. Roll ¼-inch thick on a floured surface or between floured pastry cloths. Cut with Gingerbread cookie cutter and place 1-inch apart on an ungreased cookie sheet. Bake. Cool 1 minute before removing from pan. Cool completely before decorating.

Ornamental Icing
¼ cup butter or margarine
4 cups sifted powdered sugar
2 unbeaten egg whites
1 teaspoon vanilla
¼ teaspoon cream of tartar
1 to 2 teaspoons light cream

Cut butter into sugar until it looks like coarse meal. Add egg whites, vanilla, and cream of tartar. Beat well and add cream until a good consistency is reached for decorating. This should be stiffer than regular icing. Divide and tint with food coloring and force through a pastry tube.

Variation: If you'd prefer to use raisins instead of the icing, put them on the Gingerbread Boys before baking.

Pack cookies in popcorn to assure they won't arrive in crumbs. The popcorn protects and is good to eat too.

molasses peppernuts

Yield: 12 dozen

15 minutes freezing time
Temperature: 325°
Baking time: 15 minutes

"Fun to make and fun to eat"

1/2 cup butter or margarine
2 1/2 cups sugar
1/2 cup molasses
1/2 cup light corn syrup
1 cup evaporated milk
8 cups flour, sifted
1/2 teaspoon salt
1/2 teaspoon nutmeg
1/2 teaspoon ginger
1/2 teaspoon cinnamon
1/2 teaspoon mace
1/2 teaspoon cloves
1/2 teaspoon allspice
Dash pepper
1 1/3 teaspoons baking powder

Cream butter and sugar. Add molasses, corn syrup, and milk, stirring well. Combine flour with remaining ingredients and add a little at a time to molasses mixture until thoroughly blended. Form a portion of dough into a roll 1/2-inch thick and 12 inches long. Place on cookie sheet and freeze. When ready to bake a portion, snip off 1/2-inch pieces and place on ungreased baking pan. Bake until as brown as you wish. The longer you leave these in the oven, the crunchier they will be. For chewy cookies, watch carefully and don't bake too long.

Note: **The amount of spices may be altered to suit your own taste.**

Popcorn pops better if stored in freezer before using.

cigarettes russes

Temperature: 400°
Baking time: 5 minutes

"Very impressive"

2 egg whites
2/3 cup sugar
4 Tablespoons butter,
melted
3/4 cup flour, sifted
1/4 teaspoon vanilla
Grated lemon peel or
orange peel, optional

Preheat the oven to 400°. Lightly beat the egg whites. Add the sugar and beat with a fork until smooth. Add melted butter, flour, and vanilla. Spread the mixture in 6-inch oblongs on greased, floured cookie sheets, with only 4 on each sheet. Test the mixture by baking only 1 at first. If too firm, add a little melted butter. If too runny, add a little flour. Bake. Do not let them brown. Take the cookies out of the oven and let stand for 1 or 2 seconds. Remove them with a palette knife and place them upside down on the kitchen counter. Roll each one tightly around the handle of a wooden spoon. THIS MUST BE DONE VERY QUICKLY or the cookies will harden - put them back into the oven to soften if necessary. Remove immediately from the spoon and cool. Store in an airtight tin. These may also be made into "shells" by shaping them over a lightly greased orange.

Serving suggestion: Serve *Peach Ice Cream,* page 444; *Strawberry French Sorbet,* page 443; or fresh berries and cream in the shells.

cream cheese cupcakes

Yield: 48 cookies

Temperature: 300°
Baking time: 45 minutes

"Incredibly good"

**3 (8-ounce) packages
  cream cheese
1 cup sugar
5 eggs
1 1/2 teaspoons vanilla**

Cream cheese and sugar. Add eggs, 1 at a time, beating well after each. Add vanilla. Spoon mixture into midget foil baking cups. Bake for 40 minutes. Cool. A hole will be in the middle of each.

**Icing
1 cup sour cream
1/2 cup sugar
1/2 teaspoon vanilla**

Combine icing ingredients. Spoon on top of each cookie. Bake for another 5 minutes. Refrigerate.

spritz delights

Yield: 6 dozen cookies

Temperature: 350°
Baking time: 10 minutes

"Light and delicious"

**1 1/2 cups butter or
  margarine
1 cup sugar
1 egg plus one egg yolk
1 teaspoon almond extract
3 cups flour**

Cream butter and sugar until fluffy. Add eggs, almond extract, and flour. Mix well, cover, and chill dough. Press mixture through a cookie press onto ungreased cookie sheets. Bake.

Variation: Lemon extract can be substituted for the almond flavoring for a different flavor.

rosettes

**Preparation time:
30 minutes**

"Light and so pretty"

**2 eggs
2 teaspoons sugar
1/4 teaspoon salt
1 cup milk
1 cup flour
1 Tablespoon lemon extract**

Combine all ingredients and beat until smooth. Heat rosette iron in hot oil in a deep kettle or an electric skillet. Drain excess oil on brown paper. Oil should be hot enough to brown a piece of bread in 1 minute. If using an electric skillet, set at 375° for 3 minutes. Dip heated iron in batter to not more than 3/4 its height. Plunge batter-coated iron quickly into hot oil and cook for 2 to 3 minutes. Remove cookies from iron with fork. While still warm, sift powdered sugar on both sides. Store in a tin box with waxed paper between layers.

Note: **If batter becomes too thin and does not hold to iron, add a drop or two of cream; if the iron is too cold, the batter will slip off and if it's too hot, the batter will stick.**

Variation:

Richer batter
**2 whole eggs
1 egg yolk
2/3 cup heavy cream
1/2 cup sugar
1 cup flour**

tassies

Yield: 24 cookies

Temperature: 325°
Baking time: 20 minutes

"You can be so creative with various fillings!"

Pastry
1 (3-ounce) package cream
   cheese
1/2 cup butter or margarine
1 cup flour

Blend softened cheese and butter. Stir in flour and chill for 1 hour. Shape into 24 (1-inch) balls and put in ungreased miniature muffin tins. Press dough against bottom and sides to make shells.

Filling
1 cup brown sugar
1 egg
1 teaspoon vanilla
1 Tablespoon butter or
   margarine
3/4 cup chopped pecans

Mix filling ingredients well. Fill shells and bake. Cool slightly, but remove from pan while still hot.

Variation: Fill shells with strawberry jam, topped with chopped pecans.

Candy stages:
Thread stage 230°-234°
Soft-ball stage 234°-240°
Firm-ball stage 244°-248°

Hard-ball stage 250°-266°
Soft-ball stage 270°-290°
Hard-crack stage 300°-310°

bon bons

**Preparation time: 1 hour
plus overnight chilling**

"Melt-in-your-mouth good"

**5¼ cups powdered sugar
1 cup butter or margarine
1 teaspoon vanilla
1 (14-ounce) can sweetened
condensed milk
2 cups chopped pecans
1 (7-ounce) can flaked
coconut
1 (6-ounce) package semi-
sweet chocolate chips
4 Tablespoons butter or
margarine
1 teaspoon vanilla
Pinch salt**

Cream sugar with 1 cup butter.
Add 1 teaspoon vanilla, milk,
pecans, and coconut and mix
well. Chill overnight. Roll into
balls and chill. Melt chocolate, 4
Tablespoons butter, 1 teaspoon
vanilla, and salt in top of a
double boiler over hot water.
Using a toothpick, dip balls, 1 at
a time, into chocolate. Store,
covered, in the refrigerator.

microwave fudge

Yield: 18 pieces

**Microwave setting: High
Baking time: 2 minutes**

"Quick and delicious"

**1 (1-pound) box powdered
sugar
½ cup cocoa
¼ teaspoon salt
1 Tablespoon vanilla
¼ cup milk
½ cup butter or margarine
½ cup chopped nuts,
optional**

Mix all ingredients except butter
and nuts in a 2-quart non-
metallic dish. Place butter on top
of mixture and cook uncovered
for 2 minutes. Remove from
microwave and beat with mixer
until well blended. Add nuts and
pour into a greased 8-inch
square pan. Place in freezer for
20 minutes or in refrigerator for
1 hour before cutting.

Note: **If doubled, add 1 minute to microwave time.**

caramels

"Rich and creamy"

2 cups sugar
3/4 cup light corn syrup
1/2 cup butter or margarine
2 cups heavy cream,
  divided
1 teaspoon vanilla
1 cup nuts, optional

In a heavy pan, combine sugar, corn syrup, butter, and 1 cup heavy cream. Stir over medium high heat until ingredients come to a full boil. Add remaining cream very slowly. Do not let the boiling stop! Heat for 20 minutes until golden brown (242° on a candy thermometer), stirring occasionally. During the last few minutes, stir constantly. Remove from heat and add vanilla and nuts, if desired. Stir well and pour into slightly greased 8-inch square pan. Cool completely, cut into small pieces, and wrap in waxed paper.

Note: **Be patient! These are marvelous when cooked long enough.**

Avoid making candy in hot, humid weather. Candy is hard to handle and becomes sugary.

chocolate-peanut butter balls

Preparation time: 1 hour

"Fabulous"

Centers
1 (18-ounce) jar crunchy
   peanut butter
1/2 cup graham cracker
   crumbs
1 cup butter or margarine
5 1/4 cups powdered sugar

Combine ingredients for the centers and form into small balls.

Dipping chocolate
1 (12-ounce) package
   semi-sweet chocolate
   chips
1/2 cup butter or margarine
Pinch salt

Melt ingredients for dipping over, not in, boiling water in the top of a double boiler. Dip centers in the chocolate. Let harden on waxed paper. Keep refrigerated or frozen.

Note: **Crisp, dry weather is a must for successful candy-making.**

Easy Variation:
3/4 cup butter or margarine
2 1/2 cups powdered sugar
2 cups graham cracker
   crumbs
1 (12-ounce) jar peanut
   butter
1 (12-ounce) package
   semi-sweet chocolate
   chips

Melt butter and mix in sugar, graham cracker crumbs, and peanut butter over low heat. Press into a greased 13x9x2-inch pan. Melt chocolate chips and spread on top. Refrigerate, but let come to room temperature before cutting to prevent the chocolate from cracking.

mother's creamy fudge

Yield: 4 pounds

Preparation time:
45 minutes
plus 2 hours chilling time

"Absolutely fantastic"

3 cups sugar
1/2 cup light corn syrup
1 cup heavy cream
1 1/2 ounces semi-sweet chocolate
4 Tablespoons butter or margarine
1 teaspoon vanilla
1 cup chopped pecans, optional

Combine sugar, syrup, cream, and chocolate in a heavy pan over low heat. Stir until all sugar has dissolved; keep the sides of the pan wiped down with a wet brush or cloth. Increase heat to medium high and do not stir again. When a small bit dropped in cold water forms a ball, it's ready (238"). Turn off stove, add butter, and let pan stay on warm stove top until butter has melted. Set aside and let stand until cool, about 20 minutes. Add vanilla and beat until thick and heavy and will stand alone when piled up. Turn into buttered 13x9x2-inch pan. Refrigerate.

Note: If using nuts, add along with vanilla.

Two Tablespoons of cocoa and one teaspoon butter or other shortening equals one ounce of chocolate.

peanut butter fudge

Yield: 16 pieces

**Preparation time:
30 minutes
plus 2 hours chilling time**

"Creamy and delicious"

**2 cups sugar
1/2 cup evaporated milk
1/4 cup water
2 Tablespoons light corn
   syrup
1 Tablespoon butter or
   margarine
1/2 teaspoon vanilla
2 Tablespoons peanut
   butter**

Boil first 5 ingredients. Lower heat and boil gently to soft-ball stage (234°-240°), stirring constantly. Test this by dropping a small amount into cold water. Remove from heat and add vanilla. Cool and then beat with mixer for several minutes. Add peanut butter and beat again. Spread into a greased 8-inch square pan. Refrigerate.

southern pralines

Yield: 4 dozen pieces

**Preparation time:
45 minutes**

"New Orleans style"

**2 cups granulated sugar
1 (1-pound) box light
   brown sugar
1/2 cup milk
1/2 pint heavy cream
Pinch salt
2/3 cup light corn
   syrup
1/3 cup granulated sugar
1/4 pound butter or
   margarine
2 teaspoons vanilla
2 cups chopped pecans
Pecan halves**

Mix sugars, milk, cream, salt, and syrup in a heavy pan and cook until this boils. Remove from heat. Caramelize 1/3 cup sugar by cooking it over medium-high heat until it liquefies. Add caramelized sugar to syrup mixture and cook over medium high heat until it forms a soft ball when dropped in cold water. Remove from heat and stir in butter and vanilla. Beat until it begins to thicken. Add nuts and drop by teaspoons on waxed paper. Place a pecan half on each praline.

toffee

Preparation time: 1 hour
plus 15 minutes chilling
time

"Marvelous"

**2 pounds butter or
margarine
5 cups sugar
16 ounces semi-sweet
chocolate
16 ounces German sweet
chocolate
16 ounces sliced almonds**

Melt and stir butter and sugar over medium heat in heavy deep pan until sugar is dissolved and mixture begins to boil. Do not stir! Cover pan and let cook 6 minutes over medium heat. Uncover and continue cooking until candy thermometer reads 290°. Pour into an ungreased 15x10x1-inch jellyroll pan. Refrigerate for 15 minutes. Melt both chocolates in the top of a double boiler over warm water; about 30 minutes. Place almonds on cookie sheet and bake in 300° oven for 5 to 10 minutes, being careful not to burn them. Pour half of chocolate over cooled candy evenly. Sprinkle ½ the almonds over the chocolate and let set. Turn candy over onto a sheet of aluminum foil and spread remaining chocolate on other side of candy. Sprinkle almonds over chocolate. When cool, break into pieces.

Note: **Store in an airtight container. Candy will keep in the refrigerator for 2 months or in the freezer for 4.**

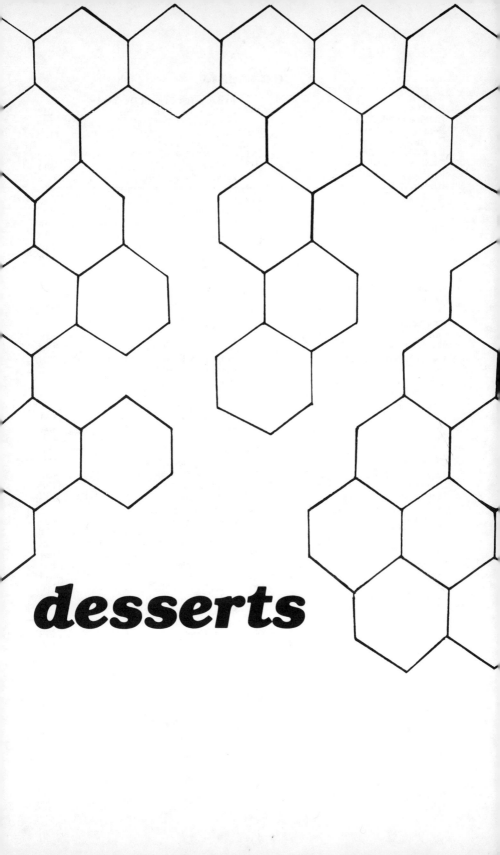

desserts

desserts

Cakes
Beer Cake 387
Belgian Mocha Cake 388
Best Ever Apple Cake 389
Carrot Cake 390
Chocolate Cream Cheese Cake 391
Danish Pudding Cake 392
Famous Chocolate Cake 393
Hummingbird Cake 394
Italian Cream Cake 395
Mississippi Mud Cake 396
Mocha Cake 397
Old-Fashioned Strawberry Shortcake 398
Rum Cake 399
Vanilla Wafer Cake 400
Zuccoto Cake 401

Pound Cakes
Coconut Pound Cake 402
Cranberry Pound Cake 403
Sour Cream or Whipped Cream 404

Fruitcakes
Unbaked Fruitcake 404
White Fruitcake 405

Cupcakes/Muffins
Fudge Cupcakes 406
Holiday Muffins 406
Pumpkin Muffins 407

Cobblers
Apple-Plum Melange 408
Deep Dish Apple Cobbler 409
Peach Cobbler 407
Southern Blackberry Cobbler 410

Cheesecakes
Chocolate Almond Cheesecake 411
Gourmet Chocolate Cheesecake 412
Miami Cheesecake 414
Party Cheesecakes 413
Praline Cheesecake 416
Strawberry Cheesecake 417

Pies
Apple Pie 418
Bourbon Pie 420
Brandy Alexander Pie 421
Chess Pie 422
Chocolate Pecan Tart 423
Chocolate Phyllo Pie 424
Cran-Apple Crumb Pie 425
Date-Chess Pie 425
Deep Dish Apple Pie 426
Fabulous Chocolate Pie 427
French Mint Pies 428
Frozen Lemonade Pie 429
Fudge Pie 426
Glazed Strawberry Pie 430
Grasshopper Pie 431
Heavenly Pie 432
Iroquois Pie 433
Lemon Cream Pie 433
Pecan Pie 434
Praline Pumpkin Pie 434
Raspberry Passion 435
Ritz Cracker Pie 437
Toffee Coffee Pie 436

Frozen/Ice Cream Desserts
Caramel Ice Cream Delight 437
Coffee Toffee Torte 438
Frozen Strawberry Dessert 439
Ice Cream Bombe
    with Raspberry Sauce 440
Mocha Toffee Delight 441
Oreo Ice Cream Pie 442
Strawberries Romanoff 440
Strawberry French Sorbet 443

Ice Cream
Chocolate Almond Ice Cream 444
Lemon Ice Cream 443
Milky Way Ice Cream 445
Peach Ice Cream 444
Vanilla Ice Cream 446

Souffles
Cold Grand Marnier Souffle
    with Strawberry Sauce 447
Cold Lemon Souffle
    with Raspberry Sauce 451
Cold Orange Souffle 448
Hot Raspberry Souffle 450
Individual Coffee Souffles 449
Raspberry Souffle 452

Fruit Desserts
Bananas Foster 453
Cantaloupe Cooler 454
Fruit Compote with Kirsch 454
Fruit Fantasy 457
Fruit Pizza 455
Poached Pears with Chocolate Sauce . 456

Custard Desserts
Amaretto Custard with Fruit 457
Caramel Custard 458
Creme Brulee 459

Assorted Desserts
Apple Fritters 460
Fantastic Chocolate Roll 461
Lemon Mousse with Blueberries 462
Meringues 464
Raspberry Mille-Feuille 466
Rum Dessert 463
Sponge Pudding 460
Walnut Crisps 465

Beverage Desserts
Blender Pot de Creme 468
Pot de Creme 469
Velvet Hammer 468

Sauces
Blueberry Sauce 470
Butterscotch Sauce 469
Caramel Sauce 470
Chocolate Sauce 472
Derby Day Mint Sauce
    with Chocolate Leaves 471
Fruit Mousseline Sauce 472
Grand Marnier Sauce for Fruit 473
Peach Melba Sauce 473
Praline Sauce 474
Witches' Brew 474

beer cake

Temperature: 350°
Baking time: 1 hour

"The beer adds something special."

2 cups brown sugar
1 cup butter or margarine
2 eggs
1 Tablespoon cinnamon
1/2 teaspoon allspice
3 cups flour
1/2 teaspoon salt
2 teaspoons baking soda
2 cups beer

Cream sugar and butter. Add the eggs and blend thoroughly. Sift dry ingredients together and add, alternating with the beer, to the sugar mixture. Mix well. Bake in a large, greased tube pan. Cool cake before icing.

Caramel Icing
1/2 cup butter or margarine
1 cup brown sugar
1/4 cup milk
1/2 teaspoon salt
1 teaspoon vanilla
2 cups powdered sugar

Melt butter and brown sugar over low heat, stirring constantly. Add milk and stir until mixture comes to a boil. Remove from heat and cool for 5 minutes before adding salt, vanilla, and powdered sugar. Stir with a wire whisk until smooth.

Note: **This icing is divine and can be used on lots of other cakes and bar cookies.**

belgian mocha cake

Yield: 12 servings

Temperature: 350°
Baking time:
25 to 30 minutes

"A really special company dessert"

2 1/2 cups granulated sugar
3 Tablespoons water
2 ounces unsweetened
   chocolate
3/4 cup butter or margarine,
   softened
1 teaspoon vanilla
4 eggs, separated
2 1/4 cups cake flour,
   sifted
1/2 teaspoon baking soda
1/2 teaspoon salt
1 cup milk
1 teaspoon cream of tartar

In a small saucepan, add 1/2 cup sugar and water to the chocolate and melt over low heat. In a large bowl, cream butter, add the remaining 2 cups sugar, and beat until fluffy. Add vanilla and then the egg yolks, 1 at a time; beating well after each addition. Add the chocolate mixture and blend well. Add flour, baking soda, and salt, alternating with the milk. Beat egg whites with the cream of tartar until stiff and then fold into chocolate mixture. Pour into 3 (9-inch) or 4 (8-inch) cake pans lined with waxed paper, greased and floured. Bake. Cool slightly, remove cake from pans, and cool completely on wire racks.

Icing
1 1/2 cups unsalted butter
1 1/2 cups powdered sugar
2 egg yolks
1 1/2 teaspoons instant
   coffee
3/4 teaspoon cocoa
3 teaspoons boiling water
1 1/2 Tablespoons almond
   extract
2 Tablespoons rum
1/2 to 3/4 cup powdered sugar

Cream butter; add 1 1/2 cups powdered sugar and the egg yolks. Beat for 5 minutes with an electric mixer. Dissolve coffee and cocoa in the boiling water. Stir in coffee mixture, almond extract, rum, and 1/2 to 3/4 cup powdered sugar to make a fairly fluid icing. Ice layers and assemble cake.

best ever apple cake

Yield: 2 loaves or 1 cake

Overnight chilling
Temperature: 325°
Baking time:
   1 hour for loaves
   1 1/2 hours for cake

"Your guests will rave!"

3 cups peeled, cored, and chopped apples
2 cups granulated sugar
3 eggs
3 cups flour
1 teaspoon baking soda
1 teaspoon salt
1 teaspoon vanilla
3 teaspoons cinnamon
1/2 teaspoon almond extract
1 cup oil
1 cup chopped nuts
1/4 cup orange juice, optional
1 cup shredded coconut, optional

Glaze
1/2 cup butter or margarine
1 cup brown sugar
1/4 cup buttermilk
1/4 to 1/2 cup Amaretto (optional)

Cover apples with sugar and let stand in a covered bowl overnight in the refrigerator. The next day, mix remaining cake ingredients in a large bowl; add the apples and sugar, mixing well. Bake in a greased and floured tube pan or 2 loaf pans. Before cake is through baking, combine butter, brown sugar, buttermilk, and Amaretto. Bring mixture to a low boil and set aside. When cake is done (cake tester comes out clean), use a sharp knife to make holes in the cake. Stir the heated glaze and pour over the cake while still in the pan. *Do not remove the cake or loaves from pans until completely cooled* (otherwise the cake will fall apart).

***Serving suggestion:* Serve this topped with whipped cream and ground nutmeg.**

carrot cake

"Delicious and different"

2 cups granulated sugar
1 cup oil
2 cups flour
1 teaspoon baking soda
1 teaspoon salt
4 eggs
3 cups grated carrots
2 teaspoons cinnamon

In a large bowl, mix sugar and oil. Sift dry ingredients and add to sugar and oil mixture. Add eggs, 1 at a time. Stir in grated carrots and cinnamon. Bake in 2 (9-inch) cake pans.

Cream Cheese Frosting
1 (8-ounce) package cream cheese, softened
1/2 cup butter or margarine, softened
1 (1-pound) box powdered sugar
2 teaspoons vanilla
1 cup chopped nuts

Beat frosting ingredients and spread between and over cooled layers.

Note: **This frosting can be frozen and used whenever needed.**

chocolate cream cheese cake

Yield: 12 to 16 servings

Temperature: 350°, 375°
Baking time:
  15, 10 minutes

"Divine"

3/4 cup butter or margarine
2 cups granulated sugar
2 ounces unsweetened chocolate, melted
2 eggs, separated
2 1/2 cups flour
1 teaspoon baking soda
1/2 teaspoon baking powder
1 1/2 cups buttermilk
1/2 cup chopped pecans
1 teaspoon vanilla

In a large bowl, cream butter and sugar. Add the melted chocolate and the beaten egg yolks; blend thoroughly. Sift the flour 3 times. Add the baking soda and the baking powder to the flour and sift again. Add dry ingredients to the sugar mixture gradually, alternating with the buttermilk. Fold in stiffly beaten egg whites, pecans, and vanilla. Bake in 3 greased 8-inch cake pans for 15 minutes at 350° and then bake for an additional 15 minutes at 375°. Remove cake from pans and cool on wire racks before frosting.

Chocolate Cream Cheese Icing
1 (8-ounce) package cream cheese
1 (1-pound) box powdered sugar
3 Tablespoons butter or margarine
3 Tablespoons cocoa
1 teaspoon vanilla

Combine icing ingredients well.

danish pudding cake

Yield: 16 servings

Temperature: 350°
Baking time: 1 1/2 hours

"Perfect for any occasion"

1 cup butter or margarine, melted
1 3/4 cups sugar
3 eggs
1 1/2 teaspoons baking soda
1 cup buttermilk
1 Tablespoon orange juice
3 cups flour
1 teaspoon salt
1 cup chopped pecans
1 pound dates, chopped

In a large bowl, mix the first 8 ingredients together thoroughly. Fold in the pecans and dates. Pour the mixture into a greased and floured tube pan lined on the bottom with waxed paper. Bake.

Glaze
1 cup sugar
1 cup orange juice

Combine the glaze ingredients together in a saucepan and heat, stirring until the sugar melts. Prick the top of the warm cake with a fork. Pour hot glaze over the cake and let stand in the pan overnight for best results. Remove from pan and slice.

Serving suggestion: Serve with hard sauce, lemon or orange sauce, or sweetened whipped cream.

famous chocolate cake

Yield: 12 to 16 servings

Temperature: 350°
Baking time: 20 minutes

"Very rich and very good!"

2 cups granulated sugar
2 cups flour
1 teaspoon baking soda
1 cup butter or margarine
4 Tablespoons cocoa
1 cup water
1/2 cup buttermilk
2 eggs
1 teaspoon vanilla

Sift sugar, flour, and soda into a large bowl. In a saucepan, melt butter with cocoa and water. Boil rapidly for a few minutes. Pour over dry ingredients and stir. Add buttermilk, eggs, and vanilla. Bake in a greased 13x9x2-inch pan.

Icing
1/2 cup butter or margarine
4 Tablespoons cocoa
1/2 cup buttermilk
1 teaspoon vanilla
1 (1-pound) box powdered sugar
1 cup chopped nuts

Bring butter, cocoa, and buttermilk to a boil in a medium saucepan. Remove from heat and add vanilla, powdered sugar, and nuts. Spread on warm cake.

To make a perfect cake:
— Position the rack in the middle of the oven.
— Let eggs, butter, and milk reach room temperature.
— Cream shortening and sugar thoroughly, until light and fluffy.
— Don't let cake pans touch each other or the sides of the oven.
— Add only 1 egg at a time and beat after each addition.
— Let the cake layers cool completely before adding filling and/or frosting.

hummingbird cake

Yield: 16 servings

Temperature: 350°
Baking time:
  25 to 30 minutes

"Heavenly!"

Cake
3 cups flour
2 cups granulated sugar
1 teaspoon salt
1 teaspoon baking soda
1 teaspoon cinnamon
3 eggs, beaten
1 1/2 cups oil
1 1/2 teaspoons vanilla
1 (8-ounce) can crushed
  pineapple, undrained
4 medium bananas, chopped
1 cup chopped pecans

Preheat oven. In a large bowl, combine dry ingredients. Add eggs and oil; stir until moistened. Stir in vanilla, pineapple, bananas, and nuts. Spoon batter into 2 (9-inch) or 3 (8-inch) greased and floured round cake pans. Bake. Cool completely and then remove from pans.

Frosting
1 (8-ounce) package cream
  cheese, softened
1/2 cup butter or margarine,
  softened
1 (1-pound) box powdered
  sugar
1 teaspoon vanilla
1 cup chopped pecans

Blend frosting ingredients thoroughly. Frost cake.

Note: Garnish the top of the frosted cake with pecan halves.

italian cream cake

Temperature: 350°
Baking time: 30 minutes

"Delightful cake"

½ cup butter or margarine
2 cups granulated sugar
½ cup shortening
5 eggs, separated
2 cups flour
1 cup buttermilk
1½ teaspoons vanilla
1 teaspoon baking soda
1 cup coconut
1 cup chopped pecans

In a large bowl, cream butter, sugar, and shortening. Add beaten egg yolks. Add flour alternating with milk and vanilla in which soda has been dissolved. Fold in beaten egg whites. Add coconut and nuts. Bake in 3 (8-inch) cake pans.

Icing
2 (8-ounce) packages cream cheese
1 cup butter or margarine
2 (1-pound) boxes powdered sugar
2 teaspoons vanilla

Beat icing ingredients well. Ice cake when layers have cooled. Refrigerate until ready to serve.

Mash overripe bananas, add lemon juice, and freeze for later use in baking.

mississippi mud cake

Yield: 18 servings

Temperature: 300°
Baking time: 40 minutes

"A chocolate lover's delight!"

2 cups granulated sugar
1 cup butter or margarine
4 eggs
1 1/2 cups flour
1/4 teaspoon salt
1/3 cup cocoa
3 teaspoons vanilla
1/2 to 1 cup chopped
   pecans or walnuts
1 (6 1/4-ounce) package
   miniature marshmallows

Cream sugar and butter. Add eggs, 1 at a time. Sift dry ingredients together and add to egg mixture. Add vanilla and nuts. Pour into a greased 13x9x2-inch pan and bake for 30 minutes. Remove from oven and spread marshmallows over top. Bake 10 minutes more. Let cake cool. Marshmallows will fall.

Chocolate Icing
1 (1-pound) box powdered
   sugar
1/3 cup cocoa
1 1/4 cups butter or
   margarine, melted
1/2 cup evaporated milk
1 teaspoon vanilla
1/2 cup chopped nuts,
   optional

In a medium bowl, mix sugar and 1/2 the cocoa with the melted butter. Stir in the remaining ingredients with a wire whisk until smooth. Frost cooled cake and wait for at least 4 hours before cutting.

Cakes iced with butter-cream or cream cheese icings should be covered and stored in the refrigerator.

mocha cake

Yield: 16 servings

Temperature: 375°
Baking time:
    25 to 30 minutes

"Not the same old chocolate cake"

**5 ounces unsweetened
    chocolate
1 cup milk
1 cup granulated sugar
3 eggs, separated
1/2 cup butter or margarine
1 cup brown sugar
2 cups cake flour,
    sifted
1 teaspoon baking soda
Pinch salt
1/4 cup water
1 teaspoon vanilla**

In a saucepan, combine chocolate and 1/2 cup milk. Stir over low heat until mixture is smooth. Stir in sugar and 1 egg yolk. Cook, stirring constantly, until mixture is thick and smooth, about 4 minutes. Cool. In a large bowl, cream butter until soft; add brown sugar and cream together until light and fluffy. Beat in remaining egg yolks, 1 at a time. Sift cake flour, soda, and salt and add to butter mixture in thirds, alternating with 1/2 cup milk and 1/4 cup water. Add vanilla. Stir in chocolate custard mixture and fold in stiffly beaten egg whites. Pour into 2 buttered (9-inch) cake pans and bake. Turn onto racks and cool.

Coffee Icing
**1 cup butter or margarine,
    softened
2 Tablespoons instant
    coffee
4 Tablespoons boiling water
Pinch salt
2 1/2 cups powdered sugar
1 Tablespoon rum**

Cream butter. Dissolve coffee in boiling water. Add coffee mixture and salt to butter, blending well. Gradually add sugar and beat until smooth. Add rum. Let sit a few minutes, then beat again. Frost the cooled cake.

old-fashioned strawberry shortcake

Yield: 8 to 10 servings

Temperature: 400°
Baking time:
10 to 15 minutes

"A tradition that should not be forgotten"

2 cups flour
3 teaspoons baking powder
1/2 teaspoon salt
1/4 cup sugar
1/2 cup butter or margarine
3/4 cup milk or light cream
1 quart strawberries,
stemmed, halved, and
sweetened to taste
1 cup heavy cream,
whipped and sweetened
to taste
8 to 10 strawberries for
garnish

In a medium bowl, sift flour, baking powder, salt, and sugar. Cut butter into flour with pastry blender or food processor until mixture is like coarse oatmeal. Stir in milk, but don't overmix. Turn dough onto a floured board; knead quickly to distribute ingredients evenly. With floured rolling pin, roll dough out to a thickness of 1/2 to 3/4-inch. Cut into circles with a 3-inch cookie cutter or glass dipped in flour. Place 2 inches apart on ungreased cookie sheet and bake. Split crosswise, butter bottom half while warm. Spoon strawberries over bottom half of buttered round, top with upper half of shortcake. Spoon on more strawberries. Top with whipped cream and garnish with a strawberry.

rum cake

Yield: 16 servings

Temperature: 325°
Baking time:
** 40 to 50 minutes**

"This will melt in your mouth!"

Cake
1 box yellow cake mix
1 (3³/4-ounce) package
** instant vanilla pudding**
1/2 cup oil
1/2 cup water
1/2 cup rum
4 eggs, beaten

Combine all ingredients in a large bowl. Beat with a mixer for 2 minutes. Pour into a greased and floured bundt or tube pan. Bake. Let cake cool for 10 minutes and remove from pan. Cool cake completely and then prick generously with a fork on the top and sides.

Glaze
1/2 cup butter or margarine,
** melted**
1/4 cup water
1/2 cup sugar
1 1/2 ounces rum

Combine butter, water, and sugar in a saucepan. Bring to a slow boil, stirring constantly. Remove from heat and add rum. Spoon generously over cake.

3 medium apples = 3 cups sliced
3 medium bananas = 2 1/2 cups sliced or 2 cups mashed
14 graham cracker squares = 1 cup fine crumbs
22 vanilla wafers = 1 cup finely crushed
4 medium peaches = 2 cups sliced
1 quart strawberries = 4 cups sliced
1 medium orange = 1/3 cup juice and 2 Tablespoons grated rind
1 medium lemon = 2 Tablespoons juice and 2 teaspoons grated rind

vanilla wafer cake

Yield: 12 to 16 servings

Temperature: 275°
Baking time: 1 1/2 hours

"Don't skip over this one."

1 cup butter or margarine
2 cups granulated sugar
6 eggs
1 (12-ounce) box vanilla wafers, crushed
1/2 cup milk
1 teaspoon vanilla
1 (7-ounce) can flaked coconut
1 cup chopped pecans

In a large bowl, cream butter and sugar. Beat in the eggs, 1 at a time. Add crushed vanilla wafers alternating with the milk. Add vanilla, coconut, and pecans and mix well. Pour into a greased and floured tube or bundt pan. Bake. Remove from pan and cool.

Icing
1 (8-ounce) package cream cheese
1/4 cup butter or margarine
1 (1-pound) box powdered sugar
1 teaspoon vanilla
1/2 cup chopped pecans

In a medium bowl of an electric mixer, beat the cream cheese and the butter until smooth. Add sugar and mix well. Add vanilla and beat until smooth. Spread on the cooled cake and sprinkle the top with chopped pecans.

Sprinkle cake plate with powdered sugar to prevent cake from sticking.

zuccoto cake

**Preparation time: 1 hour
plus overnight chilling**

"Out of this world"

1 (12-ounce) frozen pound
cake, thawed
3/4 cup sweet Marsala wine
4 ounces blanched almonds
1 (6-ounce) package
semi-sweet chocolate
chips
2 cups heavy cream
3/4 cup powdered sugar
3/4 cup heavy cream,
whipped
Chocolate shavings

Variation: **You may use
Amaretto, Cointreau, or any
liqueur that is not too thick
in place of the Marsala wine.**

Line the inside of a 10½-inch round-bottomed bowl, a zuccoto bowl, or a mold with plastic wrap. Extend the plastic over the edge of the bowl. Cutting the ends off of the pound cake, slice the cake into triangular-shaped pieces 3/4-inch wide. Paint 1 side of each cake section with wine. Arrange the pieces, painted side down, in the lined bowl with the pointed ends alternating up and down so that the *entire* bowl is lined with cake. Fill in any gaps with cake pieces. Brush with wine. Chop the nuts and the chocolate chips separately. Whip the heavy cream and add powdered sugar, nuts and ½ the chocolate chips. Spoon ½ the cream mixture into the cake-lined bowl, leaving the center hollow. Melt the remaining chocolate chips, cool slightly, and fold into the rest of the cream mixture. Spoon into the hollow center of the mold. Cover the top with cake slices and brush with wine. Trim edges, cover, and refrigerate overnight or at least for 8 hours. To serve, invert the cake onto a flat dish and remove mold and plastic wrap. Decorate with piped whipped cream and chocolate shavings.

coconut pound cake

**Yield: 1 bundt cake
or 2 loaves**

**Temperature: 350°
Baking time:
45 to 50 minutes**

"Marvelous flavor"

**2 cups sugar
1 cup oil
2 cups flour
1 1/2 teaspoons baking
powder
1 teaspoon salt
5 eggs, separated
1 cup buttermilk
1 teaspoon coconut
flavoring
3/4 cup coconut**

Topping
**1 cup sugar
1/2 cup water
1 teaspoon coconut
flavoring**

In a large bowl, beat sugar and oil together. Sift flour, baking powder, and salt. Add egg yolks to buttermilk; beat well. Alternately add flour mixture and milk mixture to sugar and oil; beating until smooth. Add coconut flavoring and coconut. Beat egg whites until stiff and fold into batter. Pour into a well greased large bundt pan or 2 (9x5x3-inch) loaf pans. Bake for 45 to 50 minutes. *Don't overbake.* Check for doneness. Large cake takes longer than loaves. About 5 minutes before cake is ready, mix the topping ingredients in a small saucepan. Stir continuously until it comes to a boil. Lower heat and simmer for 3 minutes. Pour over cake as soon as it comes out of the oven. Allow cake to cool in pans.

cranberry pound cake

Yield: 16 servings

Temperature: 325°
Baking time: 55 minutes

"Quite a combination of flavors"

1 box yellow cake mix
3 eggs
3/4 cup water
1/2 cup orange juice
1/4 cup butter or margarine,
 softened
2 Tablespoons grated
 orange rind
1 (14-ounce) jar
 cranberry-orange relish
Powdered sugar
2 Tablespoons granulated
 sugar
3 Tablespoons butter or
 margarine
1 cup heavy cream,
 whipped, optional

Preheat oven to 325°. Grease a bundt pan and dust with flour. In a large bowl, blend the cake mix with the next five ingredients and beat for 2 minutes at medium speed. Fold in 1/2 cup relish. Pour into pan and bake. Cool until lukewarm and turn out. Sprinkle with powdered sugar. Combine remaining relish with sugar and 3 Tablespoons butter in small saucepan and heat thoroughly. Spoon topping on cake slices. A dollop of whipped cream is good, too.

If you don't have buttermilk on hand, add 1 Tablespoon white vinegar or lemon juice to 1 cup milk. Let stand for 5 minutes.

sour cream or whipped cream pound cake

Yield: 16 servings

Temperature: 300°
Baking time: 1 1/2 hours

"Both are so good, it's hard to decide."

1 cup butter or margarine
3 cups sugar
6 eggs, separated
3 cups flour
1/4 teaspoon salt
1/4 teaspoon baking soda
2 cups sour cream or
   1 cup heavy cream
1 teaspoon vanilla or
   almond extract

In a large bowl, cream butter and sugar. Stir in yolks, 1 at a time. Sift flour, salt, and soda together and add to the butter mixture, alternating with the sour cream or the heavy cream. Add extract. Beat egg whites until stiff and fold in. Pour batter into a greased bundt pan. Place in a cold oven, turn oven to 300° and bake.

unbaked fruitcake

Yield: 16 servings

**Preparation time:
   30 minutes**

"Easy and delicious"

1 pound miniature
   marshmallows
1 cup heavy cream
1 pound dates, finely
   chopped
1 pound pecans, chopped
1/4 pound maraschino
   cherries, chopped
1/4 teaspoon salt
1 teaspoon vanilla
1 pound graham crackers,
   crushed

Melt marshmallows in cream in the top of a double boiler. In a medium bowl, mix dates, pecans, and cherries. Add fruit mixture, salt, and vanilla to marshmallows. Add 1/2 of the crushed graham crackers to the marshmallow mixture. Turn mixture onto a surface dusted with graham cracker crumbs. Either form into a long roll or an oblong square. Wrap in waxed paper and store in the refrigerator until ready to serve.

white fruitcake

**Yield: 1 cake
or 3 loaves**

**Temperature: 275°
Baking time: 2 1/2 hours**

"Old southern recipe"

**16 ounces crystallized
   citron
8 ounces crystallized red
   cherries
8 ounces crystallized
   pineapple
4 cups flour, sifted
1 1/2 cups butter or
   margarine
2 1/4 cups sugar
1 cup water
2 teaspoons baking powder
8 egg whites
1 teaspoon almond extract
1 teaspoon lemon extract
1 teaspoon vanilla extract
1 ounce bourbon or brandy
6 to 8 ounces grated
   coconut, preferably fresh
1 pound pecans, chopped**

In a large bowl, dust fruit lightly with part of the flour listed; reserve the remaining flour. In a separate large bowl, cream the butter and sugar. Add alternately the flour and water. Add baking powder. Beat egg whites until stiff and add to the batter. Add the extracts, bourbon, coconut, and chopped nuts. Add the floured fruit and mix well. Spoon batter into a large greased and floured tube pan or 3 large loaf pans. Bake until a golden brown.

Note: **The loaves make excellent Christmas presents.**

fudge cupcakes

Yield: 1 1/2 dozen

Temperature: 325°
Baking time: 15 minutes

"Thick and chewy like brownies"

1 1/2 ounces unsweetened
  chocolate
1/2 cup butter or margarine
1 cup sugar
2/3 cup flour
1 teaspoon vanilla
2 eggs, well beaten
1 cup pecans, chopped

Melt chocolate and butter in the top of a double boiler. In a medium bowl, mix other ingredients; add to chocolate mixture. Fill cupcake papers 2/3 full and bake.

Note: **Great to keep on hand in the freezer.**

holiday muffins

Yield: 2 dozen

Temperature: 325°
Baking time:
  20 to 25 minutes

"Makes wonderful holiday gifts!"

1/2 cup butter or margarine
1 cup brown sugar
1 egg
1 1/2 cups flour
1/4 teaspoon ground cloves
1/4 teaspoon cinnamon
1/4 teaspoon nutmeg
1 cup crushed pineapple,
  with juice
1 teaspoon baking soda
1/2 cup raisins
1/2 cup coconut
1 cup pecans, chopped
1/4 cup candied cherries,
  optional

In a medium bowl, cream butter and brown sugar; beat in the egg. Add flour and spices. In a small pan, heat the pineapple and add the baking soda. Mix pineapple into the batter with the remaining ingredients. Fill greased muffin tins 1/2 full and bake.

pumpkin muffins

Yield: 14 muffins

Temperature: 350°
Baking time: 20 minutes

"Perfect for Halloween treats"

1/2 cup shortening, melted
1 cup canned pumpkin
1/2 cup chopped dates
2 eggs
1/2 cup water
1 3/4 cups flour
1/4 teaspoon salt
1 1/2 cups sugar
1 teaspoon baking soda
1/4 teaspoon baking powder
1 teaspoon cinnamon
1/2 teaspoon nutmeg
1/2 teaspoon ginger
1/4 teaspoon cloves

Blend shortening, pumpkin, dates, eggs, and water. Sift remaining ingredients and add to pumpkin mixture. Pour into greased muffin tins, about 3/4 full, and bake until set when touched.

Serving suggestion: **Top with sweetened whipped cream or lemon sauce.**

peach cobbler

Yield: 4 to 6 servings

Temperature: 375°
Baking time:
30 to 40 minutes

"Not doughy, extremely delicious"

3 cups sliced peaches
1 Tablespoon lemon juice
1 cup sugar
1/2 teaspoon salt
1 cup flour
1 egg, beaten
6 Tablespoons butter or margarine, melted

Place peaches in 8x8-inch baking dish; sprinkle with lemon juice. Sift dry ingredients; add egg, tossing the mixture with fork until crumbly. Sprinkle over peaches and drizzle with butter. Bake. Serve warm.

1/2 coconut + nutmeg good!

apple-plum. melange

Yield: 8 servings

Temperature: 375°
Baking time: 40 minutes

"Your family will love this!"

4 cups peeled and sliced
   Jonathan apples
1 Tablespoon lemon juice
1/4 cup granulated sugar
1/2 cup flour
1/2 cup rolled oats
1/3 cup brown sugar
Dash salt
3 teaspoons cinnamon
1/2 teaspoon nutmeg
1/2 cup butter or margarine,
   melted
1/4 cup orange juice
1 (7 3/4-ounce) jar baby food
   plums
1/3 cup raisins
3/4 cup chopped pecans

In a non-metallic bowl, sprinkle the apple slices with lemon juice. In a separate bowl, mix together the sugar, flour, rolled oats, brown sugar, salt, cinnamon, and nutmeg; stir in the melted butter and the orange juice and mix thoroughly. Make 2 layers of a mixture of the apples, plums, raisins, and pecans and the orange juice mixture in a buttered 2-quart casserole. Bake.

Serving suggestion: Serve warm with vanilla ice cream mixed with brandy.

408

deep dish apple cobbler

Yield: 6 to 8 servings

Temperature: 350°
Baking time: 30 minutes

"For those with a sweet tooth"

6 cups peeled and thinly sliced apples
2/3 cup granulated sugar
Dash nutmeg
Dash cinnamon
1/2 cup butter or margarine
4 Tablespoons water
1/2 cup brown sugar
1/2 cup butter or margarine
1 cup flour
Pinch salt

Grease a 13x9x2-inch glass casserole. Fill with apples. Cover apples with sugar, nutmeg, and cinnamon. Dot generously with 1/2 cup butter and sprinkle with water. Cream brown sugar and 1/2 cup butter. Add flour and salt, mixing until crumbly. Sprinkle crumb mixture on top of apples. Bake.

Variation: Other fruits that may be used are peaches, pitted cherries, or slightly sweetened rhubarb.

Soften hardened brown sugar in the microwave with 1 cup hot water. (High) 1 1/2 to 2 minutes for 1/2 pound or 2 to 3 minutes for 1 pound.

southern blackberry cobbler

Yield: 8 servings

Temperature: 350°, 425°
Baking time:
   15, 20 to 30 minutes

"A wonderful southern tradition"

4 cups fresh blackberries or
  2 (16-ounce) packages
  frozen blackberries,
  thawed
3/4 cup sugar
3 Tablespoons flour
1 1/2 cups water
1 Tablespoon lemon juice

Place berries in a lightly greased 2-quart baking dish. Combine sugar and flour in a small bowl. Add water and lemon juice, mixing well. Pour this syrup over berries and bake at 350° for 15 minutes.

Crust
1 3/4 cups flour
2 to 3 Tablespoons sugar
2 teaspoons baking powder
1 teaspoon salt
1/4 cup shortening
6 Tablespoons heavy cream
6 Tablespoons buttermilk
2 Tablespoons butter or
  margarine, melted

Combine flour, sugar, baking powder, and salt. Cut in shortening until mixture resembles coarse crumbs. Stir in cream and buttermilk. Knead dough 4 or 5 times. Roll to about 1/4 inch on a lightly floured surface. Cut dough to fit baking dish. Place crust over hot berries. Brush crust with melted butter. Bake at 425° for 20 to 30 minutes or until crust is golden brown.

Note: Serve warm with cream and sugar, sweetened whipped cream, or ice cream if you want to be really daring with the calories!

chocolate almond cheesecake

Yield: 12 to 16 servings

Temperature: 375°
**Baking time: 1 1/2 to 2 hours
    plus overnight chilling**

"Your guests will be awed."

**1 1/2 cups chocolate wafer
    crumbs**
**1 cup blanched almonds,
    lightly toasted and
    chopped**
1/3 cup sugar
**6 Tablespoons butter or
    margarine, softened**
**3 (8-ounce) packages cream
    cheese, softened**
1 cup sugar
1/3 cup heavy cream
1/2 cup Amaretto
2 teaspoons vanilla
4 eggs
2 cups sour cream
1 Tablespoon sugar

Garnish
**1 cup blanched almonds,
    lightly toasted and
    chopped**

In a mixing bowl, combine the wafer crumbs, almonds, sugar, and butter. Pat mixture on bottom and sides of a 10-inch springform pan. Cream together the cream cheese, sugar, heavy cream, liqueur, and 1 teaspoon vanilla. Beat in eggs, 1 at a time, beating well after each addition. Beat mixture until light. Pour into crumb lined pan. Bake in middle of oven for 1 1/2 hours or until top of cake cracks and knife inserted in middle comes out clean. Transfer cake to rack. Let stand 5 minutes so it will set well. Combine sour cream, 1 teaspoon vanilla, and sugar in a bowl. Mix well and spread evenly over cake. Bake for 5 more minutes. Place cake on rack and let cool completely. Cover lightly with waxed paper and let chill overnight. When ready to serve, remove sides from pan and garnish with toasted almonds around outer edge and on top of cake.

gourmet chocolate cheesecake

Yield: 12 to 16 servings

Temperature: 350°
Baking time:
   1 hour 10 minutes
   plus 5 hours chilling time

"Worth the calories"

Crust
1 (8½-ounce) box thin chocolate wafers, crushed
¾ cup butter or margarine, melted
¼ teaspoon cinnamon

Combine crushed wafers with butter and cinnamon. Press into bottom and sides of a large springform pan. Chill.

Filling
1 (12-ounce) package semi-sweet chocolate chips
4 (8-ounce) packages cream cheese, softened
2 cups sugar
4 eggs
3 teaspoons cocoa
2 teaspoons vanilla
2 cups sour cream

Melt chocolate in top of double boiler over warm water. Beat softened cheese in large bowl until fluffy and smooth. Gradually beat in sugar, then eggs, 1 at a time. Add melted chocolate, cocoa, and vanilla. Blend thoroughly. Stir in sour cream and pour into chilled crust. Bake. Cool at room temperature and then refrigerate for at least 5 hours.

party cheesecakes

Temperature: 375°
Baking time:
  15 to 20 minutes

"A beautiful dessert for a buffet"

2 (8-ounce) packages
  cream cheese
2 eggs
3/4 cup sugar
1 Tablespoon lemon juice
1 teaspoon vanilla
1 (12-ounce) box vanilla
  wafers, crushed
1 (21-ounce) can cherry pie
  filling
1 teaspoon almond extract

In a small bowl, blend cream cheese, eggs, sugar, lemon juice, and vanilla. Spoon 1 Tablespoon vanilla wafer crumbs into each muffin tin lined with paper cups. Fill 3/4 full with the cream cheese mixture and bake. Combine the cherry pie filling with the almond extract. Top each cooled cake with 1 Tablespoon of this mixture. Refrigerate until ready to serve.

To make vanilla sugar: add 2 to 3 split vanilla beans to 1 quart sugar for several weeks.

miami cheesecake

Yield: 12 to 14 servings

Temperature: 400°, 500°, 200°
Baking time:
10, 12, 60 minutes
plus 3 hours chilling time

"One of the best"

Crust
1 cup sifted flour
1/4 cup sugar
1 teaspoon grated lemon rind
1/4 teaspoon vanilla
1/2 cup butter or margarine
1 egg yolk

Mix flour, sugar, lemon rind, and vanilla with a pastry blender. Add butter and the egg yolk. Shape into a mound, wrap in waxed paper, and chill for 1 hour. Put 1/3 of the dough between floured pieces of waxed paper; pat and stretch to cover the bottom of an ungreased 9-inch springform pan with sides removed; remove paper and trim to fit. Bake in a preheated 400° oven until golden brown, about 10 minutes; cool. Raise oven temperature to 500°, grease pan sides, attach to bottom, and pat rectangular-shaped dough pieces to the inside of the pan sides. The dough should be paper-thin and completely cover the sides.

(continued)

Cheese Filling

5 (8-ounce) packages cream
   cheese, softened
1 3/4 cups sugar
3 Tablespoons flour
1/4 teaspoon salt
1/2 teaspoon grated orange
   rind
1/2 teaspoon grated lemon
   rind
1/4 teaspoon vanilla
5 medium eggs plus 2 egg
   yolks
1/4 cup heavy cream

In a large bowl, beat cream cheese until fluffy. Mix sugar, flour, salt, orange rind, lemon rind, and vanilla; slowly add to the cream cheese. Beat until smooth. Add eggs and egg yolks, 1 at a time, beating after each addition. Stir in the cream. Pour batter into the lined pan and bake in a 500° oven for 12 minutes. Lower oven temperature to 200° and bake for 1 hour. *Do not open the oven door.* Cool on a wire rack and then remove sides of the pan. Chill for at least 3 hours.

Strawberry Glaze

3 cups fresh strawberries,
   stemmed and rinsed
1 cup water
1 1/2 Tablespoons cornstarch
1/2 to 3/4 cup sugar

In a medium saucepan, crush 1 cup strawberries and add the water. Cook for 2 minutes over moderate heat. Mix cornstarch with sugar and stir into the hot berry mixture. Bring to a boil, stirring constantly. Cook until clear and thick. Remove from heat and cool to room temperature. Place remaining strawberries on the cake, spoon on the glaze, and chill for 2 hours.

Variation: Use pineapple rings on the top with a large strawberry in the center of each. Blackberry, blueberry, and cherry garnishes are also excellent.

praline cheesecake

Yield: 8 to 12 servings

Temperature: 350°
Baking time: 1 hour

"Sinfully delicious"

Crust
1 1/4 cups crushed graham crackers
1/4 cup granulated sugar
1/4 cup chopped pecans
1/4 cup butter or margarine, melted

Combine crust ingredients and press on the bottom and sides of a 9-inch springform pan. Bake for 10 minutes.

Filling
1 cup brown sugar
3 (8-ounce) packages cream cheese, softened
1 (5-ounce) can evaporated milk
2 Tablespoons flour
1 1/2 teaspoons vanilla
3 eggs
1 cup pecan halves, toasted

Beat brown sugar, cream cheese, milk, flour, and vanilla in a large bowl or in a food processor. Add eggs and beat until well blended. Pour into the baked crust and bake for 50 minutes or until almost set. Cool in the pan for 30 minutes. Loosen sides and cool completely. Decorate the top of the cake with pecan halves.

Topping
1 cup dark corn syrup
1/4 cup cornstarch
2 Tablespoons brown sugar
1 teaspoon vanilla

In a small saucepan, combine corn syrup, cornstarch, and brown sugar. Cook, stirring constantly, until thick and bubbly. Remove from heat and add the vanilla. Cool slightly and pour over cheesecake.

Note: Pass remaining sauce.

strawberry cheesecake

Yield: 8 to 10 servings

Temperature: 300°
Baking time: 1 1/2 hours
plus 3 hours chilling time

"Creamy and rich"

Crust
**1 1/2 cups graham cracker
   crumbs**
1 cup sugar
**1/2 cup butter or margarine,
   melted**
1 teaspoon cinnamon

Mix crust ingredients and press into bottom and sides of an 8-inch springform pan. Chill.

Filling
**1 (12-ounce) package cream
   cheese, softened**
3/4 cup sugar
4 eggs, separated
2 Tablespoons flour
1 1/2 teaspoons vanilla
1/2 teaspoon salt
2 cups light cream, scalded

In a large bowl beat cream cheese, sugar, egg yolks, flour, vanilla, and salt with an electric mixer on high speed until smooth. With the mixer on the lowest speed, gradually add scalded cream to the cream cheese mixture. Beat egg whites until stiff. Fold into mixture. Pour into springform pan. Place springform pan into a shallow pan with 1-inch of water. Bake until barely set. Cool.

Topping
**1 pint fresh strawberries,
   rinsed and stemmed**
**1/4 cup red currant jelly,
   melted**

Slice strawberries and place decoratively on the top of cooled cheesecake. Paint strawberries with melted jelly. Refrigerate cheesecake at least 3 hours to chill thoroughly.

apple pie

"Judged the best in the Nashville 'Better Homes and Gardens' competition"

Crust
2 1/4 cups sifted flour
1 teaspoon salt
3/4 cup shortening
5 Tablespoons cold water

Combine the flour, salt, and shortening in a medium bowl. With a pastry blender or 2 knives, cut in the shortening until well blended but fairly coarse. Sprinkle mixture with the water, a little at a time; toss with a fork. Work the dough into a firm ball with your hands. Press 1/2 the dough into a flat circle on a lightly-floured surface. Roll it into a circle 10 1/2 inches in diameter. Gently place the dough in a 9-inch pie pan. Try not to stretch the dough.

(continued)

Filling

- **6 cups pared and thinly sliced Winesap apples**
- **1 cup sugar**
- **4 Tablespoons flour**
- **1/2 teaspoon cinnamon**
- **1 1/2 teaspoons vanilla**
- **1 Tablespoon water**
- **4 Tablespoons butter or margarine**

In a large bowl, combine the apples, sugar, flour, cinnamon, vanilla, and water gently but thoroughly. Pour the mixture into the pastry-lined pie pan. Dot with butter.

Roll the remaining dough 1/8 inch thick. Cut strips of pastry 1/2 to 3/4 inch wide. Lay 1/2 the strips on the filled pie at 1-inch intervals. Place the other 1/2 of the strips in the opposite direction, forming a diamond pattern. Flute the edge of the bottom crust, securing the strips. Bake for 10 minutes at 450°, reduce temperature to 325°, and bake for 45 minutes more.

Note: **The lattice pastry strips can be twisted to create a pretty effect.**

bourbon pie

Temperature: 400°
Baking time: 5 minutes
    plus overnight freezing

"Rich and delicious"

Crust
1 1/4 cups crushed chocolate
    wafer crumbs
1/4 cup sugar
1/3 cup butter or margarine,
    melted

Mix wafer crumbs, sugar, and
butter together in a small bowl.
Press on the bottom of a 9-inch
pie pan. Bake for 5 minutes in a
400° oven.

Filling
3 egg yolks
1/2 cup sugar
1/2 envelope unflavored
    gelatin
2 1/2 Tablespoons water
1/2 ounce unsweetened
    chocolate, grated
1 cup heavy cream
2 Tablespoons bourbon
    or more
1 teaspoon vanilla
1/2 cup chopped pecans

In a large bowl, beat egg yolks
and sugar. Dissolve gelatin in
water. Add to sugar mixture.
Add chocolate, cream, bourbon,
vanilla, and nuts; mixing well.
Pour into crust and freeze
overnight.

Use blender or food processor to make granulated sugar into superfine sugar.

brandy alexander pie

Yield: 8 servings

Preparation time:
10 minutes
plus 3 hours chilling time

"Very light"

1 envelope unflavored gelatin
1/2 cup cold water
2/3 cup sugar
1/8 teaspoon salt
3 eggs, separated
1/4 cup cognac
1/4 cup creme de cacao
2 cups heavy cream
1 (9-inch) graham cracker crust
Chocolate shavings
Toasted almonds, optional

Sprinkle gelatin over cold water in the top of a double boiler. Add 1/3 cup sugar, salt, and egg yolks. Stir to blend. Stir over low heat until gelatin dissolves and mixture thickens slightly. Do not boil. Remove from heat. Stir in cognac and creme de cacao. Chill until mixture starts to mound slightly. Beat the egg whites with remaining sugar until stiff. Fold into gelatin mixture. Whip and fold in 1 cup heavy cream. Turn into the crust and refrigerate. Chill thoroughly. Before serving, top with the remaining cream that has been whipped, chocolate shavings, and almonds, if desired.

421

chess pie

"So very rich and easy"

2 eggs
1 cup sugar
¼ cup butter or margarine,
melted
1 Tablespoon milk or light
cream
1 Tablespoon bourbon
1 Tablespoon cornmeal
Dash salt
1 (8-inch) unbaked pie shell
or 6 (3-inch) unbaked
tart shells

Beat the eggs lightly in a medium bowl. Stir in the sugar, melted butter, milk, bourbon, cornmeal, and salt. Pour mixture into the pie shell and bake.

Variations: **This recipe will make 6 (3-inch) tarts. Do not fill each tart shell too full. Bake on the lowest rack of the oven at 400° for 10 minutes; move to the middle rack and bake another 10 minutes.**

Lemon Chess Pie: **Substitute 2 Tablespoons fresh lemon juice and 2 teaspoons grated lemon rind for the bourbon.**

Coconut Chess Pie: **Add ½ cup flaked coconut to the basic chess pie recipe. Use a 9-inch pie shell.**

chocolate pecan tart

Yield: 8 servings

Temperature: 350°
Baking time: 50 minutes

"Melts in your mouth"

1/4 cup butter or margarine
1/2 cup brown sugar
1/2 cup granulated sugar
1/4 cup dark corn syrup
1/2 cup light corn syrup
Dash salt
1 teaspoon vanilla
2 Tablespoons bourbon
1/4 cup semi-sweet chocolate chips
3 eggs, beaten
1/2 cup chopped pecans
1 (9-inch) deep dish pie shell

In a 1-quart saucepan, melt butter over low heat. Stir in sugars, syrups, and salt until sugars dissolve. Remove from heat and cool slightly. Add vanilla, bourbon, chocolate, eggs, and pecans; mixing well. Place pie shell in a 350° oven on the bottom rack for a few minutes. Remove and pour in the filling; return to the middle rack of the oven and bake for 50 minutes.

Note: To avoid a soggy crust, fill when still warm. Filling can be done a day or 2 ahead, brought to room temperature, poured into warm crust, and baked.

Serving suggestion: Serve warm with sweetened whipped cream.

chocolate phyllo pie

Yield: 12 servings

Temperature: 375°
Baking time: 20 minutes
   plus 3 hours chilling time

"A really special treat"

6 (18x12-inch) phyllo sheets
6 Tablespoons butter or
   margarine, melted
5 egg whites
1 Tablespoon unflavored
   gelatin
1/3 cup cold water
1 (6-ounce) package semi-
   sweet chocolate chips
1/2 cup butter or margarine
1 teaspoon instant coffee
4 egg yolks
1/4 cup brandy
1/2 cup sugar
1 Tablespoon sugar
1 cup heavy cream, whipped
Toasted sliced almonds

Grease a 9-inch springform pan. Place phyllo sheets in bottom and up sides of pan, brushing each with melted butter and overlapping pan edges. Trim dough to pan edges; crumble trimmings into pan. Bake for 20 minutes. Combine 1 egg white and 1 Tablespoon water and brush over hot crust. In small saucepan soften gelatin in cold water. Heat and stir until gelatin is dissolved. Stir in chocolate, 1/2 cup butter, and coffee; heat and stir until melted. In the top of a double boiler, combine yolks and brandy; beat with mixer until frothy. Gradually beat in 1/2 cup sugar. Place over simmering water. Cook and stir about 8 minutes or just until slightly thicker. *DO NOT OVERCOOK.* Place pan over cold water and beat for 3 or 4 minutes. Stir chocolate mixture into yolk mixture. Beat whites to soft peaks. Add sugar and beat to stiff peaks. Fold chocolate mixture into whites. Pour into baked crust. Chill, covered, for at least 3 hours. Before serving, top with whipped cream and almonds.

cran-apple crumb pie

Yield: 6 servings

Temperature: 450°, 350°
Baking time:
   10, 20 to 30 minutes

"Tart and delicious"

1 1/2 cups cranberries
1 cup granulated sugar
1 1/2 Tablespoons quick
   tapioca
2 teaspoons lemon juice
Dash salt
4 cups *thinly sliced*
   tart apples
1 unbaked (9-inch) pie shell
1/2 cup flour
1/4 cup brown sugar
1 teaspoon cinnamon
1/4 cup butter or margarine

Coarsely chop cranberries. Mix
sugar, tapioca, lemon juice, and
salt. In a large bowl, combine
with apples and cranberries.
Pour into pie shell. Combine
flour, brown sugar, and
cinnamon; cut in butter to make
a coarse crumb mixture.
Sprinkle mixture on top of pie.
Bake at 450° for 10 minutes.
Reduce temperature to 350° and
bake for 20 to 30 minutes more
or until apples are tender.

date-chess pie

Yield: 8 servings

Temperature: 350°
Baking time: 55 minutes

"Well worth dieting tomorrow"

3 egg yolks
2/3 cup sugar
1 Tablespoon flour
1/2 teaspoon salt
1 1/3 cups heavy cream
1 teaspoon vanilla
1 cup chopped dates
1 cup chopped walnuts
1 (9-inch) pie shell
1 cup heavy cream, whipped
   and sweetened to taste

In a small bowl of an electric
mixer, beat egg yolks, sugar,
flour, and salt on medium speed
until thickened and lemon-
colored. With mixer on low
speed, blend in 1 1/3 cups cream
and the vanilla. Stir in dates and
walnuts and pour into the pie
shell. Bake in a 350° oven for 50
to 60 minutes, or until top is
golden brown. Cool. Serve
topped with whipped cream.

deep dish apple pie

Yield: 8 to 10 servings

Temperature: 425°, 350°
Baking time:
   10, 45 minutes

"Just like Mom made"

5 to 6 tart apples, peeled and sliced
2 (9-inch) deep dish pie shells
4 Tablespoons butter or margarine
1 1/4 cups sugar
1/2 cup flour
1 teaspoon cinnamon
1/2 teaspoon nutmeg
1/2 teaspoon ground cloves
1/2 teaspoon allspice
2 Tablespoons fresh lemon juice

Place 1/2 of sliced apples into a (9-inch) pie shell. Dot apples with 2 Tablespoons butter. Mix sugar, flour, cinnamon, nutmeg, cloves, and allspice. Sprinkle half of the mixture over apples. Repeat the entire procedure with remaining ingredients. Cover with lattice pie crust, using remaining pie shell. The pie may be frozen at this point. Bake pie at 425° for 10 minutes. Reduce heat to 350° and bake for 45 minutes.

fudge pie

Yield: 6 servings

Temperature: 375°
Baking time: 35 minutes

"So good"

2/3 cup evaporated milk
2 Tablespoons butter
1 (6-ounce) package semi-sweet chocolate chips
2 eggs, beaten
1 cup sugar
2 Tablespoons flour
3/4 teaspoon salt
1 cup chopped pecans
2 teaspoons vanilla
1 (9-inch) unbaked pie shell

In the top of a double boiler over medium heat, combine milk, butter, and chocolate; stir until melted. Add the eggs and stir until thoroughly mixed. Combine sugar and flour in a large bowl. Stir in the chocolate mixture, salt, pecans, and vanilla. Pour into the pie shell and bake. Serve warm.

fabulous chocolate pie

Yield: 10 servings

Temperature: 350°
Baking time: 25 minutes

"This truly deserves its name."

- **8 ounces semi-sweet chocolate**
- **1/4 cup freshly-brewed coffee**
- **8 eggs, separated**
- **2/3 cup granulated sugar**
- **2 1/2 teaspoons vanilla**
- **1/8 teaspoon salt**
- **2 Tablespoons butter or margarine**
- **1/2 cup Zwieback crumbs**
- **3/4 cup salted, chopped almonds**
- **1 1/3 cups heavy cream**
- **1/4 cup sifted powdered sugar**
- **Chocolate shavings**

Let chocolate and coffee stand in the top of a covered double boiler over low heat until chocolate melts. Beat egg yolks in a bowl until thickened; then gradually add 2/3 cup sugar. Add to chocolate mixture. Add 1 teaspoon vanilla. In another bowl, beat egg whites with salt until stiff, but not dry. Fold whites into chocolate until blended. Butter and dust a 9-inch pie plate with Zwieback crumbs. Fill with chocolate mixture until just level with edge of pie plate. Refrigerate remaining mixture. Bake pie for 25 minutes. Turn off oven and let stand for another 5 minutes. Cool on racks for 2 hours. Fold almonds into chilled chocolate mixture and pour into pie where baked chocolate has sunk to make a shell. Whip cream with remaining vanilla and powdered sugar and pour onto pie. Shave chocolate on top and keep refrigerated.

french mint pies

Yield: 30 servings

Temperature: 325°
Baking time:
   20 minutes plus
   3 hours freezing time

"Wonderful to have on hand for an emergency"

Crust
15 soda crackers, crumbled
1 cup granulated sugar
3 egg whites, beaten
1 cup chopped nuts
1 teaspoon vanilla

Filling
1 1/2 cups butter or
   margarine, softened
3 cups powdered sugar
5 ounces unsweetened
   chocolate, melted
6 eggs
1 1/2 teaspoons peppermint
   extract
3 teaspoons vanilla

Combine crust ingredients and pour a spoonful into each cupcake paper. Bake. In a mixing bowl, beat butter and sugar for 5 minutes. Add chocolate and beat for 3 minutes. Add eggs, 1 at a time, beating well after each one; add peppermint and vanilla. Beat mixture 5 more minutes. Spoon into cups lined with crust. Freeze until half an hour before serving.

To make a non-soggy pie crust, brush the crust with lightly beaten egg white or with apricot glaze for added flavor in sweet pastries. Bake the pie in the lower third of your oven.

frozen lemonade pie

**Preparation time:
30 minutes
plus overnight freezing**

"A light dessert with a rich flavor"

Crust

**1 1/4 cups crushed vanilla
   wafers
2 Tablespoons sugar
4 Tablespoons butter or
   margarine, melted**

Combine crushed wafers, sugar, and butter. Press firmly on the bottom and sides of a 10-inch pie pan. Chill.

Filling

**1 (6-ounce) can lemonade
   concentrate, thawed
4 eggs, separated
1 (14-ounce) can sweetened
   condensed milk
4 Tablespoons sugar
1 cup heavy cream
Grated lemon rind, optional**

In a large bowl of an electric mixer or a food processor, combine the lemonade, egg yolks, and the condensed milk. With clean beaters, beat the egg whites, adding the sugar slowly until stiff. Fold into lemonade mixture. Pour filling into crust and freeze overnight or for at least 8 hours. Before serving; whip cream, sweeten to taste, and garnish the top of the pie. Sprinkle with grated lemon rind, if desired.

glazed strawberry pie

Yield: 6 to 8 servings

**Preparation time:
30 minutes plus
3 hours chilling time**

"So pretty, you'll hate to cut it."

1 quart strawberries
1 cup sugar
3 Tablespoons cornstarch
1/2 cup water (if liqueur is used, decrease water by 2 Tablespoons)
1 Tablespoon fresh lemon juice
1/4 teaspoon salt
2 Tablespoons kirsch, optional
1 (9-inch) baked pie shell
1 cup heavy cream, whipped

Wash and stem strawberries. Divide strawberries into 2 groups, reserving the better looking berries to keep whole. Put half of the berries and sugar in a food processor or blender and puree. Add cornstarch and water, blending well; add lemon juice and salt. Blend well. Put the mixture in a medium saucepan and cook until it thickens, stirring constantly. Add the liqueur, if desired, and mix well. Cool. Arrange the reserved berries inside the pie shell. Strain the mixture over the berries in the pie shell. Chill the pie thoroughly, at least 3 hours. Garnish or serve with whipped cream.

grasshopper pie

Temperature: 400°
Baking time: 5 minutes
   plus 2 hours chilling time

"Refreshing!"

Crust
1 1/4 cups crushed chocolate
   wafers
1/4 cup sugar
1/3 cup butter or margarine,
   melted

Filling
1 envelope unflavored
   gelatin
1/2 cup sugar
Dash salt
1/2 cup cold water
3 eggs, separated
1/4 cup green creme de
   menthe
1/4 cup white creme de cacao
1 cup heavy cream, whipped

Garnish
1 cup heavy cream,
   whipped, optional
Chocolate shavings,
   optional

Mix crust ingredients and press against the bottom and sides of a 9-inch pie pan. Bake. Cool. Mix gelatin, 1/4 cup sugar, and the salt in the top of a double boiler. Add water and egg yolks, 1 at a time, blending well. Place over boiling water and stir constantly until gelatin dissolves and mixture thickens slightly, about 5 minutes. Remove from heat; stir in liqueurs. Chill, stirring occasionally, until mixture has the consistency of an unbeaten egg white. Beat egg whites until stiff. Gradually add remaining sugar. Fold into gelatin mixture. Fold in the whipped cream. Turn into crust and chill for at least 2 hours (best chilled overnight). Garnish with whipped cream and shaved chocolate, if desired.

heavenly pie

Temperature: 275°
Baking time: 1 hour plus
24 hours chilling time

"Light as a cloud!"

1 1/2 cups sugar
1/4 teaspoon cream of tartar
4 eggs, separated
3 Tablespoons fresh lemon juice
1 Tablespoon grated lemon rind
2 cups heavy cream, whipped
1 pint fresh strawberries, raspberries, or blueberries

Sift together 1 cup sugar and cream of tartar. Beat egg whites until stiff, gradually adding the sugar mixture. Continue beating until thoroughly blended. Line a 9-inch pie plate with parchment paper or dust with baking powder. Line the bottom and sides of the pie plate with the meringue mixture. Do not spread too close to the rim. Bake. Cool completely. Beat egg yolks slightly, stir in 1/2 cup sugar, lemon juice, and lemon rind. Cook in the top of a double boiler, stirring constantly, until very thick (8 to 10 minutes). Cool. Combine 1/2 of the whipped cream with the lemon mixture. Fill shell. Place fruit on top of the lemon filling and cover with remaining whipped cream. Chill for 24 hours. The pie may be frozen; however, put on whipped cream topping after removing from freezer.

iroquois pie

Yield: 12 to 16 servings

Temperature: 350°
Baking time:
    45 to 50 minutes

"Always a winner"

2 unbaked (9-inch) pie shells
1/2 cup butter or margarine,
    melted
1 cup sugar
1 cup light corn syrup
4 eggs, beaten
3 Tablespoons bourbon
1 (6-ounce) package semi-
    sweet chocolate chips
1 1/4 cups chopped pecans
	Preheat oven to 350°. Remove
	pie shells from freezer and allow
	them to reach room
	temperature. In a large bowl,
	combine the remaining
	ingredients, adding them 1 at a
	time and stirring after each
	addition. Pour into pie shells and
	bake until firm.

Variation: Sweet chocolate chips may be used for a sweeter-tasting pie. Serve either version with a whipped cream topping.

lemon cream pie

Yield: 6 servings

Preparation time:
    20 minutes plus
    2 hours chilling time

"A rich taste treat"

5 egg yolks
1 cup sugar
5 Tablespoons water
4 Tablespoons fresh
    lemon juice
1/4 cup butter or margarine,
    melted
1 baked (9-inch) pie shell
    or 6 tart shells
1 cup heavy cream, whipped
	Beat egg yolks in a medium
	bowl until light in texture.
	Alternately, add sugar, water,
	and juice. Cook in top of a
	double boiler, stirring
	continually until thickened.
	Remove from heat and stir in
	butter. Cool. Pour in pie shell or
	tart shells. Top with whipped
	cream. Chill for at least 2 hours
	before serving.

pecan pie

Yield: 6 servings

Temperature: 450°, 350°
Baking time:
  10, 35 minutes

"Southern cooking at its best"

3 Tablespoons butter or
  margarine
3/4 cup sugar
1 teaspoon vanilla
3 eggs
1 cup white corn syrup
1/4 teaspoon salt
1 cup chopped pecans
1 (9-inch) unbaked
  pie shell

Cream with a mixer: butter, sugar, and vanilla until fluffy. Add eggs, 1 at a time, mixing thoroughly after each. Add syrup and salt; mix well. Add pecans, mix, and turn into pie shell. Bake 10 minutes at 450°. Reduce heat to 350° and bake approximately 35 more minutes. Cool on a wire rack.

Variation: **Add extra pecan halves on the top of the pie 15 minutes before it is ready.**

praline pumpkin pie

Yield: 6 to 8 servings

Temperature: 450°, 325°
Baking time:
  10, 60 to 65 minutes

"Something different for Thanksgiving!"

Praline Layer
1/2 cup finely chopped
  pecans
2 Tablespoons butter or
  margarine, melted
1/3 cup brown sugar
1 (9-inch) unbaked pie shell

Blend praline layer ingredients in a small bowl. Press the mixture gently into the bottom of the pie shell.

(continued)

Filling

2 eggs
1 (29-ounce) can pumpkin
2/3 cup brown sugar
1 Tablespoon flour
1/2 teaspoon ground ginger
1/4 teaspoon ground cloves
1/2 teaspoon cinnamon
1/2 teaspoon salt
1 cup light cream

Beat eggs until frothy and add remaining filling ingredients, 1 at a time. Mix thoroughly. Pour mixture into pie shell over praline layer. Bake for 10 minutes in a 450° oven; reduce heat to 325° and bake for 60 to 65 minutes more.

raspberry passion
Yield: 12 servings

Preparation time:
20 minutes plus
4 hours freezing time

"Great to have on hand for company"

1 (10-ounce) package frozen red raspberries
2 egg whites
1 cup sugar
1 Tablespoon lemon juice
1 Tablespoon Amaretto
1 cup heavy cream
1 teaspoon vanilla
1 Tablespoon brandy
1/4 cup sliced almonds, toasted
2 (9-inch) pie shells, baked and frozen

Place partially thawed raspberries, egg whites, sugar, lemon juice, and Amaretto in a large mixing bowl. Beat with an electric mixer at high speed for 15 minutes. Whip cream until stiff; add vanilla and brandy. Fold whipped cream and almonds into raspberry mixture. Pour into pie shells and freeze for at least 4 hours.

toffee coffee pie

Q Q Q

Temperature: 375°
Baking time: 15 minutes
   plus overnight chilling

"Delicious and beautiful"

Pastry
1/2 package pie crust mix
1/4 cup light brown sugar,
   firmly packed
3/4 cup finely chopped
   pecans
1 ounce unsweetened
   chocolate, grated
1 Tablespoon water
1 teaspoon vanilla

Combine pastry ingredients,
using a fork, a pastry blender, or
a food processor. Turn into a
well-greased 9-inch pie pan,
pressing firmly against the
bottom and sides of the pan.
Bake.

Filling
1/2 cup butter or margarine,
   softened
3/4 cup granulated sugar
1 ounce unsweetened
   chocolate, melted and
   cooled
2 teaspoons instant coffee
2 eggs

In a small bowl of an electric
mixer, beat butter until creamy
at medium speed. Gradually add
sugar; beating until fluffy. Blend
in chocolate and coffee. Add 1
egg and beat for 5 minutes. Add
another egg and beat for 5 more
minutes. Turn filling into cooled
pie shell and refrigerate
overnight.

Topping
2 cups heavy cream
1 Tablespoon instant
   coffee, dissolved in
   1 Tablespoon water
1/2 cup powdered sugar
Chocolate curls, optional

The next day, combine cream
with the dissolved coffee and the
powdered sugar. Cover and
refrigerate for 1 hour. Beat
mixture until stiff and pipe onto
the pie with a decorating tube.
Top with chocolate curls, if
desired.

ritz cracker pie

Yield: 6 servings

Temperature: 350°
Baking time: 30 minutes

"Unusual - fun for those who haven't had it before"

1/2 teaspoon baking powder
3 egg whites
1 cup sugar
1/2 teaspoon almond extract
1/2 teaspoon vanilla
2/3 cup chopped pecans
14 Ritz crackers, crushed
Ice cream or whipped cream

Add baking powder to egg whites and beat until stiff. Add sugar gradually; add almond extract and vanilla. Fold in pecans and crackers. Pour into a greased (9 or 10-inch) pie pan and bake. Top with ice cream or whipped cream.

caramel ice cream delight

Yield: 12 servings

Temperature: 375°
Baking time:
15 minutes plus
3 hours freezing time

"Great for when your time is short"

1 cup flour
1/2 cup butter or margarine, softened
1/4 cup brown sugar
1/2 cup chopped pecans
1/2 gallon vanilla ice cream, softened
1 (12-ounce) jar caramel ice cream topping

Combine flour, butter, brown sugar, and pecans in a food processor or blender. Spread on a cookie sheet. Bake at 375° for 15 minutes. Cool and crumble. Layer 1/2 the crumb mixture and the ice cream in a 13x9x2-inch pan. Cover with the caramel sauce and top with the remaining crumb mixture. Freeze for at least 3 hours or until firm. Cut into squares.

coffee toffee torte

Yield: 8 to 10 servings

Preparation time:
1 hour plus
5 hours freezing time

"Make ahead for a party"

2 1/2 to 3 dozen macaroons
1 quart chocolate almond
or Jamoca Almond Fudge
ice cream
8 Tablespoons chocolate
fudge sauce
1 quart coffee ice cream
14 small Heath bars

Garnishes
Fudge sauce
Whipped cream

Oil an 8-inch springform pan. Crush 1/2 of the macaroons and spread in bottom of the pan. Slightly soften almond ice cream and spread on top of crumbs. Drizzle 4 Tablespoons chocolate sauce over ice cream. Crush remaining macaroons and spread on top of ice cream. Soften coffee ice cream and spread over second layer of crumbs. Drizzle with 4 more Tablespoons chocolate sauce. Freeze. Crush Heath bars and sprinkle on top. Freeze for 4 to 5 hours. Remove torte from pan and place on a serving platter. Let stand at room temperature for 20 minutes. Pass fudge sauce and whipped cream when ready to serve.

Note: **This is a bit messy to serve and could be made in individual ramekins, if desired.**

frozen strawberry dessert

Yield: 12 servings

Temperature: 350°
Baking time:
15 to 20 minutes plus
6 hours freezing time

"Great to take along for a crowd"

Crust
1 cup flour
1/2 cup brown sugar
1 cup chopped pecans
1 cup butter or margarine

Blend the crust ingredients and spread in a 13x9x2-inch baking pan. Bake for 10 minutes. Stir the mixture and then bake for an additional 5 to 10 minutes or until lightly browned.

Filling
2 egg whites
1 cup granulated sugar
2 teaspoons lemon juice
2 (10-ounce) packages
frozen strawberries,
partially thawed
1/2 cup heavy cream,
whipped

In a large bowl of an electric mixer, beat the egg whites until stiff; add the sugar gradually. Add the lemon juice and berries; whip at high speed for 5 minutes. Fold in whipped cream and spread the mixture over the baked crust. Freeze for 6 hours or overnight.

Serving suggestion: **Cut into squares and garnish each portion with strawberry halves and whipped cream.**

ice cream bombe with raspberry sauce

Yield: 8 servings

Preparation time:
   30 minutes plus
   6 hours freezing time

"A showy dessert that's easy"

1 **quart vanilla ice cream**
1 **(16-ounce) package frozen peaches, thawed**
1 **cup sour cream**
1/2 **cup grenadine**

Raspberry Sauce
1 **(10-ounce) package frozen raspberries, thawed**
2 **Tablespoons Grand Marnier**

Soften ice cream. Puree peaches in blender or food processor. Add peaches, sour cream, and grenadine to ice cream. Mix well. Pour into mold and freeze, covered, for at least 6 hours. Unmold with a warm towel onto a platter and leave in the freezer until 20 minutes before serving. Combine sauce ingredients and pour over bombe before serving.

strawberries romanoff

Yield: 6 to 8 servings

Preparation time:
   5 minutes plus
   1 hour chilling time

"A special occasion dessert"

2 **quarts large ripe strawberries (do not use frozen)**
1 **cup finely granulated sugar**
1 **cup sour cream**
1 to 1 1/2 **cups vanilla ice cream, softened**
2 to 4 **Tablespoons Cointreau**

Wash, stem, and dry berries. In a large bowl, mix berries with sugar and refrigerate until ready to serve. Combine the sour cream, ice cream, and Cointreau at serving time and add to the strawberries.

440

mocha toffee delight

Preparation time:
30 minutes plus
4 hours freezing time

"Delicious and beautiful to serve"

14 ladyfingers, split
4 Tablespoons instant coffee
1 Tablespoon boiling water
1/2 gallon vanilla or coffee ice cream, softened
12 Heath bars, frozen and crushed
1/2 cup heavy cream
2 Tablespoons white creme de cacao

Line the bottom and sides of a 9-inch springform pan with the ladyfingers, cutting to fit. Dissolve coffee in boiling water. Cool. Stir ice cream and 3/4 of the crushed candy together and spoon into the pan; cover and freeze until firm. Before serving, combine cream and creme de cacao. Whip until soft peaks form. Spread over ice cream and garnish with reserved crushed Heath bars.

Note: **Take frozen dessert out of the freezer and leave in the refrigerator for 30 minutes for ease in serving.**

oreo ice cream pie

Yield: 8 to 12 servings

Preparation time:
45 minutes plus
6 hours freezing time

"Sinfully rich and you'll love every bite!"

25 Oreos, crushed
1/3 cup butter or margarine, melted
1 quart of your favorite ice cream or 1 pint each of 2 different flavors
4 ounces semi-sweet chocolate, melted
1 cup sugar
2 Tablespoons butter or margarine
2 (5-ounce) cans evaporated milk

Combine crushed oreos with 1/3 cup melted butter. Press mixture into a 13x9x2-inch glass dish to make a crust; freeze. After several hours, melt ice cream slightly and press on top of the crust (in layers, if 2 flavors are used). Refreeze. Do not melt excessively or the crust will absorb the ice cream and become soggy. In the top of a double boiler, combine chocolate, sugar, 2 Tablespoons butter, and milk. Cook, stirring continuously, until ingredients are well blended and mixture becomes thick. *Cool completely* and pour over ice cream. Refreeze.

strawberry french sorbet

Yield: 6 servings

**Preparation time:
10 minutes plus
5 hours freezing time**

"A special treat for a summer party"

4 cups fresh strawberries
2 cups sugar
2 cups buttermilk

In a large bowl, mash the strawberries and mix with the sugar. Add the buttermilk and blend well. Pour mixture into a 15x10x1-inch jelly roll pan. Freeze for 1 hour or until firm. Transfer the mixture to a blender or a food processor and whip. Refreeze for 4 hours in individual molds or in a storage container.

Serving suggestion: Serve in hollowed-out orange or melon shells or in green apples which have been cored and hollowed-out.

lemon ice cream

Yield: 1 gallon

**Preparation time:
4 1/2 hours**

"Refreshing and easy"

3 cups sugar
1 cup fresh lemon juice
4 to 8 teaspoons grated lemon rind
2 (13-ounce) cans evaporated milk, chilled
1/2 gallon whole milk (will not use all of this)

Mix sugar, lemon juice, and lemon rind together; let stand for 2 hours. Pour evaporated milk into ice cream freezer. Add lemon mixture; stir well. Add whole milk to bring mixture to 3/4 height of 1-gallon container. Stir well and freeze. Store in a refrigerator freezer for at least 2 hours.

chocolate almond ice cream

Yield: 1 quart

Preparation time: 4 hours

"Rich and delicious"

1 cup sugar
1 1/2 teaspoons unflavored
   gelatin
4 cups light cream
3 ounces unsweetened
   chocolate
1 egg, slightly beaten
1 teaspoon vanilla
Dash salt
3/4 cup toasted, slivered
   almonds

Thoroughly combine sugar and gelatin in saucepan. Add half of the cream and all the chocolate. Stir over low heat until chocolate melts. Add egg, mix well, and heat until thickened. Chill; add remaining cream, vanilla, salt, and almonds. Place in an electric or hand crank freezer and freeze.

Note: **This is better if frozen in a refrigerator freezer for at least 2 hours before serving.**

peach ice cream

Yield: 1 gallon

**Preparation time:
   3 1/2 hours**

"A summer treat"

1 quart fresh peaches,
   diced
3 cups sugar
1 Tablespoon fresh lemon
   juice
Pinch salt
1/4 to 1/2 teaspoon almond
   extract (only when
   peaches do not have
   enough flavor)
4 cups heavy cream
2 cups light cream (and
   more to fill freezer
   3/4 full)

Mix peaches, sugar, lemon juice, salt, and almond extract in a large bowl. Add heavy cream and 2 cups light cream. Pour into an electric freezer. Add enough light cream to fill freezer 3/4 full. Freeze and remove dasher. Cover and place in refrigerator freezer at least 2 hours before serving.

milky way ice cream

Yield: 1 quart

Preparation time: 3 hours

"Tastes heavenly"

8 Milky Way bars, sliced
2 cups milk
5 eggs
1 1/2 cups sugar
2 teaspoons vanilla
1 (13-ounce) can evaporated milk
1 (5-ounce) can evaporated milk
1 1/2 cups light cream

In a heavy saucepan, melt candy bars in the milk. Cool. Meanwhile, beat eggs, add sugar, and mix well. Add vanilla, evaporated milk, and light cream. Combine the chocolate mixture with the egg mixture, mixing well. Pour mixture into freezer can. Add extra milk if needed to fill to the full line. Freeze in the ice cream freezer. Stir well and freeze in a refrigerator freezer for a few hours before serving.

Ground or chopped nuts should be frozen no longer than 2 or 3 months.

vanilla ice cream

Yield: 1 quart

**Preparation time:
3 to 4 hours**

"The very best"

**1 quart milk
3 eggs
3/4 cup sugar
1 1/2 teaspoons vanilla**

Heat milk until a skin forms. Let milk cool. Beat eggs and add sugar. Slowly add a small amount of milk to the eggs and stir; add the rest with vanilla. Cook in top of a double boiler over boiling water for 5 minutes. Freeze in ice cream freezer. Remove and freeze in refrigerator freezer 2 to 3 hours.

Variations: Here are some suggestions for those with creative souls:

-Add 1 quart pureed strawberries or peaches

-Add a (6-ounce) package of semi-sweet chocolate chips or butterscotch chips to cooled ice cream mixture

-Add 1 cup chunky peanut butter

-Add 2 teaspoons peppermint extract (decrease vanilla by 1/2 teaspoon) with a few drops of green food coloring. Chocolate chips (6 ounces) may be added too

Have fun!

cold grand marnier souffle with strawberry sauce

Yield: 8 to 10 servings

**Preparation time:
1 hour plus 3 to 4
hours chilling time**

"A dramatic end to a perfect meal"

1 Tablespoon unflavored
  gelatin
1/4 cup cold water
3 eggs, separated
1 cup sugar
Dash salt
2 teaspoons grated lemon
  rind
6 Tablespoons Grand
  Marnier
2 cups heavy cream,
  whipped

Dissolve gelatin in cold water. Beat egg yolks, adding sugar slowly until mixture is thick and pale. Beat whites with salt until stiff. Add lemon rind, Grand Marnier, and dissolved gelatin to yolks. Fold mixture into whites then fold in whipped cream carefully. Pile lightly into a 6-cup souffle dish or mold. Chill or freeze.

Strawberry Sauce
1 (10-ounce) package
  strawberries, pureed
2 Tablespoons Grand
  Marnier

Combine strawberries and 2 Tablespoons Grand Marnier; serve over the chilled souffle.

Variation: Raspberries may be substituted for a delightful change.

cold orange souffle

Yield: 6 to 8 servings

**Preparation time: 1 hour
plus 3 hours chilling time**

"Light and delicate"

8 large oranges
**2 Tablespoons frozen
orange juice concentrate**
1 envelope gelatin
4 eggs, separated
1 Tablespoon orange liqueur
1 cup sugar
1 cup heavy cream

Cut a small slice off the top of each orange. Reserve the tops. Put frozen concentrate into a 2-cup measuring cup. Squeeze the oranges and add the fresh orange juice to the orange concentrate to make 2 cups. Pour orange juice into a large saucepan. Sprinkle gelatin over the juice. Place over low heat and stir until gelatin is dissolved. In a small bowl, beat egg yolks lightly and mix in a small amount of hot orange juice. Pour the egg mixture gradually into the orange juice in the saucepan. Cook, stirring, for about 3 minutes until slightly thickened. Remove from heat and let cool. Place plastic wrap on the surface of the mixture and refrigerate for 30 minutes, stirring occasionally, until mixture mounds slightly. Grate 1 Tablespoon orange rind from the reserved tops. Stir orange rind and liqueur into chilled mixture.

(continued)

In a small bowl, beat egg whites until foamy with an electric mixer. Add 1/2 cup sugar gradually and beat until stiff. Fold this into the orange mixture. In a small bowl, beat cream with remaining 1/2 cup sugar until stiff peaks form. Fold into the orange mixture. Spoon mixture into hollowed out orange shells or ramekins. Chill for at least 3 hours before serving.

individual coffee souffles

Yield: 8-12 servings

**Preparation time:
1/2 hour plus 3 to 4
hours chilling time**

"Great for a party"

3 egg whites
**3 Tablespoons instant
coffee**
Dash salt
2 Tablespoons sugar
2 cups heavy cream
1/8 cup sugar
1 teaspoon vanilla
**2 Tablespoons creme de
cacao liqueur**
**2 Heath bars, finely
chopped**
1/2 cup toasted almonds

Combine egg whites, coffee, and salt. Beat until stiff, gradually adding 2 Tablespoons sugar. Beat the cream, gradually adding 1/8 cup sugar and vanilla. Combine the 2 mixtures and add the liqueur. Fold in the candy. Fill individual ramekins and refrigerate until solid. Sprinkle chopped almonds on top of each cup. Covered with heavy foil, the cups may be frozen indefinitely. Defrost 25 minutes before serving.

Note: **This dessert may also be made in a 1 1/2-quart souffle dish.**

hot raspberry souffle

Yield: 6 servings

Temperature: 375°
Baking time:
   35 to 45 minutes

"Not a spoonful will be left."

6 Tablespoons butter or margarine
1/4 cup granulated sugar
3 Tablespoons flour
1/2 cup milk
2 Tablespoons granulated sugar
4 egg yolks, beaten
1/4 cup Amaretto
2 (10-ounce) packages frozen sweetened raspberries, thawed and drained, reserving 1/4 cup syrup
3 Tablespoons raspberry jam
6 egg whites
1/4 teaspoon cream of tartar
Pinch salt

Place a waxed-paper collar, with a few inches overlap, around a 1 1/2-quart souffle dish. Butter the dish and the collar with 3 Tablespoons butter and dust thoroughly with 1/4 cup sugar. Set aside. Melt remaining butter in a small saucepan. Add the flour and blend until smooth. Remove from heat and slowly add milk and sugar, blending thoroughly. Cook over medium heat, stirring constantly, until mixture thickens. Remove from heat. In a medium bowl, combine egg yolks, Amaretto, reserved raspberry syrup, and jam. Add 1/3 of the hot milk mixture and blend thoroughly. Add egg mixture to the remaining milk in the saucepan and cook for 1 minute over medium heat, stirring slowly. In a large bowl, combine raspberries and the hot milk mixture. Cool completely. Beat egg whites until foamy; add cream of tartar and salt and beat until stiff peaks form. Gently fold 1/2 the egg whites into the raspberry mixture and combine thoroughly. Carefully fold in the remaining egg whites and spoon into the souffle dish. Bake until golden brown.

(continued)

Sauce

**1 (10-ounce) package frozen
  sweetened raspberries,
  thawed and undrained**
2 Tablespoons Amaretto

Powdered sugar

While the souffle is baking,
partially puree the sauce
ingredients in a blender or a food
processor. Set aside. When the
souffle is ready, sprinkle it with
powdered sugar and serve
immediately with the sauce.

Note: **Best when baked in the lower 1/3 of the oven.**

cold lemon souffle with raspberry sauce

Yield: 12 servings

**Preparation time: 1 hour
  plus 3 hours chilling time**

"Light and delicate"

3 eggs, separated
1 cup sugar
2 Tablespoons gelatin
1/2 cup water
1/3 cup fresh lemon juice
1 teaspoon vanilla, optional
**4 teaspoons grated lemon
  rind**
1 egg white
1 1/2 cups heavy cream

Beat yolks with sugar until
mixture is pale and thick.
Dissolve gelatin in water; melt
over hot water and add to egg
mixture. Add lemon juice,
vanilla, and rind. Beat 4 egg
whites until stiff. Beat cream
until stiff. Fold whites into yolks
(1/3 first, then the rest). Fold in
whipped cream. Put in 1 1/2-quart
souffle dish and chill for at least
3 hours.

Raspberry Sauce
**1 (10-ounce) package
  frozen raspberries**
1 1/2 teaspoons cornstarch
1 Tablespoon lemon juice
**1 Tablespoon kirsch, or
  to taste**

Puree raspberries in a blender or
a food processor. Force through
a sieve. Mix cornstarch and
lemon juice and add to
raspberry mixture. Bring to a
boil in a medium saucepan and
cook until slightly thickened.
Add the kirsch. Spoon over the
chilled souffle.

raspberry souffle

Preparation time:
45 minutes plus 4 1/2
hours chilling time

"Perfect for any party"

2 **(10-ounce) packages**
  frozen raspberries
2 **envelopes unflavored**
  gelatin
1/2 **cup sugar**
1 **teaspoon lemon juice**
Pinch salt
4 **egg whites at room**
  temperature
2 **cups heavy cream**

Place a collar of waxed paper around a 1 1/2-quart souffle dish. In a blender, puree raspberries at low speed until smooth. In a large saucepan, sprinkle gelatin evenly over raspberry liquid. Cook over low heat until gelatin is dissolved. Remove from heat and stir in 1/4 cup sugar, lemon juice, and salt. Chill, stirring frequently, until mixture has consistency of unbeaten egg whites (about 20 minutes). Beat egg whites in large bowl with mixer at high speed until foamy. Add 1/4 cup sugar gradually and beat until egg whites stand in stiff glossy peaks. Gently fold in raspberry mixture. In a small bowl, with a mixer at medium speed, beat 1 1/2 cups cream until soft peaks form. Fold into raspberry mixture and put into souffle dish. Chill for at least 4 hours. Garnish with remaining cream, whipped.

bananas foster

**Preparation time:
15 minutes**

"Dramatic end to any meal"

**4 Tablespoons butter or
   margarine
6 Tablespoons brown sugar
1 teaspoon cinnamon
1/2 cup rum
4 bananas, sliced
   lengthwise
1/2 cup banana liqueur
1 pint vanilla ice cream**

In a large skillet or flambe pan, melt butter over low heat. Add the brown sugar and cinnamon and mix thoroughly. Put 1/4 cup rum in a small saucepan and heat to boiling while completing the next two steps. Put bananas in pan and saute until soft. Add banana liqueur and the remaining rum, continuing to cook over low heat. Pour hot rum into pan and ignite. The flame can be prolonged by tipping the pan in a circular motion and basting the bananas with flame. When the flame dies out, serve 2 banana slices over a large scoop of ice cream. Spoon sauce over the ice cream and bananas.

Separate eggs while still cold. Before beating whites, let them reach room temperature.

cantaloupe cooler

Yield: 6 to 8 servings

Preparation time:
1/2 hour plus 2
hours chilling time

"Wonderful for a hot summer night"

1 Tablespoon cornstarch
1/2 cup cold water
1 1/2 cups blueberries
1/4 cup sugar
2 Tablespoons creme de cassis
1 Tablespoon fresh lemon juice
1/4 teaspoon ground cinnamon
1 quart rainbow sherbet
2 medium cantaloupes, quartered, seeds removed

Dissolve cornstarch in water. In a large saucepan, combine cornstarch mixture, blueberries, and sugar. Cook over medium heat until thickened, stirring constantly. Pour into a covered container and refrigerate until cold, at least 2 hours. Before serving, add cassis, lemon juice, and cinnamon and blend well. To serve, place a large scoop of sherbet on each cantaloupe wedge and top with the blueberry sauce.

fruit compote with kirsch

Yield: 6 to 8 servings

Preparation time:
1/2 hour plus 2 hours
chilling time

"Refreshing!"

1 quart strawberries, washed and halved
1 pint bing cherries, stemmed, halved, and pitted
2 cups chunk pineapple
1/2 to 3/4 cup powdered sugar
3/4 cup kirsch

Combine fruit in a medium bowl. Sprinkle with powdered sugar and kirsch. Chill for 2 hours.

Variation: Other types of berries and fruits may be substituted or added.

454

fruit pizza

Temperature: 325°
Baking time: 15 minutes
  plus overnight chilling

"Unusual"

1 (16-ounce) package
  refrigerator sugar
  cookie, softened to
  room temperature
1 (8-ounce) package cream
  cheese, softened
1/2 cup sugar
1 (8-ounce) can mandarin
  oranges
1 pint frozen or fresh
  strawberries
1 (14-ounce) can chunk
  pineapple
2 bananas, sliced
1/2 cup lemon juice
1 (12-ounce) jar apricot
  preserves
1 cup heavy cream, whipped
  and sweetened to taste

Butter a large pizza pan. Roll cookie dough to within 1 inch of the edge of the pan. Bake until lightly browned. Cool. Mix cream cheese and sugar. Spread on *cooled* cookie pastry. Refrigerate overnight. Drain oranges, strawberries, and pineapple and refrigerate, covered, overnight. The next day, dip bananas in lemon juice. Arrange the fruit on top of the cookie pizza. Heat the apricot preserves in a saucepan until the consistency of syrup. Pour over pizza and chill in refrigerator until ready to serve. Slice and serve with sweetened whipped cream.

poached pears with chocolate sauce

Yield: 8 servings

Preparation time:
30 minutes plus
1 hour chilling time

"Elegant looking, but easy"

4 Bartlett pears, peeled,
  halved, and cored
2 cups water
1 cup sugar
6 Tablespoons rum or
  Amaretto, optional
1 quart ice cream
1 (6-ounce) package semi-
  sweet chocolate chips
2 Tablespoons butter or
  margarine
3 Tablespoons water
1/4 teaspoon vanilla
2 Tablespoons chopped
  pistachios

In a large, covered saucepan,
poach the pears gently in a
syrup made of the water and
sugar. Baste occasionally and
cook until pears are tender, 10 to
15 minutes. Chill the pears in
the syrup. Beat rum or Amaretto
into ice cream. Freeze mixture.
In a medium saucepan, combine
chocolate, butter, water, and
vanilla. Warm over medium heat
until the chocolate is melted. Stir
in pistachios. Serve each pear on
ice cream. Drizzle with warm
sauce.

To bake meringue pie shell or tarts, place parchment paper between
pie plate or cookie sheet and meringue or dust with baking powder.

fruit fantasy

Preparation time:
1/2 hour plus
1 1/2 hours chilling time

"A refreshing summer dessert"

1 cup plain yogurt or
   sour cream
2 Tablespoons brown sugar
2 peaches, peeled and diced
2 pears, diced
1 large apple, diced
1/2 cup fresh blueberries
1/2 cup coarsely chopped
   walnuts or pecans

In a small bowl, stir yogurt (or sour cream) until creamy. Blend in brown sugar. In a large bowl, gently toss together peaches, pears, apple, and blueberries. Pour yogurt (or sour cream) mixture over fruit. Toss gently. Sprinkle with nuts. Chill, covered, until ready to serve. Other fruits may be added or substituted for those listed.

amaretto custard with fruit

Yield: 6 servings

Temperature: 325°
Baking time: 25 minutes

"Elegant and easy"

Custard
1 (8-ounce) package cream
   cheese
1/2 cup sugar
1 Tablespoon fresh lemon
   juice
1/2 teaspoon vanilla
2 eggs

Topping
2 cups sliced strawberries,
   blueberries, chopped
   orange sections, or a
   combination
1/2 cup Amaretto

Combine all custard ingredients and beat until well blended. Pour mixture into a 1 1/2-quart casserole and bake. Cool. The custard may be stored in the refrigerator, covered. To serve, spoon custard into sherbet glasses or glass bowls and top each with fruit. Pour a heaping Tablespoon of Amaretto over each.

caramel custard

Temperature: 325°
Baking time:
1 to 1 1/2 hours
plus 2 hours chilling time

"A great way to use left-over egg yolks"

2 cups milk
1 cup sugar
6 egg yolks, well beaten
1/2 teaspoon vanilla
1/2 cup sugar

In a small saucepan, scald milk with 1 cup sugar. Let cool for 2 minutes; add slowly to egg yolks in a large bowl, stirring constantly. Add vanilla. Melt 1/2 cup sugar in a heavy skillet and cook, stirring constantly, until it darkens. Pour sugar syrup into 6 to 8 custard cups and run it around the cups until each cup is lined and the caramel hardens. Strain the custard into the cups. Set in a pan of hot water 1/3 of the way up the sides and bake until set. Chill. Serve cold either in the custard cups or turned out into dessert dishes with the caramel as sauce.

Note: **Always plan to make this a day ahead.**

Put marbles in the bottom of your double boiler. They will rattle when the water level drops too low.

creme brulee

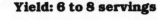

**Preparation time: 1 hour
plus 3 hours chilling time**

"Habit forming"

**3 cups heavy cream
1-inch piece vanilla bean
6 egg yolks
6 Tablespoons sugar
Ice cream salt
1/2 cup brown sugar**

Heat the cream and vanilla bean in the top of a double boiler. With an electric mixer, beat egg yolks and sugar in a large bowl until very light and creamy. Stir warm cream into egg mixture very slowly. Return mixture to top of double boiler. Bring the water in the bottom of the double boiler to a boil, making sure the water does not touch the custard pan. Stir constantly until the custard coats the spoon. Pour custard into a 1-quart glass serving dish or ramekins. Refrigerate for at least 3 hours. About an hour before serving, place custard dish(es) in a 2-inch deep pan. Pack with cracked ice and ice cream salt. Cover the custard with brown sugar until none of the custard shows through. Broil on the highest rack of the oven until the sugar melts. Watch carefully or the custard will burn. Serve immediately or refrigerate until ready to serve.

Note: **The ice cream salt prevents the custard from melting. Without it you would need to refrigerate the custard for another 3 hours.**

apple fritters

Yield: 200 fritters

Preparation time: 1 hour

"From Martha Stewart for the 'Heart of Country' Preview Party"

16 cups unbleached flour
1/2 cup baking powder
1 cup sugar
2 Tablespoons salt
24 eggs, separated
12 cups milk
3 cups unsalted butter,
  melted
25 red and green tart
  apples, cored and grated
  with skins left on
Oil

Sift flour and baking powder.
Stir in sugar and salt. Lightly
beat the egg yolks and add to the
milk. Stir in the flour mixture
until well blended. Add the
butter; mixing well. Beat the egg
whites until stiff, but not dry.
Fold into flour mixture. Add
apples; mixing thoroughly. Cook
on hot griddles with a small
amount of oil.

**Serving suggestion: Serve with honey, spicy apple butter, or
syrup.**

sponge pudding

Yield: 6 to 8 servings

Temperature: 350°
Baking time: 1 hour

"Custard-like souffle--Wonderful!"

1/2 cup flour
2 cups milk
1/2 cup butter or margarine
1/2 cup sugar
5 eggs, separated

Toppings
-Crushed fresh berries or
  fruit
-Partially drained frozen
  berries or fruit
-Amaretto
-Grand Marnier
-Fruit or berry sauce

Mix flour with a little cold milk
until smooth. Heat remaining
milk; add flour and stir for 10
minutes over medium heat. Add
butter and sugar; mixing well.
Cool. Stir in well beaten egg
yolks. Beat egg whites until stiff
and fold into mixture. Pour
pudding into a greased
1 1/2-quart souffle dish. Set dish
in a hot water bath and bake.
Top each serving with berries,
fruit, or liqueur.

fantastic chocolate roll

Yield: 12 servings

Temperature: 325°
Baking time: 20 minutes
plus 2 hours chilling time

"No better way to end a meal"

5 eggs, separated
1/2 cup sugar
2 Tablespoons cocoa
Pinch salt
Oil

Beat egg yolks until lemon-colored. Add sugar, cocoa, and salt. Fold in stiffly beaten egg whites. Line a 15x10x1-inch jelly roll pan with waxed paper. *Liberally* coat with oil so that it actually runs. Pour batter into pan and bake. Cool slightly, turn out on a damp cloth, and cover with another damp cloth.

Filling
2 cups heavy cream
1/2 cup sugar
1/2 teaspoon vanilla

Beat heavy cream; gradually add sugar and vanilla. Remove cloth from the cake and spread cake with the filling. Using the undercloth, gently roll the cake, jelly roll fashion. Refrigerate roll for at least 2 hours.

Sauce
1 cup sugar
1/2 teaspoon vanilla
1 egg
2 Tablespoons cold water
2 ounces unsweetened chocolate, melted
Milk or light cream

Heat sugar, vanilla, egg, water, and chocolate over low heat for 10 minutes; stirring constantly. Add a little milk, or, even better, cream to make the sauce the consistency of thin custard. Serve the roll sliced with hot chocolate sauce.

Note: **Remove the roll from the refrigerator 30 minutes before serving.**

lemon mousse with blueberries

Yield: 6 servings

Preparation time:
¹/₂ hour plus
2 hours chilling time

"Delightful summer dessert"

1 quart fresh blueberries
1 cup sugar
5 eggs, separated
5 Tablespoons fresh
lemon juice
1 cup heavy cream, whipped
2 teaspoons lemon rind,
grated

Wash blueberries and remove stems. Place in a 2-quart glass serving bowl, sprinkle with ¼ cup sugar, and chill. In the top of a stainless steel or enamel double boiler (aluminum will affect the flavor and color of mousse), beat egg yolks with the remaining sugar until the mixture turns a light lemon color. Add lemon juice and cook mixture over simmering water, whisking constantly, until it coats a spoon. Do not let it come to a boil. Immediately remove from heat and cool. Beat egg whites until stiff, but not dry. Fold them gently into the cooled lemon mixture. Fold in whipped cream and lemon rind. Mix until smooth. Chill for at least 2 hours. Just before serving, cover the berries with the cold mousse.

Note: **Berries can also be served in long-stemmed wine glasses with the mousse.**

Variation: **Strawberries or blackberries can be substituted for the blueberries.**

rum dessert

Yield: 12 servings

**Preparation time: 1 hour
plus overnight chilling**

"An elegant and flavorful dessert"

1 1/2 to 2 dozen ladyfingers
1/4 cup dark Jamaican rum
6 egg yolks
1 cup sugar
1 envelope gelatin
1/2 cup cold water
2 cups heavy cream
1/2 cup dark rum
Unsweetened chocolate
    curls

Soak ladyfingers slightly in 1/4 cup rum. Line bowl with split ladyfingers. A (2-quart) clear glass bowl gives the prettiest effect, although it can be made in 2 small bowls. In a large bowl, beat egg yolks until very light and add sugar. Dissolve gelatin in cold water. Bring to a boil over low heat. Pour gelatin mixture over egg mixture; stirring briskly. Whip heavy cream until stiff. Fold into egg mixture. Stir in 1/2 cup rum. Pour egg mixture into the lined bowl and chill overnight. Sprinkle top with chocolate curls.

Note: **Dark Jamaican rum has a stronger flavor. It can be made with other rums, but the flavor will not be as strong.**

meringues

Temperature: 400°
Baking time: 12 hours

"Great to have on hand in the freezer"

6 egg whites
1/4 teaspoon salt
1 teaspoon vinegar
1 teaspoon vanilla
1 1/2 cups sugar

Preheat oven to 400°. Separate the eggs while still cold. Place the whites in a large mixing bowl and bring to room temperature. Add salt, vinegar, and vanilla to the egg whites and beat with an electric mixer until stiff peaks form. Add the sugar, 1 Tablespoon at a time, scraping the sides of the bowl often. Mix at medium speed, reducing the speed as the mixture thickens. Continue beating until the mixture is very stiff. Shape meringue into nests 4 inches in diameter and place on a cookie sheet lined with aluminum foil. Turn off the preheated 400° oven and *immediately* place the meringues in the oven. *Do not open the oven door* for at least 12 hours. Store in an airtight container if not using right away.

Note: These can't be made on a rainy day.

Alternate baking method: Bake in a 275° oven for 1 hour. Turn oven off, open the door partially, and let meringues cool for 5 minutes before removing.

Variation: Miniature Meringue Shells - Make shells about 2 inches in diameter and fill with chocolate, lemon pie filling, or ice cream after they are baked. This method makes a good "pick-up" dessert for a buffet. Yield: 3 to 4 dozen.

Serving suggestion: Serve meringues filled with peppermint ice cream topped with *Chocolate Sauce,* page 472, or filled with sliced peaches or strawberries topped with sweetened whipped cream.

walnut crisps

Yield: 2 to 3 dozen shells

Temperature: 350°
Baking time:
  6 to 8 minutes

"Delightfully different"

1/2 cup butter or margarine, melted
1/3 cup light corn syrup
1/2 cup sugar
2 Tablespoons brandy
1/2 cup sifted flour
1/4 teaspoon salt
1/2 cup chopped walnuts

Mix all ingredients and drop by teaspoons on a well-greased cookie sheet. Bake. Cool for 1 minute; remove by starting spatula at edges and working in quickly, but carefully. Shape over upside down muffin tins. This is time-consuming as they must be baked a few at a time but they keep well and are good to have on hand.

Serving suggestion: Fill with either coffee or vanilla ice cream and pass Kahlua to pour over the top.

raspberry
mille-feuille

Temperature: 375°
Baking time: 40 minutes
plus 3 hours chilling time

"A patisserie specialty from your own kitchen"

Puff Pastry
3 cups bread flour
1 cup cake flour
4 cups cold butter or
margarine
1 cup ice water

Combine bread and cake flour. Cut butter into 1/2-inch pieces and drop into flour. With a pastry blender or a food processor, blend the butter and flour until the butter is the size of peas. Add ice water and mix *only enough* to moisten the flour. Cover with plastic wrap and refrigerate for 30 minutes. Turn dough onto a lightly-floured board and shape into a rectangle. Lightly dust the dough with flour and roll out until the dough measures 12x24-inches. Fold into 3 even parts (12x8-inches). Turn dough lengthwise and roll out again. Fold and repeat turning process 1 more time. Allow the dough to rest and chill for at least 2 hours before using. It may be refrigerated overnight. Roll pastry to 1/8 inch thick and cut into 6 strips, 12x4-inches each. *This is enough pastry for 2 "creations"; either freeze 1/2 the pastry at this point or double the filling and topping recipes if 12 servings are needed.* Place on a parchment-covered baking sheet in a single layer. Bake in a preheated oven for 40 minutes.

(continued)

466

If pastry is browning too fast, cover with parchment or foil or turn off the oven and leave the door closed until cool. The pastry strips need to be cool before assembling with filling and topping.

Filling
1 cup milk
1/4 vanilla bean, split
5 Tablespoons sugar
3 egg yolks
2 Tablespoons flour
1 cup heavy cream, whipped

Combine milk, vanilla bean, and 5 teaspoons sugar in a medium saucepan. Bring to a boil and then remove from heat. In a bowl, whisk egg yolks and the remaining sugar until light yellow, about 1 minute. Add flour to the egg mixture and whisk until smooth. Remove vanilla bean from the milk. Pour 1/2 the milk into the egg mixture and mix thoroughly. Pour eggs and milk back into the saucepan and bring to a boil, whisking constantly. Cook until thick as custard and cool. Refrigerate for 30 minutes. This can be done a day or 2 ahead of time up to this point. Just before assembling, fold in whipped cream.

Topping
1 pint raspberries, fresh or frozen
3/4 cup sugar (omit if frozen fruit in syrup is used)
2 Tablespoons fresh lemon juice

Puree raspberries in a blender or a food processor. Add sugar and lemon juice. Chill thoroughly. To assemble, place a sheet of baked pastry on a serving platter and cover with 1/2 the cream filling. Add another layer of pastry and top with the remaining filling. Top with a layer of pastry. Pour the fruit topping over the top layer of the pastry. To serve, cut into 6 servings crosswise, at the table.

Note: **Make puff pastry in a cool kitchen. Heat causes the butter to soften too quickly.**

blender pot de creme

Yield: 6 servings

**Preparation time:
20 minutes
plus 1 hour chilling time**

"Great for dinner parties"

**3/4 cup milk less
2 Tablespoons
1 (6-ounce) package semi-
sweet chocolate chips
1 egg
2 Tablespoons sugar
1 teaspoon vanilla
Salt
2 Tablespoons brandy, rum,
or bourbon, optional
1 cup heavy cream, whipped**

Heat milk to just below the boiling point. Place chocolate chips, egg, sugar, vanilla, salt, and brandy, if desired, in a blender and process on low speed for a few minutes. Add the hot milk and blend for 2 minutes. Pour into cups and let cool in the refrigerator for at least 1 hour. Serve with the whipped cream.

Note: **Can be made a day ahead.**

velvet hammer

Yield: 8 servings

**Preparation time:
15 minutes
plus 1 hour freezing time**

"A light end to a meal, but watch the liqueur!"

**1/2 gallon vanilla ice cream
2 ounces brandy
2 ounces creme de cacao
2 ounces triple sec**

Combine the ingredients in a blender in 2 batches. Store in the freezer until ready to serve. Blend before serving. Serve in champagne glasses or large bowled wine glasses.

pot de creme

Preparation time:
30 minutes
plus 1 hour chilling time

"Very rich"

2 cups heavy cream
1/4 cup sugar
1 1/3 cups semi-sweet
    chocolate chips
6 egg yolks
1 teaspoon vanilla
1 cup heavy cream, whipped

Put cream in top of double boiler. Add sugar and scald over hot water. Remove from stove, add chocolate and stir until melted. Beat egg yolks and add to chocolate mixture very slowly (the hot mixture will cook the bits of egg if you aren't careful). Return to stove and cook over boiling water, stirring constantly, until thickened, about 5 to 6 minutes. Remove from heat, stir in vanilla, and cool. Pour into cups (demi-tasse, pot de creme, or champagne glasses) and refrigerate for at least 1 hour before serving with the whipped cream.

Note: **Can be made a day ahead.**

butterscotch
sauce

Yield: 1 1/2 cups

Preparation time:
15 minutes plus
1 hour chilling time

"Couldn't be easier or any better"

2 cups brown sugar
1 cup heavy cream
1 cup butter or margarine

Combine the 3 ingredients and heat in the top of a double boiler until thickened, stirring constantly. Cover and refrigerate.

blueberry sauce

Yield: 1 1/2 cups

Preparation time:
1 1/2 hours plus
2 hours chilling time

"A must to have on hand"

2 cups fresh blueberries
1/3 cup sugar
1 Tablespoon fresh lemon
   juice
1/4 teaspoon salt
1/2 teaspoon vanilla

Wash and crush berries.
Combine them with sugar,
lemon juice, and salt, in a
saucepan. Bring to a boil and
boil for 1 minute. Add vanilla
and chill.

Serving suggestion: Serve over pudding, pancakes, or ice cream (especially lemon).

caramel sauce

Yield: 4 1/2 cups

Preparation time:
25 minutes

"Mmmmm mmmmm good"

2 cups light brown sugar
1 3/4 cups light corn syrup
1/2 cup butter or margarine
2 cups heavy cream
1 teaspoon vanilla
Pinch salt

In a deep heavy pan, bring
brown sugar, syrup, butter, and
1 cup of the heavy cream to the
soft ball stage (235°) over
medium high heat. Remove
from heat and cool for 5
minutes. Add remaining cream,
vanilla, and salt; stirring well.
Store in the refrigerator.

Note: When ready to serve, heat over moderate heat or in the microwave.

derby day mint sauce with chocolate leaves

Yield: 1 pint

Preparation time:
  Sauce-20 minutes
  Chocolate leaves-
  1 1/2 hours

"Refreshing"

1 cup light corn syrup
1/2 cup green creme de menthe
1/2 cup crushed pecans
Vanilla ice cream
16 fresh leaves, camelia or ficus leaves work the best
1 (6-ounce) package semi-sweet chocolate chips

Combine syrup and creme de menthe in a saucepan and bring to a boil. Remove from heat immediately. Stir in crushed pecans. Refrigerate until ready to serve. Pour over vanilla ice cream.

Chocolate Leaves

Carefully wash and thoroughly dry the leaves. In top of a double boiler, melt chocolate chips. Remove from heat. Drag the top of each leaf through the chocolate. Carefully run your fingers down the side of the leaf to the point. Excess chocolate on the back or sides will make the chocolate difficult to remove later. Place the leaves on waxed paper and place in the refrigerator for at least 1 hour. When set, carefully peel leaves from chocolate. Serve as a garnish with mint sauce.

Note: **The leaves are a beautiful garnish for most chocolate or mocha desserts.**

chocolate sauce

Yield: 2 pints

Preparation time:
   30 minutes

"Dangerous to have on hand"

1/2 cup butter or margarine
4 ounces unsweetened
   chocolate
1/2 teaspoon salt
1 (13-ounce) can evaporated
   milk
3 cups sugar

In the top of a double boiler over low heat, melt butter and add chocolate; blend. Add salt and milk; stirring until blended. Add sugar and stir over low heat for 20 minutes.

Note: **This marvelous sauce keeps in the refrigerator for up to 3 months.**

fruit mousseline sauce

Yield: 2 cups

Preparation time:
   1/2 hour plus
   1 1/2 hours chilling time

"Delicious fruit dessert"

2/3 cup sugar
2 Tablespoons flour
2 eggs, beaten
3 Tablespoons lemon juice
1 1/4 cups pineapple or
   orange juice or a
   mixture of the 2
1/2 cup heavy cream,
   whipped

Combine sugar and flour in a heavy enameled iron pan over hot water or in the top of a double boiler. Add eggs and juices; beat well. Cook, stirring constantly, until the mixture thickens. Cover and place in the refrigerator; it will thicken more as it chills. When mixture is cold, fold in the whipped cream.

Serving suggestion: **Serve with fresh pineapple, pineapple chunks packed in juice, orange sections, bananas, or a mixture of these fruits with strawberries for a fruit melange.**

grand marnier sauce for fruit

Yield: 1 pint

"Divine"

Preparation time:
  30 minutes plus
  1 1/2 hours chilling time

5 egg yolks
1/2 cup sugar
1/2 cup Grand Marnier
1 cup heavy cream
2 Tablespoons sugar

Beat egg yolks and 1/2 cup sugar with a wire whisk vigorously for 10 minutes in the top of a double boiler over boiling water. When the mixture is very thick, remove from heat and stir in 1/4 cup Grand Marnier. Cool and then refrigerate for 30 minutes. With an electric mixer, beat heavy cream with 2 Tablespoons sugar and fold into chilled mixture. Add the remaining Grand Marnier and mix well. Refrigerate until ready to serve.

peach melba sauce

Yield: 1 quart

Preparation time:
  30 minutes

"A pretty dessert"

1 (10-ounce) package frozen raspberries
1 (16-ounce) can peach slices
1/4 cup sugar
1 Tablespoon cornstarch
1/2 cup port wine
1 Tablespoon lemon juice

Defrost raspberries, drain, and reserve syrup. Drain peaches, saving 1/4 cup syrup. Combine sugar and cornstarch in a saucepan or chafing dish. Slowly add fruit syrups, wine, and lemon juice. Cook over medium heat until sauce is thick and clear. Add peaches and heat. Add raspberries and heat gently.

Serving suggestion: Serve over vanilla or peach ice cream. For an elegant effect pour over meringues filled with peach ice cream.

praline sauce

Yield: 3 1/2 cups

**Preparation time:
20 minutes**

"Delicious on ice cream"

**1 1/2 cups brown sugar
2/3 cup light corn syrup
1/4 cup butter or margarine
3/4 cup chopped pecans
1 (5-ounce) can evaporated
 milk**

In a saucepan, heat sugar, syrup, and butter to a boil. Cool. Stir in pecans and milk; blend thoroughly. Refrigerate covered.

Note: Keeps quite a long time. Marvelous when heated for a short time in the microwave.

witches' brew

Yield: 3 cups

**Preparation time:
5 minutes plus
4 days standing time**

"Marvelous over ice cream"

**1 1/2 cups brandy
2 cups sugar
1 cup fruit**

Mix 1 cup brandy and 1 cup sugar, cover, and let stand for 4 days; stirring daily. Add well-drained fruit, 1/2 cup brandy, and 1 cup sugar; cover tightly.

Note: Fruits suitable for use are: peaches, pears, peeled apricots, pineapple, and cherries. Fruit may be added every 3 or 4 days. Use a wooden spoon when stirring to avoid breaking the fruit.

substitutions

1 teaspooon baking powder = ¼ teaspoon baking soda, ½ teaspoon cream of tartar; adding 1 extra egg for each teaspoon baking powder

1 cup biscuit mix = 1 cup flour, 1½ teaspoons baking powder, ½ teaspoon salt, 1 Tablespoon shortening

1 cup brown sugar = 1 cup granulated sugar plus 2 Tablespoons molasses

1 cup buttermilk = 1 cup lukewarm milk plus 1 Tablespoon lemon juice; let stand 5 minutes, beat briskly

1 cup cake flour = 1 cup all-purpose flour less 2 Tablespoons

3 ounces semi-sweet chocolate = 2 ounces unsweetened chocolate plus 2 Tablespoons sugar or ⅓ cup cocoa plus 2 Tablespoons sugar plus 2 Tablespoons butter or margarine

1 ounce unsweetened chocolate = 3 Tablespoons cocoa plus 1 Tablespoon butter or margarine

1 cup corn syrup = ¾ cup sugar plus ¼ cup water

1 Tablespoon cornstarch = 2 Tablespoons flour

¾ cup cracker crumbs = 1 cup bread crumbs

1 cup heavy cream = ¾ cup milk plus ⅓ cup butter or margarine

1 cup light cream = ¾ cup milk plus 3 Tablespoons butter or margarine

1 cup milk = ½ cup evaporated milk plus ½ cup water

1 Tablespoon mustard = 1 teaspoon dry mustard plus 1 Tablespoon white wine or vinegar

1 cup self-rising flour = 1 cup all-purpose flour plus 1½ teaspoons baking powder plus ¼ teaspoon salt

1 Tablespoon Worcestershire sauce = 1 Tablespoon soy sauce plus dash hot sauce

Our sincere thanks to the members of the Junior League of Nashville and their friends who contributed so much to Encore! Nashville.

Martha Brown Adams
Peggy Keylon Adams
Corinne Blake Adrian
Mary Elizabeth Aiken
Beth Callaway Alexander
Mary Prue Polk Alley
Jill Coats Anderson
Milbrey Waller Andrews
Katherine Sutton Apel
Barbara Scott Asbury
Jo Ann Gourley Bainbridge
June McCoy Ball
Nancy Morris Barksdale
Vicki Hurd Bartholomew
Allison Webb Bass
Elizabeth Smith Bass
Amos Baugh
Elizabeth Core Bearden
Rebecca Turnipseed Bergquist
Katherine Davis Berry
Linda Lipscomb Berry
Mildred Tyson Bickley
Suzanne Griffith Binkley
Gwen Crow Bond
Christine Hampton Bradford
Melissa Luton Bradford
Margaret Dortch Brooks
Diane Jones Brown
Elizabeth Moorhead Brown
Lenore Taylor Brown
Margaret Dyer Brown
Rachel Blair Brown
Patricia Anderson Bryan
Sarah Lytton Buchanan
Ann Snell Bumstead
Phyllis Walker Bush
Barry Mitchiner Caldwell
Betty Rye Caldwell
Cissy Caldwell
Frances Hill Caldwell
Ginger Glass Caldwell
Helen Beatty Callahan

Lucia Landstreet Callahan
Margaret Ringland Cameron
Judy DeMoss Campbell
Ruth Early Cannon
Sylvia Felts Cantrell
Jean Dobson Caplinger
Marlyss Johnson Carlson
Mary Kay King Carmichael
Mary Cartwright
Laurine Vail Casey
Missy Campbell Casey
Annamarie Landress Cate
Nancy Coffin Cawood
Keith Campbell Cawthorne
The Centennial Club
Mary Ann Braden Chaffin
Sigourney Woods Cheek
Patricia Dick Cherry
Mary Clark
Anne Campbell Clay
Elizabeth Moughon Clements
Louise Campbell Cline
Karen Dale Coble
Anita Kirby Cochran
Martha K. Coffin
Florence Fletcher Coke
Eunice Ridley Colmore
Patricia Kirkman Colton
Jean Kirby Condrey
Ashley Whitsett Conner
Griffitha Glasser Cook
Jean Eggleston Cook
Mary Brown Cook
Ruth Brown Cook
Sally Frierson Cook
Mary Earl Cooper
Sarah Wilson Cooper
Ann Peacher Cowden
Elizabeth Wade Craig
Polly Nelson Craig
Judy Rodenhauser Crawford
Katherine Sheridan Crocker

476

Nancy Ferrier Crook
Ella Connell Cummings
Patricia Page Curry
Ann Champlin Danner
Susan McGinnis Darst
Adelaide Shull Davis
Bonnie Binning Davis
Florence Stumb Davis
Martha Dickinson Davis
Mary Follin Davis
Susan Ivie Davis
Patricia Waterfield Des Prez
Betty Smith Dobson
Sarah D'Atri Dobson
Sophia Ezzell Dobson
Carol Robinson Duncan
Bert Dunn
Gretchen Newell Edmiston
Diane Peterson Edwards
Carol Clark Elam
Mary Elam Evers
Genevieve Baird Farris
Margaret Handly Fitzgerald
Genevieve Eve Fletcher
Mary Jane Harrison Folger
Mary Coble Follin
Elizabeth Byrn Fox
Bettie Orr Franklin
Corinne Scales Franklin
Louise Bransford Frazer
Genevieve Bartlett Fricks
Patricia Champion Frist
Tootsie Black Ganick
Elizabeth Knox Gentle
Betsy Bradford Gerlach
Judy Johnson Glascock
Wilma Monypeny Godchaux
Helen Golter
Virginia Plunkett Goodson
Lilian Duke Granbery
Lesley Nield Green
Theo Newsom Greene

Ruth Wagner Griscom
Nene Shuford Gunn
Janin Sinclair Hale
Elizabeth Raebeck Hall
Grace Ward Hall
Molly McCalla Hampton
Louise Fort Hardison
Lynn Northcutt Hardison
Emma Hinton Harton
Elizabeth Creighton Harwell
Sarah Schafer Havens
Halle Fowler Hayes
Harriet Miller Haynes
Jane Van de Roovaart Haynes
Merilyn Hovey Herbert
Mary Wilson Herndon
Pat Pierce Hicks
Ann Stahlman Hill
Freeda Kitchens Hill
Darlene Batey Hoffman
Mary Jane Parham Holliday
Lisle Castleman Hooper
Jane Smith Howard
Carroll Cole Howell
Bitsy Dorris Husband
Jane Nicholas Huston
Binnie Briggs Barr Irwin
Julia Lipscomb Jarman
Nancy Maureen Jarman
Henrietta Darr Johnson
Mary Leyden Bevington
  Johnson
Anita O'Fallon Johnston
Annice Johnston
Lillias Dale Johnston
Katie Newton Jones
Gertrude Joseph
Jane Buchanan King
Gloria Edmondson Kinnard
Mary Pillow Wells Kirk
Donna Townsend Kirkpatrick
Jean Sanders Kirkpatrick

Elizabeth Oliver Kown
Susan Monaghan Lacey
Nancy Denney Lackey
Salli Shropshire La Grone
Elizabeth Weaver Lane
Meredith Mendel Leahy
Candice Winsett Ledbetter
Betty Leftwich
Louise Martin Leighton
Anna Mary Bransford
  Lenderman
Chloe Fort Lenderman
Sissie Kimbrough Lewis
Caroline Phillips Ligon
Betsy Rodenhauser Lindseth
Drane Dickinson Maddox
Barbara Nixon Maguire
Faye Walters March
Sally Fran Ross Martin
Susan Goza Martin
Linda Lavve Mason
Alice Casey Mathews
Susan Beane Mathews
Rachel Merritt McAllister
Mary Catheryne Phipps McCalla
Donna Wunderlich McCullough
Mary Day McGee
Anne Applegarth McGugin
Betsy Vinson McInnes
Donna Henderson McInnis
Martha Morrison McKeand
Jane Clements McMackin
Margaret Webb McQuiddy
Susan Gilmore McSwain
Betty Cochran Metcalf
Anne Phillips Cunningham
  Meyer
Suzanne Edwards Miller
Molly Wakefield Milner
Brenda Bloodworth Mondelli
Patricia Weisiger Morel
Carlana Moscheo
Lou Binkley Mudter

Ruth Orr Napier
Dorothy Potter Nash
Sandra Carrington Nelson
Britton Hassell Nielsen
Charles Norris Nielsen
Phoebe Clark Nischan
Hennie Johnson Noland
Ann Benson Northcutt
Anne Gayle Norvell
Jane Howard Oleksy
Mindy Thompson Orman
Louise Toll German Ottenville
Ophelia Thompson Paine
Margaret Allen Palmer
Margaret Stanford Palmer
Nancy Keen Butterworth Palmer
Jane Adair Parham
Adrienne Morgan Parker
Hope Haselden Parker
Bette Sue Jackson Parrish
Anne Caldwell Parsons
Suzanne Pate
Marsha Tanner Patterson
Theresa Godchaux Payne
Elinor Berger Peek
Virginia Stanford Perdue
Marion Brooke Philpot
Freddie Monsour Pierce
Lynn Stevenson Pilversack
Margaret Pechin Powell
Missy Holman Pride
Mary England Proctor
Doris Oetjen Raebeck
Lynn Holt Ragland
Tandy Rice
Evy Kay Rhodus Ritzen
Mary Ann Farris Robbins
Frances Wilkerson Rodenhauser
Mary Virginia Martin Rogers
Charles N. Rolfe
Margaret Oliver Rolfe
Mary Hughes Rose
Marti Maschmeier Rosenberg

478

Ralph Rowntree
Ellen Russell Sadler
Maribeth Sargent
Julia Edwards Sawyers
Lindy Beazley Sayers
Nancy Hanson Scheunemann
Patricia Scott
Jean Seate
Carolyn Parker Sheffield
Bertie Foster Shriver
Doris Schillerman Simpson
Virginia Phillips Sinclair
Virginia Vaughn Gaston Sinclair
Ellen Harrison Sloan
Angela Phillips Smith
Billie Ann Gloth Smith
Claudette Demant Smith
Dot Boren Smith
Edith Gardner Orr Smith
Judith Walton Smith
Marie Hall Smith
Mary Virginia Cecil Smith
Nancy Manier Smith
Sissy Morehead Sobel
Susan Mieher Spickard
Margaret Teas Stein
Ann Randol Stephens
Madlynn Anderson Stevenson
Martha Stewart
Mary Edwards Stokes
Nancy Baker Stroman
Hettie Lish Stuart
Bolin Kane Stumb
Holly Cochrane Sutro
Barbara Simpson Sutton
Mary Wade Sutton
Louise McKee Swain
Shirley Curtis Swartzbaugh
Jane Anderson Tarkington
Margaret Gilliam Taylor
Bernice May Fritchman Teas
Shirley Tenison
Carol Parker Thomas
Suzanne Caldwell Thomas
Mary Battle Higgins Thompson

Mary Davenport Thym
Sandra Young Tidswell
Bess Brown Tirrill
Nancy Taylor Tirrill
Robert D. Tuke
Susan Cummins Tuke
Virginia Hume Uden
Helen Warnecke Van
    de Roovaart
Connie Cook Vanderpool
Mary Nelson Wade
Lucette Frazier Wager
Mary Alice Herbert Walker
Sallie Huggins Wallace
Fran Phillips Ward
Margaret Norvell Ward
Barbara Warhurst
Jeanette Sloan Warner
Carol Orthwein Weaver
Elizabeth Carothers Weaver
Molly Leach Weaver
Nancy Johnson Weaver
Caroline Bartlett Webb
Anne Harrison Webber
Julia Harrison Webber
Ann Harwell Wells
Govan Davidson White
Peg Smith Wildner
Holly Anderson Wilds
Anne Hendricks Wiley
Linda Huisken Wilks
Donna Forcum Williams
Gwen Williams
Jerry Banks Williams
Kay Ellison Williams
Linda Christie Williams
Lynn Perry Williams
Maude Williams
Lea Tidwell Witherspoon
Mary Harrington Witherspoon
Libby Polk Wolf
Ellen Dobson Wright
Pamela Port Wylly
Denis Sarratt Yeiser

INDEX

A

Alabama's Carob Brownies 9
Almond Cheese Strips 54
Almond-Apricot Coffee Cake 351
Amaretto Custard with Fruit 457
Anderson, Bill Anderson's
    Pumpkin Ice Cream Pie 10
Appetizers, see Hors d'Oeuvres

APPLES
Apple Fritters 460
Apple Honey-Cointreau 152
Apple Pie 418
Apple-Plum Melange 408
Applesauce Bread 359
Apples with Bleu Cheese 55
Best Ever Apple Cake 389
Cran-Apple Crumb Pie 425
Deep Dish Apple Cobbler 409
Deep Dish Apple Pie 426
Tennessee Ernie Ford's Fresh
    Apple Nut Cake 16

APRICOTS
Almond-Apricot Coffee Cake 351
Apricot Bars 363
Apricot-Glazed Chicken 267
Arnold, Eddy Arnold's Coconut
    Cream Pie 11

ARTICHOKES
Artichoke-Asparagus Mold 132
Artichoke Bottom First Course 50
Artichoke-Oyster Soup 84
Artichoke-Rice Salad 112
Asparagus-Artichoke Casserole . . . 189
Marinated Artichoke and
    Mushroom Salad 120
Rib Roast with Artichoke Sauce . . . 311
Shrimp, Mushroom, Artichoke
    Fondue 73
Toasted Artichoke Rounds 53
Variety Quiches 174

ASPARAGUS
Artichoke-Asparagus Mold 132
Asparagus-Artichoke Casserole . . . 189
Asparagus Egg-Drop Soup 85
Asparagus Parisienne 190
Asparagus Roll-Ups 54
Easy Asparagus 189
Roquefort and Asparagus
    Quiche 176
Aspic, Tomato Soup 140

AVOCADOS
Avocados Stuffed with Curried
    Crabmeat 51
Avocado Vichyssoise 77
Layered Guacamole 71
Mexican Guacamole Dip 70
Stuffed Avocado Salad 130

B

BACON
Bacon-Wrapped Shrimp 55
Fluffy Bacon-Cheese Omelet 165
Hot Bacon Dressing 143
Baked Cornish Hens 289
Baked Ham with Plum Garnish 318
Baked Quail in Wine 292
Baked Red Snapper 236
Baked Sandwiches 97
Baked Stuffed Manicotti Shells 182

BANANAS
Banana Jama 152
Banana-Nut Bread 357
Bananas Foster 453
Barbara Mandrell's Seafood
    Mold 22

BARBECUE
Barbecued Beef 305
Barbecued Lamb 314
Barbecued Red Snapper 235
Barbecued Shrimp 249
Barbecued Spareribs 322
Hickory Smoked Barbecued
    Chicken 287
Kitty Wells' Barbecued Chicken
    in a Bag 35
Basic Crepes 354
Bass, Oven-Baked 237

BATTER
Beer Batter, Fried Shrimp 253
Deep-Frying Chicken Batter 286

BEANS
Black Bean Soup 87
California Baked Beans 190
Curried Bean Sprout Salad 116
Navy Bean Soup 96
Oven-Baked Beans 191
Red Beans with Rice 192
Bearnaise Sauce 267
Beau Jacques French Dressing 146

BEEF, see Meats
Beef en Gelee 304
Beef Stroganoff 306
Boeuf de Wellington 307

BEER
Beer Cake 387
Beer Cheese 62
Beer Dip, Pumpernickel
    Surprise 63
Beer Rolls 345

BEETS
Burgundy Beets 195
Belgian Mocha Cake. 388
Best Ever Apple Cake. 389
BEVERAGES
Blender Ice Tea 40
Bloody Mary Mix 41
Boiled Custard. 41
Breakfast in a Gulp 40
Cafe Mexicano. 42
Christmas Cranberry Tea. 42
Coffee Punch 43
Do-it-Yourself Kahlua 43
Eggnog 44
Frozen Whiskey Sour 44
Mint Julep. 45
Peach Smash. 45
Sangria 46
Sunshine Tea. 40
Super Slurping Punch. 46
Velvet Hammer. 468
Bill Anderson's Pumpkin
Ice Cream Pie 10
BISCUITS, see Breads
Black Bean Soup. 87
Blackberry Cobbler, Southern. 410
Blackberry Curd 153
Blender Hollandaise. 220
Blender Hollandaise, Eggs
Fox Hollow Farm. 164
Blender Ice Tea 40
Blender Mayonnaise 142
Blender Pot de Creme. 468
Bleu Cheese Dressing I 144
Bleu Cheese Dressing II. 145
Bloody Mary Mix 41
BLUEBERRIES
Blueberry Sauce 470
Fresh Blueberry Salad. 134
Lemon Mousse with Blueberries. . . 462
Tammy Wynette's Blueberry
Buckle 36
Boeuf de Wellington. 307
Boiled Custard. 41
Boiled Lobster 260
Boiled Shrimp in Beer 248
Bon Bons. 379
Bourbon Peaches 219
Bourbon Pie 420
Brandy Alexander Pie 421
BREADS
Basic Crepes. 354
Bundt Bread. 333
Buttermilk Waffles. 355
Cheese French Bread. 334

Cinnamon-Raisin Bread. 338
Coffee Can Bread. 339
Corn Bread 356
Danish Cheese Bread. 336
Easy Loaf Bread 340
French Bread. 335
Granola Bread 340
Honey Whole Wheat Bread 341
Lightest Ever French Toast 351
Onion Bread. 337
Overnight Pancakes. 355
Plain White Bread. 343
Popovers. 356
Rye Bread 344
Whole Wheat Bread 342
Biscuits
Easy Yeast Biscuits. 347
Grandpa Jones' Biscuits. 19
Coffee Cakes
Almond-Apricot Coffee Cake. 351
Sour Cream Coffee Cake 352
Spicy Marble Coffee Cake 353
Muffins
Easy Schnecker Muffins. 350
Whole Wheat Muffins 342
Rolls
Beer Rolls 345
Czechoslovakian Kolaches. 346
Graham Rolls. 348
Ice Box Potato Rolls 345
Refrigerated Rolls-Sweet Rolls 349
Tea Breads
Applesauce Bread. 359
Banana-Nut Bread 357
Date-Nut Bread 358
Lemon Bread. 358
Orange Tea Bread 360
Pumpkin Bread. 357
Strawberry Bread. 359
Zucchini Bread 360
Breakfast in a Gulp. 40
Breast of Chicken au Champagne. . . . 268
Brenda Lee's Trout Fillets. 20
Brie en Croute 49
Brisket. 308
BROCCOLI
Broccoli and Cauliflower
Casserole. 193
Broccoli Puff. 194
Broccoli Salad 113
Cream of Broccoli Soup. 81
Marinated Broccoli. 121
Variety Quiches. 174
Broiled Chicken Liver Appetizers. . . . 51
Broiled Sole. 240

481

Brown Rice Enchiladas............. 179

BROWNIES

Alabama's Carob Brownies....... 9
Brownies Divine................. 363
Oatmeal Brownies............... 370

BRUNCH

Artichoke Bottom First Course.... 50
Camembert Souffle.............. 168
Cheese Souffle.................... 169
Creole Eggs..................... 163
Curried Swiss Eggs.............. 163
Eggs Fox Hollow Farm........... 164
Fluffy Bacon-Cheese Omelet...... 165
Green Chile Souffle.............. 170
Kitchen Sink Frittata............. 166
Make-in-Advance Cheese
    Pudding...................... 171
Oven Omelet.................... 170
Quiches, see Eggs and Cheese
Savory Souffle Roll.............. 300
Ranch Eggs..................... 167
Shrimp and Cheese Casserole..... 256
Sour Cream Enchiladas.......... 172
Spiced Eggs.................... 166
Steeplechase Casserole.......... 302
Buddha's Feast.................... 206
Buffet Cauliflower................. 112
Bundt Bread....................... 333
Burgundy Beets................... 195
Buried Treasures.................. 56
Buttermilk Waffles................ 355
Butterscotch Sauce 469

C

Cafe Mexicano.................... 42
Cakes, see Desserts
Calcutta Mulligatawny Soup........ 88
California Baked Beans............. 190
Camembert Souffle 168
Camille Dressing.................. 145
Canapes, see Hors d'Oeuvres

CANDY

Bon Bons........................ 379
Caramels........................ 380
Chocolate-Peanut Butter Balls.... 381
Microwave Fudge................ 379
Mother's Creamy Fudge.......... 382
The Oak Ridge Boys' Caramel
    Corn......................... 24
Peanut Butter Fudge............. 383
Porter Wagoner's Fudge......... 34
Southern Pralines................ 383
Toffee.......................... 384
Canning Notes.................... 151
Cantaloupe Cooler................ 454
Caper Egg Sauce.................. 237

Caper Sauce...................... 323
Caramel Custard.................. 458
Caramel Ice Cream Delight........ 437
Caramel Popcorn, The Oak Ridge
    Boys......................... 24
Caramels........................ 380
Caramel Sauce................... 470
Carousel Cheese Ball.............. 64

CARROTS

Carrot Cake..................... 390
Carrot Chutney.................. 159
Carrots and Onions with
    Madeira...................... 196
Cream of Carrot Soup with Peas ... 90
Marinated Carrot Sticks.......... 58
Orange Carrots.................. 195
Cash, Johnny Cash's "Old Iron Pot"
    Family-Style Chili............. 12
June Carter Cash's Vegetable
    "Stuff"...................... 13
Mama Cash's Chocolate Bavarian
    Pie.......................... 14
Rosanne Cash's Tuna Casserole... 15

CAULIFLOWER

Broccoli and Cauliflower
    Casserole.................... 193
Buffet Cauliflower............... 112
Cheese Soup with Cauliflower..... 89

CAVIAR

Caviar Mousse.................. 67
Elegant Caviar Pie 52

CELEBRITIES

Alabama's Carob Brownies....... 9
Bill Anderson's Pumpkin Ice
    Cream Pie.................... 10
Eddy Arnold's Coconut Cream
    Pie.......................... 11
Johnny Cash's "Old Iron Pot"
    Family-Style Chili............. 12
June Carter Cash's Vegetable
    "Stuff"...................... 13
Mama Cash's Chocolate Bavarian
    Pie.......................... 14
Rosanne Cash's Tuna Casserole... 15
Tennessee Ernie Ford's Fresh
    Apple-Nut Cake............... 16
The Gatlin Brothers' Mexican
    Meatball Soup................ 17
Merle Haggard's Rainbow Stew ... 18
Grandpa Jones' Biscuits.......... 19
Brenda Lee's Trout Fillets........ 20
Loretta Lynn's Cherry Pie 21
Barbara Mandrell's Seafood
    Mold........................ 22

Ronnie Milsap's Chicken Breast
   Casserole........................ 23
The Oak Ridge Boys' Caramel
   Corn............................ 24
Dolly Parton's Brownie Pudding... 25
Minnie Pearl's Chess Pie.......... 26
Jeannie C. Riley's Texas
   Skyscraper Dessert 27
Johnny Rodriguez's Enchiladas... 28
T.G. Sheppard's Chicken-Shrimp
   Supreme....................... 29
Hank Snow's Melting Moments
   Cookies....................... 30
Ray Stevens' "Raymone's
   Salad"........................ 31
Sylvia's Flour Enchiladas......... 32
Mel Tillis' Hamburger Stew....... 33
Porter Wagoner's Fudge.......... 34
Kitty Wells' Barbecued Chicken
   in a Bag 35
Tammy Wynette's Blueberry
   Buckle........................ 36
Celery Amandine.................. 197
Chafing Dish Spinach with
   Oysters....................... 65

CHEESE, see Eggs and Cheese
Almond Cheese Strips............ 54
Apples with Bleu Cheese.......... 55
Baked Sandwiches............... 97
Beer Cheese..................... 62
Beer Dip, Pumpernickel
   Surprise...................... 63
Brie en Croute................... 49
Camembert Souffle.............. 168
Carousel Cheese Ball............ 64
Chafing Dish Spinach with
   Oysters....................... 65
Cheesecake, see Desserts
Cheesecake Delights............. 365
Cheese Delights................. 98
Cheese French Bread............. 334
Cheese Souffle.................. 169
Cheese Soup with Cauliflower..... 89
Cheese-Spinach Luncheon
   Entree....................... 173
Cheese Stuffed Peppers.......... 207
Cheesy Cake Squares............ 364
Cheesy Eggplant................ 199
Cheesy Noodles................. 183
Chicken Cheese Chowder......... 86
Chili Roll....................... 66
Christmas Cheese Spread......... 69
Danish Cheese Bread............ 336
Green Chile Souffle.............. 170
Hot Crabmeat Dip............... 67

Iced Cheese Sandwiches.......... 104
Krispie Cheese Wafers............ 57
Make-in-Advance Cheese
   Pudding...................... 171
Olive Cheese Balls............... 57
Pita-Club Supreme.............. 107
Pita-Sausage and Cheese Filling... 106
Shrimp and Cheese Casserole..... 256
Something Special Hot Cheese
   Dip.......................... 72

CHERRIES
Cherry Conserve................. 154
Loretta Lynn's Cherry Pie 21
Chess Cakes..................... 364

CHESS PIE
Chess Pie....................... 422
Date-Chess Pie.................. 425
Minnie Pearl's Chess Pie......... 26
Chewy Coconut Cookies........... 366

CHICKEN, see Poultry
Chicken and Mushroom Crepes
   Florentine.................... 265
Chicken Bombay 269
Chicken Breasts in Vermouth
   and Tarragon................. 270
Chicken Breasts with Cheese
   and Herbs.................... 276
Chicken Cheese Chowder......... 86
Chicken Cordon Bleu............. 272
Chicken Creole.................. 273
Chicken Cutlets................. 274
Chicken Divan................... 275
Chicken Jerusalem.............. 278
Chicken Liver Pate.............. 68
Chicken Plus.................... 272
Chicken Rollade................. 277
Chicken Salad-Ribbon Sandwich
   Loaf......................... 103
Chicken Stuffed with Cream
   Cheese....................... 278

CHILI
Chili........................... 295
Chili Roll....................... 66
Johnny Cash's "Old Iron Pot"
   Family-Style Chili............. 12
Chilled Picnic Ratatouille.......... 114

CHOCOLATE
Belgian Mocha Cake.............. 388
Blender Pot de Creme............ 468
Bon Bons....................... 379
Bourbon Pie.................... 420
Brandy Alexander Pie............ 421
Brownies Divine................. 363
Cafe Mexicano.................. 42
Chocolate Almond Cheesecake.... 411

Chocolate Almond Ice Cream 444
Chocolate Cream Cheese Cake 391
Chocolate-Peanut Butter Balls 381
Chocolate Pecan Tart 423
Chocolate Phyllo Pie.............. 424
Chocolate Sauce 472
Coffee Toffee Torte................ 438
Derby Day Mint Sauce with
    Chocolate Leaves 471
Dolly Parton's Brownie Pudding... 25
Fabulous Chocolate Pie........... 427
Famous Chocolate Cake 393
Fantastic Chocolate Roll.......... 461
French Mint Pies................. 428
Fudge Cupcakes 406
Fudge Drop Cookies.............. 371
Fudge Pie 426
Gourmet Chocolate Cheesecake... 412
Grasshopper Pie 431
Iroquois Pie..................... 433
Jeannie C. Riley's Texas
    Skyscraper Dessert 27
Mama Cash's Chocolate Bavarian
    Pie.......................... 14
Microwave Fudge 379
Milky Way Ice Cream 445
Mississippi Mud Cake............. 396
Mocha Cake 397
Mother's Creamy Fudge 382
Oatmeal Brownies 370
Oreo Ice Cream Pie 442
Poached Pears with Chocolate
    Sauce........................ 456
Porter Wagoner's Fudge.......... 34
Pot de Creme 469
Toffee......................... 384
Toffee Coffee Pie................ 436
Velvet Hammer.................. 468
Zuccoto Cake 401

CHOWDER
    Chicken Cheese Chowder......... 86
    Hearty Clam Chowder........... 92
Christmas Cheese Spread.......... 69
Christmas Cranberry Tea.......... 42
Cigarettes Russes................. 375
Cinderella's Golden Potato
    Casserole..................... 208
Cinnamon-Raisin Bread........... 338
CLAMS
    Hearty Clam Chowder........... 92
    Hot Clam Dip 70
    Super Simple Clam Sauce 228
Club Supreme Filling, Pita......... 107
Cobblers, see Desserts
Cocktail Sauce, Fried Oysters....... 230

COCONUT
    Chewy Coconut Cookies 366
    Coconut Chess Pie 422
    Coconut Pound Cake 402
    Eddy Arnold's Coconut Cream
        Pie......................... 11
COFFEE
    Cafe Mexicano.................. 42
    Coffee Can Bread............... 339
    Coffee Punch 43
    Coffee Toffee Torte............. 438
    Do-It-Yourself Kahlua 43
    Individual Coffee Souffles........ 449
    Toffee Coffee Pie............... 436
Coffee Cakes, see Breads
Cold Cream of Cucumber Soup...... 80
Cold Grand Marnier Souffle with
    Strawberry Sauce............... 447
Cold Lemon Souffle with Raspberry
    Sauce......................... 451
Cold Orange Souffle 448
Cold Pea Salad................... 115
Cold Spinach Soup............... 79
Colony Club Zucchini 214
Company Crab Casserole.......... 228
CONSERVES
    Apple Honey-Cointreau 152
    Banana Jama................... 152
    Blackberry Curd................ 153
    Cherry Conserve 154
    Green Pepper Jelly............. 155
    Hot Pepper Jelly 154
    Peach Rum Jam 156
    Strawberry Preserves 156
COOKIES
Bar Cookies
    Alabama's Carob Brownies 9
    Apricot Bars................... 363
    Brownies Divine 363
    Cheesecake Delights 365
    Cheesy Cake Squares............ 364
    Chess Cakes................... 364
    Chewy Coconut Cookies 366
    Lemon Squares................. 367
    Linzer Bars................... 369
    Oatmeal Bars Extraordinaires..... 368
    Oatmeal Brownies 370
Drop Cookies
    Fudge Drop Cookies............ 371
    Ginger Snaps.................. 371
    Hank Snow's Melting Moments
        Cookies 30
    Macaroons 372
    Oatmeal Crispies............... 367
Rolled Cookies

Gingerbread Boys................ 373
Sugar Cookies 366
Special-Effect Cookies
Cigarettes Russes................ 375
Cream Cheese Cupcakes 376
Molasses Peppernuts............. 374
Rosettes......................... 377
Spritz Delights................... 376
Tassies.......................... 378
Coquilles St. Jacques.............. 232

CORN
Cornmeal Mush.................. 198
Southern Corn Pudding 198
White Corn Casserole 199

CORN BREADS, see Breads

CORNISH HENS
Baked Cornish Hens.............. 289
Rock Cornish Game Hens......... 288
Country Captain.................. 279

CRAB
Avocados Stuffed with Curried
Crabmeat..................... 51
Company Crab Casserole......... 228
Crab Epicurean.................. 226
Crab Imperial.................. 224
Crab Louis....................... 117
Crabmeat Hors d'Oeuvre Mold 68
Crabmeat Supreme 227
Crab Mousse.................. 66
Crab-Shrimp au Gratin........... 225
Elegant Crabmeat Crepes........ 223
Hot Crabmeat Dip............... 67
Hot Crabmeat Sandwiches....... 100
Lobster, Shrimp, and Crab
Casserole..................... 259
Marinated Crab.................. 122
Seafood Bombay Salad 126
Seafood Gumbo.................. 83
Snowcapped Mushrooms........ 60
Variety Quiches................. 175

CRANBERRY
Christmas Cranberry Tea......... 42
Cran-Apple Crumb Pie 425
Cranberry Frappe................ 197
Cranberry-Orange Relish........ 157
Cranberry Port Wine Salad....... 133
Cranberry Pound Cake 403
Crappie, Oven-Baked Bass or........ 237
Cream Cheese Cupcakes 376
Cream of Broccoli Soup............. 81
Cream of Carrot Soup with Peas..... 90
Creme Brulee...................... 459

CREOLE
Chicken Creole 273
Creole Eggs...................... 163

Creole Shrimp................... 250

CREPES
Basic Crepes..................... 354
Elegant Crabmeat Crepes........ 223
Chicken and Mushroom Crepes
Florentine.................... 265
Croutons........................ 128
Crown Pork Roast................ 319
Crunchy Chicken Squares......... 280

CUCUMBERS
Cold Cream of Cucumber Soup.... 80
Cucumber-Sour Cream Salad..... 116
Shrimp and Cucumber
Sandwiches.................. 105

CUPCAKES, see Desserts

CURRY
Avocados Stuffed with Curried
Crabmeat..................... 51
Curried Bean Sprout Salad........ 116
Curried Chicken Salad 115
Curried Swiss Eggs.............. 163
Curry Tomato-Split Pea Soup 91
Egg-Curry Mold................. 134
Seafood Bombay Salad 126
Shrimp-Curry Casserole......... 251
Czechoslovakian Kolaches.......... 346

D
Danish Cheese Bread.............. 336
Danish Pudding Cake 392
Date-Chess Pie................... 425
Date-Nut Bread 358
Deep Dish Apple Cobbler 409
Deep Dish Apple Pie.............. 426
Deep-Frying Chicken Batter 286
Derby Day Mint Sauce with
Chocolate Leaves 471

DESSERTS
Apple Fritters................... 460
Dolly Parton's Brownie Pudding... 25
Fantastic Chocolate Roll......... 461
Jeannie C. Riley's Texas
Skyscraper Dessert 27
Lemon Mousse with Blueberries... 462
Meringues...................... 464
Puff Pastry, Raspberry
Mille-Feuille.................. 466
Raspberry Mille-Feuille........... 466
Rum Dessert..................... 463
Sponge Pudding 460
Walnut Crisps 465
Beverage Desserts
Blender Pot de Creme............. 468
Pot de Creme 469
Velvet Hammer.................. 468
Cakes

485

Beer Cake 387
Belgian Mocha Cake 388
Best Ever Apple Cake 389
Carrot Cake 390
Chocolate Cream Cheese Cake 391
Coconut Pound Cake 402
Cranberry Pound Cake 403
Danish Pudding Cake 392
Famous Chocolate Cake 393
Hummingbird Cake 394
Italian Cream Cake 395
Mississippi Mud Cake 396
Mocha Cake 397
Old-Fashioned Strawberry
   Shortcake 398
Rum Cake 399
Sour Cream or Whipped Cream
   Pound Cake 404
Tennessee Ernie Ford's Fresh
   Apple Cake 16
Unbaked Fruitcake 404
Vanilla Wafer Cake 400
White Fruitcake 405
Zuccoto Cake 401
Cheesecakes
   Chocolate Almond Cheesecake 411
   Gourmet Chocolate Cheesecake . . . 412
   Miami Cheesecake 414
   Party Cheesecakes 413
   Praline Cheesecake 416
   Strawberry Cheesecake 417
Cobblers
   Apple-Plum Melange 408
   Deep Dish Apple Cobbler 409
   Peach Cobbler 407
   Southern Blackberry Cobbler 410
Cupcakes/Muffins
   Fudge Cupcakes 406
   Holiday Muffins 406
   Pumpkin Muffins 407
Custard Desserts
   Amaretto Custard with Fruit 457
   Caramel Custard 458
   Creme Brulee 459
Frozen Desserts
   Bill Anderson's Pumpkin Ice
      Cream Pie 10
   Caramel Ice Cream Delight 437
   Coffee Toffee Torte 438
   Frozen Strawberry Dessert 439
   Ice Cream Bombe with
      Raspberry Sauce 440
   Mocha Toffee Delight 441
   Oreo Ice Cream Pie 442
   Strawberries Romanoff 440

Strawberry French Sorbet 443
Fruit Desserts
   Bananas Foster 453
   Cantaloupe Cooler 454
   Fresh Blueberry Salad 134
   Fruit Compote with Kirsch 454
   Fruit Fantasy 457
   Fruit Pizza 455
   Poached Pears with Chocolate
      Sauce 456
   Tammy Wynette's Blueberry
      Buckle 36
Ice Cream
   Chocolate Almond Ice Cream 444
   Lemon Ice Cream 443
   Milky Way Ice Cream 445
   Peach Ice Cream 444
   Vanilla Ice Cream 446
Pies
   Apple Pie 418
   Bourbon Pie 420
   Brandy Alexander Pie 421
   Chess Pie, Lemon and Coconut 422
   Chocolate Pecan Tart 423
   Chocolate Phyllo Pie 424
   Cran-Apple Crumb Pie 425
   Date-Chess Pie 425
   Deep Dish Apple Pie 426
   Eddy Arnold's Coconut Cream
      Pie 11
   Fabulous Chocolate Pie 427
   French Mint Pies 428
   Frozen Lemonade Pie 429
   Fudge Pie 426
   Glazed Strawberry Pie 430
   Grasshopper Pie 431
   Heavenly Pie 432
   Iroquois Pie 433
   Lemon Cream Pie 433
   Loretta Lynn's Cherry Pie 21
   Mama Cash's Chocolate Bavarian
      Pie 14
   Minnie Pearl's Chess Pie 26
   Pecan Pie 434
   Praline Pumpkin Pie 434
   Raspberry Passion 435
   Ritz Cracker Pie 437
   Toffee Coffee Pie 436
Sauces
   Blueberry Sauce 470
   Butterscotch Sauce 469
   Caramel Sauce 470
   Chocolate Sauce 472
   Derby Day Mint Sauce with
      Chocolate Leaves 471

Fruit Mousseline Sauce........... 472
Grand Marnier Sauce for Fruit..... 473
Peach Melba Sauce............... 473
Praline Sauce.................... 474
Raspberry Sauce, Ice Cream
    Bombe........................ 440
Witches' Brew................... 474
Souffles
Cold Grand Marnier Souffle with
    Strawberry Sauce.............. 447
Cold Lemon Souffle with
    Raspberry Sauce............... 451
Cold Orange Souffle.............. 448
Hot Raspberry Souffle............ 450
Individual Coffee Souffles......... 449
Raspberry Souffle................ 452

DIJON
Dijon Mustard Dressing........... 147
Dijon Sauce, Rack of Lamb........ 315
Quiche Lorraine Dijon............ 174

DILL
Dill Dip......................... 69
Dill Dressing.................... 146
Dilled Shrimp with Mushrooms ... 252
Do-It-Yourself Kahlua............. 43
Dolly Parton's Brownie Pudding..... 25
Dove in White Wine.............. 289

DRESSINGS, see Salads
Dressing Stuffing, Stuffed
    Pork Chops.................... 325

DUCK
Duck............................ 290
Live Oak Duck................... 291
Duke of Windsor Sandwiches....... 99

E
Easy Asparagus................... 189
Easy Loaf Bread.................. 340
Easy Schnecker Muffins............ 350
Easy Vichy...................... 77
Easy Yeast Biscuits............... 347
Eddy Arnold's Coconut Cream Pie... 11
Egg-Curry Mold.................. 134
Eggnog......................... 44

EGGPLANT
Cheesy Eggplant................. 199
Chilled Picnic Ratatouille......... 114

EGG SALAD
Egg Salad, Ribbon Sandwich
    Loaf.......................... 103
Molded Egg Salad................ 138

EGGS AND CHEESE
Creole Eggs...................... 163
Curried Swiss Eggs............... 163
Eggs Fox Hollow Farm............ 164
Fluffy Bacon-Cheese Omelet...... 165

Make-In-Advance Cheese
    Pudding....................... 171
Oven Omelet.................... 170
Ranch Eggs..................... 167
Sour Cream Enchiladas.......... 172
Spiced Eggs..................... 166
Frittatas
Kitchen Sink Frittata............ 166
Spaghetti Frittata............... 184
Quiches
Cheese-Spinach Luncheon
    Entree........................ 173
Quiche Lorraine Dijon............ 174
Roquefort and Asparagus
    Quiche........................ 176
Sour Cream Quiche.............. 177
Spinach Pie..................... 210
Tomato Pie..................... 218
Variety Quiches................. 174
Zucchini Puff Pie................ 178
Souffles
Camembert Souffle.............. 168
Cheese Souffle.................. 169
Green Chile Souffle.............. 170
Oyster Souffle.................. 230
Salmon Souffle................. 245
Savory Souffle Roll.............. 300
Spinach Souffle................. 210
Spinach Souffle Mold............ 139
Tuna Souffle................... 247
Zucchini Souffle................ 215
Elegant Caviar Pie............... 52
Elegant Crabmeat Crepes.......... 223

ENCHILADAS
Brown Rice Enchiladas.......... 179
Johnny Rodriguez's Enchiladas... 28
Sour Cream Enchiladas.......... 172
Excellent Mushroom Casserole...... 201
Eye of Round or Tenderloin
    Rib Roast...................... 309

F
Fabulous Chocolate Pie............ 427
Famous Chocolate Cake........... 393
Fantastic Chocolate Roll........... 461
Fettuccine....................... 183
Flemish Sauce................... 262
Flounder Florentine............... 242
Fluffy Bacon-Cheese Omelet....... 165
Ford, Tennessee Ernie Ford's
    Fresh Apple-Nut Cake........... 16
French Bread.................... 335
French Bread, Cheese............. 334
French Dressing, Beau Jacques..... 146
French Mint Pies................. 428
French Toast, Lightest-Ever........ 351

Fresh Blueberry Salad............. 134
Fried Oysters...................... 230
Fried Rice......................... 180
Fried Shrimp in Beer Batter........ 253
Fried Tomatoes in Golden Sauce..... 217
Frittata, Kitchen Sink.............. 166
Frittata, Spaghetti................. 184
Frozen Fruit Salad................. 135
Frozen Lemonade Pie.............. 429
Frozen Strawberry Dessert......... 439
Frozen Tomato Salad............... 136
Frozen Whiskey Sour.............. 44

FRUIT
Amaretto Custard with
  Fruit....................... 457
Cheese and Fruit Stuffing,
  Stuffed Pork Chops............ 325
Frozen Fruit Salad.............. 135
Fruit Compote with Kirsch........ 454
Fruit Fantasy................... 457
Fruit Mousseline Sauce.......... 472
Fruit Pizza..................... 455
Fruit Salad Dressing............ 147
Heavenly Pie................... 432
Hot Fruit Casserole............. 219
Prosciutto and Fresh Fruit....... 125
Witches' Brew.................. 474

FRUITCAKES, see Desserts
FUDGE
Fudge Cupcakes................. 406
Fudge Drop Cookies............. 371
Fudge Pie..................... 426
Microwave Fudge............... 379
Mother's Creamy Fudge.......... 382
Peanut Butter Fudge............ 383
Porter Wagoner's Fudge.......... 34

G
GAME
Baked Quail in Wine............. 292
Dove in White Wine............. 289
Duck.......................... 290
Live Oak Duck.................. 291
Gatlin Brothers' Mexican Meatball
  Soup........................... 17
Gazpacho...................... 82
Gazpacho Salad Mold............. 137
German Potato Salad............. 118
Gingerbread Boys................ 373
Ginger Snaps................... 371
Glazed Strawberry Pie........... 430
Golden Gravy.................... 329
Golden Mushrooms.............. 202
Gourmet Chocolate Cheesecake..... 412
Graham Rolls................... 348

Grand Marnier Souffle, Cold,
  with Strawberry Sauce.......... 447
Grand Marnier Sauce for Fowl...... 291
Grand Marnier Sauce for Fruit...... 473
Grandpa Jones' Biscuits........... 19
Granola Bread.................... 340
Grasshopper Pie................. 431
Green Chile Souffle............... 170
Green Pepper Jelly................ 155
Green Sauce..................... 261
Guacamole, Layered.............. 71
Guacamole Dip, Mexican.......... 70
Gumbo, Seafood.................. 83

H
Haggard, Merle Haggard's Rainbow
  Stew........................... 18
HAM
Baked Ham with Plum Garnish.... 318
Club Supreme Filling, Pita........ 107
Ham Salad, Ribbon Sandwich
  Loaf.......................... 103
Savory Souffle Roll.............. 301
Hank Snow's Melting Moments
  Cookies....................... 30
Hearty Clam Chowder............. 92
Hearty Sausage and Rice Soup...... 93
Heavenly Pie.................... 432
Hickory-Smoked Barbecued
  Chicken....................... 287
Holiday Muffins.................. 406
HOLLANDAISE
Blender Hollandaise.............. 220
Blender Hollandaise, Eggs Fox
  Hollow Farm.................. 164
Hollandaise Sauce, Chicken
  Divan........................ 275
Home Canning Notes.............. 151
Honey-Mustard Dressing.......... 148
Honey-Whole Wheat Bread......... 341
HORS D'OEUVRES
Appetizers
Artichoke Bottom First Course.... 50
Avocados Stuffed with Curried
  Crabmeat.................... 51
Broiled Chicken Liver
  Appetizers................... 51
Elegant Caviar Pie.............. 52
Mexican Appetizer.............. 52
Mushrooms on Toast............ 204
Oysters Chez Elise.............. 53
Canapes
Almond Cheese Strips........... 54
Apples with Bleu Cheese.......... 55
Asparagus Roll-Ups.............. 54

488

Bacon-Wrapped Shrimp.......... 55
Brie en Croute 49
Buried Treasures................ 56
Krispie Cheese Wafers........... 57
Marinated Carrot Sticks.......... 58
Marvelous Meatballs............. 58
Olive Cheese Balls............... 57
Oyster-Stuffed Mushrooms....... 59
Snowcapped Mushrooms........ 60
Stuffed Mushrooms Parmesan.... 61
Tasty Water Chestnuts........... 62
Toasted Artichoke Rounds........ 53
Dips, Sauces, and Spreads
Beer Cheese.................... 62
Beer Dip, Pumpernickel Surprise.. 63
Carousel Cheese Ball............. 64
Caviar Mousse.................. 67
Chafing Dish Spinach with
  Oysters...................... 65
Chicken Liver Pate.............. 68
Chili Dip, Bacon-Wrapped
  Shrimp...................... 55
Chili Roll...................... 66
Christmas Cheese Spread........ 69
Crabmeat Hors d'Oeuvre Mold.... 68
Crab Mousse................... 66
Dill Dip....................... 69
Hot Clam Dip................... 70
Hot Crabmeat Dip............... 67
Jezebel Sauce.................. 72
Layered Guacamole............ .. 71
Mexican Guacamole Dip......... 70
Pumpernickel Surprise.......... 63
Shrimp Cocktail Spread.......... 73
Shrimp, Mushroom, Artichoke
  Fondue..................... 73
Something Special Hot Cheese
  Dip........................ 72
Sour Cream Dip, Pumpernickel
  Surprise..................... 63
Spinach Dip.................... 74
Sweet 'n Sour Sauce............. 74
Tangy Vegetable Sauce.......... 220
Tomato Soup Aspic............. 140
Hot Bacon Dressing............. 143
Hot Clam Dip................... 70
Hot Crabmeat Dip............... 67
Hot Crabmeat Sandwiches........ 100
Hot Dogs, Super Dogs........... 105
Hot Fruit Casserole............. 219
Hot Pepper Jelly................ 154
Hot Raspberry Souffle........... 450
Houston's Italian Meat Sauce....... 297
Hummingbird Cake............... 394
Hungarian Poppy Seed Onions..... 209

I
Ice Box Potato Rolls............... 345
ICE CREAM, see Desserts
  Ice Cream Bombe with Raspberry
    Sauce....................... 440
  Iced Cheese Sandwiches......... 104
  Iced Chicken Breasts............ 282
  Iced Melon Soup................ 78
ICINGS
  Caramel Icing, Beer Cake........ 387
  Chocolate Cream Cheese Icing,
    Chocolate Cream Cheese
    Cake....................... 391
  Chocolate Icing, Mississippi
    Mud Cake.................... 396
  Chocolate Nut Icing, Famous
    Chocolate Cake............... 393
  Coffee Icing, Mocha Cake........ 397
  Cream Cheese Frosting, Carrot
    Cake....................... 390
  Cream Cheese Icing,
    Hummingbird Cake............ 394
  Cream Cheese Icing, Italian
    Cream Cake.................. 395
  Cream Cheese Icing, Vanilla
    Wafer Cake.................. 400
  Mocha Icing, Belgian Mocha
    Cake....................... 388
Individual Coffee Souffles.......... 449
Iroquois Pie.................... 433
Italian Chicken.................. 283
Italian Cream Cake.............. 395
Italian Dressing................. 148
Italian Pesto Garden Soup......... 94
J
Jeannie C. Riley's Texas
  Skyscraper Dessert............. 27
Jezebel Sauce.................. 72
Johnny Cash's "Old Iron Pot"
  Family-Style Chili............. 12
Johnny Rodriguez's Enchiladas..... 28
Jones, Grandpa Jones' Biscuits..... 19
June Carter Cash's Vegetable
  "Stuff"........................ 13
K
Kahlua, Do-It-Yourself........... 43
Kitchen Sink Frittata............. 166
Kitty Wells' Barbecued Chicken
  in a Bag..................... 35
Kolaches, Czechoslovakian......... 346
Krispie Cheese Wafers............. 57
L
LAMB, see Meats
Layered Gourmet Salad........... 119
Layered Guacamole............... 71

Layered Pickles 157
Lee, Brenda Lee's Trout Fillets 20

LEMON
Cold Lemon Souffle with
 Raspberry Sauce 451
Frozen Lemonade Pie 429
Lemon Bread 358
Lemon Chess Pie 422
Lemon Cream Pie 433
Lemoned Chicken 271
Lemon Ice Cream 443
Lemon Mousse with Blueberries . . . 462
Lemon Squares 367
Lemon Squash with Walnuts 211
Lemon Veal 326
Lettuce Soup 95
Lightest Ever French Toast 351
Linzer Bars 369
Live Oak Duck 291
Loaf Bread, Easy 340

LOBSTER
Boiled Lobster 260
Lobster, Shrimp, and Crab
 Casserole 259
Lorenzo Dressing, Molded
 Egg Salad 138
Loretta Lynn's Cherry Pie 21

M
Macaroons 372
Make-Ahead Poppy Seed Noodles . . . 184
Make-in-Advance Cheese Pudding . . 171
Mama Cash's Chocolate Bavarian
 Pie 14
Mandarin-Fried Shrimp with
 Peas 254
Mandrell, Barbara Mandrell's
 Seafood Mold 22
Manicotti Shells, Baked Stuffed 182
Marinated Artichoke and
 Mushroom Salad 120
Marinated Broccoli 121
Marinated Carrot Sticks 58
Marinated Crab 122
Marinated Eye of Round 310
Marinated Onions 121
Marvelous Meatballs 58
Maurice Salad Dressing 149

MAYONNAISE
Blender Mayonnaise 142
Mayonnaise 142
Must-Make Mayonnaise 143
Orange Mayonnaise 330
Tarragon Mayonnaise, Tomato-Egg
 Tarragon Salad 131
Meatballs, Marvelous 58

MEATS
Beef
 Barbecued Beef 305
 Beef en Gelee 304
 Beef Stroganoff 306
 Boeuf de Wellington 307
 Brisket 308
 Chili 295
 Eye of Round or Tenderloin Rib
  Roast 309
 Houston's Italian Meat Sauce 297
 Johnny Cash's "Old Iron Pot"
  Family-Style Chili 12
 Marinated Eye of Round 310
 Marvelous Meatballs 58
 Mel Tillis' Hamburger Stew 33
 Merle Haggard's Rainbow Stew . . . 18
 Mexican Appetizer 52
 Mexican Delight 124
 Moussaka 298
 Picadillo 299
 Rib Roast with Artichoke Sauce . . . 311
 Shish Kebob 312
 Spaghetti Bolognese Sauce 296
 Steak Diane 308
 Steak Teriyaki 313
 Zucchini Lasagna 303
Lamb
 Barbecued Lamb 314
 Rack of Lamb with Dijon
  Sauce 315
 Shish Kebob 312
 Special Saucy Lamb 316
 Spring Lamb Stew 317
Pork
 Baked Ham with Plum Garnish 318
 Barbecued Spareribs 322
 Crown Pork Roast 319
 Pork Chops in Wine 323
 Roast Pork with Sage 321
 Stuffed Pork Chops 324
 Stuffed Pork Loin 320
Sausage
 Hearty Sausage and Rice Soup 93
 Italian Pesto Garden Soup 94
 Kitchen Sink Frittata 166
 Ratatouille with Sausage 200
 Sausage and Cheese Filling,
  Pita 106
 Steeplechase Casserole 302
Veal
 Lemon Veal 326
 Scallopine with Mushrooms
  and White Wine 327

Veal Scallops Vermouth 326
Veal Smitane 328
MELONS
Iced Melon Soup 78
Melon Ball and Shrimp Salad 123
Prosciutto and Fresh Fruit 125
Mel Tillis' Hamburger Stew 33
MERINGUE
Meringue, Eddy Arnold's Coconut
Cream Pie 11
Meringues. 464
Merle Haggard's Rainbow Stew 18
MEXICAN
Brown Rice Enchiladas. 179
Cafe Mexicano 42
Chili Roll 66
Gatlin Brothers' Mexican
Meatball Soup 17
Gazpacho 82
Gazpacho Salad Mold. 137
Green Chile Souffle. 170
Johnny Rodriguez's Enchiladas. . . 28
Layered Guacamole. 71
Mexican Appetizer 52
Mexican Delight 124
Mexican Guacamole Dip. 70
Mexican Rice 181
Mexican Salad Filling, Pita. 106
Ranch Eggs. 167
Rice with Green Chiles 181
Something Special Hot Cheese
Dip 72
Sour Cream Enchiladas 172
South of the Border Chicken 285
Sylvia's Flour Tortillas. 32
Miami Cheesecake 414
Microwave Fudge 379
Milky Way Ice Cream 445
Milsap, Ronnie Milsap's Chicken
Breast Casserole 23
Minnie Pearl's Chess Pie 26
Mint Julep. 45
Mississippi Mud Cake. 396
MOCHA
Belgian Mocha Cake. 388
Mocha Cake 397
Mocha Toffee Delight 441
Mock Sangria. 46
Mock Turtle Doves 281
Molasses Peppernuts. 374
MOLDED SALADS, see Salads
Molded Egg Salad, Lorenzo
Dressing 138
Mother's Creamy Fudge 382
Moussaka 298

Mousseline Sauce, Poached
Salmon 244
MUFFINS, see Breads
MUSHROOMS
Dilled Shrimp with Mushrooms . . . 252
Excellent Mushroom Casserole. . . . 201
Golden Mushrooms 202
Marinated Artichoke and
Mushroom Salad. 120
Mushroom Florentine 202
Mushroom Sauce, Stuffed Sole 238
Mushrooms on Toast 204
Mushroom-Stuffed Tomatoes 216
Oyster-Stuffed Mushrooms 59
Scallopine with Mushrooms
and White Wine. 327
Sherried Peas and Mushrooms 204
Shrimp, Mushroom, Artichoke
Fondue 73
Shrimp with Mushrooms in
Wine Sauce. 257
Snowcapped Mushrooms. 60
Souffleed Mushrooms 203
Stuffed Mushrooms Parmesan 61
Toasted Mushroom Sandwiches. . . 108
Variety Quiches. 175
Mussels Provencales 234
Must-Make Mayonnaise 143
N
Navy Bean Soup 96
Navy Salad Dressing 149
Nicoise, Salade. 127
O
Oak Ridge Boys' Caramel Corn 24
OATMEAL
Oatmeal Bars Extraordinaires. 368
Oatmeal Brownies 370
Oatmeal Crispies. 367
Okra, Pickled 160
Old-Fashioned Strawberry
Shortcake 398
Olive Cheese Balls. 57
OMELETS
Fluffy Bacon-Cheese Omelet 165
Oven Omelet 170
ONIONS
Carrots and Onions with
Madeira 196
Hungarian Poppy Seed Onions 209
Marinated Onions. 121
Onion Bread. 337
Onion Soup. 96
Zucchini and Spring Onions 215
ORANGES
Cold Orange Souffle 448

Cranberry-Orange Relish 157
Orange Carrots 195
Orange Mayonnaise 330
Orange Tea Bread 360
Oreo Ice Cream Pie 442

ORIENTAL
Asparagus Egg-Drop Soup 85
Buddha's Feast 206
Lemon Squash with Walnuts 211
Mandarin-Fried Shrimp with
   Peas 254
Oriental Chicken 284
Oriental Chicken Salad Filling,
   Pita 107
Oriental Vegetable Casserole 191
Peas Oriental 205
Steak Teriyaki 313
Oven-Baked Bass or Crappie 237
Oven-Baked Beans 191
Oven Omelet 170
Overnight Pancakes 355

OYSTERS
Artichoke-Oyster Soup 84
Chafing Dish Spinach with
   Oysters 65
Fried Oysters 230
Oyster or Shrimp Boats 101
Oyster Pie 231
Oysters Chez Elise 53
Oyster Souffle 230
Oyster-Stuffed Mushrooms 59
Scalloped Oysters 229
Seafood Gumbo 83

P
Pancakes, Overnight 355
Parmesan Salad Dressing 150
Parton, Dolly Parton's Brownie
   Pudding 25
Party Cheesecakes 413
Party Wine Potatoes 208

PASTA
Baked Stuffed Manicotti Shells 182
Cheesy Noodles 183
Dilled Shrimp with Mushrooms . . . 252
Fettuccine 183
Make-Ahead Poppy Seed
   Noodles 184
Pasta Primavera 186
Rosanne Cash's Tuna Casserole . . . 15
Scallops Italian 233
Spaghetti Frittata 184
Super Simple Clam Sauce 228
Tuna Cooler 246

Zucchini Lasagna 303

PEACHES
Bourbon Peaches 219
Peach Cobbler 407
Peach Ice Cream 444
Peach Melba Sauce 473
Peach Rum Jam 156
Peach Smash 45

PEANUT BUTTER
Chocolate-Peanut Butter Balls 381
Peanut Butter Fudge 383
Pearl, Minnie Pearl's Chess Pie 26
Porter Wagoner's Fudge 34

PEAS
Cold Pea Salad 115
Cream of Carrot Soup with Peas . . . 90
Curry Tomato-Split Pea Soup 91
Mandarin-Fried Shrimp with
   Peas 254
Peas Oriental 205
Sherried Peas and Mushrooms 204

PECANS
Chocolate Pecan Tart 423
Pecan Pie 434

PEPPERS
Stuffed Peppers 207
Green Pepper Jelly 155
Hot Pepper Jelly 154
Peppernuts, Molasses 374
Picadillo 299
Pickled Okra 160

PICKLES
Layered Pickles 157
Pickled Okra 160
Seven-Day Pickles 158
Zucchini Bread 'n Butter Pickles . . 159
PIES, see Desserts
THE WELL-STUFFED PITA POCKET
Club Supreme Filling 107
Mexican Salad Filling 106
Oriental Chicken Salad
   Filling 107
Sausage and Cheese Filling 106
Plain White Bread 343

PLUMS
Apple-Plum Melange 408
Baked Ham with Plum Garnish 318
Poached Fillet of Sole with Grapes . . . 239
Poached Pears with Chocolate
   Sauce 456
Poached Salmon Mousseline 244
Popcorn, Caramel, Oak Ridge Boys . . 24
Popovers 356
PORK, see Meats
Pork Chops in Wine 323

Porter Wagoner's Fudge............ 34

POTATOES
Cinderella's Golden Potato
Casserole..................... 208
German Potato Salad............ 118
Ice Box Potato Rolls 345
Party Wine Potatoes............. 208
Sweet Potatoes Caramel......... 207
Pot de Creme 469
Pot de Creme, Blender............. 468
Poulet Etouffe en Croute........... 266

POULTRY
Apricot-Glazed Chicken.......... 267
Baked Cornish Hens............. 289
Breast of Chicken
au Champagne 268
Broiled Chicken Liver
Appetizers 51
Calcutta Mulligatawny Soup...... 88
Chicken and Mushroom Crepes
Florentine.................... 265
Chicken Bombay 269
Chicken Breasts in Vermouth
and Tarragon.................. 270
Chicken Breasts with Cheese and
Herbs........................ 276
Chicken Cordon Bleu............. 272
Chicken Creole 273
Chicken Cutlets................. 274
Chicken Divan.................... 275
Chicken Jerusalem 278
Chicken Plus................... 272
Chicken Rollade 277
Chicken Stuffed with Cream
Cheese....................... 278
Country Captain................. 279
Crunchy Chicken Squares........ 280
Curried Chicken Salad 115
Deep-Frying Chicken Batter 286
Hickory-Smoked Barbecued
Chicken...................... 287
Iced Chicken Breasts............. 282
Italian Chicken 283
Kitty Wells' Barbecued Chicken
in a Bag...................... 35
Lemoned Chicken 271
Mock Turtle Doves, Stuffed
Chicken Breasts in Mushroom
Sauce........................ 281
Oriental Chicken................. 284
Oriental Chicken Salad Filling,
Pita.......................... 107
Poulet Etouffe en Croute.......... 266
Rock Cornish Game Hens......... 288

Ronnie Milsap's Chicken Breast
Casserole..................... 23
South of the Border Chicken 285
T.G. Sheppard's Chicken-Shrimp
Supreme..................... 29
Variety Quiches.................. 174
POUND CAKES, see Desserts
Praline Cheesecake 416
Praline Pumpkin Pie 434
Praline Sauce................... 474
Southern Pralines................ 383
Prosciutto and Fresh Fruit......... 125
Puff Pastry, Raspberry
Mille-Feuille.................... 466
Pumpernickel Surprise............. 63
PUMPKIN
Bill Anderson's Pumpkin Ice
Cream Pie 10
Praline Pumpkin Pie 434
Pumpkin Bread.................. 357
Pumpkin Muffins 407

Q
Quail, Baked in Wine.............. 292
QUICHE, see Eggs and Cheese
Quiche Lorraine Dijon............ 174

R
Rack of Lamb with Dijon Sauce...... 315
Rainbow Stew, Merle Haggard's..... 18
Raisin Bread, Cinnamon........... 338
Raisin Sauce for Ham.............. 330
Ranch Eggs..................... 167
RASPBERRIES
Cold Lemon Souffle with Raspberry
Sauce........................ 451
Hot Raspberry Souffle............ 450
Ice Cream Bombe with Raspberry
Sauce........................ 440
Raspberry Mille-Feuille........... 466
Raspberry Passion 435
Raspberry Souffle................ 452
Ratatouille, Chilled Picnic 114
Ratatouille with Sausage 200
Ray Stevens' "Raymone's Salad"... 31
Red Beans with Rice.............. 192
Redfish in Wine................. 234
Red Snapper, Baked............. 236
Red Snapper, Barbecued........... 235
Refrigerated Rolls-Sweet Rolls 349
RELISHES
Carrot Chutney.................. 159
Cranberry-Orange Relish......... 157
Squash Relish 158
Ribbon Sandwich Loaf 102
Rib Roast with Artichoke Sauce 311

RICE

Artichoke-Rice Salad 112
Brown Rice Enchiladas 179
Fried Rice 180
Hearty Sausage and Rice Soup 93
Mexican Rice 181
Red Beans with Rice 192
Rice Pilaf 178
Rice with Green Chiles 181
Riley, Jeannie C. Riley's Texas
    Skyscraper Dessert 27
Ritz Cracker Pie 437
Roast Pork with Sage 321
Rock Cornish Game Hens 288
Rodriguez, Johnny Rodriguez's
    Enchiladas 28

ROLLS, see Breads

Ronnie Milsap's Chicken Breast
    Casserole 23
Roquefort and Asparagus Quiche 176
Rosanne Cash's Tuna Casserole 15
Rosettes 377
Rum Cake 399
Rum Dessert 463
Rye Bread 344

S

SALADS

Artichoke-Rice Salad 112
Broccoli Salad 113
Buffet Cauliflower 112
Chicken Salad, Ribbon Sandwich
    Loaf 103
Chilled Picnic Ratatouille 114
Club Supreme Filling, Pita 107
Cold Pea Salad 115
Crab Louis 117
Croutons 128
Cucumber-Sour Cream Salad 116
Curried Bean Sprout Salad 116
Curried Chicken Salad 115
Egg Salad, Ribbon Sandwich
    Loaf 103
German Potato Salad 118
Ham Salad, Ribbon Sandwich
    Loaf 103
Iced Chicken Breasts 282
Layered Gourmet Salad 119
Marinated Artichoke and
    Mushroom Salad 120
Marinated Broccoli 121
Marinated Crab 122
Marinated Onions 121
Melon Ball and Shrimp Salad 123
Mexican Delight 124
Mexican Salad Filling, Pita 106

Oriental Chicken Salad Filling,
    Pita 107
Prosciutto and Fresh Fruit 125
Ray Stevens' "Raymone's
    Salad" 31
Salade Nicoise 127
Seafood Bombay Salad 126
Shrimp and Cucumber Filling,
    Sandwiches 105
Slaw 125
Spinach Salad 128
Stuffed Avocado Salad 130
Tomato-Egg Tarragon Salad 131
Tuna Cooler 246
Molded Salads
Artichoke-Asparagus Mold 132
Barbara Mandrell's Seafood Mold . . 22
Cranberry Port Wine Salad 133
Egg-Curry Mold 134
Fresh Blueberry Salad 134
Frozen Fruit Salad 135
Frozen Tomato Salad 136
Gazpacho Salad Mold 137
Molded Egg Salad, Lorenzo
    Dressing 138
Spinach Souffle Mold 139
Tomato Soup Aspic 140
Vegetable Salad Mold 141
Salad Dressings
Beau Jacques French Dressing 146
Blender Mayonnaise 142
Bleu Cheese Dressing I 144
Bleu Cheese Dressing II 145
Camille Dressing 145
Dijon Mustard Dressing 147
Dill Dressing 146
Fruit Salad Dressing 147
Honey-Mustard Dressing 148
Hot Bacon Dressing 143
Italian Dressing 148
Lorenzo Dressing 138
Maurice Salad Dressing 149
Mayonnaise 142
Must-Make Mayonnaise 143
Navy Salad Dressing 149
Parmesan Salad Dressing 150
Tomato-Roquefort Dressing 144

SALMON

Poached Salmon Mousseline 244
Salmon Souffle 245

SANDWICHES

Baked Sandwiches 97
Cheese Delights 98
Duke of Windsor Sandwiches 99
Hot Crabmeat Sandwiches 100

Iced Cheese Sandwiches. 104
Oyster or Shrimp Boats. 101
Ribbon Sandwich Loaf 102
Shrimp and Cucumber
    Sandwiches. 105
Super Dogs. 105
The Well-Stuffed Pita Pocket. 106
Toasted Mushroom Sandwiches. . . 108
Sangria 46

SAUCES, see also Dessert Sauces
Artichoke Sauce, Rib Roast 311
Barbecue Sauce, Barbecued
    Shrimp. 249
Barbecue Sauce, Hickory Smoked
    Barbecued Chicken 287
Barbecue Sauce, Kitty Wells'
    Barbecued Chicken in a Bag. 35
Bearnaise Sauce 267
Blender Hollandaise. 220
Caper and Egg Sauce, Baked
    Red Snapper. 237
Caper Sauce 323
Cocktail Sauce, Fried Oysters 230
Dijon Sauce, Rack of Lamb. 315
Flemish Sauce. 262
Golden Gravy. 329
Golden Sauce, Fried Tomatoes 217
Grand Marnier Sauce for Fowl. 291
Green Sauce. 261
Hollandaise Sauce, Chicken
    Divan. 275
Houston's Italian Meat Sauce 297
Jezebel Sauce 72
Lemon Sauce, Shrimp with
    Lemon Sauce. 258
Mousseline Sauce, Poached
    Salmon 244
Mushroom Sauce, Chicken
    Cutlets. 274
Mushroom Sauce, Mock Turtle
    Doves. 281
Mushroom Sauce, Stuffed Sole 238
New Sauce Verte, Chicken Breasts
    in Vermouth and Tarragon. 271
Pesto Sauce, Italian Pesto Garden
    Soup. 95
Raisin Sauce for Ham. 330
Sauce Nantua, Shrimp Nantua 255
Shallot Cream Sauce 329
Shotgun Sauce, Baked Quail
    in Wine. 292
Spaghetti Bolognese Sauce 296
Super Simple Clam Sauce 228
Sweet and Sour Sauce, Fried
    Shrimp in Beer Batter 253

Sweet 'n Sour Sauce. 74
Tangy Vegetable Sauce. 220
Tartar Sauce. 262
Watercress Mousseline Sauce. 261
Wine Sauce, Shrimp with
    Mushrooms 257

SAUSAGE, see Meats
Savory Souffle Roll. 300
Scalloped Oysters. 229
Scallopine with Mushroms and
    White Wine. 327

SCALLOPS
Coquilles St. Jacques. 232
Scallops Elegant 231
Scallops Italian 233

SEAFOOD
Artichoke-Oyster Soup. 84
Avocados Stuffed with Curried
    Crabmeat 51
Bacon-Wrapped Shrimp. 55
Baked Red Snapper 236
Barbara Mandrell's Seafood Mold. . 22
Barbecued Red Snapper 235
Barbecued Shrimp. 249
Boiled Lobster. 260
Boiled Shrimp in Beer 248
Brenda Lee's Trout Fillets. 20
Broiled Sole. 240
Chafing Dish Spinach with
    Oysters 65
Company Crab Casserole 228
Coquilles St. Jacques. 232
Crab Epicurean. 226
Crab Imperial. 224
Crab Louis. 117
Crabmeat Hors d'Oeuvre Mold 68
Crabmeat Supreme 227
Crab Mousse. 66
Crab-Shrimp au Gratin. 225
Creole Shrimp. 250
Dilled Shrimp with Mushrooms . . . 252
Elegant Crabmeat Crepes. 223
Flounder Florentine. 242
Fried Oysters 230
Fried Shrimp in Beer Batter 253
Hearty Clam Chowder. 92
Hot Clam Dip 70
Hot Crabmeat Dip. 67
Hot Crabmeat Sandwiches. 100
Lobster, Shrimp, and Crab
    Casserole. 259
Mandarin-Fried Shrimp with
    Peas 254
Marinated Crab. 122
Melon Ball and Shrimp Salad. 123

Mussels Provencales 234
Oven-Baked Bass or Crappie 237
Oyster or Shrimp Boats 101
Oyster Pie 231
Oysters Chez Elise 53
Oyster Souffle 230
Oyster-Stuffed Mushrooms 59
Poached Fillet of Sole with
    Grapes 239
Poached Salmon Mousseline 244
Redfish in Wine 234
Rosanne Cash's Tuna Casserole . . . 15
Salmon Souffle 245
Savory Souffle Roll, Seafood
    Filling 301
Scalloped Oysters 229
Scallops Elegant 231
Scallops Italian 233
Seafood Bombay Salad 126
Seafood Gumbo 83
Shrimp and Cheese Casserole 256
Shrimp and Cucumber
    Sandwiches 105
Shrimp Boil Dinner 248
Shrimp Cocktail Spread 73
Shrimp-Curry Casserole 251
Shrimp, Mushroom, Artichoke
    Fondue 73
Shrimp Nantua 255
Shrimp with Lemon Sauce 258
Shrimp with Mushrooms in Wine
    Sauce 257
Snowcapped Mushrooms 60
Special Fish Fillets 235
Stuffed Sole with Mushroom
    Sauce 238
Super Simple Clam Sauce 228
Trout Creole 240
Trout in Foil 241
Tuna Cooler 246
Tuna Souffle 247
Turbot Turbon 243
Variety Quiches 174
Seven-Day Pickles 158
Shallot Cream Sauce 329
Sheppard, T.G. Sheppard's Chicken-
    Shrimp Supreme 29
Sherried Peas and Mushrooms 204
Shish Kebob 312
Shotgun Sauce, Baked Quail
    in Wine 292

SHRIMP
Bacon-Wrapped Shrimp 55
Barbecued Shrimp 249
Boiled Shrimp in Beer 248

Buried Treasures 56
Crab-Shrimp Au Gratin 225
Creole Shrimp 250
Dilled Shrimp with Mushrooms . . . 252
Fried Rice 180
Fried Shrimp in Beer Batter 253
Lobster, Shrimp, and Crab
    Casserole 259
Mandarin-Fried Shrimp with
    Peas 254
Melon Ball and Shrimp Salad 123
Oyster or Shrimp Boats 101
Seafood Bombay Salad 126
Seafood Gumbo 83
Shrimp and Cheese Casserole 256
Shrimp and Cucumber
    Sandwiches 105
Shrimp Boil Dinner 248
Shrimp Cocktail Spread 73
Shrimp-Curry Casserole 251
Shrimp, Mushroom, Artichoke
    Fondue 73
Shrimp Nantua 255
Shrimp with Lemon Sauce 258
Shrimp with Mushrooms in
    Wine Sauce 257
T.G. Sheppard's Chicken-
    Shrimp Supreme 29
Slaw 125
Snowcapped Mushrooms 60
Snow, Hank Snow's Melting Moments
    Cookies 30
SOLE
Broiled Sole 240
Poached Fillet of Sole with
    Grapes 239
Stuffed Sole with Mushroom
    Sauce 238
Something Special Hot Cheese Dip . . 72
**SOUFFLES, see Eggs and Cheese
and Desserts**
Souffleed Mushrooms 203
SOUPS
Cold
Avocado Vichyssoise 77
Cold Cream of Cucumber Soup 80
Cold Spinach Soup 79
Cream of Broccoli Soup 81
Easy Vichy 77
Gazpacho 82
Iced Melon Soup 78
Hot
Artichoke-Oyster Soup 84
Asparagus Egg-Drop Soup 85
Avocado Vichyssoise 77

Black Bean Soup................. 87
Calcutta Mulligatawny Soup...... 88
Cheese Soup with Cauliflower..... 89
Chicken Cheese Chowder......... 86
Cream of Broccoli Soup........... 81
Cream of Carrot Soup with Peas... 90
Curry Tomato-Split Pea Soup..... 91
Hearty Clam Chowder............ 92
Hearty Sausage and Rice Soup.... 93
Italian Pesto Garden Soup........ 94
Lettuce Soup.................... 95
Navy Bean Soup................. 96
Onion Soup...................... 96
Seafood Gumbo.................. 83
Super Simple Soup............... 86
The Gatlin Brothers' Mexican
    Meatball Soup................ 17
Zucchini Soup................... 85
Sour Cream Coffee Cake........... 352
Sour Cream Dip, Pumpernickel
    Surprise.................... 63
Sour Cream Enchiladas........... 172
Sour Cream Pound Cake........... 404
Sour Cream Quiche............... 177
Southern Blackberry Cobbler...... 410
Southern Corn Pudding........... 198
Southern Pralines................ 383
South of the Border Chicken....... 285
Spaghetti Bolognese Sauce........ 296
Spaghetti Frittata................ 184
Special Fish Fillets.............. 235
Special Saucy Lamb............... 316
Spiced Eggs..................... 166
Spicy Marble Coffee Cake.......... 253

SPINACH
Chafing Dish Spinach with
    Oysters..................... 65
Cheese-Spinach Luncheon
    Entree...................... 173
Chicken and Mushroom Crepes
    Florentine................... 265
Cold Spinach Soup............... 79
Flounder Florentine.............. 242
Mushroom Florentine............ 202
Savory Souffle Roll, Ham and
    Spinach Filling.............. 301
Spinach Dip..................... 74
Spinach Elegant................. 209
Spinach Pie..................... 210
Spinach Salad................... 128
Spinach Souffle................. 210
Spinach Souffle Mold............. 139
Stuffed Pork Chops, Spinach
    Filling...................... 324
Variety Quiches................. 175

Sponge Pudding................... 460
Spring Lamb Stew................. 317
Spritz Delights.................... 376
SQUASH
Lemon Squash with Walnuts...... 211
Squash Relish................... 158
Summer Squash au Gratin....... 212
Winter Squash Casserole......... 213
Steak Diane..................... 308
Steak Teriyaki................... 313
Steeplechase Casserole........... 302
Stevens, Ray Stevens' "Raymone's
    Salad"...................... 31
STRAWBERRIES
Cold Grand Marnier Souffle with
    Strawberry Sauce............. 447
Frozen Strawberry Dessert....... 439
Glazed Strawberry Pie........... 430
Old-Fashioned Strawberry
    Shortcake................... 398
Strawberries Romanoff.......... 440
Strawberry Bread............... 359
Strawberry Cheesecake......... 417
Strawberry French Sorbet....... 443
Strawberry Preserves........... 156
Stuffed Avocado Salad........... 130
Stuffed Mushrooms Parmesan...... 61
Stuffed Pork Chops............... 324
Stuffed Pork Loin................ 320
Stuffed Sole with Mushroom Sauce.. 238
Sugar Cookies................... 366
Summer Squash au Gratin........ 212
Sunshine Tea.................... 40
Super Dogs..................... 105
Super Simple Clam Sauce......... 228
Super Simple Soup............... 86
Super Slurping Punch............ 46
Sweet 'n Sour Sauce.............. 74
Sweet Potatoes Caramel.......... 207
Swiss Eggs, Curried.............. 163
Sylvia's Flour Tortillas........... 32
T
Tammy Wynette's Blueberry
    Buckle...................... 36
Tangy Vegetable Sauce........... 220
Tartar Sauce.................... 262
Tassies......................... 378
Tasty Water Chestnuts........... 62
TEA
Blender Ice Tea................. 40
Christmas Cranberry Tea......... 42
Sunshine Tea................... 40
TEA BREADS, see Breads
Tenderloin Rib Roast or Eye of
    Round...................... 309

Tennessee Ernie Ford's Fresh
  Apple-Nut Cake.................. 16
T.G. Sheppard's Chicken-Shrimp
  Supreme........................ 29
Tillis, Mel Tillis' Hamburger Stew ... 33
Toasted Artichoke Rounds.......... 53
Toasted Mushroom Sandwiches..... 108
Toffee 384
Toffee Coffee Pie.................... 436

TOMATOES
  Curry Tomato-Split Pea Soup 91
  Fried Tomatoes in Golden Sauce... 217
  Frozen Tomato Salad............. 136
  Mushroom-Stuffed Tomatoes 216
  Tomato-Egg Tarragon Salad 131
  Tomatoes Supreme 218
  Tomato Pie 218
  Tomato-Roquefort Dressing....... 144
  Tomato Soup Aspic.............. 140
Tortillas, Sylvia's Flour............. 32

TROUT
  Brenda Lee's Trout Fillets......... 20
  Trout Creole 240
  Trout in Foil 241

TUNA
  Rosanne Cash's Tuna Casserole... 15
  Tuna Cooler 246
  Tuna Souffle.................... 247
Turbot Turbon..................... 243

TURKEY
  Club Salad Supreme, Pita......... 107
  Duke of Windsor Sandwiches 99

U
Unbaked Fruitcake................. 404

V
Vanilla Ice Cream 446
Vanilla Wafer Cake................. 400
Variety Quiches.................... 174

VEAL, see Meats
  Veal Scallops Vermouth 326
  Veal Smitane.................... 328

VEGETABLES
  Asparagus-Artichoke Casserole... 189
  Asparagus Parisienne 190
  Broccoli and Cauliflower
    Casserole..................... 193
  Broccoli Puff.................... 194
  Buddha's Feast 206
  Buffet Cauliflower............... 112
  Burgundy Beets 195
  California Baked Beans........... 190
  Carrots and Onions with
    Madeira...................... 196
  Celery Amandine 197

  Cheese-Stuffed Peppers 207
  Cheesy Eggplant................ 199
  Cinderella's Golden Potato
    Casserole..................... 208
  Chilled Picnic Ratatouille........ 114
  Cold Pea Salad.................. 115
  Colony Club Zucchini 214
  Cornmeal Mush................. 198
  Easy Asparagus................. 189
  Excellent Mushroom Casserole.... 201
  Fried Tomatoes in Golden Sauce... 217
  Golden Mushrooms.............. 202
  Hungarian Poppy Seed Onions.... 209
  Italian Pesto Garden Soup 94
  June Carter Cash's Vegetable
    "Stuff"...................... 13
  Lemon Squash with Walnuts...... 211
  Marinated Onions................ 121
  Mushroom Florentine............ 202
  Mushrooms on Toast 204
  Mushroom-Stuffed Tomatoes 216
  Orange Carrots 195
  Oriental Vegetable Casserole...... 191
  Oven-Baked Beans............... 191
  Party Wine Potatoes............. 208
  Pasta Primavera 186
  Peas Oriental 205
  Ratatouille with Sausage 200
  Red Beans with Rice............. 192
  Sherried Peas and Mushrooms 204
  Souffleed Mushrooms............ 203
  Southern Corn Pudding 198
  Spinach Elegant................. 209
  Spinach Pie..................... 210
  Spinach Souffle 210
  Summer Squash au Gratin........ 212
  Sweet Potatoes Caramel.......... 207
  Tomatoes Supreme 218
  Tomato Pie 218
  Vegetable Salad Mold............ 141
  White Corn Casserole 199
  Winter Squash Casserole 213
  Zucchini and Spring Onions 215
  Zucchini Puree 216
  Zucchini Souffle 215
Velvet Hammer.................... 468

VICHYSSOISE
  Avocado Vichyssoise............. 77
  Easy Vichy 77

W
Waffles, Buttermilk 355
Wagoner, Porter Wagoner's Fudge... 34
Walnut Crisps 465

498

Water Chestnuts, Tasty............. 62
Watercress Mousseline Sauce....... 261
Wells, Kitty Wells' Barbecued
   Chicken in a Bag................. 35
Well-Stuffed Pita Pocket............ 106
Whipped Cream Pound Cake........ 404
Whiskey Sour, Frozen.............. 44
White Bread, Plain................. 343
White Corn Casserole 199
White Fruitcake 405
Whole Wheat Bread................ 342
Whole Wheat Bread, Honey........ 341
Whole Wheat Muffins 342
Winter Squash Casserole........... 213
Witches' Brew..................... 474
Wynette, Tammy Wynette's
   Blueberry Buckle 36

Y

Yeast Biscuits, Easy 347

Z

ZUCCHINI
   Chilled Picnic Ratatouille......... 114
   Colony Club Zucchini 214
   Zucchini and Spring Onions 215
   Zucchini Bread.................. 360
   Zucchini Bread 'n Butter Pickles .. 159
   Zucchini Lasagna................ 303
   Zucchini Puff Pie................ 178
   Zucchini Puree 216
   Zucchini Souffle 215
   Zucchini Soup................... 85
   Variety Quiches.................. 174
Zuccoto Cake..................... 401

for a list of our favorite recipes:

Send a stamped, self-addressed envelope
to:
ENCORE! NASHVILLE
2202 Crestmoor Road
Nashville, Tennessee 37215

Encore! Nashville
2202 Crestmoor Road
Nashville, Tennessee 37215

Please send_____copies of *Encore!*
Nashville at $12.50 each plus $1.50 postage and
handling per book. For Tennessee delivery, add
$.84 sales tax per book. Make checks payable to
Encore! Nashville.

Name _____

Street _____

City _____

State _____ Zip _____
          Price subject to change without notice

- -

Encore! Nashville
2202 Crestmoor Road
Nashville, Tennessee 37215

Please send_____copies of *Encore!*
Nashville at $12.50 each plus $1.50 postage and
handling per book. For Tennessee delivery, add
$.84 sales tax per book. Make checks payable to
Encore! Nashville.

Name _____

Street _____

City _____

State _____ Zip _____
          Price subject to change without notice

- -

Encore! Nashville
2202 Crestmoor Road
Nashville, Tennessee 37215

Please send_____copies of *Encore!*
Nashville at $12.50 each plus $1.50 postage and
handling per book. For Tennessee delivery, add
$.84 sales tax per book. Make checks payable to
Encore! Nashville.

Name _____

Street _____

City _____

State _____ Zip _____
          Price subject to change without notice

Encore! Nashville
2202 Crestmoor Road
Nashville, Tennessee 37215

Please send_____copies of *Encore!
Nashville* at $12.50 each plus $1.50 postage and
handling per book. For Tennessee delivery, add
$.84 sales tax per book. Make checks payable to
Encore! Nashville.

Name _____

Street _____

City _____

State _____ Zip _____
  Price subject to change without notice

Encore! Nashville
2202 Crestmoor Road
Nashville, Tennessee 37215

Please send_____copies of *Encore!
Nashville* at $12.50 each plus $1.50 postage and
handling per book. For Tennessee delivery, add
$.84 sales tax per book. Make checks payable to
Encore! Nashville.

Name _____

Street _____

City _____

State _____ Zip _____
  Price subject to change without notice

Encore! Nashville
2202 Crestmoor Road
Nashville, Tennessee 37215

Please send_____copies of *Encore!
Nashville* at $12.50 each plus $1.50 postage and
handling per book. For Tennessee delivery, add
$.84 sales tax per book. Make checks payable to
Encore! Nashville.

Name _____

Street _____

City _____

State _____ Zip _____
  Price subject to change without notice

Reorder Additional Copies